3rd
Edition

Berlin
FROM $50 A DAY

by Beth Reiber

Macmillan • USA

ABOUT THE AUTHOR

Beth Reiber, a freelance travel writer, lived for four years in Germany and for three years in Japan. Now residing in Lawrence, Kansas, she continues to write travel articles and is the author of several Frommer guides: Japan, Tokyo, Hong Kong, Walking Tours of Berlin, Walking Tours of Tokyo, and St. Louis & Kansas City.

MACMILLAN TRAVEL

A Simon & Schuster Macmillan Company
1633 Broadway
New York, NY 10019

Copyright © 1995 by Simon & Schuster, Inc.

All rights reserved. No part of this book may be reproduced or transmitted in any form or by any means, electronic or mechanical, including photocopying, recording, or by any information storage and retrieval system, without permission in writing from the Publisher.

Macmillan is a registered trademark of Macmillan, Inc.

ISBN 0-02-860633-7
ISSN 1055-5366

Editor: Robin Michaelson
Map Editor: Douglas Stallings
Design by Michele Laseau
Digital Cartography by Devorah Wilkenfeld and Ortelius Design

SPECIAL SALES

Bulk purchases (10+ copies) of Frommer's travel guides are available to corporations at special discounts. The Special Sales Department can produce custom editions to be used as premiums and/or for sales promotion to suit individual needs. Existing editions can be produced with custom cover imprints such as corporate logos. For more information write to: Special Sales, Simon & Schuster, 1230 Avenue of the Americas, New York, NY 10020.

Manufactured in the United States of America

Contents

1 Saving Money in Berlin   1

1. The $50-a-Day Premise   1
2. Fifty Money-Saving Tips   2
3. Best Bets on a Budget   5

2 Introducing Berlin   10

1. Frommer's Favorite Berlin Experiences   11
2. The City Today   11
★ *Berlin's Melting Pot*   12
3. A Look at the Past   14
★ *Dateline*   14
★ *Did You Know?*   19
4. Famous Berliners   24
5. A Cultural Capital   26
6. Architecture 101   28
7. Cuisine   29
★ *Dining Tips*   30

3 Planning a Trip to Berlin   33

1. Visitor Information & Entry Requirements   33
2. Money   34
★ *What Things Cost in Berlin*   36
3. When to Go   37
★ *Berlin Calendar of Events*   38
4. Health & Insurance   39
5. Tips for Special Travelers   39
6. Getting There   42

4 Getting to Know Berlin   50

1. Orientation   50
2. Getting Around   59
★ *Fast Facts: Berlin*   66

5 Where to Stay 72

1. Doubles for Less than 100 DM ($66) 73
2. Doubles for Less than 135 DM ($90) 77
★ *Family-Friendly Hotels* 81
3. Youth Hostels & Youth Hotels 85
4. Camping 88

6 Where to Eat 89

1. Restaurants by Cuisine 91
2. Meals for Less than 12 DM ($8) 93
★ *Family-Friendly Restaurants* 97
3. Meals for Less than 25 DM ($16.65) 104
★ *Imbisse: Meals on the Run* 112
4. Coffeehouses 114

7 What to See & Do 116

★ *What's Special About Berlin* 117
★ *Suggested Itineraries* 117
1. The Top Attractions 120
2. More Attractions 124
★ *Did You Know?* 125
3. Parks & Gardens (and a Zoo, Too) 140
★ *Time for a Picnic* 140
4. Especially for Kids 142
5. Special-Interest Sightseeing 144
6. Organized Tours 146
7. Swimming 148

8 City Strolls 149

1. Along the Ku'damm 149
2. Berlin-Mitte (Eastern Berlin) 156
3. Prenzlauer Berg 166

9 Shopping   173

   1 The Shopping Scene   173
   2 Shopping A to Z   176

10 Berlin After Dark   184

   1 The Performing Arts   185
   ★ *Church Music*   186
   2 The Club & Music Scene   188
   3 The Bar & Cafe Scene   193
   4 More Entertainment   202
   5 Late-Night Bites   203

11 Easy Excursions from Berlin   205

   1 Potsdam   205
   2 The Spreewald   212

Appendix   216

   A Basic Phrases & Vocabulary   216
   B Menu Terms   218
   C Glossary of Terms   220
   D Metric Measures   222

Index   223

List of Maps

Berlin at a Glance   54–55

The U-Bahn &
 the S-Bahn   62–63

Berlin Accommodations   78–79

Western Berlin Dining   94–95

Berlin-Mitte Dining   101

Berlin-Mitte Sights   127

Sights Around
 Charlottenburg   133

Sights Around the Tiergarten   135

Along the Ku'damm   153

Berlin-Mitte   158–159

Prenzlauer Berg   169

Shopping along the
 Ku'damm   175

Easy Excursions   209

Potsdam   211

AN INVITATION TO THE READER

When researching this book, I discovered many wonderful places—hotels, restaurants, shops, and more. I'm sure you'll find others. Please tell us about them so that we can share the information with your fellow travelers in upcoming editions. If you were disappointed with a recommendation, we'd love to know that, too. Please write to:

> Beth Reiber
> *Frommer's Berlin from $50 a Day,* 3rd edition
> Macmillan Travel
> 1633 Broadway
> New York, NY 10019

AN ADDITIONAL NOTE

Please be advised that travel information is subject to change at any time—and this is especially true of prices. We therefore suggest that you write or call ahead for confirmation when making your travel plans. The author, editors, and publisher cannot be held responsible for the experiences of readers while traveling. Your safety is important to us, however, so we encourage you to stay alert and be aware of your surroundings. Keep a close eye on cameras, purses, and wallets, all favorite targets of thieves and pickpockets.

WHAT THE SYMBOLS MEAN

✪ Frommer's Favorites

Hotels, restaurants, attractions, and entertainment you should not miss.

ⓢ Super-Special Values

Hotels and restaurants that offer great value for your money.

The following abbreviations are used for credit cards:

AE	American Express	EU	Eurocard
CB	Carte Blanche	JCB	Japan Credit Bank
DC	Diners Club	MC	MasterCard
DISC	Discover	V	Visa
ER	enRoute		

Saving Money in Berlin

It's never been easier to visit Berlin. During the Cold War, just getting to Berlin was an adventure, with passengers restricted to their trains or their cars as they traveled through Communist territory to reach Berlin, where they were then largely confined to its western half. After the Wall fell, Berlin experienced such upheaval—both emotional and physical—that it was a chore just keeping up with the changes sweeping through the city. Telephone numbers changed, bus lines were altered, and businesses closed, especially in East Berlin. Even more distressing for visitors was the fact that hotel rates shot upward, often more than 30% each year, the result of rising real estate prices.

Certainly more changes are inevitable as Berlin readies itself as the home of the German parliament. But for visitors, Berlin has become a fairly uncomplicated destination, thanks to German efficiency and the passage of time. Room rates have stabilized, museums throughout the city have instituted regular and predictable opening hours, restaurants have blossomed in what was the culinary wasteland of East Berlin, the number of tourist offices has multiplied, and shops throughout the city now observe longer store hours.

Even more striking is that more bargains exist now compared to a few years ago. With regard to transportation, budget travelers have more options in fares. Reduced admissions for clusters of museums are available, as well as up to 50% discounts off the regular price for opera, theater, and concert tickets. Granted, Germany is by no means Europe's cheapest country, but it is affordable. More importantly, a trip to Berlin can be deeply enriching as well.

1 The $50-a-Day Premise

Everyone always asks me: "Is it really possible to stay in Berlin for as little as $50 a day?" I know it is, because I do it. But as with all Frommer budget guides, $50 isn't meant to be a gauge for *all* your expenses. After all, only you know how many museums you're going to visit, when you want to splurge, and what you want to buy. Rather, this book shows how you can live in Berlin from $50 a day, per person, to cover the basics of lodging and meals.

At the time of this writing, $50 U.S. is equivalent to 75 DM. Two people traveling together would have approximately 150 DM ($100) to spend each day. If they choose an inexpensive pension that includes breakfast for 90 DM ($60), they have 20 DM ($13.35) to spend together for lunch and 40 DM ($26.65) left for dinner. Room rates often include continental breakfast, sometimes even a buffet breakfast. Lunch can be as simple as take-out Chinese or Turkish food or German sausage, which will cost considerably less than 20 DM ($13.35), or a hearty German meal offered as a daily special. As for dinner, you'll find many options in the 40-DM-range for two.

While it's easier to travel economically if there are two of you, a single traveler can live on as little as $50 a day by staying in a no-frills pension and eating at the least expensive restaurants, or, even better, staying at a hostel, which leaves more money to spend on meals. Open year-round, Berlin's hostels have no age limit, although those older than 26 pay slightly more.

2 Fifty Money-Saving Tips

AIR TRAVEL

1. Shop all the airlines that fly to your destination and keep checking, since the availability of cheap fares changes daily.
2. Read the advertisements in newspaper travel sections, which often feature special deals and packages.
3. Consider traveling off season—November through March—when airlines offer their lowest fares.
4. Travel on weekdays (Monday through Thursday), when you can save about $60 on round-trip fares.
5. Buy your ticket as early as possible, since the cheapest fares such as APEX (Advance Purchase Excursion) usually require a 21-day advance purchase.

ACCOMMODATIONS

6. Choose a room without private shower, toilet, telephone or TV, since you'll pay more for these amenities.
7. When making your reservation, ask whether a cheaper room is available than the one offered—maybe a smaller room, one on an upper floor, or one farther from the shared bathroom.
8. Climb the stairs. Pensions located on top floors of old buildings without elevators usually have less expensive rates than similar pensions in elevator buildings.
9. If it's winter, ask about off-season discounts, or if you're staying for one or two weeks—longer than the usual tourist stay—ask whether you can have a reduced rate.
10. Avoid staying in Berlin during major trade fairs (called *Messe*), when many hotels raise their rates.
11. Stay at a pension that includes breakfast in the room rate or offers it for a little extra charge. Buffet-style breakfasts are a bargain; since you can refill your coffee and eat as much as you wish, you might be able to tide yourself over to an early dinner.

12. Avoid making telephone calls, even local ones, from your hotel room phone. You'll be charged at least 50 Pfennig (35¢) instead of 30 Pfennig (20¢) per three minutes.
13. Remember that youth hostels, which have no age limit, are the cheapest way to go.
14. Camp out at several campgrounds, which are equipped with modern sanitary facilities and stores, in Berlin's vicinity.
15. If you're under 26, don't mind roughing it, and are visiting Berlin in summer, sleep in the Internationales Jugendcamp, a large tent with mattresses and sheets.

DINING

16. Stop at one of Berlin's countless food stalls (called *Imbisse*), which sell sausages, Turkish specialties, french fries, and other fast food, as well as drinks. You can eat your purchase right there, picnic in the park, or bring it back to your hotel room.
17. If you're a coffee fan, look for coffee-shop chains such as Tschibo, where you enjoy an inexpensive cup of coffee, espresso, or cappucino.
18. Go to department stores to find food bargains and inexpensive cafeterias. If you want to picnic or stock up on snacks for later, buy bread, cheese, sausages, fruit, wine, beer, milk, and other items at the store's food department, usually located in the basement. Also stop by the store's restaurants, which usually include cafeterias offering daily specials, drinks, and desserts.
19. Look for daily specials, which often include a main course and side dishes, at most German restaurants. The specials aren't usually on the regular menu; you'll find them posted at the restaurant entrance or inserted in the menu. It's especially important to ask about specials if you're reading from an English menu—as the specials are often printed only in German.
20. Order a fixed-price lunch—available from about 11am to 2pm—which usually includes an appetizer or soup, main course, and dessert, and is much cheaper than ordering a la carte.
21. For the best bargain in town, go to the student cafeteria of Berlin's Technical University, located in the center of town. You don't have to be a student to take advantage of complete meals for less than $3.
22. Splurge at a higher-priced restaurant by ordering one of the less expensive main courses (which usually comes with side dishes) and cutting out drinks, appetizers, and desserts.
23. Eat at a pub or bar; they stay open late and often serve reasonably priced snacks or complete meals.
24. As you reach for more bread from the basket in the middle of your table, keep in mind that many restaurants charge extra for each slice. Ask about the restaurant's policy. Also, a few restaurants levy a table charge (called a *Gedeck*).

25. Since service charge is already included in the bill, it's sufficient to add a mark to meals costing less than 20 DM ($13.35). For meals costing more than 20 DM, most Germans leave a 10% tip.
26. Be sure to ask the locals for recommendations—there may be a great and inexpensive restaurant right around the corner.

LOCAL TRANSPORTATION

27. If you decide to rent a car for excursions to the countryside, try to negotiate in dollars before leaving home for a better deal, and be sure to get everything in writing.
28. Check whether you can get a fly-drive package that includes your flight and car rental.
29. Ask about weekend rates for rental cars and any special promotions.
30. Be sure to check the rates offered by local, independent car-rental agencies, since they're usually cheaper than the internationally known companies.
31. Avoid taxis unless several of you can split the cost; otherwise, take buses, subways, and commuter trains.
32. If you have a Eurailpass, use it for free travel on all S-Bahn lines (commuter trains) in Berlin.
33. Save by buying four tickets at once (a *Sammelkarte*) instead of single tickets for Berlin's public transportation system. Tickets are good for up to two hours.
34. Consider buying one of several transportation passes available: a 30-hour ticket; the Group Ticket, good for two adults and three children for 30 hours of unlimited travel; or the seven-day ticket.
35. For discounts in travel and sightseeing, consider purchasing the WelcomeCard, which gives one adult and up to three children three days of unlimited travel and offers reduced admissions for sightseeing trips, museums, and attractions.
36. Remember that children under six travel free in Berlin, while children ages 6 to 14 receive reduced fares.

ATTRACTIONS AND NIGHTLIFE

37. Remember that all state museums are free on Sundays and public holidays.
38. To save money visiting several museums clustered together, take advantage of combined tickets that allow entry to several museums in one day at reduced admission prices.
39. If you're a student or a senior citizen, ask about discounts at most of Berlin's museums.
40. Receive up to 50% off opera, theater, and concert tickets by dropping by the half-price ticket booth, Hekticket, to see what's available for that evening's performances.
41. Avoid the commission charged by ticket outlets by purchasing tickets for opera and theater directly at the box office.

42. Be on the lookout for free concerts or jam sessions offered by bars or live-music venues. Many clubs have free live music at least one night a week.
43. Take advantage of Sunday brunch—quite a few bars and restaurants offer free live music.
44. Dance on weeknights when most discos and dancing clubs have cheaper admission prices. Some also offer cheaper drink prices early in the evening.

SHOPPING

45. Do all your major shopping in one store, if possible, so you can claim a refund in the value-added tax (purchases must total more than 60 DM [$40] in any one store).
46. For antiques, collectibles, unique souvenirs, and crafts, browse the the weekend market at Strasse des 17. Juni.

CURRENCY AND COMMUNICATIONS

47. Never pay for a transcontinental call if you can help it. Both AT&T and MCI, for example, allow you to speak directly to an American operator, with rates far less expensive than regular international phone calls from Germany.
48. Exchange money at banks rather than hotels.
49. If you're cashing travelers' checks, cash as many as you think you might need in the near future, since you'll usually pay a commission on each transaction.
50. If you're exchanging large sums of money, try an ATM for the most favorable exchange rate.

3 Best Bets on a Budget

Researching this book, I have spent countless hours inspecting hotels and pensions, eating at restaurants, visiting museums, and checking out Berlin's varied nightlife. Just like Berlin, this book has changed through the years, and I've worked hard to reflect what's new, ferret out those establishments that no longer meet Frommer's standards, and predict what changes might occur during the next couple of years. I've tried to include enough to suit budget travelers of all stripes, from retirees to families to backpacking students.

With the budget traveler in mind, this is just a sampling of the best Berlin has to offer:

BERLIN'S TOP ATTRACTIONS FOR FREE

1. No trip to Berlin would be complete without a leisurely stroll down the **Ku'damm,** the city's showcase shopping boulevard, and **Unter den Linden,** the historical heart of the city. For detailed walks linking the most important sights on these two boulevards, see Chapter 8, "City Strolls."

2. See Berlin's most famous treasures—the spectacular Pergamon Altar in the **Pergamon Museum** and Queen Nefertiti in the **Egyptian Museum**—on a Sunday or public holiday, when state-owned museums are free. For more information, see Chapter 7, "What to See & Do."
 3. Browse the spectacular food emporium on the sixth floor of **KaDeWe,** the largest department store on the European continent. There you'll find 1,500 types of cheese, 1,000 different kinds of sausage, lobsters in tanks, exotic teas, wines, jams, sweets, and food counters offering sit-down meals. The endless swirl of imported food products from around the world makes a stroll here an experience you won't soon forget. Refer to Chapter 9, "Shopping."
 4. Visiting a **market** is a wonderful way to spend a few hours in Berlin. My favorite is the weekend market at Strasse des 17. Juni for its endless array of antiques, collectibles, and arts and crafts. At the Turkish Market, held Tuesday and Friday afternoons, you'll find exotic spices and clothing; you'll think you've landed in Istanbul. See Chapter 9, "Shopping."
 5. For **bird's-eye-views** of the city's rooftops, climb the steps to the tower of Rathaus Schöneberg, which also houses the huge Freedom Bell given to Berlin by the American people in 1950 (see Chapter 7, "What to See & Do"), or climb to the top of the dome of the French Cathedral in Berlin-Mitte (see the Berlin-Mitte city stroll in Chapter 8).
 6. Probably the prettiest grounds in all Berlin are the formal, **baroque gardens of Charlottenburg Palace.** For more information on my favorite park, see "Parks & Gardens (and a Zoo, Too)" in Chapter 7.
 7. The Berlin Wall is no more, but a kilometer-long section of it, called **East Side Gallery** and decorated by artists upon invitation of the East German authorities in 1990, has been left standing as an open-air gallery. For information on how to get there, see Chapter 7, "What to See & Do."
 8. The **Spreewald,** a unique, natural wonderland of canals and streams, is a great place for a hike or an inexpensive boat ride. Located 60 miles from Berlin, it's been a popular destination for city dwellers for decades. For more information, refer to Chapter 11, "Easy Excursions from Berlin."
 9. Free **organ concerts** are presented in the new structure of the Kaiser-Wilhelm Gedächtniskirche, located in the center of Berlin on the Ku'damm, every Saturday at 6pm. For information on this and other church music, refer to Chapter 10, "Berlin After Dark."
10. Several bars and music clubs offer **free live music** at least one night a week. There's free jazz at the A-Trane on Tuesday and Wednesday evenings, free concerts every Sunday evening at Lucky Strike Originals, free music every evening at Wirtshaus Zum Löwen, and free concerts late Saturday at Café Swing. On weekends, Georg Brau

features free live music Saturdays and Sundays from 10am to 1pm, Eierschale has live music all Sunday from 10am, and Yorckschlössen entertains with Dixieland jazz on Sundays from 2 to 6pm. For detailed information, see Chapter 10, "Berlin After Dark."

BEST BUDGET ACCOMMODATIONS

1. Artist Renate Prasse has decorated her **Pension München,** just two subway stops from the Ku'damm. Her unerring eye for beauty is evident throughout. Flowers, original artwork, and a charming proprietress make this inexpensive pension a winner. Rates start at 60 DM ($40) for a single and 85 DM ($56.65) for a double.
2. The fact that **Arco** doesn't have an elevator saves you money. With an enviable location right on the Ku'damm, this third-floor walk-up is refined, tastefully decorated, and has an Old-World atmosphere, and is every bit worth the price of 110 DM ($73.35) for a double, including continental breakfast.
3. One of my favorites, the **Bogota,** right off the Ku'damm, is an older, old-fashioned hotel with character, each room slightly different. Rates, with continental breakfast, start at 75 DM ($50) for a single and 120 DM ($80) for a double.
4. **Hotel West-Pension,** right on the Ku'damm, occupies the second floor of a beautiful turn-of-the-century building and boasts an ambience reminiscent of old Berlin. Singles start at 75 DM ($50) and doubles at 130 DM ($86.65).
5. Looking for a splurge? **Hotel Tiergarten Berlin,** two subway stops from Bahnhof Zoo, is my number-one choice. With turn-of-the-century charm and elegance, light and airy rooms equipped with modern conveniences, and a cheerful breakfast room, it's the kind of place you'd come back to again and again. Rates are 180 DM ($120) single and 215 DM ($143.35) double, including buffet breakfast.
6. **Artemesia,** about a five-minute walk from the Ku'damm, is owned and run by women for women and is the best place in town for single female travelers. Complete with rooftop terrace, cozy hotel bar with fireplace, sunny breakfast room, and cheerful and spotless rooms, it's worth the prices starting at 109 DM ($72.66) for singles and 185 DM ($123.35) for doubles. "Last-minute" discounts of 10 to 20 DM ($6.65–$13.35) per person are available on vacant rooms by calling one or two days before your intended day of arrival.
7. **Charlottenburger Hof,** two S-Bahn stops from Bahnhof Zoo, is one of Berlin's finest budget hotels. Modern rooms come equipped with cable TVs, safes, and alarm clocks, and the staff is youthful and friendly. Rates start at 75 DM ($50) for a single and 90 DM ($60) for a double.
8. **Transit Hotel,** located in Kreuzberg, is a great choice for young travelers who like the prices of a youth hostel but don't like the accompanying curfew. It's especially good for single travelers, who pay

33 DM ($22) for a bed in a dormitory room, including buffet breakfast. There are also many single rooms for 80 DM ($53.35) and double rooms for 99 DM ($66), all with breakfast.

9. A lot of extras make **Hotel-Pension Alexandra,** located just off the Ku'damm, better than most in its price range—hair dryers, cable TVs, radios, laundry service, babysitting, and a friendly proprietress who speaks good English, to name a few. It's especially price-worthy in the off season, when singles start at 65 DM ($42.45) and doubles at 120 DM ($80), including buffet breakfast.

10. **Zimmer des Westens,** with a convenient location between Bahnhof Zoo and Wittenbergplatz, is a modestly priced, family-owned pension offering clean, quiet, and pleasant rooms. Rates, including continental breakfast, start at 70 DM ($46.65) for a single and 95 DM ($63.35) for a double.

BEST BUDGET DINING

1. **Mensa,** the student cafeteria of the Technical University, is Berlin's best-kept secret for bargain dining. Located near Bahnhof Zoo and open only for lunch, it offers complete meals to both students and non-students for less than 4 DM ($2.65).

2. **Hardtke,** just off the Ku'damm, is an old-fashioned German restaurant that has been serving hearty German fare for more than 40 years. Save money by dining before 6pm, when a platter of sausages with side dishes is offered for 10.50 DM ($7). Otherwise, a very satisfying meal can be enjoyed at this popular restaurant for about 20 DM ($13.35) per person.

3. **Opernpalais,** located in historic Berlin-Mitte, is one of Berlin's best-known restaurants and coffeehouses and occupies part of a palace built in 1733. An outdoor *Imbiss* situated in a pretty plaza serves sausages, sandwiches, and snacks for around 5 DM ($3.35). In the indoor coffeehouse, enjoy a cup of coffee for 3.50 DM ($2.35).

4. For a musical Sunday brunch, go early to **Eierschale,** across from the Gedächtniskirche, where jazz and blues bands accompany a buffet breakfast from 6 to 12 DM ($4–$8).

5. Quite simply, the best grilled chicken I've ever eaten can be found at **Henne,** located in Kreuzberg. The chicken is so good, in fact, that that's all Henne serves, along with side dishes of potato or kraut salad. A half chicken and a side order costs 13 DM ($8.65), and even though I usually avoid eating chicken skin, I can't resist it here.

6. **Oren,** located in what was once Berlin's most well-known Jewish quarters, was East Berlin's first modern Kosher restaurant when it opened a few years ago. An interesting menu draws inspiration from Asia, the Middle East, and international vegetarian cuisines. Popular, and rightfully so, it is the perfect place for a meal when visiting nearby Museumsinsel or bar-hopping on Oranienburger Strasse. A meal here will cost about 12 to 25 DM ($8–$16.65).

7. When you're tired of German cuisine, head to **Restaurant Marché Mövenpick,** right on the Ku'damm, a pleasant cafeteria with a substantial salad bar, vegetable bar, pastas, daily specials, juices, and desserts. It has the extra bonuses of a large no-smoking section (a rarity in Germany) and outdoor seating. A complete meal here will run between 15 and 20 DM ($10–$13.35).
8. **Piccola Taormina Tavola Calda,** just off the Ku'damm, is one of the cheapest and best-known Italian pizzerias, with a slice costing 2.50 DM ($1.65). Full-size pizzas, starting at 6.50 DM ($4.35), are big enough for two to share.
9. One of the most unusual places for a meal is on the sixth floor of **KaDeWe,** the continent's largest department store, which boasts one of the largest food emporiums I've ever seen. More than a dozen sit-down counters offer a variety of food, from pasta and salads to Asian cuisine. Expect to spend 10 to 15 DM ($6.65–$10) for a meal.
10. Germany and beer go together, and one of my favorite places to imbibe is at **Luisen-Bräu,** a micro-brewery near Berlin's famous Charlottenburg Palace and Egyptian Museum. You can come for just a beer, which costs 2.60 DM ($1.75) for a fifth of a liter, or order a platter of excellently prepared German food from the self-service counter, with most meals averaging 10 to 15 DM ($6.65–$10).

2

Introducing Berlin

Once again the capital of a united Germany, Berlin mirrors its nation's history more vividly than any other city. Under Bismarck, it became the capital of the newly united Germany. It blossomed culturally in the twenties, only to fall under the shadow of Hitler's Third Reich. The city was almost totally destroyed during World War II, and afterward was both victim and symbol of the Cold War. Isolated and surrounded by East Germany, Berlin was a divided city, a division made concrete with the erection of the Berlin Wall. A hideous structure more than 100 miles long and 13 feet high, it was constructed to stop the mass exodus of East Germans into West Berlin that was draining East Germany of its youngest, brightest, and best-educated citizens. No one dreamed that in 1989 another exodus would trigger the fall of the Wall and the end of East Germany's Communist regime.

Although the core of former East Berlin is showing signs of revitalization with new office buildings, shops, art galleries, bars, and restaurants, much of the eastern half of the city remains in economic shambles, with high unemployment and a rising crime rate. Buildings are decaying, pockmarked with shrapnel as though World War II had ended only yesterday. Even West Berlin is beset by new problems, such as rising rents, homelessness, and a dramatic increase in immigrants, mostly from eastern Europe. The euphoria caused by the fall of the Wall has long given way to grim economic and political realities, even disillusionment. I have never seen a city so marred by graffiti as Berlin during my last visit.

But Berliners are tough, and years of living with the Wall have taught them to survive adversity. Always Germany's least provincial city—liberal and tolerant—Berlin attracts artists, writers, students, and those in search of alternative lifestyles. Its rich culture—museums, opera, theater, symphony, jazz, international film premieres, and nightlife that never shuts down—makes Berlin one of Europe's most interesting destinations. With the sweeping curves of its art nouveau architecture, its tree-lined streets, and the refinement of its old-style cafes, Berlin is graceful, but it also has the weird, the wired, and the energy of the avant-garde. Even young Europeans—who generally skip Germany for the more liberal climes of Paris, Amsterdam, or Copenhagen—are flocking to Berlin. Berlin also serves as a perfect gateway to eastern Europe. Suddenly, Berlin is in. This is a great time to be visiting, as Berlin forges ahead in its new—and old—role as capital of Germany.

1 Frommer's Favorite Berlin Experiences

Strolling the Ku'damm and Unter den Linden No trip to Berlin would be complete without a leisurely stroll down the Ku'damm, the city's showcase boulevard, and Unter den Linden, the historical heart of the city.

Cafe Life Cafes are where people meet friends, discuss the day's events, read the newspaper, or just sit at a sidewalk table and watch the never-ending parade.

A Picnic in the Tiergarten In the heart of the city, the Tiergarten, home of the Berlin Zoo and Aquarium, is laced with hiking paths that skirt ponds and cut through meadows, a good place for a picnic or a leisurely walk.

Museum Hopping Since most museums in Berlin are located in clusters and offer combination tickets at a discount, you can literally race from one museum to the next, if only to see the great masterpieces.

The Food Emporium of KaDeWe With 1,000 different kinds of sausage, 500 different sorts of bread, 1,500 different types of cheese, and counters selling ready-to-eat dishes, this is a true culinary adventure and not to be missed.

Browsing the Market at Strasse des 17. Juni The best flea market in the city, with a wide variety of antiques, curios and junk, as well as handcrafted items such as jewelry and clothes, is held Saturday and Sunday only.

An Afternoon at the Turkish Market At the Turkish Market Tuesday and Friday afternoons, you'll find exotic spices and clothing; you'll think you've landed in Istanbul.

A Lazy Day at the Beach Europe's largest inland beach is at Wannsee, which boasts a children's playground, shops, and restaurants. This is a great place to go on a fine summer's day.

An Evening with the Berlin Philharmonic Don't miss the chance of hearing one of the world's great orchestras at the fabulous Philharmonic Hall.

Pub Crawling 'til Dawn There are no mandatory closing hours for bars in Berlin, which means you can celebrate all night long. And if you stay out all night, you'll even find cafe/bars ready to serve you breakfast in the wee hours.

Sunday Brunch Sunday brunch is very much in vogue in Berlin, and there are a number of places that offer a tempting buffet of goodies. Even more popular are those that offer live music as well, such as the Eierschale right off the Ku'damm.

2 The City Today

Today Berlin is Germany's most popular travel destination, with more than 10 million visitors a year. Now that the Wall is history, visitors are discovering the treasures Berlin has harbored all along, including some of the world's great museums, housing such gems as the bust of Nefertiti and the magnificent Pergamon Altar. Having been divided for so many decades, Berlin has two of almost everything: two major opera houses, two museums for primeval and early history, two Egyptian museums, two historical museums, two museums of modern art, two museums of European masterpieces, two sculpture collections. And that's only the beginning.

WHEN THE WALL CAME TUMBLING DOWN

No German city has been more acutely affected by reunification than Berlin. Not only did it suddenly become reunited Germany's capital, but it also faced the formidable task of integrating two separate systems that had 40 years to develop, each with its own political, social, economic, cultural, and ideological values. Everything from bus lines to telephone lines had to be coordinated and changed; streets severed by the Wall had to be rejoined. The differences between eastern and

Berlin's Melting Pot

Berlin has the largest non-German population of any city in Germany—Poles, Silesians, East Prussians, Turks, Yugoslavs, and Greeks. One of the first to arrive were the Huguenots, invited by Friedrich Wilhelm II (the "Great Elector") to Berlin in the 17th century. Traces of their influence can still be found today; for example, they introduced *Boulette*, the Berlin meatball specialty.

In Imperial times, Poles, Silesians, and East Prussians were drawn to Berlin. In the 1920s, artists and bohemians chose Berlin as their home. After World War II, Turkish, Yugoslavian, Greek, and Polish immigrants found homes and ready employment in West Berlin, while immigrants from Vietnam, Cuba, Angola, and Mozambique were drawn to East Berlin. Most recently, newcomers to Berlin have included refugees from former Eastern-Bloc countries, including Poles, refugees from former Yugoslavian states, and from the former USSR.

Today, more than 1 in 10 residents is a foreigner. One out of five children under age six has parents with foreign passports. Turks are the largest minority in Berlin, numbering more than 100,000 and living mainly in the western precincts of Kreuzberg, Neukölln, and Wedding. Although problems occasionally arise because of differences in customs and cultural backgrounds, escalating in recent times to animosity and violence toward foreign workers and their families, on the whole Berlin enjoys greater racial harmony than many parts of Germany. Decades of isolation helped forge a sense of community spirit; years of living with the Wall have bred tolerance and determination.

western Berlin are still rather shocking. Although there is no longer a physical barrier between the two halves, a psychological one still exists, and Berliners still speak of "East" or "West" Berlin as though they were two separate entities.

West Berliners, after years of living with the uncertainty posed by the Wall and an encircling hostile regime, developed a distinct "live for today" lifestyle, much more Bohemian and liberal than that of their compatriots in other German cities. West German government policies further enhanced Berlin's liberal climate. In an effort to encourage young West Germans to live in this metropolitan outpost, the government granted residents generous housing subsidies and exemption from military service, thereby attracting artists, activists, rebels, and others in search of an alternative lifestyle. Because of their isolation, West Berliners were as apt to identify themselves with Parisians or New Yorkers as they were with fellow Germans.

Thus, when the Wall came down and the initial jubilation wore off, East Berliners came as something of a shock to the liberal West Berliners. Unmistakable in their tiny, squat, Trabant automobiles and the dull sameness of Eastern-Bloc clothing, East Germans seemed so serious, so naive, so obedient to authority—so German. But West Berlin was no less shocking to East Berliners, with its decadent nightlife, availability of drugs, unabashed pursuit of capitalism, and all the ills of the Western world. West Berliners were seen as arrogant and materialistic; East Berliners felt like second-class citizens and suffered a loss of self-esteem.

It hasn't been easy resolving the differences between East and West, and although it will take time the process has begun and differences are shrinking daily. Even now, it's not always easy to tell what side of the city a Berliner hails from, and surely the day will come when a Berliner is once again simply a Berliner.

After all, Berliners are bound together by certain characteristics that are thoroughly and unmistakably German—not to mention Prussian, which means that they take pleasure in orderliness, precision, and the established order of things. But Berliners are also known for their dry wit and humor, and their penchant for nicknaming everything in sight: They call the Kongresshalle the "pregnant oyster," while the new church next to the Gedächtniskirche is known as the "lipstick and powder puff." The large global fountain in front of the Europa-Center is the "wet dumpling," while the TV tower on Alexanderplatz is the "tele-asparagus."

Berliners also have what's called "schnauze," a cocky attitude that makes them say that everything is bigger and better in Berlin. They share this trait with Bavarians and fellow Münchners and in fact, there's a story that goes like this: A Bavarian boasted to a Berliner that Bavaria was superior to Berlin because of its Alps. He then smugly asked the Berliner if Berlin had any comparable mountains.

"No," answered the Berliner calmly, "but if we did, you can be sure they'd be higher than yours."

3 A Look at the Past

Dateline

- **1200** Two settlements, Berlin and Cölln, founded on the Spree River.
- **1237** Cölln first mentioned in documents.
- **1244** Berlin first mentioned in documents.
- **1307** Berlin and Cölln unite and build a joint town hall.
- **1415** Count Friedrich von Nürnberg from the house of Hohenzollern becomes Friedrich I, Prince Elector of Brandenburg.
- **1470** Berlin becomes the official residence of the Elector of Brandenburg.
- **1539** Prince Elector Joachim II converts to Protestantism, and the Reformation comes to Berlin.
- **1618–48** The Thirty Years' War reduces Brandenburg's population by half.
- **1640–88** Friedrich Wilhelm, the "Great Elector," reigns.

continues

MEDIEVAL TOWN TO ROYAL CAPITAL

As ironic as it now seems, Berlin began life as a divided city 800 years ago, when two Wendish settlements were founded on the Spree River: Berlin, on a bank of the river, and Cölln (or Kölln), on a nearby island in the river. Located about halfway between the established fortresses of Spandau and Köpenick, the two small settlements developed as trading towns, spreading along the banks of the Spree in what is now Berlin-Mitte. A convenient stopover on a much-traveled trade route, Berlin-Cölln cleverly required all traveling tradesmen who passed through to stay several days and offer their merchandise for sale: This gave the towns' merchants an opportunity to purchase rye, wool, oak, hides, furs, and other goods and then to export them as far afield as Hamburg, Flanders, and even England. Both towns grew and prospered, and although their citizens were not particularly interested in unifying, eventually it became inevitable. In 1307 they merged under the name of Berlin and built a joint town hall. Berlin also joined the powerful Hanseatic League, a protective and commercial federation of free towns along the Baltic Sea.

During the next century, Berlin fell under the rule of various dynasties and was repeatedly attacked by robber barons and roving bandits. In desperation, Berlin finally appealed to the Holy Roman Emperor in 1411 for protection against the robber barons. To the rescue came Count Friedrich from the Hohenzollern house in Nuremberg, and by 1414 he had defeated the most notorious robber barons of the day. Shortly thereafter he proclaimed himself the Prince Elector of Brandenburg, thereby gaining control of Berlin and surrounding Brandenburg.

Although the people revolted against the Hohenzollern takeover, the rebellion was easily quashed. In 1470 Berlin became the official residence of the Elector of Brandenburg. (The German word for *Elector*, by the way, is *Kurfürst*, which literally means "Choosing Prince," one who had the right to elect the emperor.) Berlin lost the freedom it had enjoyed as an independent trading town.

The Hohenzollerns ruled from Berlin for the next 500 years, during which time Berlin changed from a town of merchants to a city of civil servants and government administrators. The tone of urban life was set by the Elector's courtiers and officials, who had a fondness for lavish festivities and feasts. Noblemen and jurists moved to this new city of opportunity, and the demand for luxury goods drew many craftspeople. In an attempt to curb the wild consumption of alcohol and loose morals that had filtered down from the privileged class to the lower classes, the authorities issued decrees against drunkenness and disturbance of the peace; they even divided the residents of Berlin into four distinct classes, each with its own restrictions on the type, price, and material of dress. As might be expected, such decrees were hard to enforce, especially as the population grew. From 1450 to 1600, residents of Berlin doubled from 6,000 to 12,000.

But then came the plague, smallpox, and the Thirty Years' War (1618–48), a religious confrontation between Protestants and Catholics. By the end of the war, half of Berlin's citizens had lost their lives and much of the city lay in ruins. Luckily for Berlin, however, Friedrich Wilhelm had come to power in 1640. One of Berlin's most able rulers, he enjoyed great popularity for his defeat of the Swedes in the decisive battle of Fehrbellin during the Thirty Years' War; to this day he is still fondly known as the Great Elector. To bolster the town's economy and rebuild its population, in 1685 he invited 6,000 Huguenots, French Protestants who were forced to flee because of religious persecution, to settle in Berlin. By 1700, nearly one Berliner in five was of French lineage.

In 1701 the Great Elector's son, Elector Friedrich III, crowned himself the first king of Prussia and became Friedrich I. Up until then, Prussia had been only a duchy under the rule of electors. In 1709, he merged Berlin and several surrounding towns into one community, declaring Berlin his royal residence and the royal capital of Brandenburg-Prussia. On the whole, however, Friedrich I was an unpopular and unloved king. Mocked for his vanity, he nevertheless did have the insight to marry Sophie Charlotte, a beautiful and intelligent woman

- **1685** The Great Elector invites 6,000 persecuted Huguenots from France to settle in Berlin.
- **1701** Elector Friedrich III crowns himself first king of Prussia, Friedrich I.
- **1709** Friedrich I names Berlin the royal residence.
- **1713–40** Friedrich Wilhelm I, the "Soldier King," reigns. He enlarges the army and fortifies Berlin.
- **1735** Berlin's population: 60,000.
- **1740–86** Friedrich II, "Frederick the Great," reigns. He builds Sanssouci Palace in Potsdam, makes Berlin a European capital, and builds the Prussian army.
- **1770** Unter den Linden constructed.
- **1791** Brandenburger Tor erected.
- **1806** Napoléon marches into Berlin, occupying the city for two years.
- **1862** Bismarck becomes

continues

Chancellor of Prussia.
- **1871** Berlin becomes capital of German Reich.
- **1918** End of World War I; Kaiser Wilhelm II abdicates, and Germany becomes a Republic.
- **1920** Greater Berlin formed and subdivided into 20 precincts with almost 4 million inhabitants.
- **1933** Hitler and Nazis seize power; Third Reich begins.
- **1936** XIth Summer Olympics held in Berlin; African-American athlete Jesse Owens wins four gold medals.
- **1939** Hitler invades Poland, World War II begins.
- **1945** German army surrenders. Berlin divided into four zones occupied by the Four Powers.
- **1948** Eleven-month Berlin Blockade. Berlin Airlift supplies West Berlin.
- **1949** Founding of the German Democratic Republic (DDR), with East Berlin as its capital.

continues

adored by the masses. An ardent advocate of intellectual and spiritual growth, she built a small summer residence where she could entertain some of the great minds of the age, holding lively discussions and debates. Upon nearing death at age 36, she said she was ready to see what the afterlife had in store. As for her husband, she predicted that her death and subsequent funeral would give him another "opportunity to demonstrate his magnificence." She was right; he enlarged the palace and named it for her. Today Schloss Charlottenburg remains the finest example of baroque architecture in Berlin.

During the 18th century, Berlin became the most important political, economic, and cultural center of the area. The town blossomed under the talents of architects Andreas Schlüter, Karl Friedrich Schinkel, and Georg Wenzeslaus von Knobelsdorff. In a flurry of activity, the Berlin Palace (destroyed in World War II) was enlarged; the boulevard of Unter den Linden was laid; the Brandenburger Tor (Brandenburg Gate) and 12 other city gates were erected; and the Supreme Court (now the Berlin Museum), the Opera, and the Arsenal were completed.

But the man credited with elevating Berlin to one of Europe's premier capitals was Friedrich II, better known as Frederick the Great, who reigned from 1740 to 1786. At first he rebelled at the idea of becoming king and tried to flee to England with an army officer. But Friedrich's father, known as the strict "soldier king," punished his disobedient son by making him watch the beheading of his friend (who, so the story goes, was also Friedrich's lover). That, perhaps more than anything, convinced Friedrich that he wanted to be king after all, and during his long reign he doubled the size of the Prussian army and made Prussia the greatest military power in Europe. He also built a charming summer residence in nearby Potsdam, Schloss Sanssouci, where he could escape the worries of an administrative life.

Under Frederick the Great's rule, Berlin became a mecca of the Enlightenment, attracting such greats as the philosopher Moses Mendelssohn, author Gotthold Ephraim Lessing, and publisher Friedrich Nicolai. Voltaire came to Potsdam as the king's guest and stayed three years. In 1763, Frederick the Great took over a failing porcelain company, banned all imports, and granted it a monopoly. The company, the Königliche Porzellan-Manufaktur (KPM) is still well-known today. By 1800, Berlin boasted 200,000 inhabitants, making it the third-largest city in Europe after London and Paris.

On October 27, 1806, Napoléon marched into the capital of a defeated Prussia, entering triumphantly through Brandenburger Tor. Knowing that it would strike at the very heart of the proud Prussians, Napoléon removed the Quadriga—a chariot drawn by four horses, and the symbol of Berlin—from the top of the gate and carted it off to Paris as part of the spoils of war. When the Prussians finally managed to rout the French a couple years later, they recovered their Quadriga—adding an Iron Cross and a Prussian Eagle—and returned it to its perch.

During the Industrial Revolution of the 19th century, Berlin emerged as a center of trade and industry, producing silk, woolens, porcelain, and machinery. But for many of the working class, industrialization brought increasing poverty and destitution. Despite the abolition of serfdom and reforms in education, peasants who flocked to Berlin to find work—including women and children—were exploited in dismal factories under harsh conditions. The middle class, meanwhile, demanded more political power to keep abreast of their newly acquired social status. Although the people rose in revolt several times—notably in the March Revolution of 1848—few concessions were gained. By the 1870s there were 70,000 homeless in Berlin out of a population of 826,000. But even those with a roof over their head often lived in gloomy and depressing flats that never saw the light of day. As many as one-tenth of the total population lived in basements; one-third lived in one-room apartments that averaged 4.3 occupants. Thus, Berlin had the dubious distinction of being one of the world's largest tenement cities.

FROM THE GERMAN REICH TO THE THIRD REICH In 1871, Prussian Chancellor Otto von Bismarck succeeded in uniting all of Germany with a nationalistic policy under the slogan "iron and blood." As Bismarck was Prussian, Berlin naturally became capital of this new German Reich, attracting even more industry and settlers so that by 1906 the city had two million inhabitants. After the turn of the century, Berlin

- 1953 Uprising in East Berlin on June 17 spreads over DDR, repressed with Soviet troops.
- 1958 USSR issues the Berlin Ultimatum, demanding that Western Allies leave Berlin, but Allies ignore the order.
- 1961 Wall constructed August 13; seals off Western Sectors.
- 1963 President Kennedy gives "Ich bin ein Berliner" speech at Rathaus Schöneberg, pledging support of a free West Berlin.
- 1971 Allies sign Four-Powers Agreement on Berlin, confirming political and legal ties between West Berlin and West Germany.
- 1972 West Berliners again allowed to visit DDR.
- 1987 750th Anniversary of Berlin.
- 1988 Berlin declared "Cultural City" of Europe.
- 1989 East Germans flee to West through

continues

- Hungary. Nov. 9 the Wall opened by DDR.
- **1990** Demolition of Wall begun; Germany reunified Oct. 3; Berlin once again becomes capital.
- East Germany adopts West German currency and drops all visa requirements for entering East Berlin.
- Reunification takes place on Oct. 3.
- Berlin is declared capital of Germany.
- Christo wraps the Reichstag in fabric.

supplanted Munich as Germany's cultural capital, attracting such artists as Max Liebermann, Lovis Corinth, and Max Slevogt. Ornate apartment dwellings lined the streets, graced with the curvilinear lines of art nouveau. Max Reinhardt came to direct the Deutsches Theater, and Richard Strauss became conductor of the Royal Opera.

In 1920, Berlin incorporated 7 formerly autonomous towns, 59 rural communities, and 27 landed estates to form a Greater Berlin, which it then divided into 20 precincts. This made Berlin the biggest industrial giant on the Continent, the nucleus of the North German railway network, as well as a commercial-banking and stock-exchange center. Through the 1920s, Berlin flourished as an intellectual and cultural center, and such architectural greats as Walter Gropius and Hans Scharoun left their marks upon the city. In 1926, a young playwright named Bertolt Brecht scored a huge success with the premiere of his *Threepenny Opera*, in this city that had 35 theaters, several opera houses, and more than 20 concert halls. Berlin's university gained a reputation as one of the best in the country, and Albert Einstein, who was director of physics at what would later become the Max-Planck Institute, received the Nobel Prize in 1921. As many as 150 daily and weekly newspapers were published in Berlin. The city rivaled Paris as one of the most exciting cities in Europe.

But behind the facade of greatness, trouble was brewing: The woes of the working class had become increasingly acute, a despair and hopelessness captured by such artists as Käthe Kollwitz and Heinrich Zille and writer Kurt Tucholsky, but otherwise largely ignored. Like the rest of Germany, Berlin had suffered hardships during World War I, with weekly rationings of one egg, 20 grams of butter, and 80 grams of meat per person. Heating fuel, lighting, and clothing were rationed as well. But the end of the war brought little relief, even though the German emperor abdicated and Germany was proclaimed a German Republic. In the winter of 1918–19, 300,000 Berliners were out of work. And yet Germany was saddled with huge war reparations, and parts of the country had been sliced off and given to the victors. Runaway inflation had made the currency virtually worthless: it took barrelfuls just to buy a loaf of bread and 600 marks just to ride the trolley. In 1921, one dollar equalled 75 marks; by November 20, 1923, one dollar was worth 4,200,000,000,000 marks. When new banknotes were finally issued, one new banknote was equal to 1,000 billion of the worthless old paper marks.

The political situation also deteriorated. Struggles between extreme rightists and leftists often resulted in street fights, militant strikes, and bloody riots. In 1929 the economic crisis went from bad to worse, with 636,000 unemployed in Berlin by 1932. Many families lost their homes; some people committed suicide.

> ### ❓ Did You Know?
>
> - In 1700, one Berliner in five was of French extraction.
> - In 1800, Berlin was the third-largest city in Europe after London and Paris.
> - In the 1920s, Berlin boasted 35 theaters, several opera houses, more than 20 concert halls, and 150 daily and weekly newspapers.
> - Founded in 1844, Berlin's Tiergarten zoo housed 10,000 animals in 1939, but only 91 survived the war.
> - Berlin is closer to Poland (60 miles) than it is to any city in former West Germany.
> - Berlin has more students than any other German university city.
> - Berlin has about 1,000 bridges—more than the city of Venice.
> - Berlin has more than 480 miles of hiking and biking trails.
> - A landlocked city, Berlin has more than 30,000 registered boats.

During this upheaval an obscure political party called the National Socialists used the social/economic situation and the harshness of the World War I treaty to gain followers with promises of making Germany great again. On January 30, 1933, Adolf Hitler became Chancellor of Germany. Hitler knew he was not a popular figure in Berlin—his Nazi party had been consistently defeated in elections here—so one of his first moves was to rid "Red Berlin" of its leftist majority. First, Berlin's Communist party headquarters was raided by police on the pretense of a planned coup d'etat. Second, on the night of February 27, 1933, the Reichstag building was mysteriously set ablaze. Although no one ever proved who set the fire—indeed, many believe it was the Nazis themselves—hundreds of Communists, Social Democrats, trade unionists, and intellectuals were rounded up, imprisoned, tortured, and murdered.

The reign of terror had only begun: After a massive book burning near the Staatsoper in May 1933, most of the country's best writers fled the country; scientists soon followed. In 1936 the Olympics were staged in Berlin; Hitler hoped to showcase his Third Reich. Although the Germans won the most gold medals, it was an African-American athlete, Jesse Owens, who stole the show by winning four gold medals.

But the Olympics could not gloss over the fact that the Nazi party reigned by terror, with much of that terror directed towards its Jewish citizens. Although the Nazi's anti-Semitic campaign had been muted during the Olympics, it resumed once the games were over. Anti-Semitic posters were put up once again, and out came more notices barring Jews from public places. On November 9, 1938, Berlin was the scene of the so-called *Kristallnacht* (Crystal Night), a night of terror directed against Jews, during which synagogues and Jewish businesses were burned to the ground. By the time Germany invaded Poland in 1939 and catapulted Europe into another world war, it had rid itself of virtually all opposition. During the next years, as many as 50,000 Berliners of Jewish faith died in concentration camps.

POSTWAR BERLIN On May 8, 1945, the German army surrendered. In Berlin, the legacy of the "Thousand Year Reich" was a wasteland of ruin and destruction. Of the 245,000 buildings in Berlin before the war, 50,000 were destroyed. As many as 80,000 Berliners had lost their lives. Of the 160,000 Jews who had lived in Berlin before 1933, only 7,247 remained. There were food shortages and fuel shortages, and everyone who had anything to sell resorted to the black market. Even drinking water had to be brought in from the country, and there was no electricity or gas. When winter came, fuel was so scarce that the Berliners cut down all their trees for firewood.

Soon Berliners were at work clearing away the rubble, too busy trying to survive and create a livable world to worry about tomorrow. But their fate had been sealed even before the end of the war: The Allies had divided Germany and Berlin into occupation zones to be governed by Great Britain, the United States, the Soviet Union, and later, France. Although each Allied Power had supreme authority in its own sector, Berlin was to be ruled jointly. This proved easier said than done.

In the summer of 1945, Churchill, Truman, and Stalin met at Potsdam, where they agreed to disarm and demilitarize Germany. There was never any intention to split the country in half or change Berlin's role as capital. Rather, they agreed that Nazism must be abolished and that local self-government should be set up on a democratic basis. Unfortunately, they had no plans for how things should proceed and harbored differing ideas of what constituted a democracy. As time went on, ideological differences and political aims created chasms between the Western and Soviet powers.

Already the Soviets had been at work setting up a Communist party in Berlin and appointing a municipal council. But when elections were held for the city parliament (Municipal Assembly) in October 1946, the Social Democrats (SPD) won almost half of the votes while the Communist party, the Socialist Unity Party, garnered only 19.8% of the votes. The Communists clearly did not have the majority.

In 1948 the Western Powers introduced the Deutsche Mark in West Berlin, thus financially separating it from East Germany and strengthening its ties with West Germany. As far as the Soviets were concerned, Berlin, with a growing democratic following, was becoming a dangerous thorn in the Soviet side. In retaliation, the Soviets introduced their own currency, declaring it legal tender throughout all of Berlin. They then imposed a road blockade of Berlin. Since food, raw materials, and necessities for 2 million people came from the Western Zones, there was no alternative but to organize an Allied airlift. Gen. Lucius D. Clay, who organized the lift, said the blockade "was one of the most brutal attempts in recent history to use mass starvation as a means of applying political pressure."

The largest airlift in history began on June 26, 1948. Within weeks, 4,000 tons of supplies were being flown into Berlin daily; in only 3 months, Tegel Airport was built. At the peak of the airlift, a plane was landing every 1 to 2 minutes, and, in April 1949, a record was set when nearly 13,000 tons of supplies were flown in on a single day. During the 11 months that the airlift lasted, more than 200,000 flights brought in 1.7 million tons of supplies.

Although the Soviets had hoped the blockade would end Western influence in Berlin, instead it drew the Western Powers together, formed a bond of friendship between Berliners and the West, and convinced the Western Powers that they must remain in Berlin to defend their concept of freedom. Soon thereafter, the Municipal Assembly and the City Council—which had had their seats in the Eastern Sector—moved to the Western Sector. The Communists responded by appointing their own City Council. The city was now divided, politically and ideologically. From then on, both sectors followed their own course of development. In 1949, East Berlin became the capital of the German Democratic Republic (DDR). In 1952, telephone communications between the two cities were cut off, tram and bus lines were severed, and West Berliners were no longer allowed into the surrounding East German countryside. However, there was still unrestricted movement throughout Berlin, with many East Berliners working in the Western sectors. In 1955, West Germany became a member of NATO; East Germany, a member of the Warsaw Pact. The Cold War was on.

And yet, few could imagine that a divided Germany was anything but temporary. As far as West Germany was concerned, its goal was reunification—with the reestablishment of Berlin as its capital. An uprising of East German workers on June 17, 1953, brutally quashed by Soviet soldiers, only reconfirmed West Germany's commitment.

Meanwhile, Berlin began to prosper again. In 1950, there were 300,000 unemployed Berliners; 7 years later it was down to 90,000. Since Berliners could still travel freely through the city, many East Berliners flocked to factories in West Berlin. Housing estates mushroomed, replacing homes that had been destroyed in the war. In 1957, West Berlin hosted a worldwide architectural competition that brought 48 leading architects from around the world to design housing for the Hansaviertel (Hansa Quarter). Clearly, West Berlin was recovering much more rapidly than East Germany, making it a popular attraction for East Germans eager for a look at the new and prosperous Berlin. Many of them liked what they saw so much that they decided to stay. Before long, East Germany was losing many of its brightest, best-educated, and most-skilled workers to the West.

In November 1958, Soviet Prime Minister Nikita Kruschchev issued the Berlin Ultimatum, demanding that the Western Powers withdraw from West Berlin. Since Berlin was seen as strategic in the "domino theory" of Communist takeovers, the Western Powers refused. Refugees continued to pour into the West. From 1949 to 1961, approximately 3 million East Germans fled their country. From the East German point of view, something clearly had to be done.

THE WALL On August 13, 1961, East Germany began erecting a wall between East and West Berlin, tearing up streets and putting up posts and barbed wire. A few days later, the wall was reinforced with concrete and brick. Movement between the two Berlins was now forbidden, leaving families and friends separated by what was soon known around the world simply as the Wall. Measuring 13 feet high and approximately 100 miles long, the Wall was backed by hundreds of guardhouses, 293 sentry towers, patrol dogs, and a vast swath of a no-man's-land that was brightly illuminated. And yet that didn't stop some East Germans willing to risk their lives for freedom. Approximately 5,000 East Germans managed to escape to West Berlin, most of them during the early years. But 78 people lost their lives trying to flee to West Berlin, most shot by East German guards.

For 28 years, the Wall stood as a constant reminder of Germany's forced division. Even for visitors, seeing the Wall for the first time was both chilling and unsettling, a feeling that intensified when crossing into East Berlin at Checkpoint Charlie. Mirrors were shoved under cars to make sure no one was hiding underneath; travelers on foot were shuttled through doors that clanged shut behind them, as though they were entering a high-security prison. Entering into East Berlin was eerie and 1984ish, as the differences between the two Berlins had became so radical with the passage of time. West Berlin was a capitalist's dream—intense, aggressive, and chaotic—a whirling blend of traffic, people, neon, and noise. East Berlin was conservative and subdued, sterile and quiet, with soldiers everywhere.

In 1971, the Four Powers signed an agreement that confirmed political and legal ties between West Berlin and West Germany. Telephone communications between the two Berlins were restored, and West Berliners were allowed to visit East Germany. For the next 18 years, conditions between East and West steadily improved, although Westerners were required to exchange a minimum amount of Western currency into East German marks, and travel into East Ger-many was still complicated and difficult for non-Germans.

In autumn 1989, Hungary opened its borders to the West and allowed East Germans to pass through. This prompted tens of thousands of East Germans to journey to freedom. This exodus was accompanied by pro-reform demonstrations throughout East Germany, which finally led to the ouster of hard-line East German leader Erich Honecker on October 18. By November 1989, approximately 175,000 East German refugees had fled, almost 1% of the total population. It was clear something had to be done to staunch the flow, but no one dreamed it was the Wall itself that would fall.

On the evening of November 9, 1989, East German authorities announced that it was permanently lifting travel restrictions on its citizens, granting them freedom of movement for the first time since the Wall was built in 1961. That evening, 50,000 East Berliners streamed into West Berlin and were welcomed on the other side with embraces and tears. Many Berliners climbed on top of the Wall to dance and celebrate.

With a story similar to others in Berlin at the time, a teacher working in West Berlin recalled what it was like in those first heady days of the Wall's opening. "On Friday, November 10, I went to the school where I work, and the director decided to cancel all classes, because history was being made in the streets and the children should see it. So

I went to Potsdamer Square, and the whole experience was so emotional, so strange, that I had goosebumps several times that day. We watched the East Berliners come through the opening in the Wall. The first ones seemed very unsure of themselves, as though they still didn't believe they could. They came slowly, with big eyes. Some of them, especially the older ones, wept. It was like they were being let out of prison after so many years."

FROM 1990 TO THE PRESENT   Soon after the Wall came down, the West German government reiterated its dedication to reunification. On March 18, 1990, democratic elections were held in East Germany that signaled the official demise of the Communist regime. Reunification of the two Germanys followed on October 3, 1990. Berlin became Germany's capital, with the seat of government remaining in Bonn for the time being.

As the jubilation of reunification wore off, new problems began to surface, and there were fears about the future in both East and West. After all, by March 1990, as many as 500,000 East Germans had settled in the West, entitling them to "adjustment money," household compensation, housing subsidies, and job retraining. In keeping with a policy that had been established years before, any East German coming to West Germany for the first time, even for just a day, was entitled to a welcoming token of 100 DM; but Bonn hadn't dreamed that virtually the entire East German population would come over to get it. Many West Germans began worrying about the financial burdens of reunification, especially the cost of East German economic development. Some West Berliners—irritated by the sudden long queues of East Germans in shops and restaurants and the soaring cost of real estate—grumbled that they wished the Wall had never come down at all. Some said that East Germans expected too much too soon, and that if East Germans wanted a more affluent lifestyle, they should have to work hard to achieve it, just as the West Germans had.

East Germans, on the other hand, were concerned about their ability to compete in a capitalist society, the impact of materialism on their youth, the appearance of a drug culture, and their treatment, both economically and socially, as second-class citizens. They worried about the loss of the old regime's cradle-to-grave benefits like controlled rents, job security, and old-age pensions. Many, especially those who had envisioned reunification as an opportunity to combine the best of socialism and democracy, felt powerless in the wave of new laws and reforms that eroded the very values they thought worth saving. Some went so far as to describe reunification as a hostile takeover.

Impressions

An immense responsibility rests upon the German people for this subservience to the barbaric idea of autocracy. This is the gravamen against them in history—that, in spite of all their brains and courage, they worship Power, and let themselves be led by the nose.
—Sir Winston Churchill, 1937

With the closing of noncompetitive, formerly subsidized enterprises, unemployment skyrocketed. By the end of 1991, unemployment in former East Germany had risen to 11%; by 1994 it was more than 13%. Many are still jobless, especially East Germany's youths. The problem has been compounded by waves of foreign asylum-seekers entering Germany (their numbers climbed from 57,000 in 1987 to 500,000 in 1992), some of whom have been the victims of attacks by right-wing extremists.

No German city has been and will be more affected by the reunification than Berlin. It faces the formidable challenge of integrating two very different systems and all of the attendant social upheavals. Skyrocketing real estate prices, homelessness, unemployment, a rising crime rate (brought on, some contend, by infiltration of Russian mobsters), and a disenchanted youth are just some of the pressing problems facing Berlin today. In addition, pitied for years as a victim of the Cold War, Berlin must also slay the ghost of its past as the capital of the Third Reich in order to take its place once again as one of Europe's great capitals.

The future will certainly continue to be one of change, especially in former eastern Berlin, as sorely needed hotels, restaurants, and service-oriented businesses set up shop. By the year 2000, Bonn is expected to relinquish its role as administrative center, with the government and parliament moving to Berlin. As the next chapter unfolds in the story of Berlin, this intense, extraordinary city is facing yet another challenging transformation.

4 Famous Berliners

Otto von Bismarck (1815–98) Known as the Iron Chancellor, Bismarck was a brilliant politician who succeeded in uniting all of Germany in 1871 and became the empire's first chancellor. Dismissed from office by Kaiser Wilhelm II in 1890, Bismarck remained popular.

Willy Brandt (1913–92) From 1957 to 1966, Brandt served as mayor of Berlin, weathering the construction of the Wall. A prominent and popular member of the Social Democratic Party (SPD), Brandt became Chancellor of West Germany in 1969 and received the Nobel Peace Prize in 1971, but in 1974 resigned after a scandal in which his close personal aide and confidant, Günter Guillaume, was unmasked as a spy for DDR.

Bertolt Brecht (1898–1956) A well-known playwright, Brecht came to Berlin in 1920 and worked with Max Reinhardt at the Deutsches Theater. An ardent Marxist, Brecht wrote epic dramas that scorned the materialistic self-absorption of the middle class and underscored the plight of the poor and the working class. In 1928 he achieved fame with *The Threepenny Opera*. Other well-known plays include *Mother Courage and Her Children* and *The Good Woman of Szechuan*. In 1933 Brecht left Berlin but returned after the war to East Berlin and founded the famous Berliner Ensemble, which continues to stage his works.

Friedrich II, "Frederick the Great" (1712–86)   The third and most well-known king of Prussia, he built the charming Sanssouci Palace in Potsdam where he could retreat to meditate and pursue philosophy. Frederick the Great was an advocate of the Enlightenment, a composer and a musician, and a friend to Voltaire.

Walter Gropius (1883–1969)   Born in Berlin, Gropius studied architecture in Munich and Berlin. In 1919 he was named director of the Weimar School of Art, which became the legendary Bauhaus. From 1928 to 1934 he worked as an architect in Berlin, immigrating in 1934 to England, and then to the United States in 1937, where he was a professor at Harvard until 1952. See the Gropius apartment building in the Hansaviertel and the Bauhaus-Archiv, built after his death according to his designs.

Georg Wenzeslaus von Knobelsdorff (1699–1753)   After studying in Italy, Paris, Spain, and Dresden, Knobelsdorff went on to become one of Germany's leading rococo architects. A friend of Frederick the Great, he actualized sketches drawn by Frederick for Sanssouci Palace in Potsdam, which remains Knobelsdorff's greatest achievement. He also designed the Deutsche Staatsoper (destroyed by fire in 1843) on Unter den Linden, as well as several buildings in the Sanssouci park.

Käthe Kollwitz (1867–1945)   A Berliner, Kollwitz was a gifted graphic artist, painter, and sculptress who expressed strong emotion in her studies of working-class Berliners. Her works can be seen at the Käthe-Kollwitz Museum on Fasanenstrasse near the Ku'damm.

Max Liebermann (1847–1935)   Liebermann, a painter and graphic artist who was born and died in Berlin, is considered the main representative of impressionism in Germany. He was founder and president of the Secession movement, a group of artists concerned with developing their own approach and impressionist style. His works are on display in the Neue Nationalgalerie in Tiergarten and the Alte Nationalgalerie on Museum Island.

Max Reinhardt (1873–1943)   Born in Vienna, Reinhardt is legendary in German theater and is credited with introducing German-language theater to the rest of the world. He served as director of the Deutsches Theater in Berlin from 1905 to 1920, and again from 1924 to 1932. Reinhardt also served as director of the Festspielhaus in Salzburg and founded the world-renowned Salzburg Festival.

Karl Friedrich Schinkel (1781–1841)   A gifted architect who received his training in Berlin, Schinkel is to Berlin what Haussmann is to Paris: the man most responsible for the city's architectural style and continuity. His works, mainly neoclassical, include the Neue Wache (New Guardhouse) on Unter den Linden, which today houses a memorial to victims of militarism; Das Altes Museum on Museumsinsel; the Schauspielhaus on Gendarmenmarkt; and the Schlossbrücke bridge over the Spree. Particularly delightful is his summerhouse behind Schloss Charlottenburg, built in the style of an Italian villa and known today as the Schinkel Pavilion. The Friedrichwerdersche Kirche in Berlin-Mitte, which he also designed, contains a museum of the architect's work and life. Schinkel also worked as a landscape painter and stage designer.

Andreas Schlüter (1660–1714) Schlüter was Berlin's top baroque architect and is credited with giving Berlin a royal appearance. Also a sculptor and influenced by Michelangelo, Schlüter is best known for his 21 masks of dying warriors in the courtyard of the Arsenal on Unter den Linden (undergoing renovation at press time) and his equestrian statue of the Great Elector now in the forecourt of Schloss Charlottenburg. As the court architect, he also rebuilt the Berlin Palace (no longer in existence) but fell out of favor when a tower he designed collapsed.

Heinrich Zille (1858–1929) A popular graphic artist and caricaturist, Zille was a chronicler of turn-of-the-century life in Berlin, which he depicted with compassionate humor. He is particularly known for his sketches of the poor and working class. Having an eye for the absurd, he contributed regularly to satirical journals. His works are on display at the Zille Museum, located in the Berliner Antik- und Flohmarkt at the Friedrichstrasse S-Bahn station.

5 A Cultural Capital

With more than 80 museums and home to the Deutsche Oper, the Staatsoper, and the Berlin Philharmonic Orchestra, not to mention a thriving and vibrant nightlife, Berlin is without question the reunified country's cultural capital.

For the most part, Berlin's artistic heritage lives on in its museums. Berlin's love affair with museums can be traced back to the 1820s, when construction of a museum complex was begun by King Friedrich Wilhelm III, who wished to make his collection of masterpieces available to the public. Located on an island in the middle of the Spree River in the heart of the city (known today as Museumsinsel, or Museum Island), the complex grew through the next century, as German archaeologists searched the world for artifacts and treasures from Persia, Greece, and Egypt. Berlin today is home of the famous bust of Nefertiti, the incredible Pergamon Altar, and the breathtaking Gate of Ishtar. Throughout Berlin there is an array of art museums, history museums, collections of applied arts, and special interest museums. Luckily for tourists, the majority of museums is concentrated in four areas of Berlin: Dahlem, Tiergarten, Charlottenburg, and Museumsinsel.

Of course, it would be wrong to assume that all Berlin's treasures originated someplace else, for Berlin was home to a great many artists in the past century. One of the earliest to gain fame was Adolph von Menzel (1815–1905), a painter who was largely self-taught and became known for his portraits. Menzel sought company in coffeehouses and is considered a forerunner of the impressionists. He was followed by a group of artists who in 1892 founded the Secession movement, headed by Max Liebermann, which was concerned with developing its own stylistic approach to impressionism. Liebermann, Lovis

Corinth, and Max Slevogt are considered foremost among German impressionists.

After the turn of the century a new generation of painters flocked to Berlin. Prominent among them was a group from Dresden known as Die Brücke (The Bridge) who arrived 1910–1911. Horrified by the industrialized urban society with its impersonal factories and grim tenements, they viewed Berlin as an industrial nightmare, a place that inspired fear, longing, unrest, and expectation of impending doom. Rather than simply imitating nature or photographing people, these painters rejected traditional subjects and style in favor of works that reflected their inner feelings and conflicts. Thus was born German expressionism. Numbered among Die Brücke was Ernst Ludwig Kirchner, Emil Nolde, Max Pechstein, and Oskar Kokoschka. Two other important artists were Käthe Kollwitz and Heinrich Zille, who portrayed the city's growing army of the poor. Visit the Brücke-Museum in Dahlem, the Käthe-Kollwitz Museum near the Ku'damm, the Alte Nationalgalerie (Old National Gallery) on Museumsinsel, and the Neue Nationalgalerie (New National Gallery) in the Tiergarten.

The Alte Nationalgalerie, specializing in painting and sculpture of the 19th century, boasts an impressive collection of works by Berlin impressionists, including early works of Max Liebermann, Lovis Corinth, and Max Beckmann. It also contains the world's largest collection of works by Adolph von Menzel. The Neue Nationalgalerie continues where the Alte Nationalgalerie ends, with art since the turn of this century and displaying works by Munch, Liebermann, Slevogt, artists belonging to Die Brücke, and artists of the former DDR.

In addition, works by contemporary Berlin artists are shown regularly in special exhibitions in the Neue Nationalgalerie and the Berlinische Galerie. And there are more than 120 galleries in Berlin, many conveniently located near the Ku'damm. Although prices are out of range for most of us, it costs nothing to look. For affordable art and crafts, there's the weekend market held on Strasse des 17. Juni, where Berliners sell everything from sketches and handmade toys to tie-dyed scarves and jewelry.

As for Berlin's performance art scene, it has a rich tradition of the stage. Much of Germany's theatrical history stems from Berlin, for it was here that playwrights Hauptmann, Ibsen, Strindberg, and Brecht made their first major breakthroughs. Max Reinhardt, recognized as the man who introduced German theater to the world, directed the Deutsches Theater from 1905 to 1920 and again from 1924 to 1932.

Impressions

Berlin is a city for artists, for the young, for the creative. Not for idyllic artists, who wish to sit on the bank of a pond, dreaming; but for those to whom a melody can come from the struggles of life . . . Berlin has taken a massive step toward becoming a center, if not the center of artistic force in Germany. —Paul Westheim, 1929

(Reinhardt also founded the world-famous Salzburg Festival.) In the 1920s, Berlin had approximately 35 theaters, several opera houses, and more than 20 concert halls.

Today Berlin is still famous for its theater, including the Schiller Theater (which now stages musicals and popular revues), the Schaubühne, and the Berliner Ensemble and cabaret. Berlin is home to three well-known opera houses, the International Film Festival, the Philharmonic Orchestra, and a number of concert halls and live-music houses. Rock stars make regular concert appearances in Berlin, and there's a strong jazz and avant-garde scene in bars and smaller music houses. As many bars remain open all night, Berlin is a mecca for nightlife revelers.

6 Architecture 101

Visually, much of Berlin is a new city, with little from before World War II remaining. In my opinion, it's hard to rave about the aesthetic charm of the Kurfürstendamm or fall in love with the sterility of Alexanderplatz, and even the city's oldest buildings such as the Nikolaikirche and the Marienkirche are usually reconstructions. The Berlin Palace, a sumptuous Renaissance residence for the Prussian kings, was deemed irreparable after World War II by the DDR and was torn down to make way for East Berlin's hideously modern Palace of the Republic with its concert halls and restaurants.

Fortunately, not all of Berlin is new. There's Schloss Charlottenburg, which served as a summer residence for Prussian kings and is considered Berlin's most beautiful baroque building. There are also fine, turn-of-the-century patrician homes throughout the city, with rich art nouveau stucco facades, projecting balconies, recessed arched windows, sweeping staircases, and high ceilings. Built during prosperous times, they sit on broad tree-lined streets that give them an even grander appearance. Fasanenstrasse and other side streets off the Kurfürstendamm boast a number of these beautiful buildings.

Many public buildings from previous centuries are in Berlin-Mitte, which was the historic heart of the city before World War II and which fell to the Communists upon the division of the city. Among these are the 17th-century Arsenal on Unter den Linden, the museums on Museumsinsel, and the Staatsoper built by Georg Wenzeslaus von Knobelsdorff in the mid-1700s (although the original Staatsoper burned in 1843, the present building is a faithful reconstruction of Knobelsdorff's design). From the same period is Berlin's most famous landmark, the Brandenburger Tor, completed in 1786 as one of 13 city gates that used to mark the entrance to Berlin.

Perhaps the most credit for Berlin's architectural greatness should be given to Karl Friedrich Schinkel (1781–1841), a protomodernist in his structural engineering, who used mainly neoclassical but also Gothic, Byzantine, and Renaissance designs in his creations. His works include the Alte Museum on Museum Island and the delightful Schinkel Pavilion on the grounds of Schloss Charlottenburg.

The most famous new quarter of postwar Berlin is the Hansaviertel, a residential area created by 48 leading architects from around the world, each of whom was asked to design one building. Among the participants were Alvar Aalto, Walter Gropius, Oscar Niemeyer, and Arne Jacobsen. Walter Gropius also left his mark on the Bauhaus-Archiv, a light and airy building housing a museum dedicated to the principles of the Bauhaus school of design.

And of course, there's also a lot of empty land waiting for development—notice the snaking scar left from the removal of the Wall. Potsdamerplatz, once the lively heart of prewar Berlin, became a wasteland of weeds and vacant lots after the Wall went up. Bordered on the west end by Hans Scharoun's impressive Philharmonie with its golden, tentlike roof, Potsdamerplatz became the focus of hot debate following the demise of the Wall as different interest groups presented their own plans for development. Some thought it should become a park; others thought it should go to the highest bidder. Today it's a maze of construction sites as Sony and Daimler-Benz construct new office buildings. More construction is taking place in former East Berlin, especially in Berlin-Mitte and along Friedrichstrasse. In fact, I have never seen so many cranes in the core of city as there are now in Berlin-Mitte; some Berliners grumble that the proliferation of high-rise office buildings in the historic heart of the city is compromising its architectural integrity. Plans are in the works to transform Alexanderplatz into a mountain of skyscrapers. The Berlin of tomorrow depends heavily on decisions made by today's city planners.

For where to go and what to see, please refer to the "For the Architecture Lover" section in "Special-Interest Sightseeing" in Chapter 7.

7 Cuisine

If you love pork, you're in the right country. Surely the Germans have invented more ways to serve pork than any other people: from simple pork sausages with a dab of mustard and a hard roll to pig's knuckle served with sauerkraut and potatoes. Berlin's KaDeWe department store, famous for its massive food floor, features 1,000 different kinds of sausage alone—most of them pork. You could have a variety of pork dishes for breakfast, lunch, and dinner.

Portions in German restaurants are huge, consisting of a main course served with a couple of side dishes on the same plate (usually sauerkraut or potatoes), accompanied by the almost obligatory rounds of beer. Because most dishes are complete meals, you can eat a satisfying meal for about 15 DM ($10), and unless you have a voracious appetite you may find yourself able to get by with only two meals a day—breakfast in your hotel, followed by one hearty meal later in the day. In any case, be forewarned that German food is not a weight-reducing cuisine. It seems to me that few worry about calories in Germany: witness the coffee shops packed at 4pm—the unofficial coffee break around the country—when everyone downs cups of coffee and sinfully fattening tortes and cakes.

BREAKFAST The typical German breakfast consists of bread or rolls topped with marmalade, cheese, or sausage. Unlike American sandwiches, which are stuffed as much as possible, in Germany it's

Dining Tips

The typical neighborhood place—popular for its beer, camaraderie, and no-nonsense cuisine—is usually crowded and lively, especially during lunchtime, when most Germans eat their big meal of the day, or after work. At these places, it's acceptable to take any free seat, even if the rest of the table is occupied. But ask first whether the seat is free and whether your fellow diners object.

At more expensive restaurants, customers are seated by the management. And in a few restaurants, usually those in former East Berlin, you may be expected to first give your coat or jacket to the coat clerk at the *Garderobe*; the clerk will expect a small tip of a mark (65¢).

As for dining etiquette, Germans use a fork and knife for almost everything, including french fries, sandwiches, pizza, chicken, and other foods that Americans are more likely to eat with their fingers. Historically, it wasn't until 1846 that forks were produced for the masses; before that, Germans ate with their fingers, too. Fifteenth-century etiquette called for using three fingers to pick up meat from plates but frowned upon stuffing food into one's mouth with both hands or keeping one's hands resting on plates for too long.

Today, Germans, like other Europeans, hold forks in the left hand and keep the knife in the right. Once you've mastered this technique, you'll find it makes a lot more sense than switching your fork from hand to hand every time you want to cut that piece of pork. If you're taking a breather from your meal and don't wish the waiter to clear your plate, lay your fork and knife down in the same position as you held them: that is, the fork on the left side of the plate and your knife on the right. If you place your knife and fork together, side by side on the plate, it's a signal to the waiter that you've finished your meal. When you get up to leave, it's considered good etiquette to say good-bye to the other diners at your table, even if they're strangers and you didn't talk to them the whole meal.

Drinking also has its rules. If you're among German acquaintances, don't take a sip until your host raises his glass. Quite often you'll bash your beer mugs or clink your wine glasses together before taking your first sip. This custom grew out of a superstition that the devil could enter the body of a person who was drinking: the clashing together of glasses was meant to create a colossal noise and scare the devil away.

---

customary to place only a single slice of cheese or sausage upon each slice of bread. Germans eat these open bread sandwiches with a knife and fork, the fork turned upside down. A soft-boiled egg—left in its shell and served in an egg cup—often accompanies these. Breakfast buffets in hotels may include cereals, such as *Muesli* (a grain cereal similar to granola) or cornflakes, fruit, juices, and coffee. German coffee is much stronger than American coffee—there's rarely a bottomless cup in Germany, though some pensions and hotels do serve extra coffee during breakfast.

If your hotel doesn't serve breakfast, choose from the many famous coffeehouses along the Ku'damm. And there are many breakfast cafes, many open all night as well.

LUNCH & DINNER For lunch or dinner, your choice ranges from the neighborhood *Gaststätte* (simple restaurants/pubs) to restaurants with cuisine from around the world. Since most Germans have their big meal of the day at lunch and restaurants may be crowded, you might want to consider eating during the off-hours.

In a traditional German restaurant, start your meal with a hearty bowl of soup, which can be quite filling. One of my favorites is *Linsensuppe* (lentil soup, often with pieces of sausage). *Leberknödelsuppe* (a dumpling soup made with beef liver, onions, and garlic) and *Kartoffelsuppe* (potato soup) are other common choices. *Gulaschsuppe,* borrowed from Hungary, is a spicy soup featuring beef, paprika, and potatoes. Appetizers include *Hackepeter* (raw minced meat, like a steak tartare) and *Soleier* (pickled eggs). There is almost an endless selection of bread: from rye to pumpernickel, and various hard rolls called *Brötchen.*

For the main dish, one of Berlin's most well-known specialties is *Eisbein* (pig's knuckle), usually served with sauerkraut and *Kartoffelpuree* (mashed potatoes) or *Erbspuree* (pureed peas). *Kasseler Rippenspeer* is smoked pork chops, created long ago by a butcher in Berlin named Kassel. A *Boulette,* introduced by the French Huguenots, is a type of cold meatball served with mustard. For pork lovers there's *Schweinebraten* (pot-roasted pork) and *Spanferkel* (suckling pig). If you come across a *Schweinshaxen,* it's grilled knuckle of pork. A *Schlachteplatte* is only for the adventuresome (roughly translated, it's "butcher's platter"), consisting of fresh blood sausage, liverwurst, pig's kidneys, and boiled pork. You'll find *Würste,* or sausages, on almost every menu, as well as at *Imbisse* (food stands), where they're served with a hard roll and mustard. Berlin's specialty sausage is the *Bockwurst,* a superlong boiled sausage, often served with *Erbsensuppe* (split-pea soup). Another favorite is grilled *Bratwurst* from Nürnberg, often prepared with beer, and the *Wiener.* A *Currywurst* is a sausage served with a curry-flavored sauce.

For something other than pork, there's *Sauerbraten* (marinated beef in a thick sauce), *Schnitzel* (breaded veal cutlet), *Brathering* (grilled herring), *Brathuhn* (roast chicken), *Aal grün* (boiled eel in a dill sauce), and *gebratene Kalbsleber Berliner Art* (sautéed calves' liver with onions and apples). Other main courses you may come across include *Tafelspitz* (boiled beef with vegetables), *Leberkäs* (a type of German meat loaf,

Impressions

Think of the man who first tried German sausage.
    —Jerome K. Jerome, 1889

common to southern Germany), and *Sülze* (jellied meat). Vegetarians should look for a *Gemüseplatte,* a dish of assorted vegetables.

In addition to traditional German fare, Berlin boasts an astounding assortment of international cuisines, thanks, in part, to the Wall. In order to attract businesses to pre-unification Berlin, the West German government offered generous subsidies that induced immigrants from Turkey, Greece, Italy, and other countries to open up shop. With time, Berliners have grown more and more appreciative of and interested in foreign food. With the largest Turkish population of any city outside Istanbul, Berlin is especially known for its Turkish restaurants. There are *Imbisse* all over town offering *doner kebab* (pita bread filled with grilled lamb, lettuce, and garlic sauce), and restaurants serving everything from lamb in a spicy sauce to shish kebab. Italian eateries—especially those specializing in inexpensive pizzas—seem to be on every street corner. Beware, however, that if you order a *peperoni pizza,* you'll get one with hot jalapeño peppers; order a *salami* pizza if you want an American-style pepperoni pizza.

DRINK Germany is known for its wines and beers, both of which are plentiful in Berlin. Berlin itself, however, is not a wine-producing region. Frederick the Great tried his hand at winemaking at Sanssouci, but the rows of grapevines are all that remain of his efforts. When in Berlin, you should try wines from other regions in Germany, such as the Rhine (Rheingau, Rheinhessen, and Rheinpfalz), Baden-Württemberg, and Franken. Wines range from the Riesling (white wine) to *Sekt* (a sparkling wine), from dry (*trocken*) to sweet (*süss*). Unless you know your German wines or simply want to experiment, ask your sommelier or waiter for a recommendation.

As for beer, Berlin's most famous brew among tourists is the *Berliner Weisse,* a draft wheat beer served with a shot of raspberry or a green woodruff syrup—a summertime drink. Strangely enough, Berliners rarely drink the stuff. If you simply order *ein Bier,* you'll get either a draft beer (*vom Fass*) or bottled beer (*eine Flasche*). An *Export* is slightly stronger but is still considered light; a *Bock* beer is dark and rich. A *Pils* or *Pilsener* is light and slightly bitter. One of my favorites is *Hefe-Weizen,* a wheat beer.

Although it's considered safe, Germans don't drink their tap water, preferring bottled water. A *Mineralwasser* is bottled mineral water, usually carbonated; if you don't like the bubbly stuff, add the words "*ohne Kohlensäure.*"

3

Planning a Trip to Berlin

Read this chapter before leaving home, and you'll be ahead of the game when it comes to preparing for your trip, packing, and getting the most for your money. However, don't stop here. By reading the other chapters, you'll be familiar with Berlin before you even arrive and may already know what you want to see and do. Knowing that Berlin has many lakes great for swimming may prompt you to pack your swimsuit; on the other hand, learning that there are many nude beaches may prompt you to leave your suit at home.

1 Visitor Information & Entry Requirements

VISITOR INFORMATION The **German National Tourist Office (GNTO)** publishes a wealth of free, colorful brochures available for travelers, including a map of Germany, general information about travel in Germany, a brochure on Berlin itself, and a pamphlet on Berlin's hotels.

If you'd like information and literature before leaving home, contact one of the GNTO offices:

United States: GNTO, 122 E. 42nd St., 52nd floor, New York, NY 10168 (☎ **212/661-7200**).

GNTO, 11766 Wilshire Blvd., Suite 750, Los Angeles, CA 90025 (☎ **310/575-9799**).

Canada: GNTO, Office National Allemand du Tourisme, 175 Bloor St. E., North Tower, Suite 604, Toronto, Ontario M4W 3R8 (☎ **416/968-1570**).

England: GNTO, Nightingale House, 65 Curzon St., London W1Y 7PE (☎ **071/495-0081**).

Australia: GNTO, Lufthansa House, 9th floor, 143 Macquarie St., Sydney 2000, Australia (☎ **012/367-3890**).

ENTRY REQUIREMENTS Citizens of the United States, Canada, Australia, and New Zealand need only a valid passport for entry to Germany and stays up to three months. Visitors from the United Kingdom need only an identity card.

Students should be sure to bring an International Student Identification Card as well; if you plan to rent a car, be sure to bring a valid driver's license (a U.S. license is fine for stays up to a year; after that you must apply for a German driver's license).

You can bring duty-free into Germany 200 cigarettes or 50 cigars or 250 grams of tobacco, 1 liter of spirits, and 2 liters of wine. You may bring gifts into Germany totaling 620 DM ($413.35).

A Note on Customs for British Citizens On January 1, 1993, the borders between European countries were relaxed as the European markets united. When you're traveling within the EC, this will have a big impact on what you can buy and take home with you for personal use.

If you buy your goods in a duty-free shop, then the old rules still apply—you're allowed to bring home 200 cigarettes and 2 liters of table wine, plus 1 liter of spirits or 2 liters of fortified wine. If you don't want the fortified wine, you can take an extra 2 liters of table wine. The perfume allowance is 60 ml, and you can take home £36 worth of other assorted goodies.

But now you can buy your wine, spirits, or cigarettes in an ordinary shop in France or Belgium, for example, and bring home *almost* as much as you like. U.K. Customs and Excise does set theoretical limits: 10 liters of spirits, plus 110 liters of beer, 20 liters of fortified wine, 90 liters of ordinary wine (no more than 60 liters of this can be sparkling wine), 800 cigarettes, 400 cigarillos, 200 cigars, and 1 kilo of tobacco. But remember, this applies only to goods bought in ordinary shops. If you buy in duty-free shops, these new rules don't apply to you.

If you are returning home from a non-EC country, the allowances are the standard ones from duty-free shops. You must declare any goods in excess of these allowances.

You cannot buy goods and take them with you to sell to others. This is a criminal offense in the U.K., and customs officers claim to be looking out for those making repeated trips or those laden down with goods.

2 Money

CURRENCY The basic unit of currency in Germany is the **Deutsche Mark (DM).** One DM equals 100 Pfennig. Coins come in denominations of 1, 2, 5, 10, and 50 Pfennig, and 1, 2, and 5 DM. Bills are issued in denominations of 5, 10, 20, 50, 100, 200, 500, and 1,000 DM.

Although rates fluctuate continually, all conversions in this book are based on a rate of 1.50 DM to U.S. $1 (and then rounded off to the nearest nickel). To help you with money in Germany, see "The Deutsche Mark" below. At press time, the pound sterling exchanged at the rate of £1 = 2.30 DM. Keep in mind that the rates may have changed, so plan your budget accordingly.

In addition, keep in mind that prices themselves will change in Berlin during the lifetime of this book—which means that they will go up. Prices for hotels, for example, rose dramatically after the Wall came down and people flocked to Berlin, simply because there was more demand than there was supply. Real estate prices also skyrocketed, resulting in higher rents. Since most proprietors of Berlin's budget

The Deutsche Mark

For American Readers At this writing $1 = approximately 1.50 DM (or 1 DM = 65¢), and this was the rate of exchange used to calculate the dollar values given in this chapter (rounded to the nearest nickel).

For British Readers At this writing £1 = approximately 2.30 DM (or 1 DM = 43p), and this was the rate of exchange used to calculate the pound values in the table below.

Note: The rates given here fluctuate from time to time and may not be the same when you travel to Germany. Therefore this table should be used only as a guide:

DM	U.S.$	U.K.£	DM	U.S.$	U.K.£
			20	13.35	8.70
			25	16.65	10.85
			30	20.00	13.05
1	.65	.43	35	23.35	15.20
2	1.33	.87	40	26.65	17.40
3	2.00	1.30	45	30.00	19.55
4	2.65	1.80	50	33.35	21.70
5	3.35	2.17	60	40.00	26.10
6	4.00	2.60	70	46.65	30.45
7	4.65	3.05	80	53.35	34.80
8	5.35	3.47	90	60.00	39.15
9	6.00	3.90	100	66.65	43.45
10	6.65	4.35	125	83.35	53.35
15	10.00	6.50	150	100.00	65.20

restaurants and pensions are renters rather than landowners, some of the increased costs have been passed on to customers. Prices given in this book, therefore, should be used only as a guideline.

TRAVELER'S CHECKS Traveler's checks issued in U.S. dollars and other foreign currencies can be exchanged only in banks, major hotels, some large department stores, and the American Express office. If you plan to spend all your time in Germany, you may wish to buy traveler's checks in German marks, available through American Express or MasterCard traveler's checks. Be aware, however, that such traveler's checks are not commonly used in Europe and will probably not be accepted as payment at small stores or restaurants.

CREDIT CARDS As for credit cards, American Express, Diners Club, MasterCard, and Visa are the ones most readily accepted (and JCB, of course, in case you happen to have a Japanese credit card). All

What Things Cost in Berlin U.S. $

Taxi from Tegel Airport to Bahnhof Zoo train station	20.50
Underground from Kurfürstendamm to Dahlem	2.45
Local telephone call (for three minutes)	.20
Double room at the Hotel Tiergarten Berlin (deluxe)	143.35
Double room at Arco (moderate)	73.35
Double room at Pension Fischer (budget)	53.35
Lunch for one at Café Hardenberg (moderate)	10.00
Lunch for one at Ashoka (budget)	6.00
Dinner for one, without wine, at Fofi's (deluxe)	35.00
Dinner for one, without wine, at Hardtke (moderate)	16.00
Dinner for one, without wine, at Athener Grill (budget)	6.50
Half-liter of beer	2.65
Glass of wine	3.30
Coca-Cola in a restaurant	1.80
Cup of coffee	2.35
Roll of ASA 100 Kodacolor film, 36 exposures	6.00
Admission to Pergamon Museum	2.65
Movie ticket	6.65
Theater ticket to Berlin Philharmonic Orchestra	8.65

major hotels and many shops and restaurants accept credit cards, particularly in western Berlin. In eastern Berlin, however, credit cards are usually accepted only in places frequented by international tourists, such as hotels and restaurants near major tourist attractions. In addition, smaller locales in both east and west are not equipped to deal with credit cards, including the majority of budget establishments listed in this book.

GETTING CASH WHILE YOU'RE THERE If you want to exchange a large amount of cash at one time (say, at least $500), the best currency exchange is offered by an Automated Teller Machine (ATM), found at many convenient locations in Berlin. A larger fee is charged for the transaction than that charged by a bank, but the exchange rate is more favorable because it's based on the wholesale exchange rate. Before leaving home, make sure you obtain a Personal Identification Number (PIN) consisting of four numbers.

And how much money should you bring with you? Plan on a minimum of $50 a day per person for lodging in a shared double room and meals. A much more comfortable allowance is $60 a day, including transportation costs, admission to museums and attractions, and drinks in a neighborhood pub. To be on the safe side, bring your credit card with you or bring a bit more in traveler's checks than you think you'll need—you can always use them later when you return home.

3 When to Go

Berlin is a tourist destination throughout the year, although the busiest season is from spring through autumn and during Berlin's major festivals and events.

THE CLIMATE Berlin is at the same latitude as Vancouver and enjoys the changes of the four seasons. Its summers are generally mild and even pleasantly cool, which accounts for the fact that very few hotels and establishments in Berlin are equipped with air conditioning. Spring and autumn can be glorious times of the year—my favorite time of year is October. Winters, on the other hand, can be quite severe, though not as bad as in the northern regions of the United States. I've been to Berlin in April when it snowed; I've also been to Berlin in February when it was so warm that plants and grass started turning green. In other words, be prepared for all kinds of weather, since temperatures and the amount of rainfall seem to vary from year to year. The following averages, however, may help you plan your trip.

Berlin's Average Daytime Temperature & Rainfall

	Jan	Feb	Mar	Apr	May	June	July	Aug	Sept	Oct	Nov	Dec
Temp. °F	30	32	40	48	53	60	70	62	56	49	40	34
°C	–1	0	4	9	12	16	20	17	13	9	4	1
Rainfall (in.)	2.2	1.6	1.2	1.6	2.3	2.9	3.2	2.7	2.2	1.6	2.4	1.9

HOLIDAYS Because Berlin is predominantly Protestant instead of Catholic, it doesn't have nearly as many holidays as Germany's Catholic regions, such as Bavaria. There are a few official bank holidays, however, to keep in mind. Some museums and restaurants are closed certain holidays of the year. State museums, for example, are closed on New Year's Day, May 1, and December 24, 25, and 31. To avoid disappointment, be sure to telephone in advance if you wish to visit a certain establishment on a holiday.

Holidays in Berlin are New Year's (January 1), Good Friday, Easter Sunday and Monday, Ascension Day, Whitsunday and Whitmonday, Labor Day (May 1), German Reunification Day (October 3), Day of Prayer and Repentance (third Wednesday in November), and Christmas (both December 25 and 26).

THE YEAR IN BERLIN If you're lucky, your trip may coincide with one of Berlin's cultural events. But if you do arrive in Berlin during any of the major events described below, it's a good idea to reserve a room in advance. For other events that may be happening, including sporting events, art exhibits, or other one-time happenings, contact the German National Tourist Organization nearest you. In Berlin, the organization in charge of arranging all of Berlin's major festivals is the **Berliner Festspiele GmbH,** near the Europa-Center at Budapester Strasse 50 (☎ 030/25 48 90). You can also purchase tickets here. The **Verkehrsamt Berlin** (tourist office), located in the Europa-Center on Budapester Strasse (☎ 030/262 60 31), is another invaluable source of information.

BERLIN CALENDAR OF EVENTS

February

✪ **International Film Festival** The calendar year starts off with a bang with this festival, which attracts stars, directors, movie critics, and film lovers from all over the world. Established back in 1951 and known locally as the Berlinale, it lasts almost two weeks and usually features about 700 films from some 20 countries at the main showing. In addition, other movies are shown round the clock under such headings as the "International Forum of Young Filmmakers" and "New German Movies."

Where: Various theaters. **When:** Late Feb. **How:** Tickets, 10 DM to 25 DM ($6.65–$16.65), can be purchased up to three days in advance at a special booth set up on the first floor of the Europa-Center, open daily from 11:30am to 6:30pm. The best showings sell out quickly, but something is always available. On the day of performance, tickets must be bought at the theater box office; check to see whether the performance is sold out.

May

- **Theatertreffen.** This drama festival, or "Theater Meeting," features German-language productions from throughout the German-speaking world, including Austria and Switzerland. It serves as a workshop for new forms of expression and performance. You have to understand German, therefore, to appreciate the various offerings. If you do and you love theater, you'll be in heaven.

June/July

- **Serenade concerts in Charlottenburg Palace.** Call Verkehrsamt Berlin (☎ 26/2 60 31) for information.

September

✪ **Berliner Festwochen** The Berlin Festival Weeks is one of the biggest events of the year and recognizes excellence in all fields of the arts, including opera, theater, music, and art.

Where: Various theaters. **When:** End of Aug. through Sept. **How:** Ticket cost depends on the venue, and may be purchased at the box offices.

October/November

✪ **Jazz-Fest Berlin** A colorful mix of avant-garde and classical jazz musicians from around the world, a must for jazz fans. There's everything from blues and swing to bebop, cool jazz, and free jazz.

Where: Haus der Kulturen der Welt. **When:** End of Oct. or Nov. **How:** Tickets, costing between 10 DM ($6.65) and 45 DM ($30), may be purchased at the box office.

December

- **Weihnachtsmarkt.** The traditional Christmas market is the number-one attraction in Berlin during December. Although several markets are held around the city, the most popular and most convenient is at the heart of the city—from the Gedächtniskirche all the way to Wittenbergplatz. It's open daily from 11am to 9pm, and features more than 150 stalls selling cookies, candied apples, mulled wine, Christmas ornaments, candy, and more. Other Christmas markets include those in the Spandau Altstadt, open only on weekends in December from 10am to 7pm, with some 500 market stands set up in the Old City district; and Schlossplatz (formerly Marx-Engels-Platz) in Berlin-Mitte, which features children's rides in addition to market stalls. It takes place Monday to Thursday from 1 to 9pm and Friday to Sunday from 1 to 10pm from the end of November to Christmas Eve.

4 Health & Insurance

No shots or inoculations are required for entry to Germany. If you need special medications, however, it's a good idea to bring them with you. Otherwise, German pharmacies are well-equipped with their own brands of medicine. If a pharmacy cannot fill your American prescription, it will give you a German substitution.

Medical and hospital services are not free in Germany, so ask your insurance company before leaving home if you are covered for medical treatment abroad. If not, you may wish to take out a short-term traveler's medical policy that covers medical costs and emergencies. If an emergency arises during your stay in Berlin, consult "Fast Facts" in Chapter 4 for emergency telephone numbers.

You may also want to take extra precautions with your possessions. Is your camera or video equipment insured anywhere in the world through your home insurance? Is your home insured against theft or loss if you're gone longer than a month (some insurance companies will not cover loss for homes unoccupied longer than a month)? If you are not adequately covered, you may wish to purchase an extra policy to cover losses.

INSURANCE FOR BRITISH TRAVELERS Most big travel agents offer their own insurance, and will probably try to sell you their package when you book a holiday. Think before you sign. Britain's Consumers' Association recommends that you insist on seeing the policy and reading the fine print before buying travel insurance. You should also shop around for better deals. Try **Columbus Travel Insurance Ltd.** (☎ 071/375-0011) or, for students, **Campus Travel** (☎ 071/730-3402). If you're unsure about who can give you the best deal, contact the **Association of British Insurers,** 51 Gresham St., London EC2V 7HQ (☎ 071/600-3333).

5 Tips for Special Travelers

FOR TRAVELERS WITH DISABILITIES Due to a skiing accident, I researched the first edition of this guide while confined to crutches. I found Berliners extremely polite and helpful, holding doors open for me and offering me their seats on buses and trains (special seats for people with disabilities are marked on buses, subways, and trains). But probably the biggest obstacle is stairs. Some of the larger subway stations have escalators and elevators, but most do not. As a plus, employees of the Berlin transportation system will call a taxi for any passengers with disabilities between the hours of 8pm and 4am. It's best to inform an employee that you need a taxi at the start of your journey by public transportation, so that a taxi will be waiting for you at the station or bus stop to drive you the rest of the way to your final destination (you, of course, pay for the taxi).

Keep in mind, too, that most inexpensive pensions are located in upper floors of multistory buildings, many without elevators or bathrooms large enough to accommodate a wheelchair. When making your hotel reservation, make sure the hotel is equipped to handle your needs.

There are many organizations in Berlin for people with disabilities. For more information, including where to rent wheelchairs and which hotels are best equipped for people with disabilities, contact **Landesamt für zentral soziale Aufgaben,** Landesversorgungsamt, Sächsische Strasse 28-30 (☎ 030/867 61 14 or 867 63 71). The **Verband Geburts & andere Behinderter** offers free use of wheelchairs, including Sundays and holidays. Call 030/341 17 97 and leave a message. In addition, **Service-Ring-Berlin** (☎ 030/859 40 10 or 924 21 18) offers advice to people with disabilities and wheelchairs for rent.

FOR SENIORS Some museums offer discounts of up to 50% to senior citizens—even though such discounts may not be posted. Men must be 65; women, 60. Carry your passport with you at all times as proof of your age.

If you wish, you can stay at youth hostels in Berlin—that is, if you can put up with the noise and exuberance of the youth and the inconvenience of shared bathrooms. There's no age limit, but "seniors"—defined as those 27 years and older—pay a slightly higher rate.

FOR SINGLE TRAVELERS Although it doesn't seem fair, single travelers usually pay more than half the price of a double room. Expensive hotels may even charge the same price for single or double occupancy. If you're alone, look for hotels that offer single rates; some even have a few single rooms, usually the smallest on the premises. An alternative is to live dormitory-style at a youth hostel, where your chances are good of meeting other single travelers.

Women traveling alone to Berlin may want to contact the **Fraueninfothek Berlin,** located in eastern Berlin at Dircksenstrasse 47 (☎ 030/282 39 80 or 28 27 57; fax 030/228 28 57). An organization managed by women for women, it can provide general travel information about Berlin, help find accommodations in private quarters for short stays of up to two weeks, and provide more information about women's groups and meetings.

As for establishments that cater only to women, Artemisia is a bright and cheery hotel geared towards the needs of female travelers, while Extra Dry is a women-only cafe selling snacks and nonalcoholic beverages. Refer to chapter 5, "Where to Stay," and chapter 10, "Berlin After Dark," for more information on these establishments.

If you plan on traveling by public transportation at night, it's good to know that between the hours of 8pm and 4am, you can ask an employee of the Berlin public transportation system to call a taxi for you, which will pick you up at your last subway station or bus stop and drive you to your final destination (you, of course, pay for the taxi).

FOR FAMILIES I took my six-month-old son along to update the second edition of this book and found Berlin easily accessible by stroller. Buses have marked doors for strollers, as well as a special area near the door where strollers can be parked and secured. Children younger than six travel for free on public transportation; those younger than 14 travel at a discounted rate.

Restaurants are a bit more problematic; except in those that cater especially to families, high chairs are virtually nonexistent and children's menus a rarity. Children would be out of place at Berlin's better restaurants; no-smoking sections are few and far between. If you have a young child, you may find yourself eating at McDonald's, Burger King, or one of the other hamburger chains more frequently than you ever thought possible.

Berlin has many attractions that appeal to children, including a wonderful zoo and several museums (see "Especially for Kids," in Chapter 7). Children usually pay half fare for attractions that charge admission; admission is usually free for children younger than 3.

FOR STUDENTS Most museums in Berlin offer student discounts, and some theaters and opera houses (including the Deutsche Oper Berlin) offer unsold tickets to students for up to 50% off.

A student's key to cheaper prices is the **International Student Identity Card (ISIC),** available to all students enrolled full- or part-time in a degree program. In addition to gaining discounted admission fares to museums and other attractions, ISIC members can also receive special airline fares and discounted rail, bus and ferry prices. Another benefit of the card is that it gives all holders free access to a worldwide traveler's assistance hotline, a toll-free service available 24 hours a day for use in medical, financial, and legal emergencies. Valid for one year, the card is available from the **Council on International Educational Exchange (CIEE),** 205 East 42nd Street, New York, N.Y. 10017 (☎ 212/661-1414). Applications must include a $16 registration fee (plus $1 postage and handling), one passport-size photo, and proof of current student status (an official letter from the school, school transcript, or registrar's receipt). Allow four weeks when applying for the card by mail.

Tips for British Students Europe is full of InterRailing students during the summer months. Eurotrain and Route 26 (☎ 071/834-7066) provide other options for cheap train fares for travelers under 26 to and from European destinations. Campus Travel, 52 Grosvenor Gardens, London SW1W 0AG (☎ 071/730-3402) provides a wealth of information and offers for the student traveler, ranging from route-planning to flight insurance, and including railcards.

The **International Student Identity Card** (ISIC) is an internationally recognized proof of student status that will entitle you to savings on flights, sightseeing, food, and accommodation. For inexpensive accommodations, youth hostels are the place to stay. You'll need an International Youth Hostels Association card, which you can purchase directly at the youth hostel in which you stay or from the youth hostel store at 14 Southampton Street, London (☎ 071/836-8541) or **Campus Travel** (☎ 071/730-3402). Be sure to bring your passport and some passport-sized photos of yourself. If you're traveling in summer, many youth hostels will be full, so it's best to book ahead. In London, you can make advance reservations for other locations from the hostel on Oxford Street or the one at 36 Carter Lane (for a £1 fee).

6 Getting There

For most readers, a trip to Berlin is likely to begin with a plane trip across the Atlantic to the European continent. Berlin itself is easily accessible by plane, train, or car. Following are some pointers.

BY PLANE

Airlines that fly between North America and Germany include **Lufthansa,** the German national airline (☎ 800/645-3880); **American** (☎ 800/433-7300); **Continental** (☎ 800/231-0856); **Delta** (☎ 800/241-4141); **TWA** (☎ 800/892-4141); **United** (☎ 800/538-2929); and **USAir** (☎ 800/622-1015). Contact your travel agent or specific carriers for current information.

To get a head start on your travel adventure, it seems only fitting to fly Germany's own Lufthansa, known throughout the world for its punctuality, dependability, and high-quality service. It operates frequent flights from the United States and Canada to Germany, with more than 120 weekly flights from 14 North American gateways, and it also flies to the greatest number of cities in Germany. Of course, Lufthansa also offers the most flights to Berlin from all major cities in Germany and elsewhere.

TRANSATLANTIC AIRFARES   Researching airfares from North America to Germany can be difficult and time-consuming, since the cheapest fares vary depending on the season and even the day of the week you travel. In addition, airlines sometimes lower prices at the last minute to fill empty seats; or they have special promotional fares—valid at certain times—and may include car-rental options. It pays, therefore, to invest time shopping around.

While first- and business-class fares are the same year round, the cheapest tickets vary with the season. The most expensive time to fly is during peak season, usually June through September. The lowest fares are available during the winter months, usually November through March (with the exception of December 12–24). Fares vary from high to low during the shoulder season, usually April, May, and October. In addition, during all seasons there are different rates for weekday and weekend flights.

APEX (Advance-Purchase Excursion)   You can cut the cost of your flight to Germany by purchasing your ticket in advance and complying with certain restrictions. These are known as APEX fares, and the restrictions may vary with the airline but always require an advance purchase and minimum and maximum stays. Lufthansa's nonrefundable APEX fares require reservations be made at least 21 days prior to departure. Payment and ticketing must be completed within 72 hours of reservation or 21 days prior to departure, whichever comes first. There is a minimum 7-day stay and a maximum 1-month stay. Rates on all nonrefundable APEX fares vary according to the season, with peak season in effect from June through September. Round-trip weekday (Monday through Thursday) flights are approximately $60 cheaper than weekend flights. At press time, Lufthansa's nonrefundable APEX fares ranged from as low as $638 round trip from New York to Berlin on a weekday in winter, to a high of $928 for the same flight in summer.

For those who wish to stay in Germany a little longer than a month, Lufthansa also offers a Special APEX fare for just $100 more than the prices just quoted; it allows a maximum 2-month stay, requires only a 14-day advance purchase, permits no stopovers, and carries a cancellation penalty.

If you prefer to fly an American airline, you may be able to fly onward to Berlin at no extra charge, even if the American airline itself flies only into Frankfurt. In 1995, for example, Continental offered an $828 round-trip fare on weekday flights in summer from Newark, regardless of whether you were flying to Frankfurt or Berlin; since Continental doesn't fly into Berlin, the final leg of your journey from Frankfurt to Berlin is on Lufthansa.

Economy Fares In addition to its APEX fares, Lufthansa also offers some other options for budget travel that allow for greater flexibility. If you are unable to plan your trip and purchase your ticket in advance or wish to stay fewer than seven days or longer than two months, you may, for example, want to take advantage of Lufthansa's **Instant Purchase (PEX) fare**. You cannot return prior to the first Sunday after departure, and stays are good for up to 6 months. At press time, PEX fares ranged from as low as $838 round trip from New York to Berlin on a weekday in winter, to a high of $1,128 for the same flight in summer. One stopover is permitted for an additional charge of $50, and there's a $150 cancellation fee.

Lufthansa also offers an **Excursion fare** that requires no advance purchase, carries no cancellation penalty, has no minimum stay, and is valid for stays up to one year. This fare permits one free stopover and an additional one at an extra $50 charge. At press time, the round-trip fare was $1,308 from New York to Berlin. In contrast, Lufthansa's regular economy round-trip ticket, which carries no restrictions and allows one free stopover en route, costs $2,482 from New York to Berlin year round.

Lufthansa's **Youth Fare,** available to those aged 12 to 24, is a good value for students going to Germany for a year's study, since its round-trip ticket allows for a maximum stay of one year. It has a 72-hour advance purchase requirement, allows no stopovers, and requires that the return reservation be left open but made 72 hours before flying.

At press time, the one-way weekday fare from New York to Germany was $294 in low season and $434 in peak season.

Other Options   Certainly the best strategy for securing the lowest airfare is to shop around. Consult the travel section of major newspapers, since they often carry advertisements for cheap fares. You may, for example, find advertisements offered by so-called bucket shops that sell discounted tickets at reductions of about 20% to 30%. Tickets are usually restrictive, valid only for a particular date or flight, nontransferable, and nonrefundable. Since some of these so-called consolidators may be selling awards purchased from frequent-fliers (an illegal action that may see your ticket confiscated at the airport), it would be wise to check up on the company by contacting the local Better Business Bureau or the state attorney general's office.

Otherwise, a safer bet is to find a travel agent who deals directly with a consolidator. Council Travel, for example, is a travel agency that deals directly with reliable consolidators, with about 40 offices nationwide. You might also consider booking a charter flight, which may offer a combination package that includes land transportation such as rental car and hotel accommodation. One reputable charter company is Condor, a Lufthansa subsidiary, which is located in Chicago and sells tickets to tour operators throughout the country.

AIRFARES FROM THE U.K.   Daily papers often carry advertisements for companies offering cheap flights. London's *Evening Standard* has a daily travel section, and the Sunday editions of almost any newspaper will run many ads. Highly recommended companies include **Trail-finders** (☎ 071/938-3366) and **Platinum Travel** (☎ 071/937-5122).

In London, there are many "bucket shops" around Victoria and Earls Court that offer cheap fares. Make sure that the company you deal with is a member of the IATA, ABTA, or ATOL. These umbrella organizations will help you out if anything goes wrong. Finally, **CEEFAX,** a British television information service included on many home and hotel TVs, runs details of package holidays and flights to Europe and beyond. Just switch to your CEEFAX channel and you'll find a menu of listings that includes travel information.

FARES FROM FRANKFURT TO BERLIN   Although it's much cheaper to purchase a ticket that will take you from North America all the way to Berlin, you may find yourself in Frankfurt. At press time, the cheapest round-trip fare from Frankfurt to Berlin was 381 DM ($254) for a night flight leaving after 7:30pm. Otherwise, the regular economy round-trip fare is a steep 496 DM ($330.65), and one-way tickets are available only in business class for 381 DM ($254).

BERLIN'S AIRPORTS

TEGEL AIRPORT   (☎ 030/41 01-1) is located in northwest Berlin only 5 miles from the main train station and the city center. It serves as the major airport for flights from Western Europe and North America. It's rather small as airports go, consisting of one main hall and a circular-shaped passenger terminal. Stop by the Berlin information counter, located in the main terminal, and pick up a free map of the city and sightseeing brochures. If you don't yet have a hotel reservation, the tourist office here will book one for you for a 5-DM ($3.35) fee. It's open from 8am to 11pm daily.

Other facilities at the airport include banks for money exchange, luggage storage, a post office from which you can make international calls, a first-aid station, a police station, car-rental firms, a restaurant, and shops selling film, newspapers, souvenirs, and travel necessities.

Getting to and from Tegel Airport The best and least expensive way to get into town is on **city bus no. 109,** which departs about every 10 to 15 minutes from just outside the arrival hall. Fare is 3.70 DM ($2.45) one way, collected by the bus driver when you board the bus. The trip to the city center takes approximately a half hour. The bus travels to Stuttgarter Platz and along the Kurfürstendamm, where most of Berlin's hotels are concentrated, all the way to Bahnhof Zoologischer Garten (Berlin's main train station) and Budapester Strasse. At the airport tourist information counter, ask which stop is most convenient to your hotel. Once inside the bus, look for a panel at the front of the bus, which clearly displays the name of each upcoming stop. A **taxi** costs approximately 30 DM ($20) one way to the city center.

SCHÖNEFELD AIRPORT (☎ 030/6091-0), formerly East Berlin's major airport, serves intercontinental flights from Asia and Latin America as well as those from Eastern Europe and the Soviet Union. It's situated less than 3 miles south of Berlin. Note that a major expansion of the airport is slated to begin in 1996.

Getting to and from Schönefeld Airport You can get into town by both **S-Bahn** and **U-Bahn.** Berlin-Schönefeld S-Bahn station is about a 5-minute walk from the airport. From there, S-Bahn 9 (usually abbreviated to S-9) travels through Alexanderplatz to Bahnhof Zoo, Savignyplatz, and Charlottenburg stations. If you don't want to walk the 5 minutes to the S-Bahn station, an alternative is to board Bus no. 171 from Schönefeld Airport for the short ride to Rudow, where you can then board U-Bahn 7 for a ride into the city. Regardless of the transportation method you choose, both routes cost 3.70 DM ($2.45) one way.

BERLIN-TEMPELHOF AIRPORT (☎ 030/6951-0), western Berlin's oldest airport, was resurrected for commercial use after the Wall fell and Berlin found itself unable to handle increased flights to the new capital. Serving flights from both European and German cities, it is located just a few miles south of the city center.

Getting to and from Tempelhof Airport The **U-Bahn 6** line connects the airport's station, Platz der Luftbrücke, with Friedrichstrasse station. If your destination is Bahnhof Zoo, take U-6 two stops to Hallesches Tor, transferring there to U-1 going in the direction of Ruhleben. The fare is 3.70 DM ($2.45).

Bus 119 travels directly from the airport to the Kurfürstendamm, where most of Berlin's hotels are located. The fare is 3.70 DM ($2.45).

BY TRAIN

It's easy to get to Berlin by rail, with good connections from Frankfurt, Hamburg, and other major European cities. Prices depend on the speed of the train you're traveling on, with the fastest trains costing the most. The normal train from Frankfurt to Berlin, for example, takes about 7 hours and, at press time, costs 130 DM ($86.65) one way for second class. The InterCity Express (ICE), Germany's high-speed train with speeds up to 250 km (155 miles) per hour, travels between Frankfurt and Berlin in five hours and costs 161 DM ($107.35) one way. From Munich, a one-way second-class ticket on a regular train costs 146 DM ($97.35); on the ICE it's 220 DM ($146.65). Travelers under age 26 are entitled to reduced train fares: a one-way ticket from Frankfurt to Berlin is 122 DM ($81.35), and from Munich to Berlin it's 101 DM ($67.35). Youth tickets are available at travel agencies, especially those that cater to students.

The price of a second-class one-way train ticket between London's Victoria Station and Berlin is 286 to 345 DM (£124 to £150), depending on the train, route, and time of travel; for youths under 26 the fare starts at 212 DM (92£).

RAIL PASSES FOR U.S. CITIZENS   If you plan on visiting other cities in Germany or are traveling to Berlin from, say, Munich, you may be able to save on train fare by purchasing a **GermanRailpass.** A particularly good deal is the **Flexipass,** available for any 5, 10, or 15 days of travel inside Germany within a 1-month period. At press time, a 5-day Flexipass cost $178 for second-class travel and only $138 for travelers under age 26. That's about the same price as a regular round-trip ticket between Munich and Berlin. What's more, with a rail pass you don't have to stand in line each time to buy a ticket. If there are two of you traveling together, you can save even more money with the **Twinpass,** which costs $267 for two adults traveling together any 5 days within a 1-month period.

GermanRailpasses, which must be purchased before leaving the United States, are available at travel agencies or from GermanRail offices. For more information, call GermanRail in Rosemont, Ill. (☎ 708/692-6300).

If you plan to travel extensively outside Germany, you may want to take advantage of a **Eurailpass**—which must also be purchased before entering Europe and is good for travel through 17 European countries. A number of options are available, including passes good for unlimited travel from 15 days to 3 months; passes that allow two or three adults to travel together for 15 days, 21 days, or 1 month; and Flexipasses good for any 5, 10, or 15 days of travel within 2 months. Eurail Youthpasses are available to travelers under age 26. At press time, a 15-day Eurailpass valid for 15 days of consecutive travel cost $498; a Eurail Flexipass good for 5 days of travel within 2 months cost $348; and a 1-month Eurail Youthpass cost $578. For information on these and other fares, contact a travel agent.

RAIL PASSES FOR U.K. RESIDENTS   Many different rail passes are available in the U.K. for travel in Britain and Europe. Stop by

British Rail International's office, the International Rail Centre, located in Victoria Station, London SW1V 1JY (☎ 071/834-2345), or Wasteels, 121 Wilton Rd., London SW1V 1JZ (☎ 071/834-7066). They can help you find the best option for the trip you're planning.

The most popular rail ticket for young U.K. residents is the **InterRail pass,** available for travelers under 26 years of age and available for various "zones," or areas, of Europe. The most extensive pass, valid for one month and entitling you to unlimited second-class travel in 26 European countries, costs £240. It also gives you a 34% discount on rail travel in Britain and Northern Ireland, and a 50% discount on the rail portion of travel from London to various continental ports. You'll also get a reduction (between 30% and 50%) on most sailings to Europe, and a variety of other ferry services around the Mediterranean and Scandinavia. If your destination is Germany, you might wish to purchase a **Freedom pass,** which allows you to travel any 3, 5, or 10 days in Germany within a restricted time period; the 3-day Freedom pass costs £131.

If you're older than 26, you can purchase the **InterRail 26 Plus,** which costs £209 for 15 days of consecutive travel or £209 for 1 month. If you're not a resident of the U.K., you can buy an InterRail card if you've been in Britain for six months.

Eurotrain tickets are another good option for travelers under 26. Valid for two months, they allow you to choose your own route to a final destination and stop off as many times as you like along the way. Eurotrain "Explorer" tickets are slightly more expensive, but allow you to cover more ground, traveling to your final destination along one route and back on another. Eurotrain travels to over 2,000 destinations in Europe and North Africa, and the price includes round-trip ferry crossing as well as round-trip rail travel from London to the port. **Campus Travel,** 52 Grosvenor Gardens, London SW1W 0AG (☎ 071/730-3402) can give you prices and help you book tickets.

Route 26 (☎ 071/834-7066) provides cheap train fares for students (or those under 26) to and from European destinations.

BERLIN'S TRAIN STATIONS

BAHNHOF ZOOLOGISCHER GARTEN   If you're arriving by train from Western Europe, you'll probably end up at Bahnhof Zoologischer Garten, Berlin's main train station and popularly called Bahnhof Zoo. It's located in the center of town, not far from the Kurfürstendamm with its hotels and nightlife. An underground, S-Bahn, and bus system connects the train station to the rest of the city. Bus no. 109, for example, travels along Kurfürstendamm and continues to Tegel Airport; bus no. 100 travels to Alexanderplatz.

Your first stop at Bahnhof Zoo, however, should be at the tourist information center, open daily from 8am to 11pm. In addition to picking up maps and brochures on Berlin, you can also have your hotel reservation made here for a 5-DM ($3.35) fee. Both a post office and money-exchange office are also located in the train station. For information on train schedules, call 194 19 or stop by the information office in the station.

BERLIN HAUPTBAHNHOF & BERLIN-LICHTENBERG

Formerly eastern Berlin's main train stations, the **Berlin Hauptbahnhof** (once called Ostbahnhof) and **Berlin-Lichtenberg** stations now serve trains from both Eastern and Western Europe. Some trains stop at Bahnhof Zoologischer Garten in addition to both these train stations, so decide beforehand where you want to get off (Bahnhof Zoo is most convenient in most instances, since the majority of the city's hotels are located here). Both the Hauptbahnhof and Berlin-Lichtenberg stations are connected to the S-Bahn 5, with direct service to Bahnhof Zoo. If you have any questions, stop by the tourist information counter located in the Berlin Hauptbahnhof, open from 8am to 8pm daily.

BY BUS

Daily bus service is available between Berlin and a number of German cities, including Bremen, Frankfurt, Hamburg, Munich, and Nürnberg. Buses are modern coaches, equipped with Pullman seats and toilets. Tickets—cheaper than train fares—can be purchased at all DER travel agencies. A one-way trip from Frankfurt to Berlin costs 99 DM ($66) and takes slightly less than 11 hours. The 9-hour trip from Munich to Berlin costs 123 DM ($82). Prices are even cheaper if you're younger than 27. The price of a one-way youth fare from Munich to Berlin, for example, is only 66 DM ($44). From Frankfurt to Berlin it's 63 DM ($42).

If you travel by bus, you'll arrive at the Omnibusbahnhof am Funkturm (Central Bus Station), located near the Radio Tower at Messedamm. From there you can board a taxi or another bus for your hotel; the nearest subway station is Kaiserdamm U-Bahn station. If you need omnibus information, dial 301 80 28.

BY CAR

Traffic can be the main obstacle to car travel. Germans are keen on exploring new territories in their unified country, and congestion in eastern Germany is further compounded by poor road maintenance (look out for those ruts and potholes). How long it takes you to drive to Berlin will therefore depend on the roads you select, the day you travel (avoid holidays and weekends if you can, especially during fine weather), and how fast you drive. Berlin is 343 miles from Frankfurt, 184 miles from Hamburg, and 363 miles from Munich. Be sure to observe all speed limits: Although there is no speed limit on Autobahns in former West Germany, eastern Germany still imposes a 100-kph (62-mph) speed limit and enforces it with radar. In addition, do not drink and drive because penalties are severe and fines high. Keep alcoholic beverages in the trunk to be on the safe side.

If you're driving to Berlin, you may want a hotel that offers parking space. Otherwise, there are many parking garages in the inner city open day and night. These include Parkhaus am Zoo, Budapester Strasse 38; Parkhaus Europa-Center, Nürnberger Strasse 5-7; Parkhaus Los-Angeles-Platz, Augsburger Strasse 30; and Parkhaus Metropol, Joachimstaler Strasse 14-19. All four are located within a few minutes' walk of the Ku'damm, the Gedächtniskirche, the Europa-Center, and Bahnhof Zoo. When making your hotel reservation, be sure to ask which parking garage is closest or most convenient to your hotel.

BY CAR AND FERRY TO EUROPE FROM THE U.K. Ferry/drive reservations can be made with any good travel agent. There are many different options, so, as always, it's advisable to shop around for the best deals.

Brittany Ferries is the U.K.'s largest ferry/drive company, sailing from the south coast of England to five destinations in France and Spain. **Stena Sealink Lines** runs ferries from Dover to Calais; Southampton to Cherbourg; Newhaven to Dieppe; and Harwich to the Hook of Holland. **P&O Ferries** sails from Portsmouth to Cherbourg and Le Havre in France; from Dover to Calais and Ostend; and from Felixstowe to Zeebrugge, Belgium. Finally **Scandinavian Sea Ways** allows you to travel farther afield, including to Germany.

With any ferry trip you can buy "open jaw" tickets, which allow you to depart from and return to different ports in the U.K., as long as you travel both ways with the same ferry company. Be sure, too, to ask whether there are any discounts for traveling certain days, how many people can ride in the same car for a standard ticket, and whether there are student discounts.

TO EUROPE FROM THE U.K. VIA THE EUROTUNNEL The 31-mile Eurotunnel opened in 1994 for passenger service, reducing the travel time from Folkestone to Calais to 20 minutes. Two different types of service are available. For those driving their own cars, Le Shuttle is a half-mile-long double-deck train that transports cars and their passengers between Folkestone and Calais, linking drivers to motorway systems on both sides of the Channel. Shuttles depart approximately every 15 minutes, and no reservations are required. No foot passengers are allowed, and the only facilities are toilets, since it's assumed people will remain in their cars.

For passenger service, the plush Eurostar operates from Waterloo International Terminal in London to Paris and Brussels in about three hours, with trains presently departing every hour. Contact your travel agent for an update on prices, services, and departures.

4

Getting to Know Berlin

This chapter will answer any questions you might have upon arrival in Berlin and during your stay, from how to get to your hotel from the airport to numbers to call during an emergency.

1 Orientation

Located in northeast Germany, Berlin occupies the geographical center of Europe, about halfway between Moscow and Lisbon. It shares the same latitude with London and Vancouver, Canada, and has the same longitude as Naples, Italy. With about 3.5 million people and a total area of 340 square miles, it is Germany's largest and most densely populated city. In fact, it's larger in area than New York City, and could easily accommodate the cities of Atlanta, Boston, Cleveland, and San Francisco within its boundaries. Its boundaries are so encompassing that the western half of Berlin alone has close to 60 square miles of woods, lakes, rivers, and parks—which served as an important breathing space for West Berliners during the decades of the Wall. After the division of Germany following World War II, Berlin was closer to Poland (60 miles) than it was to West Germany (100 miles). Berlin is 184 miles from Hamburg, 343 miles from Frankfurt, and 363 miles from Munich.

VISITOR INFORMATION

There are several branches of the **Verkehrsamt Berlin,** Berlin's tourist information office, ready to serve you. The main office is conveniently located in the Europa-Center, with its entrance on Budapester Strasse (☎ 030/262 60 31), just a couple minutes' walk from Bahnhof Zoo and the Ku'damm. In addition to stocking maps (which, unfortunately, cost 1 DM, or 65¢, each) and brochures about the city, the tourist office will also book a hotel room for you for a 5-DM ($3.35) fee. It's open Monday to Saturday from 8am to 10:30pm and Sunday from 9am to 9pm.

Other tourist offices are located at Tegel Airport (☎ 030/41 01-31 45) and Bahnhof Zoo train station (☎ 030/313 90 63). Both are open daily from 8am to 11pm, and both will also book your hotel room. There's also a tourist information office at the Hauptbahnhof in East Berlin (☎ 279 52 09), open daily from 8am to 8pm, as well as at Brandenburg Gate, a main tourist attraction, open daily from 10am to 6pm (☎ 229 12 58 or 229 20 07).

For information in English on the latest cultural events in Berlin, your best bet is *BerlinBerlin*, written in both English and German and published every three months. It's sold at the Verkehrsamt Berlin for 3.50 DM ($2.35). In addition to information on events, concerts, and special exhibitions, it also has a good city map and subway map. Also available at the tourist office and at magazine kiosks is an excellent publication called *Berlin Programm,* published only in German but valuable for its listings of plays, operas, concerts, and other happenings. Costing 2.80 DM ($1.85) and issued monthly, it also lists museums and their hours. Even if you can't read German, you may be able to decipher what's being performed where.

If you do read German, you'll want to pick up a copy of either *tip* or *zitty,* two German city magazines published in alternate weeks with information on alternative theater, film, rock, and folk. *zitty* costs 3.60 DM ($2.40); *tip* costs 4 DM ($2.65).

FOR STUDENTS Berlin's oldest university, now called Humboldt University, was founded in 1810. Unfortunately, after World War II most departments and institutes of Humboldt fell within the Soviet Sector; when some students were suspended for political reasons in 1948, teachers and students founded the Free University in West Berlin. Also in western Berlin is the University of Technology, located near Bahnhof Zoo.

Today, with a population of well over 100,000 students, Berlin is Germany's largest "university city." Berlin has student cafeterias with budget-priced meals (see Chapter 6, "Where to Eat"); most museums offer student discounts. In addition, some theaters (such as the renowned Schiller-Theater) offer half-price discounts on unsold tickets to students on the night of the performance.

For student discounts, you'll need an International Student Identity Card. It's easiest to apply for the card before leaving home (refer to Section 5, "Tips for Special Travelers," in Chapter 3), but if you've arrived in Berlin without one and can show proof of current student status, you can obtain one at **ARTU,** a travel agency located at Hardenbergstrasse 9 (☎ 313 04 66)—not far from Bahnhof Zoo. ARTU also offers discount plane fares for youths and students around the world; it's open Monday to Friday from 10am to 6pm (on Wednesday from 11am to 6pm), and on Saturday from 10am to 1pm.

FOR GAY MEN & WOMEN Berlin has a very active alternative scene, with many different organizations for gay men and women. **Kommunikations- und Beratungszentrum für Homosexuelle Männer und Frauen** is a support group and counseling center for both gay men and women and is located at Kulmerstrasse 20 in Schöneberg. Call 215 90 00 for the Schwulenberatung (counseling for gay men) and 215 20 00 for Lesbenberatung (counseling for lesbians); hours are Monday, Tuesday, and Thursday from 4 to 8pm and Wednesday from 10am to 2pm.

FOR WOMEN **Fraueninfothek Berlin,** Dircksenstrasse 47, Berlin-Mitte (☎ 030/28 27 57), is a women's information center run by and for women. The center, located near Alexanderplatz, provides sightseeing information, recommends counseling centers sensitive to women's issues, and even gives advice on transportation routes and tips about restaurants and bars. It can also help with private accommodations for short stays of up to two weeks. If you need help or advice and don't know where to turn, this is the best place to start. It's open Monday through Friday from 10am to 6pm.

Artemisia, Brandenburgische Strasse 18 (☎ 87 89 05), is a bright and cheery hotel open only to women and has a well-informed staff that can steer guests to organizations and events of interest to women. **Extra Dry,** Pariser Strasse 3 (☎ 885 22 06), is a women-only cafe selling snacks and nonalcoholic beverages in a comfortable, friendly, and pleasant atmosphere. Refer to the accommodations (Chapter 5) and nightlife (Chapter 10) chapters for more information on these establishments.

CITY LAYOUT

With no more Wall slicing the city in half, the Berlin of today is markedly different from what it was, and becoming more so every day. And yet, even though there are no physical barriers between east and west, there is still a psychological one, and for most Berliners there is still an East and a West Berlin. In a rudimentary sketch of the city, West Berlin fanned westward from Brandenburger Tor; East Berlin was everything east of Brandenburger Tor.

Greater Berlin is composed of 23 precincts, each with its own town hall, market squares, and shopping streets. Of these, Charlottenburg in former West Berlin and Berlin-Mitte in former East Berlin evolved as the main financial, shopping, and entertainment centers for Berliners on both sides of the Wall. Today these two precincts remain the most important for visiting tourists. Charlottenburg contains the famous Kurfürstendamm Boulevard, most of the city's hotels, the main train station, the Europa-Center shopping and restaurant complex, many museums, and Schloss Charlottenburg (Charlottenburg Palace). Berlin-Mitte, so named because it was once the middle and social heart of old Berlin, was where the city was founded more than 800 years ago. It contains Museumsinsel (Museum Island) with its outstanding museums; a famous boulevard called Unter den Linden; a replica of old Berlin called the Nikolaiviertel; and Alexanderplatz, once the heart of Communist East Berlin. If you want, you can walk from Charlottenburg to Berlin-Mitte in less than 2 hours, a pretty stroll that takes you through the Tiergarten, the largest park in the city.

Berlin's other important museum districts, Tiergarten and Dahlem, are within easy reach of the city center by subway or bus. Spread along

Impressions

It is distressing to see the multitude of soldiers here—to think of the nation's vitality going to feed 300,000 puppets in uniform. In the streets one's legs are in constant danger from officers' swords.
—George Eliot, 1854

the southwestern edge of the city and accessible by S-Bahn are Berlin's most famous woods, the Grünewald, and waterways, the Havel and Wannsee. In the east, the Spreewald is a huge refuge of waterways and woods.

Cutting a diagonal path through the city is the Spree River. From the Grosser Müggelsee at the southeast end of Berlin, the Spree runs through Köpenick, where it picks up the Dahme River; through eastern Berlin, where it's joined by the Panke River; past the Reichstag building and the Tiergarten; and on to Spandau, where it empties into the Havel River. It was on the banks of the Spree River—halfway between Köpenick and Spandau—that two villages called Berlin and Cölln sprang up centuries ago, growing and merging and eventually becoming the city we know today.

MAIN STREETS & SQUARES

The most famous street in western Berlin is the **Kurfürstendamm,** affectionately called the **Ku'damm.** About $2^1/_2$ miles long, it begins at the Kaiser-Wilhelm Gedächtniskirche (Memorial Church), a ruined church left standing as a permanent reminder of the horrors of war. This is the eastern end of the boulevard, where nearby you'll find Bahnhof Zoo (western Berlin's main train station); a large park called the Tiergarten; and the Europa-Center, a 22-story building with shops and the Verkehrsamt (tourist information office). From the Europa-Center, **Tauentzienstrasse** leads straight to **Wittenbergplatz,** the location of the KaDeWe, the largest department store on the Continent.

From the Gedächtniskirche, the Ku'damm stretches toward the west and is lined with many of the city's smartest boutiques, as well as many of its hotels. Just a 5-minute walk north of the Ku'damm, off Knesebeckstrasse, is a square called **Savignyplatz,** noted for its bars and restaurants.

Wilmersdorfer Strasse, located west of Savignyplatz and north of the Ku'damm, is a pedestrian street lined with department stores, boutiques, and restaurants. Locals shop here; it's easily accessible from the Wilmersdorfer Strasse U-Bahn station.

Berlin's other famous boulevard—and historically much more significant—is **Unter den Linden** in eastside Berlin. This was the heart of pre–World War II Berlin, its most fashionable and liveliest street. Its most readily recognized landmark is the Brandenburger Tor (Brandenburg Gate), and buildings along the tree-lined street have been painstakingly restored. Unter den Linden leads to Museumsinsel (Museum Island), which boasts the outstanding Pergamon Museum among its number of great museums. North of Museumsinsel is the old Scheunenviertel, formerly the Jewish district of old Berlin and now home to a beautiful synagogue (undergoing extensive renovation), avant-garde art galleries, and some of Berlin's hippest bars. Only a 5-minute walk away from Museumsinsel is also the modern center of eastern Berlin, **Alexanderplatz,** with its tall television tower. Southwest of Alexanderplatz and only a few minutes' walk away is the Nikolaiviertel (Nikolai Quarter), a reconstructed neighborhood of shops, bars, and restaurants resembling old Berlin.

Berlin at a Glance

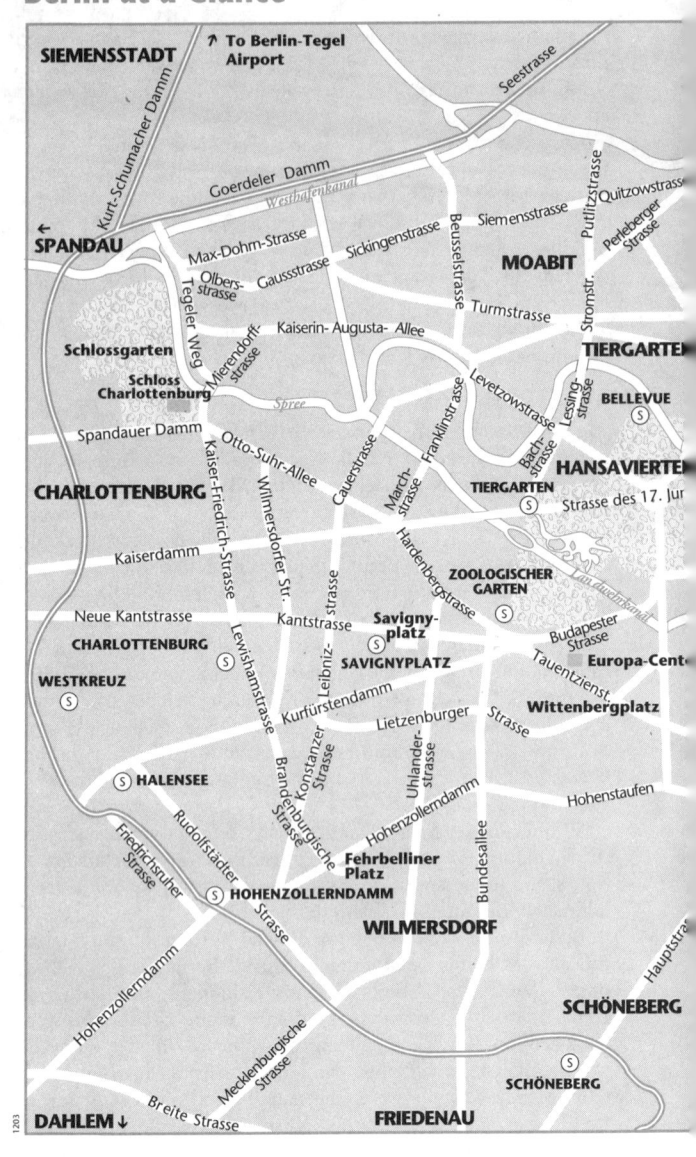

FINDING AN ADDRESS

Although some of Berlin's streets are numbered with the evens on one side and the odds on the other, many others are numbered consecutively up one side of the street and continuing back down the other. The numbering system of the Ku'damm, for example begins at the Gedächtniskirche and increases on the same side of the street all the way to end of the boulevard, and then jumps to the other side of the street and continues all the way back: Thus, Ku'damm 11, site of a Tschibo coffee shop, is across the street from Ku'damm 231, location of the Hertie bei Wertheim department store. It's a bit complicated at first, but numbers for each block are posted on street signs.

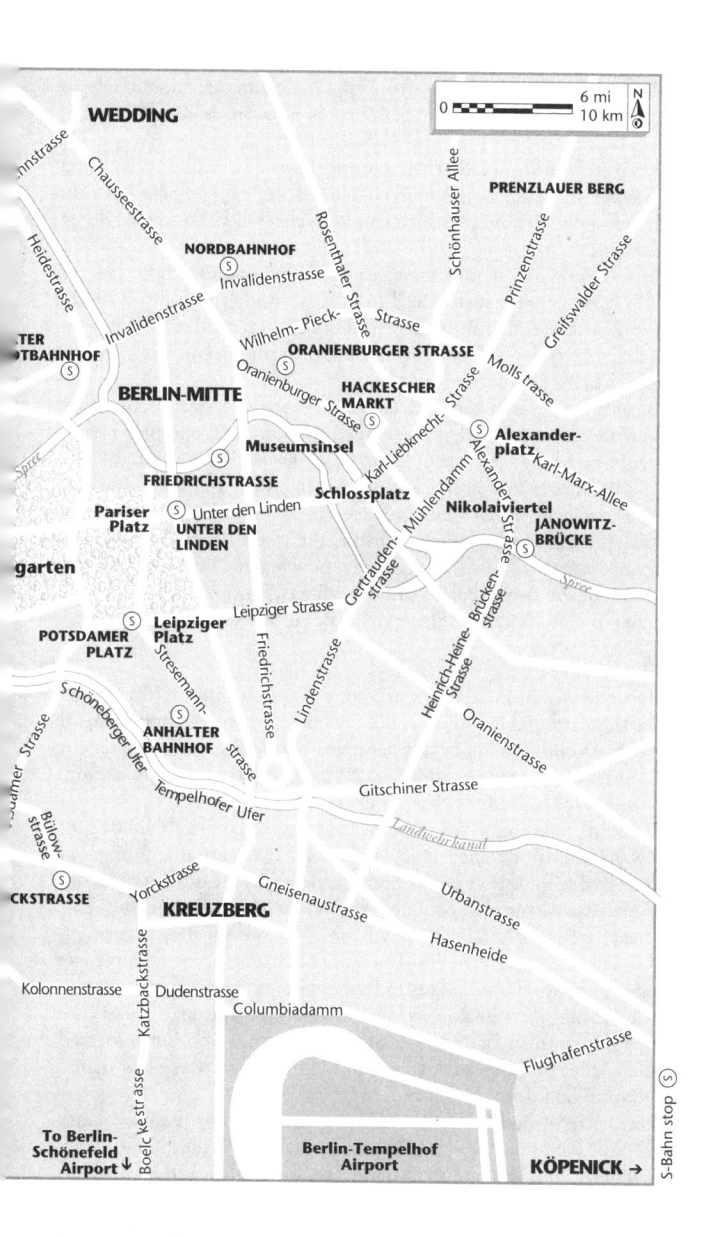

In German, *Strasse* means "street" and *Platz* means "square." Generally speaking, streets south of the Ku'damm are named after important towns and regions, such as Augsburger Strasse, Nürnberger Strasse, and Pariser Strasse. Streets north of the Ku'damm are more likely to be named after famous Germans, such as Kantstrasse, Goethestrasse, and Schillerstrasse.

Keep in mind, too, that the ground floor of a building is called *Erdgeschoss* in German and marked *E* on elevators. The next floor up is therefore the first floor (which would be the American second floor) and so on.

In searching for an address, it helps to know that new zip codes for all of Germany were introduced in 1993 to unify the country under one postal system. Similar to the United States, Berlin now has five-digit zip codes, which vary according to the precinct and appear before the city's name.

Be aware, too, that some streets and stations in eastern Berlin have been renamed, particularly those named after former Communist party leaders who have fallen out of favor. Some have reverted back to their original names before Berlin was divided following the war. Most notably, these include Marx-Engels-Platz station, now Hackescher Markt; Platz der Akademie, now Gendarmenmarkt; Marx-Engels-Forum, now Rathausstrasse; and Marx-Engels-Platz, now renamed Schlossplatz and once site of the Berlin Palace (most Berliners, however, still refer to it as Marx-Engels-Platz). All these are in Berlin-Mitte.

MAPS

Unless the situation changes, the map issued by the Berlin tourist office that costs 1 DM (65¢) is not adequate for an in-depth study of the city. Luckily, many hotels have free maps that help supplement the tourist-office map. In addition, *BerlinBerlin,* a tourist publication, contains maps of Berlin's city center.

If you're planning to spend more than several days in Berlin or simply want a more detailed map of the city, there are many maps of greater Berlin for sale at bookstores. Both Falk and Euro City put out folding maps of the city, complete with an index of street names. Less unwieldy is Rand McNally's "City Flash," which is smaller, waterproof, and shows only central Berlin (Dahlem and Spandau, for example, are not on the map). Good places to look for maps are the Europa Presse Center, a magazine and newspaper store in the Europa-Center; the Presse Zentrum in Bahnhof Zoo; and Kiepert, a bookstore located at the corner of Knesebeckstrasse and Hardenbergstrasse less than a 10-minute walk from Bahnhof Zoo.

For a map of Berlin's transportation system, stop by the BVG kiosk in front of Bahnhof Zoo, where you can purchase a detailed map showing all bus, tram, and S- and U-Bahn lines for 3 DM ($2). If you want a detailed listing of every bus line, pick up a copy of the VBB Atlas for 5 DM ($3.35), published by the Berlin-Brandenburg transportation company. More information on BVG is given in section 2, "Getting Around."

NEIGHBORHOODS IN BRIEF

Charlottenburg This is western Berlin's most important precinct, stretching from the Tiergarten all the way to the Havel River in the west and including the Ku'damm within its boundaries. This is where the majority of Berlin's hotels are, along with Bahnhof Zoo (the main train station), the Europa-Center, and such well-known theaters as the Deutsche Oper, Schiller-Theater, and Theater des Westens. The precinct takes its name from Sophie Charlotte, wife of Prussian King Friedrich I. Schloss Charlottenburg (Charlottenburg Palace), built for Sophie Charlotte, is here with a cluster of fine museums nearby—including the Ägyptisches Museum (Egyptian Museum), with its famous bust of Nefertiti, and the Bröhan Museum, with its art nouveau collection.

Savignyplatz Actually a part of Charlottenburg and just a couple minutes' walk north of the Ku'damm, Savignyplatz is a pleasant square lined with restaurants and bars, many with outdoor seating. It's a great place to relax over a beer. Radiating out from Savignyplatz, only a few minutes' walk away, are a number of other streets important for all you nightlife bloodhounds, including Kantstrasse, Schlüterstrasse, and Bleibtreustrasse.

Berlin-Mitte The cultural and political heart of pre–World War II Berlin, Berlin-Mitte fell on the eastern side of the Wall after the city's division. It was here that Berlin began in the 13th century, when two settlements called Berlin and Cölln sprang up on opposite banks of the river. Included in this district—known as the First Precinct—is Museumsinsel (Museum Island) with its famous museums, the restored Nikolaiviertel (Nikolai Quarter), and the boulevard Unter den Linden. Unfortunately, both the war and postwar years took their toll on this historic area: What wasn't bombed during the war was largely destroyed later under Communist rule, including Berlin's former royal palace, which had been the home of the Prussian monarchy for centuries; the ancient buildings on Fischerinsel, which were replaced by high rises; and the old Academy of Architecture designed by Schinkel. Today, the transformation of Berlin-Mitte continues unabated, as socialist-era buildings are torn down to make way for modern office buildings in anticipation of the city's new role as the nation's capital. Fortunately, those edifices along Unter den Linden that have been painstakingly restored still stand as reminders of the city's grand past, and Berlin-Mitte remains Berlin's most historically significant precinct.

Tiergarten Tiergarten, which literally means "animal garden," refers to both Tiergarten park and the precinct of the same name. Sandwiched in between Charlottenburg and Berlin-Mitte, it encompasses a residential district called Hansaviertel (Hansa Quarter), the Zoologischer Garten (Berlin Zoo), the Reichstag (Parliament), Bauhaus-Archiv, the Philharmonie (home to the Berlin Philharmonic Orchestra), and a cluster of museums such as the Neue Nationalgalerie (New National Gallery), the Kunstgewerbe Museum (Museum of Applied Arts), and the Musikinstrumenten Museum (Museum of Musical Instruments). By the end of the century, several museums now in Dahlem will move to new homes in this district, making it the center for European art in western Berlin.

Hansaviertel Stretching along the northern edge of Tiergarten park, the Hansaviertel (Hansa Quarter) is a residential district of housing projects—from one-family dwellings to apartment buildings. Each building was designed by a different architect as the result of an international gathering in 1957 by 48 leading architects from 13 countries, including Alvar Aalto, Walter Gropius, and Le Corbusier.

Dahlem Once its own village and now a part of Zehlendorf precinct, Dahlem is home of western Berlin's Free University (formed after World War II, when the division of Berlin gave the city's only university to the eastern sector), the Max-Planck Institute, and, most important for visitors, a number of fine museums. These include the world-renowned Gemäldegalerie (Picture Gallery), with its European masterpieces from the 13th to 18th centuries, the Skulpturengalerie (Sculpture Gallery), the Museum für Volkerkunde (Ethnological Museum), Museum für Deutsche Volkskunde (Museum of German Ethnology), the Museum für Indische Kunst (Museum of Indian Art), and the Museum für Ostasiatische Kunst (Museum of Far Eastern Art). After the Gemäldegalerie and the Skulpturengalerie move to new homes in Tiergarten by the end of this decade, Dahlem will showcase Berlin's collection of non-European art.

Spandau Located on the western edge of the city at the juncture of the Spree and Havel rivers, Spandau is older than Berlin itself, but only by five years. An independent city until engulfed by Greater Berlin in 1920, Spandau retains its own flavor and character, including an Altstadt (Old Town) and an Italian-style citadel dating from the 16th century. Notable for its Christmas market in December, its shops in the Altstadt, and its woods and water recreation, Spandau is a popular destination for both Berliners and visitors alike.

Kreuzberg Once a poor neighborhood with a high concentration of immigrants, students, and artists drawn by the low rents, Kreuzberg was West Berlin's most alternative address, with a funky mix of counterculture bars, Turkish grocery stores, ethnic restaurants, and houses occupied by squatters. After the fall of the Wall, however, the once-isolated precinct smack-dab against the Wall became prime real estate. High rents are forcing much of Berlin's counterculture to flee to the city's east side and many new restaurants are now rather gentrified. Kreuzberg, however, still boasts pockets of the avant-garde, with smoke-filled cafes, music stores, ethnic eateries, and communes. It is the most densely populated precinct of western Berlin, with approximately one-third of its inhabitants stemming from Turkey, Greece, and former Yugoslavia. About 65% of its apartments were built around the turn of the century. It's fun to visit the Turkish Market, held here every Tuesday and Friday afternoon. Also in Kreuzberg is the Berlin Museum, depicting the city's history (now undergoing renovation); the Martin-Gropius-Bau with its gallery of modern art; and the Museum Haus am Checkpoint Charlie, which documents the history of the Wall and nonviolent revolutions around the world.

Museumsinsel Located in the middle of the Spree River, this island is the home of Berlin's oldest museum complex. Begun in the 1820s and under East German jurisdiction after the war, this amazing collection of museums includes the outstanding Pergamon Museum with its architectural treasures.

Alexanderplatz   Originally serving as a market for oxen, Alexanderplatz became the heart of the East German capital during Communist rule. A large, rather sterile square, Alexanderplatz is dominated by a soaring TV tower. There's also a large S-Bahn and U-Bahn station here. One of the few old buildings remaining from prewar Berlin is the Rathaus on the square's south side, built in 1930 and now serving as the home for Berlin's central government.

Nikolaiviertel   Located just southwest of Alexanderplatz and bordered by the Spree River, Nikolaiviertel has been re-created to show what Berlin might have looked like centuries ago. It's named after the Nikolaikirche (St. Nicholas's Church), Berlin's oldest church, which rises from the middle of the quarter. Grouped around the church are about 30 town houses with 788 apartments (some with ceilings as high as 12 feet), as well as a number of restaurants, pubs, and shops—all faithfully reconstructed down to the minutest historical details.

Prenzlauer Berg   Located just north of Berlin-Mitte, Prenzlauer Berg developed as a working-class district in the 19th century and remains largely working class today. Home to dissidents, rebels, and political activists even during the days of Communist rule, it is slowly beginning to flourish as a new alternative cultural center, with hip coffee shops, restaurants, and low-rent art galleries.

Köpenick   Located in eastern Berlin at the southeast end of the city, Köpenick dates back to the 9th century and still has a rather provincial atmosphere. An important industrial area, it is home primarily to the working class. The 17th-century Köpenick Palace now houses the Kunstgewerbe Museum (Museum of Applied Arts). With its wealth of woods and lakes (including the Müggelsee, one of Berlin's largest lakes), it's a pleasant place for a stroll.

2 Getting Around

Berlin has an excellent public transportation network, including buses, the U-Bahn (underground), and the S-Bahn (overhead inner-city railway). All are run by Berlin's **BVG** (☎ 752 70 20), the largest public transportation department in Germany. You can ride farther for less money in Berlin than anywhere else in Germany. In fact, even a trip to Potsdam is included in Berlin's transportation network, costing only 3.70 DM ($2.45) one way, the normal price of a ticket. If you have any questions regarding public transportation throughout Berlin, drop by the BVG information booth located in front of Bahnhof Zoo on Hardenbergerplatz. It's open daily from 8am to 8pm. In addition to giving information on how to get where, it sells the various tickets described in the next sections, including the 30-hour ticket, the 7-day ticket, and the Sammelkarte. It also has a free map of Berlin's S- and U-Bahn system.

BY PUBLIC TRANSPORTATION   One of the best things about Berlin's public transportation system is that the same ticket can be used throughout Greater Berlin for every branch of it, including the S-Bahn, U-Bahn, and buses. Furthermore, you can use the same ticket to transfer from one line to another anywhere in Greater Berlin. But even better is the fact that your ticket is good for up to 2 hours, allowing for transfers, round trips, or even interruptions of your trip (you could, for example, go to Spandau for an hour or so and then return with the same ticket, as long as your entire trip is completed in two hours).

An important thing to remember is that prices are expected to rise during the lifetime of this book. If you have any questions, contact the BVG. At press time, a single ticket good for two hours costs 3.70 DM ($2.45); children between 6 and 14 pay 2.50 DM ($1.65). If you're traveling only a short distance (only six stops by bus or three stops by subway), you can purchase a **Kurzstreckenkarte** for 2.50 DM ($1.65) for adults and 2 DM ($1.35) for children.

If you plan on traveling frequently by bus or subway, you're much better off buying a **Sammelkarte,** a card with four tickets at discounted rates. A normal Sammelkarte costs 12.50 DM ($8.35); a Sammelkarte with short-distance tickets costs 8.50 DM ($5.65). Even more convenient, especially if you're going to be traveling more than 4 times on public transportation during one day and that evening, is the **30-Stunden-Karte** (30-hour ticket) for 15 DM ($10), good for Greater Berlin, including trips to and throughout Potsdam. If there are two of you, you can save even more money with the 30-hour **Gruppenkarte** (Group Ticket), which costs 20 DM ($13.35) and allows 2 adults and up to 3 children to travel together throughout Berlin for 30 hours.

If you're going to be in Berlin at least three days and plan on doing a lot of sightseeing, you might consider purchasing a **WelcomeCard**, available at all tourist offices and at the BVG information booth for 29 DM ($19.35). It allows one adult and up to three children unlimited travel in Greater Berlin for three days, as well as providing 20 to 50% reductions on sightseeing trips, museums, and attractions in Berlin and Potsdam. Attractions and museums offering reductions with the WelcomeCard include all state-owned museums, such as the Egyptian Museum, Gemäldegalerie, and Neue Nationalgalerie (which offer a 50% reduction), and the Berlin zoo. Keep in mind, however, that c hildren under 6 years of age always travel free on Berlin's public transportation system and that children from 6 to 14 years of age receive reductions on both public transportation and at museums and attractions. Ask for a brochure of the WelcomeCard to determine whether the sights offering reductions are on your list of things to see. Finally, if you're going to be in Berlin for at least a week, of excellent value is the 7-day ticket for 40 DM ($26.65), valid for any 7 consecutive days.

You can purchase tickets from automatic machines at all S- and U-Bahn stations, from bus drivers, and even at some machines located at bus stops (most common at bus stops on the Ku'damm). Some of the larger stations, such as Zoologischer Garten at Bahnhof Zoo, have ticket windows staffed with personnel. You can also purchase tickets from the BVG kiosk in front of Bahnhof Zoo. Since the automatic machines are in German only and can be quite confusing, you may be best off heading for the BVG kiosk or a ticket window to purchase a Sammelkarte or one of the many other tickets available.

Impressions

This place recalls to the beholder at every step, the image, genius, and the actions of the reigning Sovereign. . . . If however, Berlin strikes by its regularity and the magnificence of its public buildings, it impresses not less forcibly with a sentiment of melancholy. It is neither enriched by commerce, enlivened by the general residence of the Sovereign, nor animated by industry, business and freedom. An air of silence and dejection reigns in the streets, where at noon-day scarcely any passengers are seen except soldiers. The population, much as it has augmented during the present reign, is still very unequal to the extent and magnitude of the city. . . . The splendid fronts of the finest houses, frequently conceal poverty and wretchedness . . . . We are at first disappointed, and then disgusted with this deception. —Sir N.W. Wraxall, 1779

By U-Bahn & S-Bahn   The fastest and easiest way to get around Berlin, especially during rush hour, is by underground (U-Bahn) and the inner-city rail system (S-Bahn). The U-Bahn has 10 lines with more than 130 stations. The S-Bahn stretches through Greater Berlin, and is useful for trips to Wannsee and even Potsdam. Note that the stretch of S-Bahn between Bahnhof Zoo and the Hauptbahnhof is being renovated: the installation of new rails will connect it to the European high-speed train system; and outdated stations, particularly Alexanderplatz and Friedrichstrasse, are being redesigned—transformed into regional stations.

Trains run from about 4am until midnight or 1am, except on Saturday night, when they run about an hour later. Two subway lines, the U-12 (the major east-west axis) and the U-9 (the north-south axis) run all night on Friday and Saturday nights, with departures from Bahnhof Zoologischer Garten approximately every half hour. Some stations have ticket windows where you can purchase a single ticket or Sammelkarte; most, however, have only automatic vending machines for tickets. In any case, you must validate your ticket yourself at one of the little red boxes before boarding the train. This is the honor system—and if you're caught without a ticket you'll be charged a 60-DM ($40) fine. If you have a valid Eurailpass, note that you can use it on Berlin's S-Bahn but not the U-Bahn.

To board the right U- or S-Bahn line for your destination, you have to know that line's final stop. If, for example, you're in Bahnhof Zoologischer Garten and you wish to board the U-1 to Nollendorfplatz, you have to know that Nollendorfplatz is in the direction of Schlesisches Tor because you won't find Nollendorfplatz mentioned on any signs. If you board U-1 headed toward Ruhleben, you'll end up going the wrong direction. Refer to the subway map in this book or the subway map in all stations to determine the direction you need to go. It's not complicated, but Berlin has yet to figure out that everything would be a lot easier if directional signs included a list of stations along the way in addition to the final stop.

Another good thing to know is that if you're a woman traveling alone or if you have a disability, you can ask any subway personnel to

The U-Bahn & the S-Bahn

U1	Krumme Lanke/Schlesisches Tor		U5	Alexanderplatz/Hönow		U8	Leinestr./Paracelsus-Bad
U2	Ruhleben/Vinetastr.		U6	Alt-Mariendorf/Alt-Tegel		U9	Rathaus Steglitz/Osloer Str.
U4	Innsbrucker Platz/Nollendorf-platz		U7	Rudlow/Rathaus Spandau		U15	Uhlandstr./Schelesisches

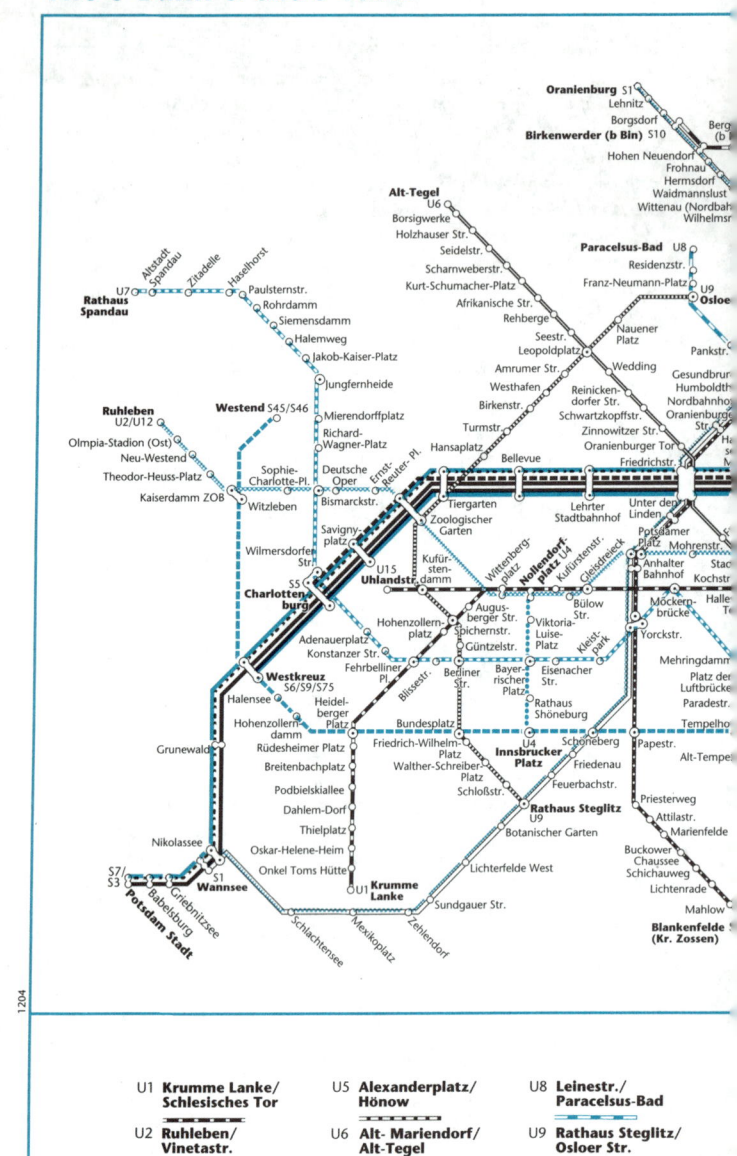

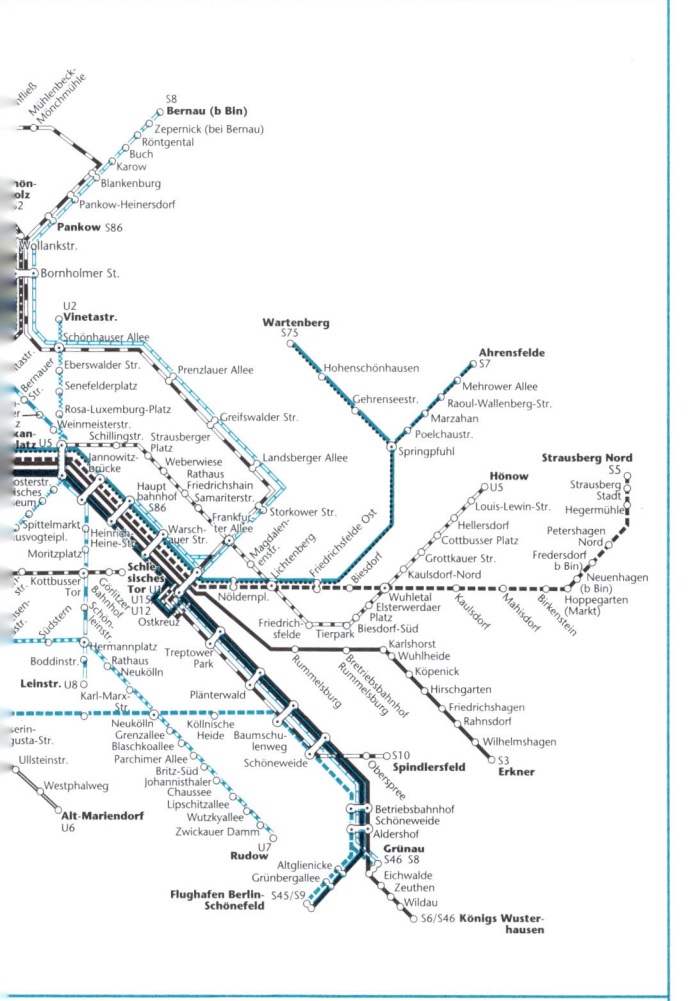

S1	**Wannsee/Oranienburg**
S2	**Blankenfelde (Kr. Zossen)/Waidmannslust**
S3	**Potsdam Stadt/Erkner**
S5	**Charlottenburg/Strausberg Nord**
S6	**Westkreuz/Königs Wusterhausen**
S7	**Potsdam Stadt/Ahrenfelde**
S8	**Bernau (b Bln)/Grünau**
S9	**Flughafen Berlin-Schönefeld/Westkreuz**
S10	**Birkenwerder (b Bln)/Spindlerfeld**
S45	**Westend/Flughafen Berlin-Schönefeld/**
S46	**Westend/Königs Wusterhausen**
S75	**Westkreuz/Wartenberg**

call you a taxi after 8pm, which will be waiting for you at your last station or bus stop to drive you the rest of the way to your final destination. You, of course, pay for the taxi ride.

By Bus With more than 170 routes, buses are the most widely used mode of transportation in Berlin. They are easy to use, and many are double-deckers, affording great views of the city. Some of the newer buses even have lighted panels at the front of the bus, clearly displaying the next stop. In any case, a list of all stops is posted in each bus as well as at bus stops. One of my favorite buses is no. 100, which travels around the clock from Bahnhof Zoo to Alexanderplatz, passing the Reichstag building and Brandenburger Tor and traveling the length of Unter den Linden along the way. It's a great way to travel to eastern Berlin's most important sites since you can see much more on a bus than via S-Bahn. You may also wish to take advantage of the buses that run along the Ku'damm (nos. 109, 119, 129, and 219) If you have any questions regarding which bus to take or where a bus stop is located, drop by the BVG booth at Bahnhof Zoo.

You can purchase only a single ticket from the bus driver. Otherwise, stamp your Sammelkarte in the red machine on the bus or use one of the other ticket options (described in the preceding sections). If you're transferring, simply show the bus driver your ticket. Apart from the normal day services, more than 60 Nachtbusse (night buses, marked with an "N" before their number) run all night, most from Bahnhof Zoo. You can pick up a brochure of their routes and schedules from the BVG booth at Bahnhof Zoo. In summer, special excursion buses marked with a triangle make express trips from Theodor-Heuss Platz to recreation areas at Grunewald, from Wannsee station to Pfaueninsel, and from Nikolassee station to Wannsee Beach.

BY TAXI You shouldn't have to take a taxi, but if you do, you can find one at the many taxi stands in the city, or you can telephone one of several taxi companies: 690 22, 26 10 26, 69 10 01, 21 01 01, or 21 02 02. The meter starts at 4 DM ($2.65), then increases according to a complicated tariff system. A 6-DM ($4) surcharge is added for taxis ordered by phone. Luggage costs an extra 1-2 DM (65¢–$1.35).

BY CAR You don't need a car for trips within Berlin: Public transportation is excellent, traffic jams are horrendous, and being burdened with a car means having to find a parking space (for a list of parking garages in the city center near the Ku'damm, consult the "By Car" section in Chapter 3). What's more, you have to pay for street parking along most streets in the middle of town (especially around the Ku'damm), with one mark per half hour levied between 9am and 7pm during the week and until 2pm on Saturdays.

You may, however, wish to rent a car for forays to the outskirts of town or destinations such as Potsdam. You'll find driving in the outskirts of Berlin no more complicated than elsewhere in Germany. Driving is on the right side of the street, and standard international road signs are used. Be sure to obey the speed limit, which is 100 kilometers per hour (60 m.p.h.) on the expressways surrounding Berlin.

If you wish to rent a car, you'll need a valid driver's license (your U.S. license is fine for stays in Germany up to one year) or an international driving license. Third-party insurance is compulsory in Germany. Foreign visitors, with the exception of most European drivers, must either present their international insurance certificate (Green Card) or take out third-party insurance.

There are several well-known car-rental agencies in Berlin. **Avis** has a counter at Tegel Airport (☎ 030/410 13 148), as well as an office near Bahnhof Zoo at Budapester Strasse 43 (☎ 030/261 18 81). The latter office is open Monday to Friday from 7am to 6pm and Saturday from 8am to 2pm. Prices here start at 169 DM ($112.65) for one day in an Opel Corsa Swing, including 15% sales tax and unlimited mileage.

Hertz, another big name, also has a counter at Tegel Airport (☎ 030/410 13 315) and at Budapester Strasse 39 (☎ 030/261 10 53). The downtown office is open Monday to Friday from 7am to 6:30pm, Saturday from 8am to 2pm. Its rates are comparable to Avis's.

Keep in mind, however, that you should always shop around for cheaper prices. Weekend prices are always cheaper than weekday prices; Avis's weekend price (from Friday noon to 9am Monday) for an Opel Corsa Swing, for example, is just 99 DM ($66), including tax and unlimited mileage. Often there are also special promotionals. Hertz, for instance, recently offered a Fiat Punto for 55 DM ($36.65), including tax and mileage. In addition, lesser-known companies often have cheaper prices than international rental agencies.

BY BICYCLE   You'll probably want to forgo the experience of riding a bicycle in the heart of Berlin with its traffic-clogged streets, but it is a fast and pleasant way to see other parts of the city. You're allowed to take bicycles onto certain compartments of both the U- and S-Bahn for an extra 3.70 DM ($2.45). Thus, you may wish to rent a cycle, take the subway to the outskirts, and then begin your ride from there. Note that you cannot take your bike on the S- or U-Bahn during rush hour, which is Monday to Friday before 9am and again in the afternoon between 2 and 5:30pm.

Fahrradstation/Berlin by Bike, Möckernstrasse 92 (☎ 216 91 77), is located in Kreuzberg near the Yorckstrasse and Möckernbrücke U-Bahn stations. From the Ku'damm, you can also reach the shop by taking bus no. 119 to the Katzbachstrasse stop. Rental prices for bikes begin at 20 DM ($13.35) for one day or 110 DM ($73.35) for one week. Students receive a 15% discount. Mountain bikes, racers, and tandems are also available. The staff gives advice on sightseeing, dispenses a free map with recommended routes, and also organizes

Impressions

Berlin is not a city at all. Berlin simply provides the arena for a number of people of intellect to gather, to whom the place is no matter. These people create the spirit of Berlin.   —Heinrich Heine, 1828

bike tours. It's open Monday through Friday from 10am to 6pm and Saturday from 10am to 2pm.

FAST FACTS: Berlin

This section is designed to make your stay in Berlin as problem free as possible. Keep in mind, however, that the information may have changed by the time you arrive. The concierge at your hotel may be able to help you if problems arise; another invaluable source is the Berlin tourist information office in the **Europa-Center** (☎ 262 60 31), with branches at Tegel Airport, Bahnhof Zoo, the Hauptbahnhof in East Berlin, and Brandenburg Gate.

Airport   See "Getting There" in Chapter 3.

American Express   The office is located in the center of town at Uhlandstrasse 173-174 (☎ 88 45 880), just off the Ku'damm. It's open Monday through Friday from 9am to 5:30pm and on Saturday from 9am to noon. There's a branch in East Berlin at Friedrichstrasse 172 (☎ 201 74 00), open Monday through Friday from 9am to 5:30pm and Saturday from 10am to 1pm.

Area Code   The area code for Berlin is 030 if you're calling from within Germany; 30, if you're calling from outside Germany. The country code for Germany is 49 if you're calling from the United States; 0049, if you're calling from most of Europe.

Bookstores   Kiepert, within a 10-minute walk from Bahnhof Zoo, near the Technical University at the corner of Knesebeckstrasse and Hardenbergstrasse (☎ 311 00 9-0), carries a good stock of maps and travel books in English and is open Mon–Fri 9am–6:30pm and Sat 9am–2pm. The nearest U-Bahn station is Ernst-Reuter-Platz.

Even more extensive is the selection offered by the British Book Shop, Mauerstrasse 83-84 (☎ 238 46 80), located just a couple minutes' walk from Museum Haus am Checkpoint Charlie near the Kochstrasse or Stadtmitte U-Bahn stations. It's open Mon–Fri 9am–6:30pm and Sat 9am–2pm (to 4pm the first Sat of the month in summer, to 5pm in winter).

Business Hours   Downtown businesses and shops are open Mon–Fri 9 or 10am–6 or 6:30pm and Sat 9am–1 or 2pm. On the first Sat of the month (called *langer Samstag*), shops remain open until 6pm in winter and 4pm in summer. In addition, some shops and most department stores remain open later on Thursdays till 8:30pm. Banks are open Mon–Fri 9am–1 or 3pm, with slightly later hours one or two days of the week, depending on the bank. Most bars stay open until 2am; some remain open until 6am. Refer to Chapter 10, "Berlin After Dark," for more information.

Car Rentals   See "Getting Around" earlier in this chapter.

Climate   See "When to Go" in Chapter 3.

Currency   See "Money" in Chapter 3.

Currency Exchange You can exchange money at any bank or at the American Express office (see listing above). There's an exchange counter at Tegel Airport open daily 8am to 10pm. You can also exchange money at the Wertheim and KaDeWe department stores, and at major hotels, but the best exchange rate is offered at banks.

Banks are open only Mon–Fri 9am–1 or 3pm, with slightly later hours one or two days of the week, depending on the bank. If you need to exchange money outside these hours try the **Deutsche Verkehrs-Kredit-Bank** (☎ 881 71 17), an exchange office at Bahnhof Zoo. It's open Mon–Sat 7:30am–10pm and Sun and holidays 8am–7pm. You can also send or receive money here via Western Union.

The Deutsche Verkehrs-Kredit-Bank will also accept major credit cards for cash, including DC, MC, and Visa; bring your passport. International credit cards will also be accepted at various ATMs (called Geldautomat in German) throughout the city, most open 24 hours a day. You'll find a Geldautomat in front of the Deutsche Verkehrs-Kredit-Bank at Bahnhof Zoo, as well as at banks up and down the Ku'damm, including in front of the Deutsche Bank at Ku'damm 28 and at the Dresdner Bank on the corner of the Ku'damm and Fasanenstrasse. You must have a four-digit PIN number, and though transaction fees are high (about 12 DM, or $8), the exchange rate is better than that offered at banks.

Dentists and Doctors The Berlin tourist office in the Europa-Center has a list of English-speaking doctors and dentists in Berlin. Your embassy can also supply you with information regarding medical care in Berlin. If you need a doctor in the middle of the night or in an emergency, call 31 00 31. Call an emergency dentist at 011 41.

Documents Required The only document needed for travel to Berlin is a valid passport. Refer to "Visitor Information & Entry Requirements," in Chapter 3.

Driving Rules See "Getting Around" earlier in this chapter.

Drugstores Called *Apotheken* in Germany, drugstores have normal business hours; a few stay open all night and on the weekends and holidays. All drugstores post the addresses of those that are open, or you can call 011 41.

Electricity Berlin's electrical current is 220 volts AC, 50 cycles, which is different from the American current of 110 volts, 60 cycles. In addition, plugs are different from those in the United States, so you'll need an adapter if you're bringing a hair dryer, an electric razor, or other electrical appliance.

Embassies/Consulates The **U.S. Consulate** is in Dahlem at Clayallee 170 (☎ 832 40 87 or 819 74 54). It's open Mon–Fri 8:30am–noon for Americans who have lost their passports, while its visa section is open Mon–Fri 8:30–10:30am.

The **British Embassy,** located on Unter den Linden 21 (☎ 201 840) in Berlin-Mitte, is open Mon–Fri 9am–noon and 2–4pm (visa section, only in the morning).

The **Canadian Embassy,** located at Friedrichstrasse 95 in Berlin-Mitte (☎ 261 11 61), is open Mon–Fri 1:30–3pm, with extra morning hours for visa matters. Call first to make sure the department you need is open.

The **Australian Consulate** is at Markgrafenstrasse 46 in Berlin-Mitte (☎ 392 21 09 or 392 15 58), open Mon–Fri 9am–noon and 2–4pm.

Emergencies The emergency number for police is 110; for fires and ambulances, it's 112. For an emergency doctor, dial 31 00 31. To find out which pharmacies are open nights, call 011 41.

Eyeglasses If you need a pair of eyeglasses, visit the opticians in the area of the Ku'damm and Tauentzienstrasse. Apollo Optik, at Kurfürstendamm 40-41 (☎ 882 52 58), is open Mon–Fri 9:30am–6:30pm (to 8pm on Thurs), and Sat 9am–2pm (to 4pm first Sat of the month in summer, 6pm in winter). It's best to carry your prescription with you from home.

Holidays See "When to Go" in Chapter 3.

Hospitals If you need to go to a hospital, the ambulance service will deliver you to the one best suited to your case. In western Berlin, summon an ambulance by dialing 112. Otherwise, if you wish to check into a hospital and it's not an emergency, contact your embassy for recommendations.

Information See "Visitor Information" earlier in this chapter and in Chapter 3.

Language See the Appendix. If you wish to learn German in more depth, *German for Travellers* published by Berlitz is quite useful.

Libraries The Amerika-Gedenkbibliothek, Blücherplatz 1 in Kreuzberg (☎ 6905-0), located near the Hallesches Tor U-Bahn station, is open Tues-Sat 11am–7pm and Mon 4–7pm. In addition, the Amerika-Haus, located at Hardenbergstrasse 20 (☎ 31 10 99 10) next to Bahnhof Zoo, houses a small library and is open Mon, Wed, and Fri 11:30am–5:30pm and Tues and Thurs 11:30am–8pm. In both cases, out-of-town visitors may read books only inside the library.

Liquor Laws The minimum drinking age is 16 if accompanied by parents; 18, if alone. Laws against drunk driving in Germany are strictly enforced and respected. Don't drink more than one beer if you intend to drive.

Lost Property Berlin's general-property office is at Platz der Luftbrücke 6 (☎ 699-0). For property lost on public transportation services, check the BVG lost-and-found at Lorenzweg 5, Tempelhof (☎ 751 80 21).

Luggage Storage/Lockers There's luggage storage at both Tegel Airport and at the main train station, Bahnhof Zoologischer Garten, where you'll find lockers.

Mail Mailboxes are yellow in Germany. Airmail letters to North America cost 3 DM ($2) for the first 20 grams, while postcards cost 2 DM ($1.35). On the average it takes anywhere from 5 to 7 days for an airmail letter to reach North America. For nonlocal mail, including air mail, be sure to use the *Andere Richtungen* slot of the mailbox. Letters up to 20 grams sent anywhere in Germany and much of Europe cost 1 DM (60¢); postcards require a 80-Pfennig (55¢) stamp.

The **post office** in Bahnhof Zoo is open Monday through Saturday from 6am to midnight and Sunday and holidays from 8am to midnight for mail, telephone calls, and telegrams. You can have your mail sent here in care of Hauptpostlagernd, Postamt 120 Bahnhof Zoo, 10623 Berlin 12 (☎ 313 97 99 for inquiries). You can also have your mail sent to you via the American Express office at Uhlandstrasse 173-174 (☎ 88 45 880), a service that is free if you have American Express traveler's checks or an American Express card. Otherwise, the service costs a steep 2 DM ($1.35) *per inquiry.*

If you want to mail a package, you'll have to go to one of the city's larger post offices: There's one at Goethestrasse 2-3, and another at Marburger Strasse 12-13, which is near the Europa-Center. Both are open Mon–Fri 8am–6pm and Sat 8am–1pm. Both sell cardboard boxes—complete with string and tape—which come in six sizes ranging in price from 2.90 DM ($1.95) to 5.50 DM ($3.65).

Maps See "City Layout" earlier in this chapter.

Money See "Money" in Chapter 3.

Newspapers/Magazines There are no English-language newspapers published in Berlin, but the *International Herald Tribune* and *USA Today,* as well as news magazines *Time* and *Newsweek,* are available at newsstands such as Europa Presse Center, located on the ground floor of the Europa-Center (☎ 216 30 03) and open daily 9am to 11pm, and at the Presse Zentrum at Bahnhof Zoo, open daily from 5am to 10pm.

If you read German, Berlin dailies are the *Berliner Morgenpost, Der Tagesspiegel, Berliner Zeitung,* and *BZ.* National dailies include *Frankfurter Allgemeine Zeitung, Süddeutsche Zeitung,* and *Die Welt. Der Spiegel* and *Stern* are weekly news magazines.

Pharmacies (Late-Night) See "Drugstores" above.

Police The emergency number for police throughout Berlin is 110.

Post Office See "Mail" above.

Radio Tune in to 90.2 FM (87.6) cable for the BBC World Service.

Restrooms If you ask for the "bathroom" in Germany, your host will wonder why you want to take a bath. A restroom in Germany is called a *Toilette* and is often labeled *WC* (which stands for water closet) in public places. Women's toilets are often marked with an *F* for *Frauen* or *D* for *Damen,* while men's are identified with an *H* for *Herren* or *M* for *Männer.*

In the center of Berlin, there are public facilities at Wittenbergplatz and near the Europa-Center on Tauentzienstrasse. Other places to look for facilities include fast-food outlets, department stores, hotels, restaurants, and pubs. If there's an attendant, it's customary to tip 30–50 Pfennig (20¢–35¢).

Safety Berlin is a safe city, particularly in places frequented by tourists such as the Ku'damm. Crime, however, has been on the increase in Berlin since the fall of the Wall, so it's a good idea to avoid parks after dark and to wear a money belt if you're carrying large sums of cash. I often travel to Berlin alone and have never had any problems using public transportation or walking the streets after dark. Germany, however, has recently seen a number of violent acts committed against minorities by right-wing extremists. Although Berlin has remained relatively untouched by these crimes, it would be wise to avoid the outskirts of former East Berlin (an area of little touristic interest) if this is of concern to you.

Taxes Germany's 15% governmental tax is included in the price of restaurants, hotels, and goods in Germany. On many goods, however, tourists can obtain a refund of the Value-Added Tax (see Chapter 9, "Shopping," for information on how to obtain a refund). There is no airport departure tax.

Taxis See "Getting Around" earlier in this chapter.

Telephone Berlin's telephone system is not much different from that in the United States when it comes to a dial tone and busy tone, but it does differ in the amount of telephone digits. Some telephone numbers have four digits, others may have seven or eight. Area codes in Germany are often enclosed by parentheses—such as (030) for Berlin—and the rest of the digits are simply grouped into twos or threes. Thus, a seven-digit number for Berlin might be written (030) 881 47 68. If you come across a number with a dash, the number following the dash is the extension number, which you can reach directly simply by dialing the entire number.

Local telephone calls cost 30 Pfennig (20¢) for the first 3 minutes; at restaurants and other private establishments, the minimum charge is usually 50 Pfennig (35¢). To make sure you don't get cut off in the middle of a conversation, insert more coins—unused coins will be returned to you at the end of the call. If you want to make an international call, look for phone booths with the green "International" sign, and make sure you have a handful of change. Otherwise, you can purchase a telephone card, available at post offices. They come in values of 12 DM ($8) and 50 DM ($33.35). Simply insert them into the telephone slot. Telephone cards are becoming so popular in Germany that many public telephones no longer accept

Impressions

The two principles of Berlin architecture appear to me to be these. On the house-tops, wherever there is a convenient place, put up the figure of a man; he is best placed standing on one leg. Wherever there is room on the ground, put either a circular group of busts on pedestals . . . or else the colossal figure of a man killing, about to kill, or having killed a beast . . . a dragon is the correct thing, but if that is beyond the artist, he may content himself with a lion or a pig. —Lewis Carroll, 1867

---

coins. The 12-DM card gives you approximately 40 minutes of local telephone calls; the 50-DM card is useful for long-distance calls.

You can also make long-distance calls from a post office, where you can also send telegrams. The main post office at Bahnhof Zoo is open until midnight. It costs 7.20 DM ($4.80) to make a 3-minute long-distance phone call to the United States. Try to avoid making telephone calls from your hotel room—a surcharge added to the bill may double or even triple the rate. You can save money making transatlantic calls by using U.S. telephone calling cards. To reach an AT&T operator in Germany, dial 0130-0010. MCI has a similar service.

Time Zone Berlin is 6 hours ahead of Eastern standard time in New York, 7 hours ahead of Chicago, and 9 hours ahead of Los Angeles. Berlin operates on Central European time—except that it's officially 6 minutes and 22 seconds behind Central European time. Germany goes on and off daylight saving time at slightly different dates than the United States, with the result that Berlin is 7 hours ahead of New York for short periods in spring and fall. As this can affect rail schedules, if you're traveling during spring or fall, make sure you double-check times.

Tipping Since a service charge is usually included in hotel and restaurant bills, you are not obliged to tip. However, it is customary to round up restaurant bills to the nearest mark; the check is handed directly to the waiter or waitress rather than left on the table. If your bill is 14 DM, tell the waitress "15 DM"; if you hand her a 20-DM note, you'll receive 5 DM in change. If your meal costs more than 20 DM ($13.35), most Germans will add a 10% tip. For taxi drivers, it's customary to tip a mark. Tip hairdressers or barbers 10%. Porters receive 2 DM ($1.35) per bag.

Water Although the water is technically safe to drink in Berlin, take your cue from the Germans, who almost never drink their tap water. Instead, they ask for bottled water, either carbonated or noncarbonated.

5

Where to Stay

Although Berlin is no longer the bargain it was, it still offers a wide range of accommodations for the budget traveler. What's more, most of its cheapest accommodations are in the heart of the city, conveniently located near subway stations, restaurants, and the city's many bars. The majority of hotels and pensions are clustered along and around the Ku'damm. Even those a bit farther from the Ku'damm are never more than a short bus or subway ride from Bahnhof Zoo.

Many of Berlin's inexpensive hotels and pensions are small establishments, in what were once grand apartments. Many haven't changed over the decades. You'll find them on the upper floors of older buildings that usually have no elevator. Generally speaking, the higher up your room, the cheaper it is, especially if it's a walk-up.

Your private room is likely to contain a sink, as well as the usual bed, table, and chairs. Your room will be heated in winter, but you won't find any air conditioning: except for an occasional two weeks in August, it rarely gets hot enough to warrant it. Rooms are generally sparsely decorated, and rarely do they include such amenities as telephones or televisions. If your room does have a telephone or television, you can bet you're paying extra. You will also pay more if you stay in a room with its own private shower and toilet (a WC or water closet). Bathtubs are generally even more expensive, simply because they are rare and are considered a luxury. If you're on a budget, therefore, request a room without private facilities. Unlike many European cities, in Berlin you do not have to pay extra to use the shower down the hall.

The hotels and pensions in this chapter are divided according to price, with the least expensive presented first, and listed by location. Most convenient is the area around the Ku'damm, which is close to Bahnhof Zoo, the Europa-Center, and Savignyplatz, with its many restaurants and bars.

Note that in Germany, floors are counted beginning with the ground floor (what would be the American first floor) and go up to the first floor (the American second floor) and beyond. Directions from Tegel Airport or Bahnhof Zoo to each establishment are listed, as well as from the nearest U-Bahn or S-Bahn station when applicable.

All rates given include the 15% government tax and the service charge. Many hotels and pensions also include breakfast in their rates. This is usually a continental breakfast consisting of coffee and rolls; a few of the more expensive accommodations offer all-you-can-eat breakfast buffets. Many visitors report that they eat so much for breakfast that it tides them over until an early dinner, saving on lunch. If you like a big breakfast, it makes sense to pay slightly more for a room that includes breakfast in its rates. On the other hand, if all you want is a quick cup of coffee at a coffee shop down the street, you may opt for one of the cheaper accommodations where breakfast is either optional or not offered at all.

Keep in mind that although every effort was made to be as accurate as possible, the rates listed here may change during the lifetime of this book—that means they may go up. Prices quoted here should therefore be taken as an approximation. Be sure to ask the current rate when making your reservation. It's best to first telephone and make your reservation, and follow up with a letter reconfirming your date of arrival, departure, and the price of your room.

It's always a good idea to reserve a room in advance. Rooms become scarce during the International Film Festival (end of February) and the Berlin Festival (running from the end of August to October), as well as during international conferences, trade fairs (called *Messe* in German), and conventions—all frequently held in Berlin. Some hotels even raise their rates during major trade fairs. In any case, remember that if the recommended accommodations here are full, the tourist office (☎ 262 60 31) will find you a room for a 5-DM ($3.35) fee. Otherwise, if you decide to strike out on your own, good hunting grounds for inexpensive hotels and pensions are the side streets radiating from the Ku'damm, especially at its eastern end near the Kaiser-Wilhelm Gedächtniskirche (Memorial Church). Other places to look include Savignyplatz and Bahnhof Charlottenburg. Unfortunately, eastside Berlin does not yet have an adequate number of inexpensive accommodations. Hopefully that will change in the near future.

1 Doubles for Less than 100 DM ($66)

ON OR NEAR THE KU'DAMM & BAHNHOF ZOO

Most of these hotels and pensions are within a 10-minute walk from the Ku'damm and Bahnhof Zoo.

❸ Pension Cortina
140 Kantstrasse, 10623 Berlin. ☎ **030/313 90 59.** Fax 030/312 73 96. 21 rms (5 with shower). 65–70 DM ($43.35–$46.65) single without shower; 90–100 DM ($60–$66.65) double without shower, 110–130 DM ($73.35–$86.65) double with shower; 120–130 DM ($80–$86.65) triple without shower, 150–165 DM ($100–$110) triple with shower. Rates include continental breakfast. Additional person 40–50 DM ($26.65–$33.35) extra. No credit cards. Bus 109 from Tegel Airport to Schlüterstrasse, then a 6-minute walk. S-Bahn: Savignyplatz, a 2-minute walk.

A native Berliner and her Italian husband have managed this small pension for more than 25 years. Located just west of Savignyplatz about a five-minute walk from the Ku'damm, it occupies part of the first floor of a century-old building and features mostly large rooms, no two alike. Some rooms have telephones, and two family-size rooms can sleep up to six people, including one facing the front that even has a balcony.

74 Where to Stay

The breakfast room, pleasantly remodeled, is a good place to start the day. Reception is up on the first floor.

Hotel Crystal

Kantstrasse 144, 10623 Berlin. ☎ **030/312 90 47** or **312 90 48.** Fax 030/312 64 65. 33 rms (7 with shower, 21 with tub or shower and WC). TEL. 70 DM ($46.65) single without bathroom, 80 DM ($53.35) single with shower only, 80–120 DM ($53.35–$80) single with tub or shower and WC; 90 DM ($60) double without bathroom, 110 DM ($73.35) twin with shower only, 120 DM ($80) double with shower only, 130–150 DM ($86.65–$100) double with tub or shower and WC; 170–190 DM ($113.35–$126.65) triple with tub or shower and WC. Crib available. Rates include continental breakfast. AE, MC, V. Free parking. Bus 109 from Tegel Airport to Bleibtreustrasse stop; or bus 149 from Bahnhof Zoo to Savignyplatz (2 stops). S-Bahn: Savignyplatz, a 2-minute walk.

Located just off Savignyplatz about a five-minute walk from the Ku'damm, this older hotel, with a striking facade, is in a building dating from the early 1900s. Yet the interior seems like a relic from the 1950s: old-fashioned, comfortable, and endearingly German. Owners John and Dorothee Schwarzrock (John is an American) are friendly, outgoing, and happy to see American guests. Rooms, supplied with just the basics, are spotlessly clean; televisions are available. All employees speak English, and there's a small bar for hotel guests just off the lobby. Its rooms with bathrooms are among the cheapest in the city center.

ⓢ Pension Fischer

Nürnberger Strasse 24a, 10789 Berlin. ☎ **030/218 68 08.** Fax 030/213 42 25. 10 rms (8 with shower). 60–65 DM ($40–$43.35) single without shower, 70–75 DM ($46.65–$50) single with shower; 80–90 DM ($53.35–$60) double without shower, 100–110 DM ($66.65–$73.35) double with shower; 130–150 DM ($86.65–$100) triple with shower. Breakfast 8–10 DM ($5.35–$6.65) extra. No credit cards. Directions: An 8-minute walk from Bahnhof Zoo. Bus 109 from Tegel Airport to Joachimstaler Strasse, then a 5-minute walk. U-Bahn: Augsburger Strasse, less than a 1-minute walk.

There's no better location than this, especially at these prices. You'll find this pension on the second floor of a simple building not far from the Europa-Center. There's no elevator. Clean and pleasant, the rooms have high ceilings and large windows letting in plenty of sunshine. Each room has an old-fashioned tiled heater, the kind that once heated all German homes. If you like quiet, ask for a room on the courtyard. The cozy breakfast room, filled with plants and flowers, has a TV. There's an automatic machine for coffee or hot chocolate, and a refrigerator for guest use.

Hotel-Pension Funk

Fasanenstrasse 69, 10719 Berlin. ☎ **030/882 71 93.** Fax 030/88 333 29. 14 rms (11 with shower only, 1 with shower and WC). TEL. 60–75 DM ($40–$50) single without shower or WC, 75–80 DM ($50–$53.35) single with shower; 100–110 DM ($66.65–$73.35) double without shower or WC, 120–130 DM ($80–$86.65) double with shower; 135–150 DM ($90–$100) double with shower and WC. Rates include continental breakfast. Additional person 40 DM ($26.65) extra. No credit cards. Directions: A 10-minute walk from Bahnhof Zoo. Bus 109 from Tegel Airport to Uhlandstrasse stop, then a 2-minute walk. U-Bahn: Uhlandstrasse, a 1-minute walk.

Fasanenstrasse is one of my favorite streets because of its elegant, turn-of-the-century houses and the Käthe-Kollwitz Museum. Walk up the sweeping white-marble staircase to reach this first-floor pension, once the home of famous silent-film star Asta Nielen. Clean and orderly, the pension is decorated with flowered wallpaper and French provincial reproduction furniture. The staff speaks English. Its location is convenient to the Europa-Center, the Ku'damm, and Bahnhof Zoo.

✪ Pension München
Güntzelstrasse 62, 10717 Berlin. ☎ **030/857 91 2-0.** Fax 030/853 27 44. 8 rms (3 with shower and WC). 60 DM ($40) single without shower or WC, 110 DM ($64.70) single with shower and toilet; 85–95 DM ($56.65–$63.35) double without shower and WC, 130–140 DM ($86.65–$93.35) double with shower and WC. Additional person 35 DM ($23.35) extra. Breakfast 9 DM ($6) extra. No credit cards. Parking 12 DM ($8). U-Bahn: U-9 from Bahnhof Zoo to Güntzelstrasse station (three stops), then a 3-minute walk.

You can tell upon entering this third-floor pension that it belongs to an artist: original artwork by Berlin artists fill the walls, there are vases of flowers, and everything is tastefully arranged and decorated. Frau Renate Prasse, the charming proprietress, is a sculptress (her work adorns the corridor) and has updated this older pension without losing its original character. Rooms are bright, white, and spotless, with nice firm beds. The building, serviced by an elevator, is only two subway stops or a 20-minute walk south of the Ku'damm. I highly recommend this pension.

Hotel-Pension Stephan
Güntzelstrasse 54, 10717 Berlin. ☎ **030/873 41 21.** 6 rms (3 with shower only). 70 DM ($46.65) single without shower; 100–110 DM ($66.65–$73.35) double without shower, 110–120 DM ($73.35–$80) double with shower. Rates include continental breakfast. Additional person 30 DM ($20) extra. No credit cards. U-Bahn: U-9 from Bahnhof Zoo to Güntzelstrasse stop, then a 3-minute walk.

Housed on the second floor of an older building equipped with an elevator and boasting super-tall ceilings, it offers clean and comfortable rooms—a few are wonderfully decorated with old-fashioned furniture. Some of the rooms are small, so if you're claustrophobic ask for a large room. Breakfast is served in a cozy living room with a color TV.

ⓢ Pension Zimmer Des Westens
Tauentzienstrasse 5, 10789 Berlin. ☎ **030/214 11 30.** 8 rms (1 with shower only, 2 with shower and WC). 70 DM ($46.65) single with shower only, 85–90 DM ($56.65–$60) single with shower and WC; 95–105 DM ($63.35–$70) double without shower or WC, 100–110 DM ($66.65–$73.35) double with shower and WC. Rates include continental breakfast. Additional person 40 DM ($26.65) extra. No credit cards. Directions: About a 7-minute walk from Bahnhof Zoo, past Europa-Center. U-Bahn: Wittenbergplatz, a 1-minute walk.

Tauentzienstrasse, a busy thoroughfare, seems like an unlikely address for this modestly priced pension. You'll find it tucked away in an inner courtyard, up three flights of rickety stairs. But the pension itself is pleasant, clean, and quiet. All in all, this is a good value in a great location, between the Europa-Center and KaDeWe department store.

Where to Stay

> **Impressions**
>
> *The Wall is a kind of masterpiece of the squalid, the cruel and the hideous, the most naked assertion one could find anywhere that life was not intended to be anything but nasty, brutish, and short.*
> —Goronwy Rees, *Diary from Berlin to Munich*, 1964

NEAR WILMERSDORFER STRASSE & BAHNHOF CHARLOTTENBURG

ⓢ Hotel Charlottenburger Hof

Stuttgarter Platz 14, 10627 Berlin. ☎ **030/32 90 70** or **324 48 19.** Fax 030/323 37 23. 45 rms (38 with shower and WC). TEL. TV. 75–80 DM ($50–$53.35) single without shower or WC, 90–120 DM ($60–$80) single with shower and WC; 90–120 DM ($60–$80) double without shower or WC, 120–160 DM ($80–$106.65) double with shower and WC; 180–240 DM ($120–$160) quad with shower and WC. Discounts in winter or for longer stays. No credit cards. Bus 109 from Tegel Airport or Bahnhof Zoo to Bahnhof Charlottenburg, then a 1-minute walk. S-Bahn: Charlottenburg, a 1-minute walk.

One of Berlin's finest budget hotels, it's great in terms of price, facilities, and location—only two S-Bahn stops from Bahnhof Zoo. Rooms are bright and modern, with cable TVs, safes, alarm clocks, and large posters featuring the works of Kandinsky, Miró, Picasso, and other artists. The staff is young and friendly. Facilities include a laundry room and drink-vending machine. Breakfast is not included in its rates, but go to the adjoining Café Voltaire, open 24 hours, for a continental breakfast, costing 5 to 8 DM ($3.35–$5.35) for hotel guests. The triples and quads are particularly good value.

NEAR RATHAUS SCHÖNEBERG

Studenten-Hotel Berlin

Meininger Strasse 10, 10823 Berlin. ☎ **030/784 67 20** or **784 67 30.** Fax 788 15 23. 50 rms (none with bath). 82–86 DM ($54.65–$57.35) double; 37 DM ($24.65) per person for bed in multibed dormitory room. Rates include continental breakfast. No credit cards. Bus 146 from Bahnhof Zoo to Rathaus Schöneberg, then a 4-minute walk. U-Bahn: Rathaus Schöneberg.

Although it calls itself a student hotel and occupies a former dormitory, this simple establishment also welcomes nonstudents and guests of any age and has no curfew. The dormitory-style rooms have 4 to 5 beds each, and there are 20 double rooms. There's a game room. It's located near Rathaus Schöneberg and John-F.-Kennedy Platz.

IN KREUZBERG

Pension Kreuzberg

Grossbeerenstrasse 64, 10963 Berlin. ☎ **030/251 13 62.** Fax 030/251 06 38. 12 rms (none with bath). 60–65 DM ($40–$43.35) single; 90–100 DM ($60–$66.65) double; 120–130 DM ($80–$86.65) triple; 160 DM ($106.65) quad. Rates include continental breakfast. No credit cards. Bus 119 or 219 from the Ku'damm to Grossbeerenstrasse stop; from Tegel Airport, bus 109 to Adenauerplatz, then bus 119 to Grossbeerenstrasse. U-Bahn: Möckernbrücke, about a 6-minute walk, or Mehringdamm, about a 3-minute walk.

A pension for more than 50 years and located on the second floor of an older building that still shows traces of grander days (there is no elevator), the Kreuzberg was recently renovated and has a bright and airy breakfast room complete with plants and artwork. The tall-ceilinged guest rooms are comfortably furnished and each has a wardrobe, table, and chairs. It caters largely to young backpackers.

Hotel Transit

Hagelberger Strasse 53-54, 10965 Berlin. ☎ **030/785 50 51.** Fax: 030/785 96 19. 49 rms (all with shower only). 80 DM ($53.35) single; 99 DM ($66) double; 150 DM ($199) triple; 170 DM ($113.35) quad; 33 DM ($22) per person in six-bed dormitory rooms. Rates include buffet breakfast. AE, MC, V. U-Bahn: U-1 from Bahnhof Zoo to Möckernbrücke, then U-7 to Mehringdamm. Bus 119 or 219 from Ku'damm to Yorck-Grossbeerenstrasse or Mehringdamm stop; from Tegel Airport, bus 109 to Adenauerplatz, then bus 119 to Mehringdamm.

Under youthful ownership, Hotel Transit opened in 1987 in what was a tobacco factory; ever since it's been a hit with young international travelers, who exchange travel advice and tips. The buffet breakfast offers unlimited coffee and tea, and facilities include a hotel bar open 24 hours with a big-screen cable TV and a laundry room. Guest rooms are painted white, a bit stark and factorylike in style, but have huge windows and tall ceilings. Although the single and double rooms are a bit pricey, there are also triples, quads, and dormitory-style rooms sleeping six that are very economical for individual budget travelers. It's great for the price.

2 Doubles for Less than 135 DM ($90)

ON OR NEAR THE KU'DAMM & BAHNHOF ZOO

✪ Hotel-Pension Alexandra

Wielandstrasse 32, 10629 Berlin. ☎ **030/881 21 07.** Fax 885 77 818. 9 rms (4 with shower only, 4 with shower and WC). TEL. TV. 65–75 DM ($42.45–$50) single without shower or WC, 95–135 DM ($63.35–$90) single with shower only, 110–155 DM ($73.35–$103.35) single with shower and WC, 120–155 DM ($80–$103.35) double with shower, 125–185 DM ($83.35–$123.35) double with shower and WC. Extra bed 45–65 DM ($30–$43.35). Rates include buffet breakfast. No credit cards. Bus 109 from Tegel Airport or Bahnhof Zoo to Olivaer Platz, then a 2-minute walk. S-Bahn: Savignyplatz, a 5-minute walk. U-Bahn: Adenauerplatz, a 5-minute walk.

Located near the western end of the Ku'damm, this pension offers spotless, cheerful rooms, decorated with either modern or antique furniture and equipped with cable TVs, radios, curtains that can block sunlight (useful for that first day of jet lag), and shaving/makeup mirrors and hairdryers in the bathroom. The stucco-ceilinged breakfast room sets the mood for your trip—it's lined with pictures of old Berlin. Frau Kuhn, the friendly proprietress, speaks good English. Unusual for a pension this size, laundry service and babysitting are available. You'll find the reception on the second floor, while rooms are on the third (there's an elevator). The wide range of prices above reflect the seasons.

Berlin Accommodations

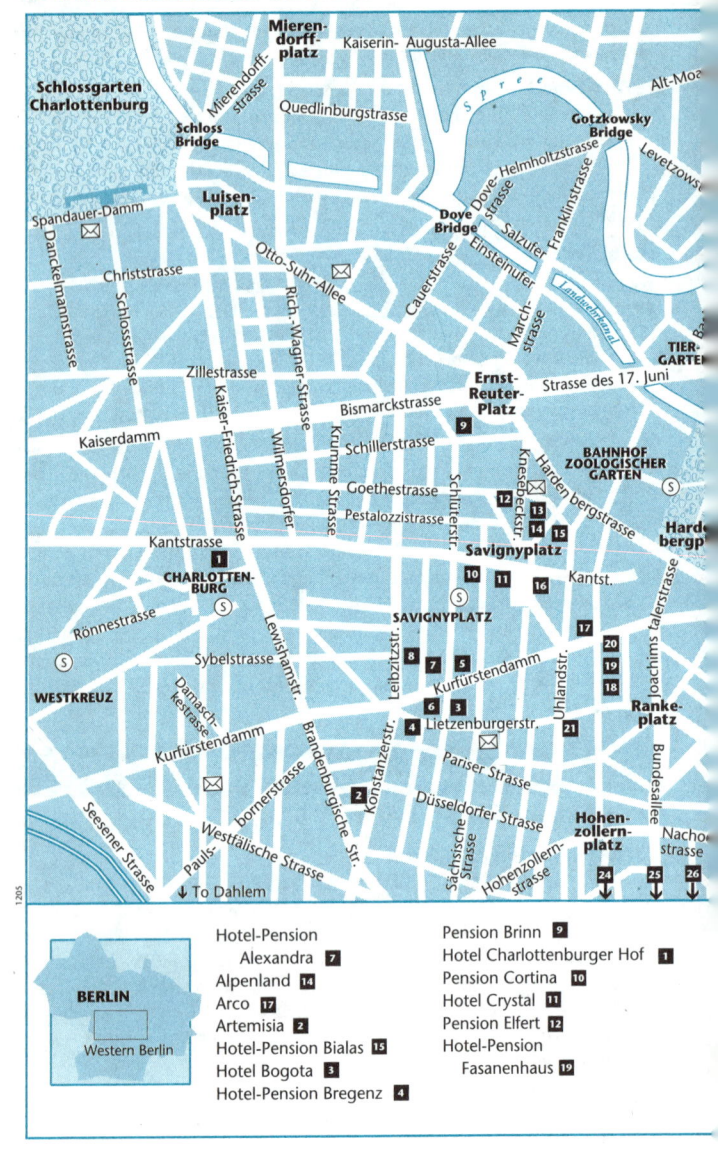

Hotel-Pension
  Alexandra [7]
Alpenland [14]
Arco [17]
Artemisia [2]
Hotel-Pension Bialas [15]
Hotel Bogota [3]
Hotel-Pension Bregenz [4]
Pension Brinn [9]
Hotel Charlottenburger Hof [1]
Pension Cortina [10]
Hotel Crystal [11]
Pension Elfert [12]
Hotel-Pension
  Fasanenhaus [19]

If you stay here in summer, you're going to spend a lot more than our budget allows, but it's a bargain in winter.

Alpenland

Carmerstrasse 8, 10623 Berlin. ☎ **030/312 39 70** or **312 48 98.** Fax 030/313 84 44. 40 rms (5 with shower only, 20 with shower and WC). 90–95 DM ($60–$63.35) single without shower or WC, 110 DM ($73.35) single with shower only, 140–160 DM ($93.35–$106.65) single with shower and WC; 120–130 DM ($80–$86.65)

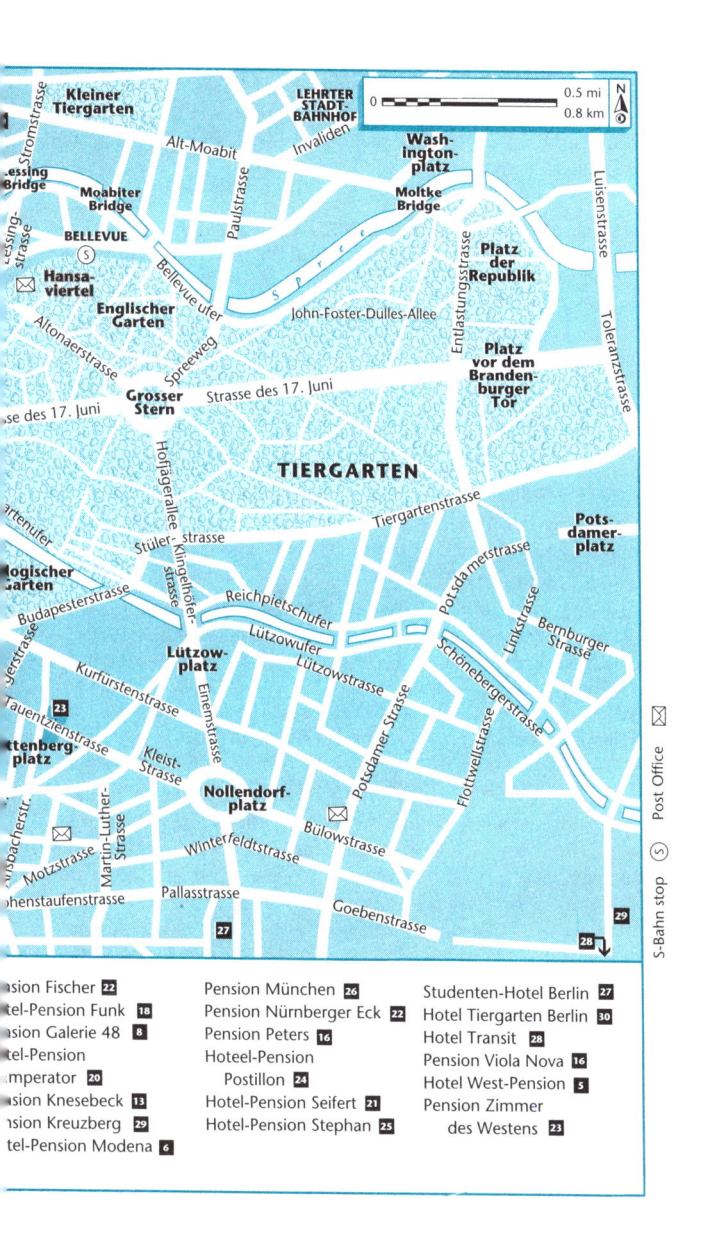

sion Fischer **22**	Pension München **26**	Studenten-Hotel Berlin **27**
tel-Pension Funk **18**	Pension Nürnberger Eck **22**	Hotel Tiergarten Berlin **30**
sion Galerie 48 **8**	Pension Peters **16**	Hotel Transit **28**
tel-Pension	Hoteel-Pension	Pension Viola Nova **16**
mperator **20**	Postillon **24**	Hotel West-Pension **5**
sion Knesebeck **13**	Hotel-Pension Seifert **21**	Pension Zimmer
sion Kreuzberg **29**	Hotel-Pension Stephan **25**	des Westens **23**
tel-Pension Modena **6**		

double without shower or WC, 180–210 DM ($120–$140) double with shower and WC. Extra bed 55–65 DM ($36.65–$43.35). Rates include continental breakfast. MC, V. Directions: A 10-minute walk from Bahnhof Zoo. Bus 109 from Tegel Airport to Uhlandstrasse, then a 6-minute walk. S-Bahn: Savignyplatz, a 3-minute walk.

This hotel occupies a century-old building that boasts a beautifully ornate facade studded with busts and figurines. Incontrast, the remodeled interior is very simple, with rooms spread over four floors

80 Where to Stay

and decorated with Scandinavian-style wood furniture. There's no elevator. Most rooms are equipped with telephones, TVs, room safes, and tiny bathrooms; and those that face the back are quieter, but the view is duller. Its restaurant serves German food.

✪ Arco

Kurfürstendamm 30, 10719 Berlin. ☎ **030/882 63 88**. Fax 881 99 02. 20 rms (10 with shower only, 6 with shower and WC). TEL. 120 DM ($80) single with shower, 150 DM ($100) single with shower and WC; 110–120 DM ($73.35–$80) double without shower or WC, 150 DM ($100) double with shower, 185 DM ($123.35) double with shower and WC. Rates include continental breakfast. AE, DC, MC, V. Bus 109 from Tegel Airport to Uhlandstrasse, then a 1-minute walk. U-Bahn: Uhlandstrasse, a 1-minute walk.

Located right on the Ku'damm, this delightful and refined third-floor pension would certainly cost more if it had an elevator. Rooms are spacious and tastefully decorated, and the reception and breakfast room serve as an art gallery. Four rooms overlooking the Ku'damm have balconies, but those facing the back courtyard are much quieter. If you like being in the center of things, this is a good choice.

Hotel-Pension Bialas

Carmerstrasse 16, 10623 Berlin. ☎ **030/312 50 25** or **312 50 26.** Fax 030/312 43 96. 38 rms (2 with WC only, 10 with shower and WC). 70–75 DM ($46.65–$50) single without shower or WC, 80–85 DM ($53.35–$56.65) single with WC, 105–115 DM ($70–$76.65) single with shower and WC; 105–115 DM ($70–$76.65) double without shower or WC, 165–180 DM ($110–$120) double with shower and WC. Rates include continental breakfast. Extra bed 40 DM ($26.65) in room without shower or WC, 50 DM ($33.35) in room with shower and WC. MC, V. Directions: A 6-minute walk from Bahnhof Zoo. S-Bahn: Savignyplatz, a four-minute walk.

There's sometimes a fine distinction between a hotel and pension; the Bialas calls itself both. It's located on a quiet, tree-lined street between Savignyplatz and Steinplatz. Reception is on the first floor. Rooms are simply furnished and spread over four floors—those at the top are quite a climb, since there's no elevator. No frills here, it's just a place to sleep.

✪ Hotel Bogota

Schlüterstrasse 45, 10707 Berlin. ☎ **030/881 50 01**. Fax 030/883 58 87. 130 rms (12 with shower, 65 with shower and WC). TEL. 75–80 DM ($50–$53.35) single without shower, 105 DM ($70) single with shower, 135–140 DM ($90–$93.35) single with shower and WC; 120–130 DM ($80–$86.65) double without shower or WC, 160 DM ($106.65) double with shower, 195 DM ($130) double with shower and WC. Extra person 40–45 DM ($26.65–$30). Rates include continental breakfast. AE, DC, MC, V. Bus 109 from Tegel Airport or Bahnhof Zoo to Bleibtreustrasse stop, then a 1-minute walk. U-Bahn: Adenauerplatz, a 6-minute walk.

The Bogota is an older hotel with character, with such architectural quirks as a stairway that wraps itself around an ancient elevator. Each floor has its own slightly different lobby; the rooms vary greatly in size and style. The quiet ones face an inner courtyard. There's a cozy TV room where you can spend a relaxing evening, and the English-speaking staff is friendly and accommodating. If you like old-fashioned, well-maintained hotels, you'll like this place, conveniently located near Olivaer Platz.

> ### 👪 Family-Friendly Hotels
>
> **Hotel-Pension Alexandra** *(see p. 77)* Not only do rooms here have radios and cable TVs (good distractions for older kids), but babysitting is available upon request as well.
>
> **Artemisia** *(see p. 87)* This women-only hotel allows children under 8 to stay free with their mother, while children up to 12 pay half price.
>
> **Hotel-Pension Bregenz** *(see p. 81)* Families are welcome at this centrally located family-owned establishment, and cribs are available.
>
> **Pension Cortina** *(see p. 73)* This pension offers a large family room that sleeps six persons.

Hotel-Pension Bregenz

Bregenzer Strasse 5, 10707 Berlin. ☎ **030/881 43 07.** Fax 030/882 40 09. 21 rms (5 with shower, 12 with shower and WC). TEL. TV. MINIBAR. 75–85 DM ($50–$56.65) single without shower or WC, 120–135 DM ($80–$90) single with shower and WC; 110–130 DM ($73.35–$86.65) double without shower or WC, 140–160 DM ($93.35–$106.65) double with shower, 170–190 DM ($113.35–$126.65) double with shower and WC; 200 DM ($133.35) quad with shower, 230 DM ($153.35) quad with shower and WC. Crib available. Rates include continental breakfast. MC. Bus 109 from Tegel Airport or Bahnhof Zoo to Leibnizstrasse, then a 3-minute walk. U-Bahn: Adenauerplatz, a 5-minute walk.

The rooms in this family-run pension, located on a residential street, are clean and spacious and have cable TV. They have double doors, which help cut down on noise. The friendly staff will make bookings for the theater and sightseeing tours, and families are welcome. The only disadvantage to staying here is that it's a bit far from Bahnhof Zoo and the east end of the Ku'damm.

Pension Brinn

Schillerstrasse 10, 10625 Berlin. ☎ **312 16 05.** Fax 030/312 16 05. 6 rms (1 with shower and WC). TEL. 100 DM ($66.65) single without shower or WC; 130 DM ($86.65) double without shower or WC, 150 DM ($100) double with shower and WC. Extra person 50 DM ($33.35). Rates include continental breakfast. No credit cards. U-Bahn: Ernst-Reuter-Strasse, a 2-minute walk.

Located about a 10-minute walk north of the Ku'damm near the Schiller-Theater and Deutsche Oper, this small and intimate pension is bright and cheerful, with tall ceilings. Period furniture in some rooms creates an Old World atmosphere. The ornate building dates from the turn of the century; the pension itself has been around for almost 50 years but was recently acquired by friendly and personable Heidi Koppe. It has one single, three double, and two large rooms perfect for families.

Pension Elfert

Knesebeckstrasse 13/14, 10623 Berlin. ☎ **030/312 12 36.** Fax 030/312 12 36. 13 rms (6 with shower). TV. 85–90 DM ($56.65–$60) single without shower, 130 DM ($86.65) single with shower; 130 DM ($86.65) double without shower, 160 DM

($106.65) double with shower. Extra person 50–60 DM ($33.35–$40); children under 6 stay free with parents. Rates include continental breakfast. No credit cards. Bus 109 from Tegel Airport to Bahnhof Zoo, then a 7-minute walk. S-Bahn: Savignyplatz, a 3-minute walk.

This simple pension offers clean, large rooms. There's no elevator to its first-floor reception, but the entryway is so ornate and the carved staircase so unusual that the mostly middle-aged clientele don't mind. It's close to the restaurants and nightlife on Savignyplatz.

Hotel-Pension Fasanenhaus

Fasanenstrasse 73 10719 Berlin. ☎ **030/881 67 13.** Fax 030/882 39 47. 14 rms (4 with shower only, 2 with shower and WC). 80–85 DM ($53.35–$56.65) single without shower or WC, 90–100 DM ($60–$66.65) single with shower only; 130–140 DM ($86.65–$93.35) double without shower or WC, 150–160 DM ($100–$106.65) double with shower only, 180–200 DM ($120–$133.35) double with shower and WC; 190–210 DM ($126.65–$140) triple with shower only, 240–260 DM ($160–$173.35) triple with shower and WC. Rates include continental breakfast. No credit cards. Directions: A 10-minute walk from Bahnhof Zoo. Bus 109 from Tegel Airport to Uhlandstrasse, then a 2-minute walk. U-Bahn: Uhlandstrasse, a 1-minute walk.

On the fashionable Fasanenstrasse just a minute's walk from the Ku'damm, this simple establishment is reached by a grandly ornate stairway. Rooms vary in size but are mostly large, some with antique furniture, and about half have TV and telephone (the management said all its rooms will eventually have TVs). Breakfast is served in your room, which may suit some of you fine. Otherwise, this pension is a bit high-priced for what it offers.

Pension Galerie 48

Leibnizstrasse 48, 10629 Berlin. ☎ **030/324 26 58** or **323 23 51.** Fax 030/324 26 58. 8 rms (3 with shower). 85 DM ($56.65) single without shower; 120 DM ($80) double without shower, 130 DM ($86.65) double with shower; 160 DM ($106.65) triple with shower. Rates include continental breakfast. No credit cards. Bus 109 to Olivaer Platz. U-Bahn: Adenauerplatz, a 5-minute walk.

This small and personable pension offers clean and cheerful rooms, all on the first floor. The breakfast room is especially nice, with a long wooden bar that serves as the reception desk. Paintings line the corridor, giving it the feel of an art gallery. It's in a good location, north of the Ku'damm.

✪ Hotel-Pension Imperator

Meinekestrasse 5, 10719 Berlin. ☎ **030/881 41 81.** Fax 030/885 19 19. 11 rms (8 with shower only, 1 with shower and WC). 75 DM ($50) single without shower or WC, 105 DM ($70) single with shower, 110 DM ($73.35) single with shower and WC; 130 DM ($86.65) double without shower or WC, 150–160 DM ($100–$106.65) double with shower, 175 DM ($116.65) double with shower and WC; 190–210 DM ($126.65–$140) triple with shower. Breakfast 12–20 DM ($8–$13.35) extra. No credit cards. Directions: A 8-minute walk from Bahnhof Zoo. Bus 109 from Tegel Airport to Uhlandstrasse, then a 2-minute walk. U-Bahn: Uhlandstrasse or Kurfürstendamm, each a 2-minute walk.

Just a stone's throw off the Ku'damm, this small pension is located on the second floor of a grand, turn-of-the-century building, reached via an ornate and gilded ground-floor entryway and elevator. A pension since 1930, it has a variety of mostly large rooms, all with tall ceilings

Doubles for Less than 135 DM ($90)

and wooden floors and with modern or antique furniture. One room even has the luxury of a sun room (called a winter garden in German). Since all rooms face an inner courtyard, they are quieter than what you'd expect from its central, busy location. Original artwork decorates the walls, and a pleasant breakfast room has the extras of a TV and sofa, but if you wish you can have breakfast delivered to your room.

Pension Knesebeck

Knesebeckstrasse 86, 10623 Berlin. ☎ **030/312 72 55.** Fax 030/313 95 07. 12 rms (none with bath). 85–90 DM ($56.65–$60) single; 130 DM ($86.65) double; 160 DM ($106.65) family room. Breakfast 10–20 DM ($6.65–$13.35) extra. AE, MC, V. S-Bahn: Savignyplatz, a 3-minute walk. Bus 109 from Tegel Airport or Bahnhof Zoo to Uhlandstrasse (or a 7-minute walk from Bahnhof Zoo).

Owned by English-speaking and friendly Jutta Jorende, this older pension has some modern twists, including artistic light fixtures in the breakfast rooms, and flowers and plants that make the place more livable and pleasant. Ten rooms face an inner courtyard, making them very quiet, and there's a large family room with four beds. Two rooms have telephones, and TVs are available. The place is less than a 10-minute walk north of the Ku'damm, past Savignyplatz.

Hotel-Pension Modena

Wielandstrasse 26, 10707 Berlin. ☎ **030/881 52 94** or **88 57 01-0.** Fax 030/881 52 94. 21 rms (9 with shower only, 5 with shower and WC). TEL. 75–80 DM ($50–$53.35) single without shower or WC, 90–95 DM ($60–$63.35) single with shower, 110–115 DM ($73.35–$76.65) single with shower and WC; 130–140 DM ($86.65–$93.35) double without shower or WC, 150–160 DM ($100–$106.65) double with shower, 175–185 DM ($116.65–$123.35) double with shower and WC. Additional person 50 DM ($33.35) extra. Rates include continental breakfast. No credit cards. Bus 109 from Tegel Airport or Bahnhof Zoo to Leibnizstrasse, then a 1-minute walk. U-Bahn: Adenauerplatz, a 6-minute walk.

This pension is on the second floor of a lovely building dating from the turn of the century; it's in a good location, near Olivaer Platz, at a good price. It's managed by Frau Kreutz, who keeps rooms spotless. Upon check in, she'll give you a key to operate the elevator, an ancient-looking box; you may prefer the stairs.

Pension Nürnberger Eck

Nürnberger Strasse 24a, 10789 Berlin. ☎ **030/218 53 71.** Fax 030/214 15 40. 8 rms (none with bath). 80 DM ($53.35) single; 130 DM ($86.65) double; 180 DM ($120) triple. Rates include continental breakfast. No credit cards. Directions: An 8-minute walk from Bahnhof Zoo. Bus 109 from Tegel Airport to Joachimstaler Strasse, then a 5-minute walk. U-Bahn: Augsburger Strasse, a 1-minute walk.

Tucked on a side street not far from the Europa-Center, this prewar-style pension has comfortable Biedermeier-reproduction furniture and massive doors to each guest room. It could have been used as a set for *Cabaret*. It has a good atmosphere and location, though it's a bit overpriced.

✪ Pension Peters

Kantstrasse 146, 10623 Berlin. ☎ **030/312 22 78.** Fax 030/312 33 14. 8 rms (none with bath). 80–85 DM ($53.35–$56.65) single; 110–120 DM ($73.35–$80) double; 140–150 DM ($93.35–$100) triple; 200–210 DM ($133.35–$140) quad. Rates include continental breakfast. AE, DC, MC, V. S-Bahn: Savignyplatz, a 2-minute

84 Where to Stay

walk. Bus 109 from Tegel Airport to Bleibtreustrasse, or 149 from Bahnhof Zoo to Savignyplatz (second stop).

Located just east of Savignyplatz and within a 10-minute walk of Bahnhof Zoo, this small pension occupies the second floor of a building dating from 1890; there's no elevator. It has stucco ceilings and double-paned windows. You'll find its modern reception and breakfast room on the ground floor. It offers four single rooms, as well as four doubles that can sleep up to four persons, making them perfect for families or small groups. One room has a television.

Hotel-Pension Seifert
Uhlandstrasse 162, 10719 Berlin. ☎ **030/884 19 10.** Fax 030/884 19 30. 52 rms (14 with shower only, 20 with shower and WC). TEL. 85 DM ($56.65) single without shower or WC, 100–105 DM ($66.65–$70) single with shower, 110–115 DM ($73.35–$76.65) single with shower and WC; 110–125 DM ($73.35–$83.35) double without shower or WC, 140 DM ($93.35) double with shower, 170 DM ($113.35) double with shower and WC. Additional person 40 DM ($26.65) extra. Rates include continental breakfast. AE, MC, V. U-Bahn: Uhlandstrasse, then a 3-minute walk. Bus 109 from Tegel Airport to Uhlandstrasse.

This simple pension, which is a bit worn around the edges with old carpeting and wallpaper, has a convenient location near the Ku'damm. With a reception on the second floor, its rooms are clean and spread on three floors, serviced by an elevator. Fifteen rooms are singles, making it a good bet if you're traveling alone. Some rooms have radios. Breakfasts are generous, and a small house bar is open evenings.

Pension Viola Nova
Kantstrasse 146, 10623 Berlin. ☎ **030/313 14 57.** Fax 030/312 33 14. 15 rms (2 with shower, 4 with shower and WC). TEL. 85–90 DM ($56/65–$60) single without shower or WC, 110–115 DM ($73.35–$76.65) single with shower, 130–140 DM ($86.65–$93.35) single with shower and WC; 110–120 DM ($73.35–$80) double without shower or WC, 130–140 DM ($86.65–$93.35) double with shower, 150–160 DM ($100–$106.65) double with shower and WC. Additional person 30 DM ($20) extra. Rates include continental breakfast. AE, DC, MC, V. S-Bahn: Savignyplatz, a 2-minute walk. Bus 109 from Tegel Airport to Bleibtreustrasse, or 149 from Bahnhof Zoo to Savignyplatz (second stop).

Located in the same building as Pension Peters (see above) and under the same ownership, this updated pension has a cheerful breakfast room and reception on the ground floor. It offers bright and modern accommodations with sleek black furniture, modern lighting, and tall stucco ceilings. Several rooms sleep three to four people. TVs are provided in some rooms and are available for rent in others. This is good place to stay.

✪ Hotel West-Pension
Kurfürstendamm 48-49, 10707 Berlin. ☎ **030/881 80 57** or **881 80 58.** Fax 030/881 38 92. 33 rms (8 with shower, 15 with shower and WC). TEL. 75–80 DM ($50–$53.35) single without shower or WC, 100 DM ($66.65) single with shower, 110 DM ($73.35) single with shower and WC; 130 DM ($86.65) double without shower or WC, 150 DM ($100) double with shower, 175–220 DM ($116.65–$146.65) double with shower and WC. Extra bed 30 DM ($20). Buffet breakfast 12 DM ($8) extra. MC, V. Bus 109 from Tegel Airport or Bahnhof Zoo to Bleibtreustrasse. U-Bahn: Uhlandstrasse, a 3-minute walk.

With a great location right on the Ku'damm, this pension occupies the second floor of a beautiful turn-of-the-century building, which has an elevator and Old World feel. There's a pleasant breakfast room with a high stucco ceiling as well as a comfortable bar for hotel guests. Some rooms have antique furnishings; others have modern. Some double rooms with shower and toilet face the Ku'damm; the rest face toward the back. Since a variety of rooms are available, specify what you want when making your reservation.

Hotel-Pension Postillon

Gasteiner Strasse 8, 10717 Berlin. ☎ **030/87 52 32.** Fax 030/87 38 59. 24 rms (5 with shower, 4 with shower and WC). TEL. 70–75 DM ($46.65–$50) single without shower or WC, 80–85 DM ($53.35–$56.65) single with shower, 90–100 DM ($60–$66.65) single with shower and WC; 120 DM ($80) double without shower or WC, 140 DM ($93.35) double with shower, 165 DM ($110) double with shower and WC. Extra bed 40–45 DM ($30–$33.35). Rates include buffet breakfast. No credit cards. U-Bahn: U-9 from Bahnhof Zoo to Berliner Strasse, then U-7 to Blissestrasse. Bus 109 from Tegel Airport to Jakob-Kaiser-Platz (first stop), then U-7 to Blissestrasse.

This hotel-pension is less conveniently located than the others above (about a 20-minute walk from the Ku'damm), but is worth a try if other establishments are full. It's owned by English-speaking Herr Bernd Lucht, who offers simple but large rooms in this older building. Those that face the front have balconies.

3 Youth Hostels & Youth Hotels

YOUTH HOSTELS

Youth-hostel cards are required for stays at Berlin's youth hostels; these cards are available at hostels for 36 DM ($24). There's no age limit, but "seniors" (27 years and older) pay slightly higher rates. Berlin youth hostels have a midnight curfew, which can be painfully early in the city that never sleeps.

Jugendgästehaus am Wannsee

Badeweg 1, 14129 Berlin. ☎ **030/803 20 34.** Telex 186606. 264 beds. 29 DM ($19.35) per person for ages 26 and younger; 38 DM ($25.35) per person for ages 27 and older. Rates include breakfast and sheets. Dinner 8.50 DM ($5.65) extra. No credit cards. S-Bahn: S-1, -3 or -7 to Nikolassee, then a 7-minute walk.

This is Berlin's newest and most modern youth hostel, a handsome brick building with red trim. It's close to Wannsee, a lake popular for swimming and boating in summer, with bathing facilities nearby. Rooms have four beds each, with showers for every two rooms. It's a relaxing place in summer.

Jugendgästehaus Berlin

Kluckstrasse 3, 10785 Berlin. ☎ **030/261 10 97.** 364 beds. 29 DM ($19.35) per person for ages 26 and younger; 38 DM ($25.35) per person for ages 27 and older. Rates include breakfast and sheets. Dinner 8.50 DM ($5.65). No credit cards. Bus 129 from Bahnhof Zoo to Kluckstrasse, then a 1-minute walk. U-Bahn: Kurfürstenstrasse, a 12-minute walk.

This is the most popular youth hostel because of its convenient location—just three subway stops from the Ku'damm. Write at least

1 month in advance to reserve a room. All rooms are dormitory style, with four to six beds, and everyone gets a locker with key.

Jugendherberge Ernst Reuter

Hermsdorfer Damm 48-50, 13467 Berlin. ☎ **030/404 16 10.** 110 beds. 24 DM ($16) per person for ages 26 and younger; 31 DM ($20.65) per person for ages 27 and older. Rates include breakfast and sheets. Dinner 8.50 DM ($5.65) extra. No credit cards. Directions: From Tegel Airport, bus 128 to Kurt Schumacher Platz, then U-6 to Tegel stop, then bus 125 to Jugendherberge stop; from Bahnhof Zoo, U-9 to Leopoldplatz, then U-6 to Tegel station, then bus 125 to Jugendher berge stop.

Although this is Berlin's cheapest, it's at least 35 minutes from the city center (longer if connections are bad and you have to wait for the bus). However, it's surrounded by woods in a peaceful part of town and offers table tennis and a TV lounge. All rooms have eight beds.

YOUTH HOTELS

Catering mostly to youth and school groups, most of these youth hotels will also take individual travelers of any age. Youth-hostel cards are not required, and most have single and double rooms in addition to multibed dormitory rooms.

Jugendgästehaus am Zoo

Hardenbergstrasse 9a, 10623 Berlin. ☎ **030/312 94 10.** 58 beds. 50 DM ($33.35) single; 90 DM ($60) double; 35 DM ($23.35) per person in dormitory room. No credit cards. Directions: A 10-minute walk from Bahnhof Zoo.

It's easy to overlook this place as there just a tiny sign outside this nondescript building. But take the elevator up to the fourth floor (if it's working) and you'll find a no-frills establishment that appeals to backpackers and youth groups. Although this hostel is intended for people 27 and younger, any age is welcome if there's room. Note, however, that those over 27 pay a 5-DM ($3.35) supplement per night to the prices quoted above. No reservations are accepted for single or double rooms, so you have to inquire when you arrive in town. There are also larger, dormitory-style rooms that sleep three to eight persons. This hostel, which has the best location, even has a bar that's open from 9:30pm to an astonishing 7am. It's across the street from Technical University with its Mensa student cafeteria, one of the cheapest places to eat in town.

Jugendgästehaus Central

Nikolsburger Strasse 2-4, 10717 Berlin. ☎ **030/87 01 88.** Fax 030/861-34 85. 456 beds. 34 DM ($22.65) per person. Sheets 7 DM ($4.65) extra for stays of 1 or 2 nights, free for stays of 3 nights or longer. Rates include breakfast. No credit cards. U-Bahn: Güntzelstrasse, Spichernstrasse, or Hohenzollernplatz, all a 5-minute walk.

This large, dormitory-style accommodation caters to school groups but will accept single travelers if there's room. It's open only to those under 25 or bona-fide students, and there's a 1am curfew. There are a few double rooms available (used mostly by teachers and group leaders), but most rooms are equipped with bunk beds sleeping 8 to 12 people per room. You'll need your own towel here. If you wish, you can prepare your own box lunch to take with you for the day for an extra 4 DM ($2.65). It's located two subway stops south of the Ku'-damm, or a 20-minute walk.

Jugendgästehaus Feurigstrasse
Feurigstrasse 63, 10827 Berlin. ☎ **030/781 52 11.** Fax 030/788 30 51. 200 beds. 40 DM ($26.65). Sheets 5 DM ($3.35) extra for stays of one to two nights, free for stays of three nights or longer. Rates include buffet breakfast. No credit cards. Bus 146 from Bahnhof Zoo to Dominicusstrasse. U-Bahn: Kleistpark, about a 5-minute walk.

This youth hotel, located in Schöneberg, caters primarily to school groups, but will take individual travelers if there's room, giving preference to younger people. There's no curfew here, and the bunk beds are a bit sturdier than elsewhere. Two-, four-, and six-bed rooms are available, as well as a few single and double rooms.

WORTH A SPLURGE

These establishments offer more luxurious surroundings and more personal service than those listed above.

ON OR NEAR THE KU'DAMM & BAHNHOF ZOO

✪ Artemisia
Brandenburgischestrasse 18, 10707 Berlin. ☎ **030/87 89 05.** Fax 030/861 86 53. 8 rms (7 with shower and WC). TEL. 109 DM ($72.66) single without shower or WC, 165 DM ($110) single with shower and WC; 185 DM ($123.35) double without shower or WC, 220 DM ($146.65) double with shower and WC. Last-minute discount 10–20 DM ($6.65–$13.35) Children under 8 stay free, children 8 to 12 pay half price. Rates include buffet breakfast. AE, MC, V. Bus 109 from Tegel Airport or Bahnhof Zoo to Adenauerplatz, then a 5-minute walk. U-Bahn: Konstanzer, a 1-minute walk.

This wonderful pension, named after Italian artist Artemisia Gentileschi, is *for women only*. In 1989 a team of four women bought and renovated a run-down pension and turned it into this modern, spotless, and thoughtfully planned establishment. Reception is up on the fourth floor; there's an elevator. There's also a sunny breakfast room, a rooftop terrace and winter garden, a small library, and a hotel bar with a fireplace. Rooms are decorated with antiques and modern furniture. Each room is dedicated to a famous "forgotten" woman, such as the composer/pianist Fanny Mendelssohn-Hensel, who lived in her brother's shadow and whose room contains a few items in memory of her. Boys up to 14 years of age can stay here with their mothers. Note that a "last-minute" discount is available—call just one or two days before your intended day of arrival, and if there's a room you can have it for 10 to 20 DM ($6.65–$13.35) less per person than the rates quoted above. I highly recommend this establishment, especially for single women travelers.

NORTH OF TIERGARTEN PARK
This establishment is centrally located just north of the Tiergarten and the Hansaviertel (Hansa Quarter), just two stops from Bahnhof Zoo on the U-Bahn.

✪ Hotel Tiergarten Berlin
Alt-Moabit 89, 10559 Berlin. ☎ **030/391 30 04** or 399 89 600.Fax 030/393 86 92. 40 rms (all with shower and WC). TEL. TV. MINIBAR. 180 DM ($120) single; 215 DM

($143.35) double. Additional person 35 DM ($23.35) extra. Children under 10 free in parents' room. Weekend discounts available. Rates include buffet breakfast. AE, DC, MC, V. U-Bahn: U-9 to Turmstrasse, then a 3-minute walk.

This small, intimate hotel has all the makings of a first-rate establishment: polite and efficient staff, turn-of-the-century charm and elegance, and light and airy rooms. Bathrooms are modern and spotless, complete with magnifying glass for shaving or applying makeup. There are four no-smoking rooms. The breakfast room with its buffet spread is a cheerful place to start the day. In short, this is the kind of place that appeals to both business and pleasure travelers, the kind you'd come back to again and again. It's certainly one of my favorites in Berlin. The small reception is on the ground floor; there's an elevator to the rooms above.

4 Camping

If you're between 14 and 26 years of age and you don't mind roughing it, you might try the **Internationales Jugendcamp**, Ziekowstrasse 161, 13509 Berlin (☎ 030/433 86 40). Take U-Bahn 6 to Alt-Tegel and continue by bus 222 to the fourth stop, Titusweg stop. This camp has a large tent, with mattresses and sheets provided. Showers are free. Open only from mid-June to the end of August, it costs 9 DM ($6) per person per night. Guests must leave the premises during the day, from 9am to 5pm. No written reservations are accepted, so call when you get to Berlin.

There are five campgrounds in the vicinity of Berlin, all open year round, but they fill up fast in summer. They are equipped with modern sanitary facilities and stores, and all charge the same rates: 7.50 DM ($5) per adult; 3 DM ($2) per child from 7 through 14 years of age; 8.50 DM ($5.65) for the camping site; and 5.50 ($3.65) per tent. **Dreilinden** (in Wannsee), Albrechts-Teerofen, 14109 Berlin (☎ 030/805 12 01), has about 100 tent sites and is reached by bus 118, followed by a 20-minute walk. **Haselhorst** (in Spandau), Pulvermühlenweg, 13599 Berlin (☎ 334 59 55), offers both tent and camper sites and is reached by taking the U-Bahn to Haselhorst, followed by a 15-minute walk. **Kladow** (in Spandau), Krampnitzer Weg 111-117, 14089 Berlin (☎ 030/365 27 97), is the largest, with 300 tent and camper-vehicle sites, and is reached by taking bus 149 and 135 followed by a 30-minute walk. Other camping sites are **Krossinsee,** Wernsdorfer Strasse 45, 12527 Berlin (☎ 030/675 86 87), reached by taking streetcar 68 from Grünau, followed by a bus going in the direction of Ziegenhals; and **Kohlhasenbrück,** Neue Kreis Strasse 36, 14109 Berlin (☎ 030/805 17 37), located in Wannsee and reached by taking the S-Bahn to Griebnitzsee and then a 10-minute walk.

6

Where to Eat

To me travel and dining are synonymous: The atmosphere of a restaurant and the celebration of a meal can make it as culturally enriching as a visit to a museum—and in Berlin it doesn't have to cost much. Crowded and lively neighborhood pubs (or *Gaststätten*) offer generous platters of German cuisine and the opportunity to strike up conversations with fellow diners. Outdoor cafes are perfect for enjoying drinks, dessert, and lighter meals while watching the endless parade of people. Even a simple picnic of bread, cheese, and wine in the middle of the Tiergarten park can be a unique Berlin experience.

The choices for dining in Berlin seem endless—even for the budget traveler—with more than 6,000 pubs and restaurants. And there is an astounding diversity of ethnic restaurants. Only half the Germans recently surveyed said they preferred their own heavier native cuisine over international fare.

The vast majority of Berlin's restaurants are found on and around the Ku'damm, including Savignyplatz, Wilmersdorfer Strasse, and the Europa-Center. In addition to the many take-out establishments here, there are also a number of *Imbisse* (food stands) serving everything from sausages to french fries. An insider's tip for sit-down bargains are department stores, all of which have food counters, cafeterias, or inexpensive restaurants with waitress service.

The restaurants that follow are listed according to cost: meals less than 12 DM ($8), meals less than 25 DM ($16.65), and those "Worth a Splurge." Unless otherwise stated, prices given for each restaurant are for main courses, which for German cuisine almost always include one or more side dishes and are often complete meals in themselves. Thus, don't assume a restaurant is beyond your budget just because it's listed in a more expensive price category. If you opt for the less expensive items on the menu and cut out alcohol, appetizers, and desserts, you can enjoy a fine restaurant. Keep in mind that many restaurants offer daily specials, usually complete meals that include a soup or appetizer, main dish, and sometimes coffee and dessert. Some of the more expensive restaurants also offer a cheaper menu during lunch hours, usually available until 2:30pm.

Each price category is further divided according to geographical location. After all, if you're visiting the museums in Dahlem or are shopping on Wilmersdorfer Strasse, you're probably much more interested in knowing what's readily available in the immediate area. And if you're craving a certain cuisine, refer to the "Restaurants by Cuisine" index. An explanation of German cuisine is given in Chapter 2; a translation of menu items appears in the Appendix.

Keep in mind that most Germans eat their big meal of the day at lunch, which is served in most restaurants from about 11:30am to 2 or 3pm and may include lunch specials at reduced prices. The most popular dinner hours are from 7 or 8pm to 10pm. Remember to arrive well ahead of the actual closing time, since restaurants stop serving food about 30 minutes and sometimes an hour before the posted closing hours. Since the vast majority of restaurants are open throughout the day, try to eat in the off-hours to avoid having to wait for a table. This is especially prudent in east Berlin, since there are still too few restaurants to meet the demand.

Although tax and service charge are included in all restaurant bills, you should still leave a small tip for your server. For meals costing less than 20 DM ($13.35), simply round off to the nearest mark or add a mark tip. For meals costing more than 20 DM, most Germans will add a 10% tip. Unlike in the United States where tips are left on the table, in Germany tips are indicated to the server before change is given back. Thus, if your bill is 14 DM and you want to give your waiter a 1-DM tip, say "15 DM" when you hand over your 20-DM bill. If she doesn't understand English (or your high-school German), simply hand back the 1-DM.

Though increasingly rare, some of the larger tourist-oriented restaurants in Berlin charge extra for use of their public facilities—usually 30 Pfennig (20¢). In eastern Berlin, it is sometimes expected to give your coat or jacket to the coat clerk at the *Garderobe,* for which the clerk expects a small tip of a mark or so (65¢).

In addition to the restaurants listed in this chapter, check Chapter 10, "Berlin After Dark," for pubs and locales that serve food in addition to wine and beer as well as places that serve "Late-Night Bites." For information on buying picnic fare and where to eat it, see the "Time for a Picnic" box in Chapter 7, "What to See & Do."

Most hotels and pensions in Berlin include breakfast in their rates, but in case yours doesn't, you might try **Eierschale,** Rankestrasse 1 (☎ 882 53 05), which offers a breakfast brunch with music. **Café Bleibtreu,** a pleasant cafe/bar at Bleibtreustrasse 45 (☎ 882 47 56), and **Zillemarkt,** Bleibtreustrasse 48a (☎ 881 70 40), have outdoor seating in summer. **Schwarzes Café,** Kantstrasse 148 (☎ 313 80 38) makes a specialty of breakfast, which is served all day. You can shop at the Winterfeldplatz morning market in Nollendorfplatz on Wednesday and Saturday and breakfast at **Café Sidney,** at Winterfeldstrasse 40 (☎ 216 52 53). One of the most popular places to be on Sunday is **Yorckschlösschen,** Yorckstrasse 15 (☎ 215 80 70), when live Dixieland jazz serenades a largely young clientele from 2 to 6pm.

1 Restaurants by Cuisine

AMERICAN
Jimmy's Diner (On or near the Ku'damm)
Lucky Strike Originals (Berlin-Mitte)
T.G.I. Friday's (Berlin-Mitte)

CHICKEN
Henne (Kreuzberg)

CHINESE
Asia-Quick (On or near the Ku'damm)
China Imbiss Dali (On or near the Ku'damm)
Chung (On or near the Ku'damm)

COFFEEHOUSES
Café Kranzler (On or near the Ku'damm)
Café im Literaturhaus (On or near the Ku'damm)
Café Möhring (On or near the Ku'damm)
Einstein (Near Nollendorfplatz)
Operncafé (Berlin-Mitte)

CONTINENTAL
Lutter & Wegner (On or near the Ku'damm)
Operncafé (Berlin-Mitte)

FRENCH
Ty Breizh Savoie Rire (Near Wilmersdorfer Strasse & Bahnhof Charlottenburg)

GERMAN
Berliner Stube (On or near the Ku'damm)
Café Hardenberg (On or near the Ku'damm)
Casino (Berlin-Mitte)
Club Culinare (On or near the Ku'damm)
Dahlem Restaurant-Café (Dahlem)
Grossbeerenkeller (Kreuzberg)
Hardtke (On or near the Ku'damm)
Ihre Frisch-Backstübe (On or near the Ku'damm)
Joseph Langer (Near Wilmersdorfer Strasse & Bahnhof Charlottenburg)
Kasino Beim Senator für Wirtschaft und Verkehr (near Rathaus Schoneberg)
Le Buffet (On or near the Ku'damm, near Wilmersdorfer Strasse & Bahnhof Charlottenburg)
Luise (Dahlem)
Luisen-Bräu (Near Schloss Charlottenburg)
Mensa (On or near the Ku'damm)
Operncafé (Berlin-Mitte)
Opernpalais Self-Service Terrace (Berlin-Mitte)
Restaurant-Café (Near Wilmersdorfer Strasse & Bahnhof Charlottenburg)
Rogacki (Near Wilmersdorfer Strasse & Bahnhof Charlottenburg)
Wienerwald (Berlin-Mitte)
Wilhelm Hoeck (Near Wilmersdorfer Strasse & Bahnhof Charlottenburg)
Wirtshaus Zum Löwen (On or near the Ku'damm)
Zum Nussbaum (Berlin-Mitte)
Zur Letzten Instanz (Berlin-Mitte)

GREEK
Ano Kato (On or near the Ku'damm)
Athener Grill (On or near the Ku'damm)
Taverna Plaka (On or near the Ku'damm)

INDIAN
Ashoka (On or near the Ku'damm)
Kalkutta (On or near the Ku'damm)

INTERNATIONAL
Café Hardenberg (On or near the Ku'damm)
Club Culinare (On or near the Ku'damm)
KaDeWe (On or near the Ku'damm)
Luise (Dahlem)
Mövenpick (On or near the Ku'damm)
Restaurant Marché Mövenpick (On or near the Ku'damm)
Shell (On or near the Ku'damm)

ITALIAN
Athener Grill (On or near the Ku'damm)
Avanti (On or near the Ku'damm)
Ciao Ciao (On or near the Ku'damm)
Piccola Taormina Tavola Calda (On or near the Ku'damm)
Pizza Bleibtreu (On or near the Ku'damm)
San Marino (On or near the Ku'damm)

JAPANESE
Udagawa Japan Imbiss (Near Wilmersdorfer Strasse & Bahnhof Charlottenburg)

KOSHER
Arche Noah (On or near the Ku'damm)
Oren (Berlin-Mitte)

MEXICAN
Jimmy's Diner (On or near the Ku'damm)

MIDDLE EASTERN
Orient (On or near the Ku'damm)

SANDWICHES
Ihre Frisch-Backstübe (On or near the Ku'damm)

SEAFOOD
Nordsee (Berlin-Mitte, near Wilmersdorfer Strasse & Bahnhof Charlottenburg)

SNACKS
Opernpalais Self-Service Terrace (Berlin-Mitte)
Zum Nussbaum (Berlin-Mitte)

THAI
Grung Thai (On or near the Ku'damm)

TURKISH
Angora (On or near the Ku'damm)
Istanbul (On or near the Ku'damm)
Karavan (On or near the Ku' damm)

VEGETARIAN
Einhorn (On or near the Ku'damm)
Higher Taste (On or near the Ku'damm)
Shell (On or near the Ku'damm)

2 Meals for Less than 12 DM ($8)

Many restaurants in this category serve ethnic food, including Turkish, Italian, Indian, and Chinese. For German fare, your best bets are the food counters and cafeterias in Berlin's larger department stores, as well as the Würste sold at Berlin's many stands. Be sure to also check the listings under "Meals for Less than 25 DM ($16.65)," since some of these offer some main courses or stews for less than 12 DM.

ON OR NEAR THE KU'DAMM

🟢 Ashoka
Grolmanstrasse 51. ☎ **313 20 66.** Main courses 5–14 DM ($3.35–$9.35). No credit cards. Daily 11am–midnight. S-Bahn: Savignyplatz, less than a 4-minute walk. INDIAN.

Located just north of Savignyplatz, this minuscule Indian establishment with outdoor seating has an open kitchen that takes up half the restaurant. It's popular with students living in the area, who come for its vegetarian or meat dishes. For an appetizer, try the *pakoras,* a kind of biscuit with cauliflower and other vegetables, with a dash of chutney. Also recommended are the vegetarian platter served with either rice or Indian bread and the lamb biryani.

Asia-Quick
Lietzenburger Strasse 96. ☎ **882 15 33.** Main courses 9–15 DM ($6–$10). No credit cards. Mon–Fri 11:30am–11:30pm, Sat 2pm–1am. U-Bahn: Uhlandstrasse, about a 6-minute walk. CHINESE.

Located south of the Ku'damm near Bleibtreustrasse, this clean, fast-food establishment (aptly named) has a TV in the corner just like in Asia. It offers soups and appetizers for less than 6 DM ($4), while most main dishes are less than 12 DM ($8). Fish, pork, beef, and chicken dishes come in several styles, including chop suey (with soy sauce) and sweet-and-sour. There are also rice, noodle, and vegetarian dishes. You can either dine in or take out.

🟢 Athener Grill
Kurfürstendamm 156. ☎ **892 10 39.** Main courses 7–15 DM ($4.65–$10). AE, DC, MC, V. Sun–Thurs 11am–4am, Fri–Sat 11am–5am. U-Bahn: Adenauerplatz, a 1-minute walk. GREEK/ITALIAN.

Located on the western end of the Ku'damm past Adenauerplatz, this cafeteria occupies a modern brick building with a spacious interior—and it's not garishly bright like most fast-food joints. Various counters offer different cuisines; the menu is on a wall near the front door. You can find pizza, spaghetti, moussaka, souvlaki, gyros, ice cream, and salads, to name only a few. After deciding what you want, pay the cashier and then hand your ticket to the cook at the appropriate counter. Greek wines are available starting at 3.20 DM ($2.15).

Avanti
Rankestrasse 2. ☎ **883 52 40.** Main courses 6.50–17.50 DM ($4.35–$11.65). No credit cards. Daily 11am–2am. U-Bahn: Kurfürstendamm, a 2-minute walk. ITALIAN.

Italian fast-food restaurants are so popular that they seem to occupy every corner. This one has a great location just off the Ku'damm, near

Western Berlin Dining

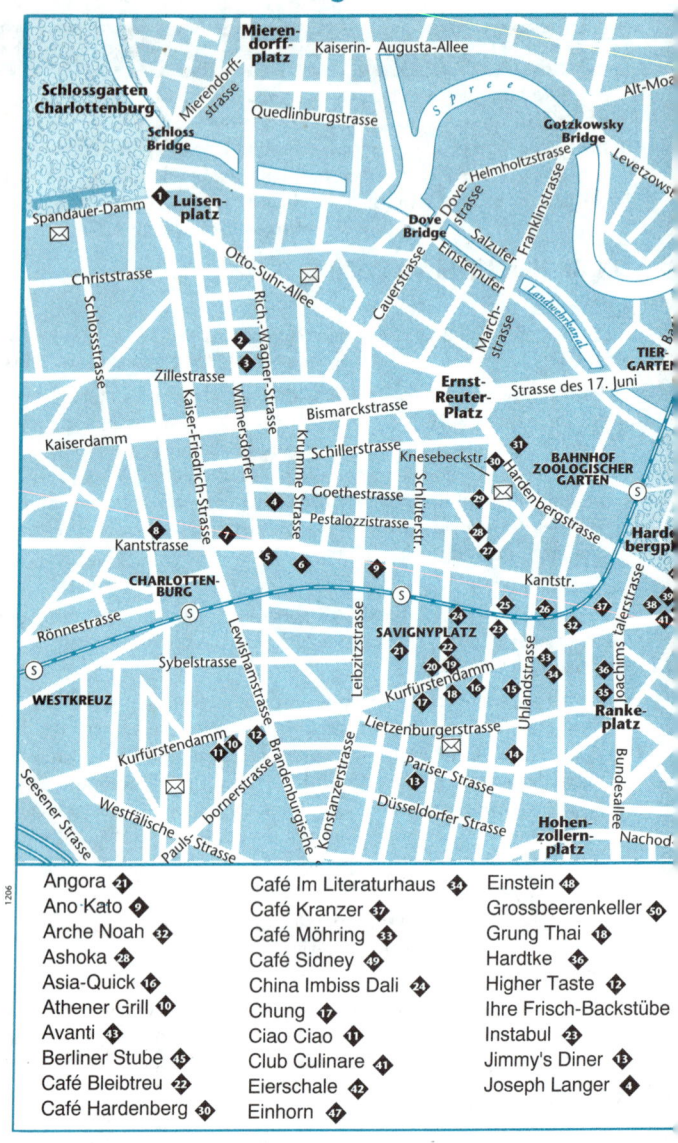

Angora ㉑	Café Im Literaturhaus ㉞	Einstein ㊽
Ano Kato ❾	Café Kranzer ㊼	Grossbeerenkeller ㊿
Arche Noah ㊷	Café Möhring ㉝	Grung Thai ⓲
Ashoka ㉘	Café Sidney ㊾	Hardtke ㊱
Asia-Quick ⓰	China Imbiss Dali ㉔	Higher Taste ⓬
Athener Grill ❿	Chung ⓱	Ihre Frisch-Backstübe
Avanti ⑮	Ciao Ciao ⓫	Instabul ㉓
Berliner Stube ㊺	Club Culinare ㊶	Jimmy's Diner ⓭
Café Bleibtreu ㉒	Eierschale ㊸	Joseph Langer ❹
Café Hardenberg ㉚	Einhorn ㊹	

the Gedächtniskirche and Wertheim department store. It's clean and modern, with contemporary artwork on the walls and an espresso bar. Pizzas and pastas are all priced under 11 DM ($7.35), and there's a salad bar where you can help yourself for 6.50 DM ($4.35) for a small plate. The antipasta is great, and costs only 6.50 DM ($4.35) for a choice of four. Daily specials are also offered.

Map Legend

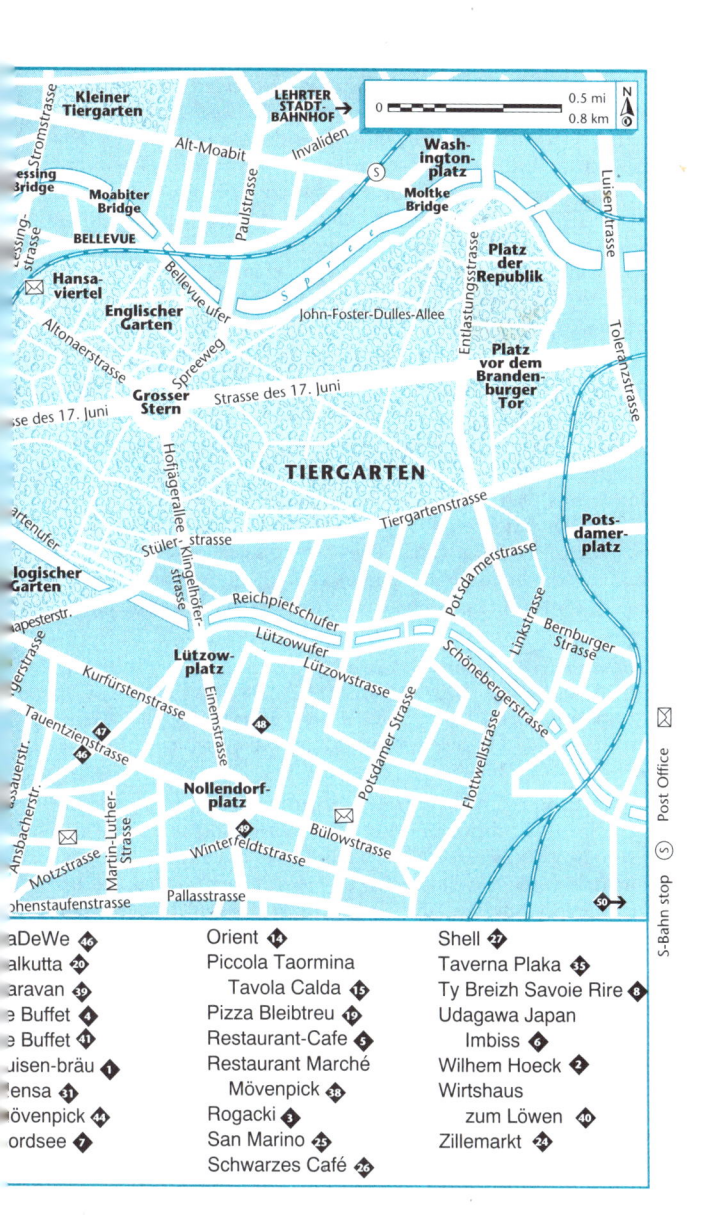

aDeWe 46	Orient 12	Shell 27
alkutta 20	Piccola Taormina	Taverna Plaka 35
aravan 38	Tavola Calda 15	Ty Breizh Savoie Rire 8
e Buffet 4	Pizza Bleibtreu 19	Udagawa Japan
e Buffet 11	Restaurant-Cafe 5	Imbiss 6
uisen-bräu 1	Restaurant Marché	Wilhem Hoeck 2
ensa 31	Mövenpick 18	Wirtshaus
övenpick 44	Rogacki 3	zum Löwen 40
ordsee 7	San Marino 25	Zillemarkt 24
	Schwarzes Café 26	

Café Hardenberg

Hardenbergstrasse 10. ☎ **312 33 30.** Main courses 8–14 DM ($5.35–$9.35). No credit cards. Daily 9am–midnight. U-Bahn: Ernst-Reuter-Platz, less than a 3-minute walk. GERMAN/INTERNATIONAL.

Located across from the Technical University less than a 6-minute walk from Bahnhof Zoo, this popular cafe is always packed with students and people who work nearby. Decorated with museum posters, plants, and ceiling fans, it serves as a coffeehouse and restaurant; in the evening, it's a bar. In summer there are tables and chairs outside. Classical music is played through the sound system until 4pm, after which is music of the 20th century. It's a good place for a meal, since portions are hearty and the menu has an interesting range of dishes that change daily and can include spaghetti, Schnitzel, Greek salads, omelets, dolmades, pork chops, and chili con carne. Breakfast is served to a late 5pm, with prices starting at around 5.50 DM ($3.65).

China Imbiss Dali

Savignyplatz S-Bahn-Bogen 604. ☎ **312 64 23.** Soups and appetizers 3–6.50 DM ($2–$4.35); entrées 9–15 DM ($6–$10). No credit cards. Daily noon–midnight. S-Bahn: Savignyplatz, less than a minute's walk. CHINESE.

Savignyplatz Bogen is a string of establishments located in the arches under the S-Bahn tracks between Savignyplatz and Bleibtreustrasse. China Imbiss Dali, just off Bleibtreustrasse, is a simply decorated Chinese restaurant offering rice and noodle dishes, as well as hearty pork, duck, beef, chicken, fish, and vegetable dishes. There's an English menu, and candles on each table make for slightly more intimate dining than what is usually offered at fast-food Chinese restaurants.

Club Culinare

Basement of Hertie bei Wertheim department store, Kurfürstendamm 231. ☎ **88 20 61.** Main courses 7–20 DM ($4.65–$13.35). No credit cards. Mon–Wed and Fri 9:30am–6pm, Thurs 9:30am–8pm, Sat 9am–1:30pm (to 5:30pm first Sat of the month in winter, to 3:30pm in summer). U-Bahn: Kurfürstendamm, a 1-minute walk. GERMAN/INTERNATIONAL.

Most department stores have grocery departments in their basements, and Hertie bei Wertheim is no exception. What's unique here are several sit-down counters, each serving different cuisine. Simply walk around until you find what tempts you most. Among your choices are several dozen kinds of salads, scrambled eggs, stews, pasta, grilled chicken, daily specials, desserts, and wines. Wertheim is conveniently located on the Ku'damm, across the street from the Kaiser-Wilhelm Gedächtniskirche.

Einhorn

Wittenbergplatz 5-6. ☎ **218 63 47.** Main courses 7–11 DM ($4.65–$7.35). No credit cards. Mon–Fri 9am–6pm, Sat 10am–1:30pm. U-Bahn: Wittenbergplatz, a 1-minute walk. VEGETARIAN.

This natural-foods shop, on the north end of Wittenbergplatz, offers vegetarian daily specials, such as curry risotto with vegetables, spinach cannelloni, vegetarian lasagna, stews, salads, spinach casserole, and vegetarian moussaka. Tempting fruit juices are also available. If you've been dying for some wholesome cereal or snacks, this is your best bet. You can eat at a stand-up counter inside, but if the weather is nice, you'll want to sit on a bench lining the square.

Higher Taste

Kurfürstendamm 157/158. ☎ **892 909 17.** Main courses 6–10 DM ($4–$6.65). No credit cards. Mon–Fri 11am–6:30pm, Sat 11am–2pm (to 6pm first Sat of the month). U-Bahn: Adenauerplatz, less than a 2-minute walk. VEGETARIAN.

> ### 👪 Family-Friendly Restaurants
>
> **Jimmy's Diner** *(see p. 97)* Is your teenager bugging you for a hamburger or some "real" food? Head for this '50s-style diner, which offers hamburgers, sandwiches, chicken, spaghetti, and Mexican food. The clientele—mainly Berlin teenagers striving for just the right look—are an entertaining eyeful.
>
> **Piccola Taormina Tavola Calda** *(see p. 99)* You won't go broke feeding your whole family at this inexpensive Italian restaurant. You can order takeout or eat at one of the simple wooden tables.
>
> **T.G.I. Fridays** *(see p. 111)* This American chain, newly opened in eastern Berlin, offers a children's menu as well as a varied regular menu with selections ranging from fajitas and fettucine Alfredo to blackened Cajun chicken, burgers, and sandwiches. Sure to please adults and children alike.

Operated by the Hare Krishna organization, this bright, clean, and cheerful vegetarian restaurant/health-food store is located on the west end of the Ku'damm (look for its entrance on Albrecht-Achilles-Strasse). Snacks include samosas, pakoras, and various breads, while warm dishes usually range from vegetable dishes called *sabji* to quiche and rice casseroles. Daily specials have included polenta with tomato and zucchini and cauliflower *sabji* with potatoes. There's also a soup of the day, a salad bar, and desserts and drinks. Food is available for take out or for eating at one of its stand-up tables.

💲 Ihre Frisch-Backstübe

Knesebeckstrasse 12. ☎ **31 06 00.** Main courses 4.50–12 DM ($3–$8). No credit cards. Mon–Sat 6am–6:30pm, Sun 1–5pm. S-Bahn: Savignyplatz, a 4-minute walk. U-Bahn: Ernst-Reuter-Platz, about a 5-minute walk. GERMAN/SANDWICHES.

Located on the corner of Knesebeckstrasse and Goethestrasse north of Savignyplatz, this neighborhood bakery has a self-service counter. You can take out food or eat in the cheerful dining area. In addition to breads and cakes, it offers pizza by the slice, sandwiches, and a changing menu of warm dishes—from smoked pork chops to Leberkäs and sauerkraut. With competitive prices and well-prepared food, this place is a good alternative to the usual fast-food joint. It's an easy 10-minute walk north of the Ku'damm.

There are several branches throughout the city, including a convenient corner *Imbiss* at Wilmersdorfer Strasse and Pestalozzistrasse (☎ **310 600**), open Monday to Friday from 6am to 6:30pm (to 8:30pm on Thursday), and Saturday from 6am to 2pm (to 4pm first Saturday of the month). Much smaller than the above store, it sells take-out sandwiches, cakes, desserts, and breads.

Jimmy's Diner

Pariser Strasse 41. ☎ **882 31 41.** Main courses 7–15 DM ($4.65–$10). No credit cards. Mon–Thurs noon–4am, Fri noon–6am, Sat 11am–6am, Sun 11am–3am. Directions: A 5-minute walk south of the Ku'damm, on the corner of Sächsischer and Pariser streets. AMERICAN/MEXICAN.

Where to Eat

If you're dying for a hamburger or Mexican tacos—especially in the middle of the night—this '50s-style American diner with bright-red plastic furniture and lots of chrome is just the place. Drive-in speakers dangle above the windows. The eclectic menu offers from corn on the cob to Aunt Mary's chicken, as well as sandwiches, spareribs, spaghetti, tacos, enchiladas, and chili con carne. The burgers, served with fries, are gigantic. There's even Mexican beer. It's popular with Berlin's young student crowd.

✪ KaDeWe

Wittenbergplatz. ☎ **212 10**. Main courses 5–20 DM ($3.35–$13.35). No credit cards. Mon–Fri 9:30am–6pm (to 8pm on Thurs), Sat 9am–1pm (to 5:30pm first Sat of the month in winter, to 3:30pm in summer). U-Bahn: Wittenbergplatz, less than a 1-minute walk. INTERNATIONAL.

Every visitor to Berlin should visit KaDeWe, simply for the experience. KaDeWe is the popular name for Kaufhaus des Westens, the largest department store on the European continent. And its top attraction is the food emporium on the sixth floor. It's massive, with row after row of gourmet foods, including exotic teas and coffees, spices, jams, sweets, vegetables, fruits, and an amazing array of sausages and cuts of pork. Spread throughout are more than a dozen sit-down counters, each specializing in a different type of food—such as pasta, Asian cuisine, grilled chicken, salads, sandwiches, oysters, and more. One counter is devoted to the potato—you can order it baked or fried in a number of styles. There's also a wine bar and a coffee bar. It's easy to get lost in this huge place, and you'll find the abundance of food either wonderful or decadent.

Karavan

Kurfürstendamm 11. ☎ **881 50 05**. Main courses 4–10 DM ($2.65–$6.65). No credit cards. Daily 9am–midnight. U-Bahn: Kurfürstendamm or Bahnhof Zoo, each less than a 2-minute walk. TURKISH.

A good place to sample Turkish cuisine—at very inexpensive prices—faces the Kaiser-Wilhelm Gedächtniskirche. It's tiny and informal, consisting of a glass counter displaying the various dishes available. You can eat your meal sitting on stools along the wall, or better yet, order take-out and sit at the restaurant's outdoor tables or public benches on the plaza, a great spot for people-watching. Try the Turkish pizza, which has a thick, soft crust with a thin spread of minced meat and spices, the *kofti* burger, a Turkish-style burger, or the *Spinat-Tasche*, a spinach-filled pastry. There's also a changing daily special, such as meat-filled eggplant, as well as Turkish sandwiches and salads.

There's another branch nearby called Meister Snack, located under the eaves of the Bilka department store on the corner of Joachimstaler Strasse and Kantstrasse, not far from Bahnhof Zoo. It offers the same Turkish food.

Le Buffet

6th floor of Hertie bei Wertheim department store, Kurfürstendamm 231. ☎ **88 20 61**. Main courses 6–15 DM ($4–$10). No credit cards. Mon–Wed and Fri 11am–6pm, Thurs 11am–8pm, Sat 11am–1:30pm (to 5:30pm first Sat of the month in winter, to 3:30pm in summer). U-Bahn: Kurfürstendamm, a 1-minute walk. GERMAN.

With a great location on the Ku'damm across the street from the Kaiser-Wilhelm Gedächtniskirche, this department-store cafeteria is spacious, with the added plus of a rooftop view of the surrounding area. In addition to a salad bar, vegetable bar, desserts and sandwiches, it offers daily specials of warm meals, such as stuffed green pepper, turkey filet, or spaghetti. Since many of the dishes are on view, ordering is easy.

🅢 Mensa

Technische Universität, Hardenbergstrasse 34. ☎ **3140**. Main courses 3–9 DM ($2–$6). No credit cards. Year-round Mon–Fri 11:30am–2:30pm. U-Bahn: Ernst-Reuter-Platz, a few minutes' walk. GERMAN.

Every German university has a Mensa, a student cafeteria offering inexpensive meals for its enrolled students. What's special about this one, located in Berlin's Technical University, is that it serves non-students as well, at slightly more expensive prices. This is by far the cheapest place for a warm meal near the Ku'damm. Upstairs you'll find the bustling cafeteria, with complete meals ranging from about 3 to 4 DM ($2 to $2.65) and consisting of dishes such as Schnitzel with noodles and vegetables or spaghetti with salad. On the building's top floor is the slightly more expensive and upscale restaurant, offering a greater choice of changing main courses such as an *Eintopf* (stew), Gulasch, curry rice, turkey breast, or vegetarian ragoût, priced between 3.40 and 9 DM ($2.25 and $6). Side dishes, priced under 2 DM ($1.35), include salads, sauerkraut, and rice. The Mensa is about a six-minute walk from Bahnhof Zoo.

Orient

Lietzenburgerstrasse 77. ☎ **881 24 60**. Main courses 8–20 DM ($5.35–$13.35). No credit cards. Daily 11am–4am. U-Bahn: Uhlandstrasse, about a 3-minute walk. MIDDLE EASTERN.

Located south of the Ku'damm, the Orient specializes in Middle Eastern and Mediterranean dishes. Although it does a brisk business in take-out orders, there is a dining area—nothing fancy but pleasant. On the menu are about two dozen items, many priced under 12 DM ($8). There's falafel, kebab, *maali* (a vegetarian dish of cauliflower, potatoes, and eggplant), gyros, and spiced grilled meatballs with potatoes and salad. Daily specials are displayed behind the take-out counter.

🅢 Piccola Taormina Tavola Calda

Uhlandstrasse 29. ☎ **881 47 10**. Main courses 6.50–15 DM ($4.35–$10). No credit cards. Daily 11am–2am. U-Bahn: Uhlandstrasse, a 2-minute walk. ITALIAN.

Located just south of Ku'damm is one of the cheapest places in town for quick Italian pizza, pasta, and risotto. This establishment is especially popular for its pizza by the slice for 2.50 DM ($1.65), attracting hungry customers around the clock. A menu on the wall lists more than 25 different personal-size pizzas (big enough for two), omelets, risotto, beefsteak, and pasta. The cooks, all Italian, will have your order ready in no time. Wine and beer are also available, and there's plenty of dining space in the back or you can order takeout.

Pizza Bleibtreu

Bleibtreustrasse 41. ☎ **883 47 78**. Main courses 6–20 DM ($4–$13.35). No credit cards. Daily 11am–1am. S-Bahn: Savignyplatz, about a 2-minute walk. ITALIAN.

This tiny place, with only four stools outside and two tables inside, offers more than 20 kinds of pizza, as well as omelets, salads, pasta, meat dishes, and fish. All its pizza and pasta dishes are priced below 12 DM ($8), with a slice of pizza at 2 DM ($1.35). You can dine in or order takeout.

BERLIN-MITTE (EASTERN BERLIN)

These budget-priced establishments are located in eastside Berlin, convenient if you're visiting Museumsinsel. In addition to the restaurants listed here, several restaurants listed under "Meals for Less than 25 DM ($16.65)" offer some dishes for less than 12 DM ($8), such as Würste or omelets.

❸ Casino

In the Staatsbibliothek, Unter den Linden 8. ☎ **2037 83 10**. Soup or salad 3–6 DM ($2–$4); main courses 6–11 DM ($4–$7.35). No credit cards. Mon–Fri 9am–6pm, Sat 10am–4pm. Bus 100 or 157 to the Staatsoper stop. GERMAN.

This inexpensive cafeteria, located in a public library right on Unter den Linden, is convenient for sightseeing jaunts along Unter den Linden and to Museumsinsel with its many museums. Daily specials, written on a board, may include Schnitzel, Rumpsteak, fish, chicken or Boulette, plus a limited number of soups and a salad of the day. Coffee is a cheap 1.50 DM ($1) a cup. It's a small place, so you may want to avoid the lunch-hour rush.

Nordsee

Spandauer Strasse 4. ☎ **242 68 81**. Main courses 7–13 DM ($4.65–$8.65). No credit cards. Mon–Sat 10am–9pm, Sun 11am–9pm. S-Bahn and U-Bahn: Alexanderplatz, a 3-minute walk. Bus 100 to Spandauer Strasse. SEAFOOD.

One of the first chain restaurants to open in what was formerly East Berlin, this Nordsee just off Alexanderplatz is bigger than most, offering plenty of tables and doing a brisk business. An illustrated menu behind the self-service counter makes ordering easy. There are more than a half dozen choices available, including fish soup, paella, fried haddock, fish sticks, and salads. Fish sandwiches are available for takeout.

✪ Opernpalais Self-Service Terrace

Unter den Linden 5. ☎ **200 22 69**. Main courses 3.50–7 DM ($2.35–$4.65). No credit cards. Summer daily 11am–midnight; autumn and spring daily noon–6pm. Closed: Jan–March. U-Bahn: Französische Strasse, about a 7-minute walk. Bus 100 to Staatsoper stop. GERMAN/SNACKS.

The Opernpalais (formerly Operncafé) is one of Berlin's best-known restaurants and coffeehouses, with prices well over 12 DM ($8). Outside the cafe, however, in a pretty, tree-shaded square, is a self-service *Imbiss* selling sandwiches, Würste, and Boulette, as well as coffee, wine, beer, and other drinks. Eat your purchase at one of the tables beside the *Imbiss*—but don't wander to the tables on the terrace, since those are reserved for coffeehouse customers with waitress service.

Berlin–Mitte Dining

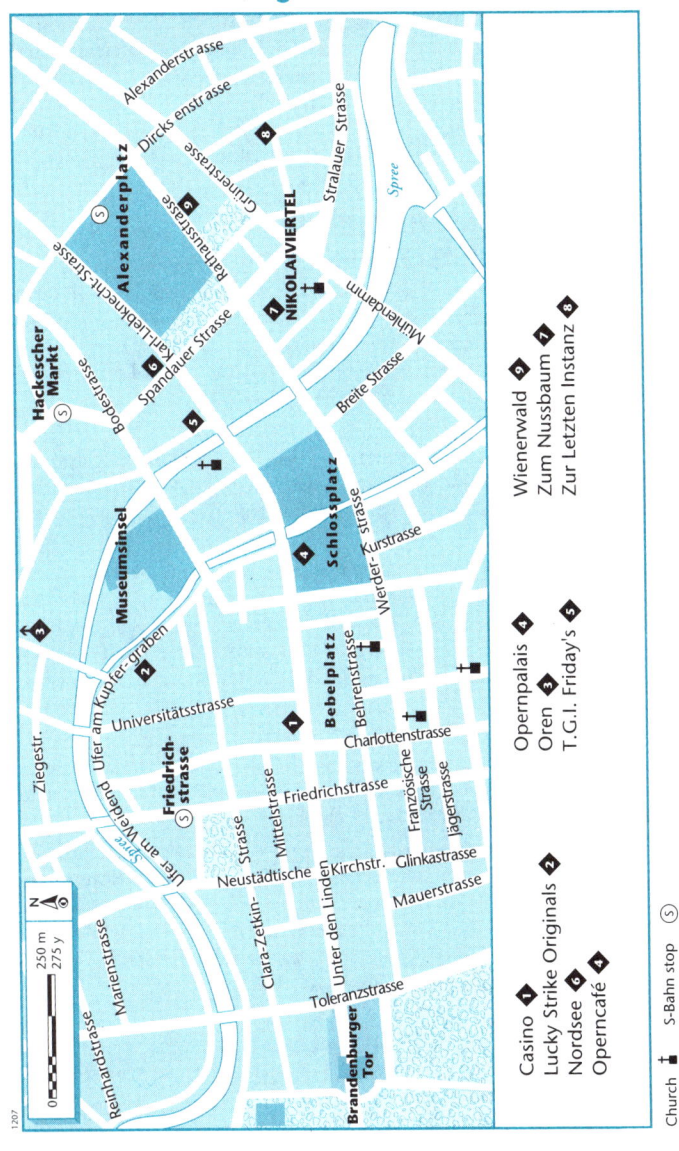

- Casino **1**
- Lucky Strike Originals **2**
- Nordsee **6**
- Operncafé **4**
- Opernpalais **4**
- Oren **3**
- T.G.I. Friday's **5**
- Wienerwald **9**
- Zum Nussbaum **7**
- Zur Letzten Instanz **8**

Zum Nussbaum

Am Nussbaum 3. ☎ **242 30 95.** Main courses 6–15 DM ($4–$10). No credit cards. Daily noon–10pm. S-Bahn and U-Bahn: Alexanderplatz, about a 5-minute walk. GERMAN/SNACKS.

Located in the restored historic Nikolai Quarter just a few minutes' walk from Alexanderplatz, this cozy tavern is modeled after a famous inn dating from 1507 that was destroyed in World War II. Rooms are tiny, with wood-paneled walls, and a limited menu offers German and Berlin specialties, including Würste, Boulette, lentil stew, *Berliner Eisbein* with sauerkraut and pureed peas, *Sülze* (jellied meat) with fried potatoes, Kasseler with potato salad, and *Rote Grütze* (cooked fruits with vanilla sauce, a North German specialty). A half liter of beer to wash it all down costs 5 DM ($3.35).

NEAR WILMERSDORFER STRASSE & BAHNHOF CHARLOTTENBURG

All these budget-priced restaurants and stand-up eateries are located on Wilmersdorfer Strasse, Berlin's main pedestrian-only shopping lane. A few are located in department stores, always a good bet for budget-priced meals; at Hertie, no. 118–119, there's **Le Buffet** on the first floor. A branch of **Nordsee** is at no. 58.

Joseph Langer

Wilmersdorfer Strasse 118. ☎ **31 67 80.** Main courses 2–9 DM ($1.35–$6). No credit cards. Mon–Fri 9am–6:30pm, Sat 8:30am–2pm (to 6pm first Sat of the month in winter, to 4pm in summer). U-Bahn: Wilmersdorfer Strasse, a 1-minute walk. GERMAN.

Joseph Langer is a butcher shop that specializes in inexpensive, simple meat dishes. You can order takeout or eat standing up at one of its chest-high tables. Various kinds of Würste are always available, from Munich's famous Weisswurst to the thick Bockwurst; other offerings include Leberkäs, soups, Schnitzel, Eisbein, Boulette, and potato salad.

Restaurant-Café

Karstadt, Wilmersdorfer Strasse 109-111. ☎ **31 891.** Main courses 8–15 DM ($5.35–$10). No credit cards. Mon–Fri 9:30am–6pm (Thurs to 8pm), Sat 9:30am–1:30pm (to 5:30pm first Sat of the month in winter, to 3:30pm first Sat of the month in summer). U-Bahn: Wilmersdorfer Strasse, a 1-minute walk. GERMAN.

One of several large department stores on Wilmersdorfer Strasse, Karstadt has an inexpensive cafeteria on the fourth floor, with several counters offering differing food. The main counter serves German specials ranging from fish and Sauerbraten to Schnitzel, while other counters are devoted to pasta, salads, vegetables, and desserts. Wonder of wonders, its no-smoking section is large.

Rogacki

Wilmersdorfer Strasse 145-146. ☎ **341 40 91.** Main courses 5–15 DM ($3.35–$10). No credit cards. Mon–Fri 9am–6pm, Sat 8am–2pm. U-Bahn: Bismarckstrasse, a 1-minute walk. GERMAN.

This butcher shop—in business more than 60 years and famous throughout Berlin for its meats—is a great place if you want to dine like a king on less than 12 DM ($8) and don't mind standing up. This large store is devoted mostly to retail sales of Würste, fish, cheeses, and breads, but it also has self-service counters offering main courses such as pig's knuckle, fish, grilled chicken, Würste, salads, and stews. The shop is located north of Bismarckstrasse; look for a lighted sign of a fish on its facade.

IN DAHLEM

Since Dahlem is primarily residential, the museum cafeteria and the Gaststätte below are your best bets for an inexpensive meal. For even cheaper dining, head for Inge Drei Sterne Imbiss, a thatched-roof food stall across from the Dahlem U-Bahn station on Königin-Luise-Strasse. Open daily from 6:30am to 8pm, it offers a variety of Würste, Boulette, noodle salad, potato salad, french fries, beer, and soft drinks, most priced under 3 DM ($2). In addition to its stand-up tables, there are a couple park benches where you can sit down.

Right beside the U-Bahn station is another food stall, called Imbiss am U-Bahnhof Dahlem-Dorf. It also offers a variety of Würste, as well as Boulette, Hähnchen Schnitzel (chicken Schnitzel) with french fries and salad, and a gyros hamburger with kraut salad and tzatziki. Prices here range from about 2.50 to 6 DM ($1.65–$4).

Dahlem Restaurant-Café
In the Gemäldegalerie, Lansstrasse 8. ☎ **831 48 84.** Main courses 7–15 DM ($4.54–$10). No credit cards. Tues–Sun 11:30am–3pm. U-Bahn: Dahlem-Dorf, about a 3-minute walk. GERMAN.

Located in the basement of the large Dahlem-museum complex, this simple but pleasant cafeteria is a convenient place for a quick meal if you're visiting Dahlem's many museums. With outdoor courtyard seating in summer, it offers German specialties, including Bauernfrüstück (scrambled eggs with potatoes, ham, and vegetables), Sülze with fried potatoes, chicken Schnitzel with potatoes and salad, and Leberkäse with fried egg and potatoes. Other choices include spaghetti, Boulette, a soup of the day, stews, salads, desserts, and beer and wine.

Luise
Königin-Luise-Strasse 40. ☎ **832 84 87.** Main courses 8–17 DM ($5.35–$11.35). No credit cards. Daily Mon–Fri 10am–11pm, Sat–Sun 9:30am–11pm. U-Bahn: Dahlem-Dorf, about a 1-minute walk. GERMAN/INTERNATIONAL.

To reach this extremely popular watering hole and informal dining establishment, turn right out of the Dahlem-Dorf U-Bahn station, and cross the street. Almost immediately to your right you'll see a large baroque-style building, with a large beer garden. Although people living in the area come here mainly to drink and socialize, Luise also serves snacks and main courses—including onion soup, spaghetti, eggplant casserole, cordon bleu, garlic chicken, and changing daily specials. Breakfast is served until 2pm. Its substantial drinking menu includes wines, grog, champagne, schnapps, liqueur, brandy, and long drinks. I'm fond of the Weissbier, a wheat beer. And of course, the wonderful beer garden is open in fine weather. Indoor dining tends to be a bit smoky, since every other German seems to smoke.

NEAR RATHAUS SCHÖNEBERG

🟢 Kasino Beim Senator für Wirtschaft und Verkehr
Martin-Luther-Strasse 105. ☎ **784 77 24.** Fixed-price lunches 5.50–8 DM ($3.65–$5.35). No credit cards. Mon–Thurs 11:30am–2:30pm, Fri 11am–1:30pm. U-Bahn: Rathaus Schöneberg, about a 2-minute walk. GERMAN.

This simple cafeteria on the fifth floor of the administration building for trade and industry—look for the sign on the front door that says "Senatsverwaltung für Wirtschaft"—is open to the general public. Take the elevator and then follow the sign that says "Kantine" to the end of the corridor (it won't look like there's a restaurant when you exit the elevator). Popular with young and old alike, this no-smoking canteen offers two fixed-price lunches a day, with a menu that changes daily, as well as a small selection of snacks, desserts, and a soup of the day. Dishes have included Schweinebraten with red cabbage and potatoes, stuffed cabbage rolls with potatoes, Gulasch with mushrooms and noodles, and grilled trout with salad and potatoes. Be sure to clear your own tray when you leave.

IN KREUZBERG

✪ Henne

Leuschnerdamm 25. ☎ **614 77 30.** Reservations imperative. Main course 10 DM ($6.65). No credit cards. Wed–Sun 7pm–midnight. U-Bahn: Moritzplatz, an 8-minute walk. CHICKEN.

You'll never get a table if you don't have a reservation—proof that here you'll find the best grilled chicken in town (*Henne* means hen). In fact, that's all it serves besides potato salad and kraut salad. The chickens are milk-fed, and their skins are deliciously crispy. A half chicken costs 10 DM ($6.65), while potato salad or kraut salad is an extra 3 DM ($2). The beer's good, too, especially the dark Klosterschwarzbier, and the ambience is even better. Packed with everyone from students to professionals, the restaurant looks ancient, with brown spotted walls, a clock that runs late, antlers everywhere, an elaborate wooden bar, and small wooden barrels that used to hold grog and raspberry juice. Behind the bar hangs a photo of John F. Kennedy, who was invited to Henne during his Berlin trip. He didn't eat here, but he did send a letter of apology.

3 Meals for Less than 25 DM ($16.65)

You can expect to pay 15 to 25 DM ($10 to $16.65) for meals at places listed in this category, excluding alcoholic beverages but including an appetizer or soup and a reasonably priced main course. On the other hand, if you want to splurge, you could easily spend more than 30 DM ($20) by indulging in a more expensive dish. Remember that main courses usually include one or two side dishes, making them complete meals.

ON OR NEAR THE KU'DAMM

Angora

Schlüterstrasse 29/30. ☎ **323 70 96.** Appetizers 8–14 DM ($5.35–$9.35); main courses 17–28 DM ($11.35–$18.65). V. Sun–Thurs 5pm–2am, Fri–Sat 5pm–4am. S-Bahn: Savignyplatz, a 2-minute walk. TURKISH.

Named after Turkey's ancient capital, the upscale Angora is coolly decorated; on stone walls are carved reproductions of stone reliefs dating from 1300 B.C. Candles are on each table, the staff is courteous and efficient, and the clientele is well dressed. The menu includes all the national favorites, including shish kebab, rack of lamb, veal, fish, and grilled dishes.

Ano Kato
Leibnizstrasse 70. ☎ **313 04 70.** Main courses 11–22 DM ($7.35–$14.65). No credit cards. Daily 6pm–12:30am. S-Bahn: Savignyplatz, a 4-minute walk. U-Bahn: Wilmersdorfer Strasse, a 4-minute walk. GREEK.

This unpretentious Greek restaurant with its white tablecloths, candles, and cheerful Greek music is a popular choice for a casual meal, which can range from moussaka, souvlaki, lamb, and gyros to calamari. Most dishes average 16 DM ($10.65); a half liter of retsina (a resin-flavored wine) is 10 DM ($6.65).

Arche Noah
Jüdischen Gemeindehaus, Fasanenstrasse 79. ☎ **882 61 38.** Fixed-price meals 16–26 DM ($10.65–$17.35); Sabbath fixed-price meals 39–49 DM ($26–$32.65); Tues buffet 33 DM ($22). AE, MC, V. Sun–Fri 11:30am–3pm and 6:30–11pm; Sat 11:30am–2:30pm. U-Bahn: Uhlandstrasse, a 2-minute walk. KOSHER.

On the first floor of the Jewish Community House, this simple dining hall is one of the few places in town for kosher food. It offers Jewish and Israeli specialties, with about three choices of fixed-price meals that change daily and include soup, dessert, and a main course that ranges from Gulasch to roast veal to lamb chops. If you have a big appetite, you might like the Tuesday night buffet with warm and cold dishes, 33 DM ($22) per person; Sabbath fixed-price meals must be ordered at least a day in advance. It's located north of the Ku'damm, not far from the Bristol Hotel Kempinski.

Berliner Stube
Steigenberger Hotel, Los-Angeles-Platz 1. ☎ **210 80.** Appetizers and soups 7–22 DM ($4.64–$14.65); main courses 14–37 DM ($9.35–$24.65). AE, DC, MC, V. Daily noon–3pm and 6–11:30pm. U-Bahn: Kurfürstendamm, a 2-minute walk. GERMAN.

I usually recommend eating outside of hotels, as local places better represent the city's cuisine. But this rustic-looking restaurant—located in one of Berlin's best-known hotels and designed to resemble an old-style Berliner pub—is a favorite with visiting and native businesspeople, especially for lunch. Conveniently located near the Ku'damm and the Europa-Center, it offers seasonal German specialties that include smoked eel, Swabian ravioli, lamb stew, veal roulade, fresh fish, and knuckle of pork. There are always several choices for fish, from poached halibut to roasted salmon steak. Take advantage of the changing lunch special, a complete meal usually priced between 15 and 20 DM ($10–$13.35). In summer there's outdoor seating.

Chung
Kurfürstendamm 190. ☎ **882 15 55.** Appetizers 5–16 DM ($3.35–$10.65); main courses 16–30 DM ($10.65–$20); fixed-price lunches 11–15 DM ($7.35–$10). AE, DC, MC, V. Daily 11:30am–midnight. U-Bahn: Uhlandstrasse or Adenauerplatz, each a 6-minute walk. CHINESE.

This ornate Chinese restaurant with hanging lanterns and a red-and-black ceiling occupies a prime spot on the Ku'damm—its glass-enclosed front dining room extends right over the sidewalk and affords a wonderful view. Lunch is the best time to come, when fixed-price meals are available Monday to Friday (excluding holidays) from 11:30am to 3pm. These consist of a choice of soup or spring roll, along with almost two dozen choices of a main dish. The menu in English has a seemingly endless list of dishes, including roast duck and chicken Shanghai style. The waitstaff is friendly and obliging.

Ciao Ciao

Kurfürstendamm 156. ☎ **892 36 12.** Reservations recommended in summer. Appetizers and soups 7.50–25 DM ($5–$16.65), pizzas and pastas 16–24 DM ($10.65–$16). MC, V. Sun–Thurs noon–2am, Fri–Sat noon–3am. U-Bahn: Adenauerplatz, a 1-minute walk. ITALIAN.

This lively, informal Italian restaurant is a great place to dine, with an animated waitstaff and plenty to watch on the Ku'damm if you can sit outside in summer. In fact, it gets so crowded in summer, you should make a reservation for dinner. Since its main dishes are a bit pricey for what they offer, your best bet is to order the carpaccio and one of the dozen pizza or pasta choices. It's located west of Adenauerplatz, past Athener Grill.

Grung Thai

Ku'damm Passage, Kurfürstendamm 202. ☎ **881 53 50.** Appetizers and soups 6–14 DM ($4–$9.35), main courses 17–30 DM ($11.35–$20). AE, DC, MC, V. Mon–Fri 6pm–3am, Sat–Sun noon–3am. U-Bahn: Uhlandstrasse, less than a 4-minute walk. THAI.

Located in a small mall on the corner of the Ku'damm and Knesebeckstrasse, this restaurant strives for an exotic atmosphere with elephant statues and Thai artifacts. The menu features more than 100 items and includes my favorites: chicken soup with coconut milk and lemongrass, Thai noodles with seafood, and spicy beef salad. There are also curries, salads, and fish, pork, and beef dishes. Try Singha beer, Thailand's national drink. Live music starts at 9pm every Friday and Saturday. After midnight, you must enter the restaurant through the passage on Knesebeckstrasse.

✪ Hardtke

Meinekestrasse 27 A & B. ☎ **881 98 27.** Appetizers and soups 6.50–18 DM ($4.35–$12), main courses 15–30 DM ($10–$20). No credit cards. Daily 11am–12:30am. U-Bahn: Uhlandstrasse, less than a 2-minute walk. GERMAN.

Just a minute's walk south of the Ku'damm, this establishment has been serving hearty German fare for more than 40 years. One of Berlin's best-known restaurants, it's very popular with German visitors to Berlin, especially retired men and women, and is packed almost every night of the week. Hardtke boasts its own butcher shop, assuring the freshest cuts, and its sausages are excellent. The dining area is divided into two separate halls (hence the two addresses A and B), both with the same menu and rustic appearance of a Gaststätte. Specialties include Berliner Eisbein with vegetables, sauerkraut, and potatoes; Brathering with potatoes; Sauerbraten or Schweinebraten with red cabbage and potato dumplings; and Berliner Boulette with red cabbage and potatoes. You could easily spend 30 DM ($20) on a great meal, or dine on sausages for 10.50 DM ($7) if you come during the day (after 6pm, the price of sausages increases to 15 DM or $10). Try the fresh bloodwurst and liverwurst, gigantic Bockwurst with potato salad, Bratwurst with potatoes and sauerkraut, or the Würste platter—all Hardtke's homemade sausages. All around, this is one of the best places in town for a typical German meal.

Istanbul

Knesebeckstrasse 77. ☎ **883 27 77.** Soups and salads 8–10 DM ($5.35–$6.65); appetizers 7–13 DM ($4.65–$8.65); main courses 22–30 DM ($14.65–$20). AE, DC, MC, V. Daily noon–midnight. S-Bahn: Savignyplatz, less than a 2-minute walk. TURKISH.

Located between the Ku'damm and Savignyplatz, this family-run establishment remains one of the oldest and best of Berlin's Turkish restaurants. Try to get a seat in one of the back rooms, dreamily decorated like a mosque. On Friday and Saturday, a belly dancer entertains after 9:30pm. You might start your meal with the Turkish aperitif *raki*, which is sun-ripened raisins flavored with anise. For an appetizer, try the *yaprak dolmast* (grape leaves stuffed with rice, pine nuts, currants, and herbs) or *hummus* (chick peas with garlic). Main courses range from so-called Turkish pizza (flat bread with chopped meat, at 13 DM, or $8.65, the cheapest entrée on the menu) to *donner Kebab* (veal grilled on a rotating spit and served with rice), shish kebab (skewered meat and vegetables), and a wide variety of lamb dishes. There's an English version of the menu.

✪ Kalkutta

Bleibtreustrasse 17. ☎ **883 62 93.** Main courses 16–25 DM ($10.65–$16.65); fixed-price lunches 10–17 DM ($6.65–$11.35). AE, DC, MC, V. Daily noon–midnight. S-Bahn: Savignyplatz, about a 2-minute walk. INDIAN.

Located a block north of the Ku'damm, this tiny and unpretentious restaurant has been serving great curries for more than 25 years and claims to be Berlin's first Indian restaurant. It is the only Indian restaurant in Berlin licensed to operate an original clay oven imported from India, which it uses for its breads and excellently prepared grilled foods and tandoori. With painted murals on the wall and Indian music, it attracts a young well-traveled clientele, many of whom have been to India. Dinner offers a wide assortment of tandoori, vegetable curries, and fish, as well as pork, chicken, beef, and veal dishes. Lunch is more economical, with fixed-price meals offered Monday to Friday from noon to 3pm. Top off your meal with mango schnapps or a Darjeeling tea liqueur.

✪ Restaurant Marché Mövenpick

Kurfürstendamm 14-15. ☎ **882 75 78.** Main courses 10–20 DM ($6.65–$13.35). AE, MC, V. Daily 8am–midnight. U-Bahn: Kurfürstendamm, a 1-minute walk. INTERNATIONAL.

Run by the Swiss-owned Mövenpick, this chain of cafeterias has been a huge success in Germany, and with good reason. Imitating the neighborhood market, it has various stands offering fresh meals—most prepared in front of the customers. My favorite is the salad bar with a variety of salads; the price determined by the size of the plate you select. There's also a vegetable buffet, and the grill stand offers meat dishes that may include grilled chicken or pork cutlets. Other stands serve a tempting array of homemade soups, pasta, daily specials, cheeses, freshly squeezed fruit and vegetable juices, ice cream, and desserts. Simply wander around and load your tray with whatever looks good; a meal here will probably run between 15 and 20 DM ($10–$13.35). You can sit in several dining areas, including a large no-smoking section and sidewalk seating. This is a great place for a casual meal on the Ku'damm.

Mövenpick

Europa-Center. ☎ **262 70 77.** Pizzas and pastas 10.50–17 DM ($7–$11.35); main courses 11.50–34 DM ($7.65–$22.65). AE, DC, MC, V. Sun–Thurs 8am–midnight, Fri–Sat 8am–1am. U-Bahn: Kurfürstendamm or Wittenbergplatz, each about a 3-minute walk. INTERNATIONAL.

Another in this popular Swiss chain, this restaurant appeals to families and a slightly older clientele, with waitress service and a huge dining area on the second floor of the Europa-Center, divided into sections serving different kinds of food. The Backstübe specializes in pizza and quiche, and offers seating on a terrace overlooking the inner atrium of the Europa-Center. Le Caveau, a wine cellar with more than 100 different kinds of wine from around the world, is more upscale and offers a changing menu that might include shrimp, roast hare, or turkey breast—with most main dishes from 18 to 34 DM ($12 to $22.65). The largest dining area, called Café des Artistes, offers herring, smoked salmon, pasta dishes, curries, steaks, fish, and pork cutlets, as well as a self-service salad bar. In summer, there's outdoor seating with views of the Gedächtniskirche at Mövenpick's ground-floor coffeehouse, which sells snacks and desserts.

San Marino

Savignyplatz 12. ☎ **313 60 86.** Pizza and pasta 8–18.50 DM ($5.35–$12.35), main courses 18–38 DM ($12–$25.35). AE, MC. Daily 11am–midnight. S-Bahn: Savignyplatz, a 1-minute walk. ITALIAN.

This upscale Italian restaurant is ideally located right on Savignyplatz, just north of the Ku'damm. In summer, you can dine outside on the square, enjoying a pleasant view, and afterward go for a drink in one of the neighborhood's many bars. In winter, you dine indoors surrounded by artwork and flowers. Although there are steaks and seafood on the English menu, all you need to order is a personal-size pizza or pasta dish, most priced under 14 DM ($9.35). Even better, come for the three-course set lunch, priced less than 20 DM ($13.35) and served Monday to Friday. It's hard to resist a glass or two of Lambrusco or Chianti.

Shell

Knesebeckstrasse 22. ☎ **312 83 10.** Soups and salads 9–22 DM ($6–$14.65); main courses 18–34 DM ($12–$22.65). AE, MC, V. Mon–Sat 9am–midnight, Sun 10am–midnight. S-Bahn: Savignyplatz, less than a 2-minute walk. INTERNATIONAL/VEGETARIAN.

Since a corner gas station used to occupy this site, it seemed only natural that when it changed into a restaurant, its name should be Shell. A simple and pleasant restaurant popular with the area's many young residents, it has a curved facade of huge windows. The main menu—available throughout the day and evening—has such dishes as risotto with wild rice, crab, vegetables and piñon nuts; almond steak with saffron; and a vegetable plate with hollandaise, potatoes, and salad. For more economical dining, order from the lunch menu, available until 6pm, with daily specials for less than 20 DM ($13.35). An evening menu offers daily specials for less than 30 DM ($20). Service is sometimes slow, so come here only if you have time or for just a cup of coffee or a beer.

Taverna Plaka
Joachimstaler Strasse 14. ☎ **883 15 57.** Appetizers and salads 7–13 DM ($4.65–$8.65); main courses 16–30 DM ($10.65–$20). No credit cards. Mon–Fri 4pm–1am, Sat–Sun and holidays noon–1am. U-Bahn: Kurfürstendamm, less than a 2-minute walk. GREEK.

This first-floor Greek restaurant, just south of the Ku'damm, is decorated in a cheerful Mykonos white-and-blue. The waiters are friendly, and the food is good no matter what you order or how much you spend. There's the usual moussaka, fish, souvlaki, and gyros on the menu, but if you're on a budget, order the Mesedes Plaka for 12 DM ($8). Although it's an appetizer plate, it's plentiful, with *dolmades* (stuffed grape leaves), eggplant salad, feta cheese, and a sampling of other Greek delicacies. An alternative is to order the huge Greek salad (called *choriatiki*) for about the same price. This is a fun place to dine, especially if you indulge in Greek wine.

Wirtshaus Zum Löwen
Hardenbergstrasse 29. ☎ **262 10 20.** Main courses 11–20 DM ($7.35–$13.35). AE, MC, DC, V. Sun–Thurs 10am–midnight, Fri–Sat 10am–2am. U-Bahn: Bahnhof Zoo or Kurfürstendamm, each a 1-minute walk. GERMAN.

This beer hall, tucked away in a plaza, is ingeniously constructed to resemble a tree-filled Bavarian plaza. Like the beer halls of Munich, they serve Bavarian beer, Löwenbräu. It's unabashedly tourist-oriented but is conveniently located behind the Gedächtniskirche, in the direction of Bahnhof Zoo. As with most beer halls, there's live music beginning at 7pm, and hearty platters of Bratwurst, Schnitzel, and Berliner Eisbein.

BERLIN-MITTE (EASTERN BERLIN)
These restaurants are convenient if you're visiting the many museums on Museumsinsel.

Lucky Strike Originals
Georgenstrasse, S-Bahnbögen 177-180. ☎ **201 774 22.** Breakfast and lunch 9.50–20 DM ($6.35–$13.35); dinner main courses 18–40 DM ($12–$26.65). AE, DC, MC, V. Daily 10am–2am–11:30am–midnight. S-Bahn: Friedrichstrasse, about a 5-minute walk. AMERICAN.

For years under the Communist regime, the area around the Museumsinsel was a culinary wasteland. How ironic that the closest two restaurants to Berlin-Mitte's museum district specialize in American food. Located under the arches of the elevated S-Bahn tracks just a stone's throw from the Pergamon Museum, Lucky Strike is an American-owned New Orleans-style restaurant/music club. It's decorated like an American diner (even the diner chairs and bar are original, imported from the United States), the recorded music is jazz, and an adjoining room serves as a live music venue nightly. Breakfast and lunch are the best choices for the bargain hunter, both served from 10am to 5pm and much cheaper than the dinner menu. This is the place to come if you're hungering for blueberry or buckwheat pancakes, bacon and eggs, or even just a bowl of cornflakes. Lunch dishes include burgers, sandwiches, chicken wings, and sloppy joes, but best is the so-called "business lunch" served Monday through Friday from 11am to 5pm. It costs 13.50 DM ($9) for meals featuring fajitas, barbecue meatballs, or wild duck.

✪ Operncafé

Opernpalais, Unter den Linden 5. ☎ **200 22 69.** Main courses 10–20 DM ($6.65–$13.35). AE, DC, MC, V. Summer, daily 8:30am–midnight. Winter, Sun–Thurs 8:30am–7pm, Fri–Sat 8:30am–midnight. S-Bahn: Friedrichstrasse or Französische Strasse, about a 10-minute walk. Bus 100 to Staatsoper. GERMAN/CONTINENTAL.

The Operncafé is one of Berlin's most famous coffeehouses, occupying part of a palace originally built in 1733, destroyed during World War II, and recently renovated at a great cost. A sumptuous breakfast buffet is offered until noon for 16.50 DM ($11), followed by an à la carte menu offering filet mignon, pork médallions, fish, and daily specials. As many as 25 different tortes are prepared daily. If the weather is nice, you may wish to dine on the outdoor terrace.

In addition to the Operncafé, the Opernpalais contains several other restaurants, all under the same management. Schinkelklause is a cafeteria offering Berliner specialties; Fridericus is a basement restaurant specializing in grilled fish. There's also a sophisticated cocktail bar. If you feel like splurging, head for the first-floor restaurant, Königin Luise, which offers German fare at higher prices and a view of the famous Unter den Linden boulevard.

✪ Oren

Oranienburger Strasse 28. ☎ **282 82 28.** Appetizers and soups 7.50–16 DM ($5–$10.65); main courses 11–25 DM ($7.35–$16.65). No credit cards. Daily 10am–midnight. S-Bahn: Oranienburger Strasse, a 3-minute walk. KOSHER.

About a 6-minute walk north of Museumsinsel and located next to a towering gold-domed synagogue currently under renovation, this is eastern Berlin's first modern Kosher restaurant. It's quickly become one of the city's most popular. Decorated in the fashion of a 1920s Berlin coffeehouse and catering to an intellectual crowd, it offers excellently prepared food, with an interesting inspired by Asian, Middle Eastern, and international vegetarian cuisines. Perhaps you'll want to start with the Russian borscht or falafel with humus and pita, followed by vegetarian lasagna, stuffed eggplant, potato and spinach casserole, or grilled fish. The Orient Express platter, with its assortment of Middle Eastern vegetarian food, is especially good.

T.G.I. Friday's

Karl-Liebknecht-Strasse 5. ☎ **2382 79 60**. Soups and soups 7–15 DM ($4.65–$10); main courses 15–30 DM ($10–$20). AE, DC, MC, V. Daily noon–midnight. S-Bahn: Alexanderplatz or Hackesher Markt, each about a 5-minute walk. AMERICAN.

Americans should feel instantly at home in this well-known chain, located across the Spree River from Museumsinsel in the shadow of the Berlin Dom and offering great outdoor seating in summer. This is one of Berlin's best places for American bar food, cocktails (more than 400 mind-boggling concoctions), and cuisine. Buffalo wings, potato skins, spinach and artichoke dip, nachos, black-bean soup, fajitas, Mexican pizza, fettuccine Alfredo, baby back ribs, filet mignon, blackened Cajun chicken, burgers, club sandwiches, and salads are just some of the choices on an extensive menu that's sure to attract the homesick in droves. There's also a children's menu, and Monday to Friday from 11am to 5pm a set lunch is available for less than 12 DM ($8). There's even a Häagen-Dazs ice cream parlor right next door.

Wienerwald

Rathausstrasse 5. ☎ **242 32 91**. Soups and salads 4–13 DM ($2.65–$8.65); main courses 12–22 DM ($8–$14.65). AE, DC, MC, V. Daily 10am–midnight. S-Bahn and U-Bahn: Alexanderplatz, a 1-minute walk. GERMAN.

A successful chain of restaurants specializing in grilled chicken, this comfortable, family-style restaurant offers a variety of chicken dishes, fish, soups, and a salad bar. An especially good deal is the quarter chicken with a choice of side dish for 8.90 DM ($5.95). There's a no-smoking section. It's located just off Alexanderplatz, near a post office.

✪ Zur Letzten Instanz

Waisenstrasse 14-16. ☎ **242 55 28**. Main courses 15–20 DM ($10–$13.35). AE, DC, MC, V. Daily noon–midnight. U-Bahn: Klosterstrasse, about a 2-minute walk. GERMAN.

Open since 1621, this tiny restaurant claims to be Berlin's oldest *Gaststätte*. Its rooms are rustic, with plank floors, wainscoting, and a few antiques here and there. The menu features Berlin specialties, including Boulette, *Gefüllte Kohlroulade* (stuffed cabbage rolls), Schnitzel, and Berliner Eisbein. For dessert there's *Rote Grütze* (cooked fruits with a vanilla sauce). In summer, a few tables are tucked into a tiny garden under spreading trees. You might have trouble finding this place—it's located about a 5-minute walk behind the red-colored Rathaus (city hall).

NEAR WILMERSDORFER STRASSE & BAHNHOF CHARLOTTENBURG

✪ Ty Breizh Savoie Rire

Kantstrasse 75. ☎ **323 99 32**. Main courses 18.50–27 DM ($12.35–$18). No credit cards. Mon–Fri 5pm–midnight, Sat 6pm–midnight. U-Bahn: Wilmersdorfer Strasse, about a 4-minute walk. FRENCH.

If you're craving French cuisine, try Ty Breizh Savoie Rire, which looks more like a campus pizza parlor than a restaurant specializing in dishes from Brittany. Owner-chef Patrick Mattei—fluent in English, German, Italian, and his native French—is outgoing and friendly, and even sings *chansons* to entertain his guests most evenings. For an appetizer, try Mattei's creation of mushrooms with shrimp and cheese or one of his other specialties—homemade pâté, cheese imported from Savoie, or the fish soup. Entrees include orange duck with pepper sauce, oysters, pork filet, beef cooked in a burgundy-wine sauce with onions, pork filet, and seafood. There are also changing specials, which may include couscous, lamb, duck, mussels, or tripe. This is a fun place to dine; the clientele ranges from the middle class to punks and the avant-garde. Even the bills are unusual and can be a scrapbook memento—if he has time, Mattei illustrates each by hand with a tally of soups, main courses, and glasses of wine.

ⓈUdagawa Japan Imbiss
Kantstrasse 118. ☎ **312 30 14.** Main courses 10–28 DM ($6.65–$18.65). No credit cards. Wed–Mon 12:30pm–midnight. U-Bahn: Wilmersdorfer Strasse, about a 3-minute walk. JAPANESE.

This tiny, self-service restaurant serves Japanese food at reasonable prices, from about 15 DM to 20 DM ($10 to $13.35) for most dishes.

Imbisse: **Meals on the Run**

If you're looking for the absolute cheapest food in town, want a meal on the run, or want to take a snack back to your hotel room, your best bet is an *Imbiss*. An *Imbiss* is a food stand or a tiny locale, where food is served for takeout or to customers who eat standing up at chest-high counters. Würste, Berliner Boulette, hamburgers, and french fries are common fare, along with ethnic choices such as pizza by the slice, Turkish pizza, gyros, doner kebab, and other finger foods. Of course, most *Imbisse* also sell beer, as well as soft drinks. You can easily dine for less than 5 DM ($3.35).

Imbisse are just off the Ku'damm—where sausages or cans of beer are sold for about 3 DM ($2)—including a stand on Knesebeckstrasse. *Imbisse* are also found on Wittenbergplatz, Savignyplatz, Alexanderplatz, Pariser Platz near Brandenburger Tor, at Friedrichstrasse S-Bahn station, in Dahlem across from the U-Bahn station, in the Tiergarten park, and at Berlin's many markets. During my last visit to the weekend market on Strasse des 17. Juni, I found stands selling everything from Turkish pizza to Würste, chili con carne, and hamburgers.

In addition, restaurants in this chapter that serve take-out food or offer stand-up tables include Ashoka (Indian), Asia-Quick (Chinese), Einhorn (Vegetarian), Higher Taste (Vegetarian), Ihre Frisch-Backstübe (German), Joseph Langer (German), Karavan (Turkish), Nordsee (Seafood), Orient (Middle Eastern), Piccola Taormina Tavola Calda (Italian), Pizza Bleibtreu (Italian), and Rogacki (German).

An informal place with only a few counters and tables, it offers a wide selection, including teriyaki chicken, *yakisoba* (fried noodles) with chicken, *tempura udon* (deep-fried food served in broth), sashimi, *nabe* (stews), and complete set meals. Here you'll find great food at great prices.

ⓢ Wilhelm Hoeck
Wilmersdorfer Strasse 149. ☎ **341 31 10.** Soups and salads 3–5 DM ($2–$3.35); main courses 9–20 DM ($6–$13.35). No credit cards. Mon–Sat 11am–11pm. U-Bahn: Bismarckstrasse, about a 2-minute walk. GERMAN.

If you want a traditional meal at modest prices, head for this well-known establishment north of Bismarckstrasse. You'll find two doors at this address—the door on the left leads to the simple family-style restaurant; the one on the right leads to the bar, first opened in 1892. The bar has more character, but the restaurant isn't as smoky. In any case, both offer the same menu of home-cooked foods "from Grandmother's kitchen," including *Sülze* (jellied meat) with potatoes, Bratwurst with sauerkraut and potatoes, Schnitzel, Eisbein with kraut, pureed peas and potatoes, and Boulette. Most platters are priced between 10 and 15 DM ($6.65 to $10), but you can eat even more cheaply if you order sausages or Boulette, priced under 5 DM ($3.35).

NEAR SCHLOSS CHARLOTTENBURG

✪ Luisen-Bräu
Luisenplatz 1. ☎ **341 93 88.** Main courses 8–20 DM ($5.35–$13.35). No credit cards. Daily 11am–midnight. Bus 109 from Bahnhof Zoo to Schloss Charlottenburg, then a half-minute walk. GERMAN.

Where better to round off a day of sightseeing than at a brewery? This one is conveniently located southeast of Charlottenburg Palace, at the corner of Spandauer Damm. Nice, cheerful, and rustic, it has large windows and paneled walls—with stainless steel tanks of beer brewing at one end of the room. You sit at long wooden tables, which makes it easy to strike up conversations with those around you—especially after a few beers. In summer you can sit outside. Order your food from the self-service counter, where you are charged by the weight of the meat slice you order, just as in a butcher shop, with slices priced at 100-gram ($3^{1}/_{2}$ oz.) increments. The food changes daily but typically includes such German favorites as Schweinebraten, Kasseler Rippenspeer, Leberkäs, Boulette, or Schweinshaxen. During my last visit, I had a huge platter of stuffed cabbage rolls and potatoes for less than 12 DM ($8). There are also stews and salads, but if all you want is a beer, that's perfectly acceptable at this brewery. Beer is available only in small .2 liter mugs, costing 2.60 DM ($1.75) each, due to the belief that it remains fresher that way.

IN KREUZBERG

✪ Grossbeerenkeller
Grossbeerenstrasse 90. ☎ **251 30 64.** Main courses 14–30 DM ($9.35–$20). No credit cards. Mon–Fri 4pm–2am, Sat 6pm–2am; closed holidays. U-Bahn: Möckernbrücke, less than a 5-minute walk. GERMAN.

There used to be hundreds of places like this in prewar Berlin—simple, smoky bars peopled by the famous and the infamous. Most were destroyed during World War II, but this one survived and is now more than a century old: evident in its aged walls, hardly visible with all the photos of theater personalities who have been here. Theatergoers drop in for a late-night meal of home-style cooking. This basement establishment serves simple and inexpensive dishes such as Berliner Würste salad with grilled potatoes, Leberkäs, omelets, and Bauernfrühstück, as well as Schnitzel, Rumpsteak, fish, and Sülze. After 7pm, make a reservation.

4 Coffeehouses

Along with beer, wine, and bottled water, coffee is probably the most popular drink in Germany. Not only a breakfast drink, coffee is also the star of that national obsession, the afternoon coffee break—a wonderful opportunity to indulge in cakes, tortes, and desserts. Of course, you could always order sparkling water or a sparkling wine.

If you're on a budget, try **Tschibo**, which offers a cup of coffee or an espresso starting at 1.90 DM ($1.25) or a cappuccino for 2.80 DM ($1.85). You can drink it standing up at one of the chest-high tables. Two convenient locations are at Kurfürstendamm 11 (☎ 883 11 94), across from the Gedächtniskirche, and at Wilmersdorfer Strasse 117 (☎ 312 80 23). They're open Monday to Friday from 9am to 6:30pm, and on Saturday from 9am to 2pm (to 6pm the first Saturday of the month).

ON OR NEAR THE KU'DAMM

✪ Café Kranzler

Kurfürstendamm 18-19. ☎ **885 77 20.** Coffee from 3.70 DM ($2.45). AE, DC, MC, V. Daily 8am–midnight. U-Bahn: Kurfürstendamm, less than a 1-minute walk.

Most of Berlin's many cafes were destroyed in World War II. One of the few to have survived is Café Kranzler, one of the city's most famous coffeehouses. Founded in 1825 and formerly located on Unter den Linden, today it occupies a modern building on the Ku'damm (shaped, some say, like a huge cake)—a premier people-watching spot, especially in summer when there are sidewalk tables. In winter, it's wonderful to sit near the huge floor-to-ceiling windows. In addition to breakfasts, German meals, and snacks, this cafe offers cakes and tortes, including *Sachertorte* (a Viennese chocolate cake) and *Rote Grütze,* cooked fruits with a vanilla sauce, a specialty of northern Germany.

✪ Cafe im Literaturhaus

Fasanenstrasse 23. ☎ **882 54 14.** Coffee from 3.50 DM ($2.35). No credit cards. Daily 9:30am–1am. U-Bahn: Uhlandstrasse, a 1-minute walk.

Just off the Ku'damm and away from the maddening crowd is this refined oasis, a cafe above a bookstore in a neighborhood of restored turn-of-the-century villas and art galleries. The Käthe-Kollwitz Museum is next door. In summer you can sit outside; in winter, in its greenhouse-like room. A decidedly artsy crowd comes for breakfast, served until 1pm, as well as salads, snacks, and desserts such as apple strudel with vanilla sauce, rice pudding with kiwi puree, and *Rote Grütze*.

Café Möhring
Kurfürstendamm 213. ☎ **881 20 75.** Coffee from 3.50 DM ($2.35). No credit cards. Daily 7am–midnight. U-Bahn: Uhlandstrasse, less than a 1-minute walk.

When Café Möhring first opened here in 1898, it was out in the countryside. Now, of course, it sits on prime real estate in one of the most exclusive neighborhoods; it was rebuilt after a fire in 1973. In addition to coffees and cakes, including spiked coffees, it offers breakfasts starting at 6 DM ($4), daily specials, and a menu that lists soups, salads, and main courses.

BERLIN-MITTE (EASTERN BERLIN)

✪ Operncafé
Opernpalais, Unter den Linden 5. ☎ **200 22 69.** Cup of coffee 3.50 DM ($2.35). AE, DC, MC, V. Summer, daily 8:30am–midnight; winter, Sun–Thurs 8:30am–7pm, Fri–Sat 8:30am–midnight. U-Bahn: Friedrichstrasse or Französische Strasse, about a 7-minute walk. Bus 100 to Staatsoper.

Located on one of Berlin's most famous boulevards is this well-known cafe. It occupies part of a palace, the Opernpalais, originally built in 1733, destroyed during World War II and recently painstakingly and lovingly restored. Elegant with chandeliers and a panoramic mural of Berlin architecture, it offers a grand breakfast buffet for 16.50 DM ($11) daily until noon, as well as 25 different tortes made fresh daily. It's especially nice on the outdoor terrace underneath the trees of this pretty square.

NEAR NOLLENDORFPLATZ

Einstein
Kurfürstenstrasse 58. ☎ **261 50 96.** Cup of coffee 4.40 DM ($2.95). AE, DC, MC, V. Daily 10am–2am. U-Bahn: Nollendorfplatz, about a 3-minute walk.

Einstein probably wouldn't object to lending his name to this cafe, located in a beautiful high-ceilinged town house from the 1920s—the former residence of Henny Porten, one of Germany's first silent-film stars. Popular with Berlin's younger, yuppie generation, it's a good place for coffee, especially Viennese varieties like an *Einspänner* (black coffee with whipped cream) or a *Melange* (coffee with milk). Breakfast is served until 2pm, with prices ranging from about 8 DM ($5.35) to 17 DM ($11.35). There's also champagne, wine, and cakes. As in Viennese coffeehouses, newspapers and magazines are provided—many in English, like *Time*. In summer, there's seating for as many as 180 outside. It's located on Kurfürstenstrasse (not to be confused with the Ku'damm), north of Nollendorfplatz.

7

What to See & Do

Berlin is sightseeing heaven for people who love museums—so spectacular that they alone are worth the trip to Berlin. The city's collections are richly diverse, ranging from Egyptian art treasures to contemporary art, from musical instruments to traditional German clothing, from architectural wonders to Islamic and African art. With more than 80 public museums and 200 galleries, Berlin offers something for everyone. I can't imagine being bored here even for a minute.

Berlin has actively sought treasures from around the world since the early 1800s, when it first began developing a museum complex on Museumsinsel. After World War II, most of the city's treasures were divided between East and West; that's why there are two of almost everything, giving visitors a bewildering choice of museums with similar and overlapping collections. The city plans to merge some of its collections once the more pressing unification problems are addressed.

Thankfully, museum-hopping in Berlin isn't the chore it can be in other major cities. The city is surprisingly compact—a savings in time and transportation costs. Furthermore, most of its major museums and attractions are clustered together in four distinct parts of the city, all conveniently reached by an efficient public transportation system and easily seen in a few days.

Of Berlin's four major museum centers, Museumsinsel in Berlin-Mitte is the oldest and best-known. This island in the middle of the Spree River is so laden with the treasures of the Pergamon Museum that I'm surprised it isn't sinking. Not to be outdone is Dahlem, which boasts the largest collection of museums in Berlin, including the famous Gemäldegalerie (Picture Gallery) and museums of non-European art. Charlottenburg is home of Schloss Charlottenburg (Charlottenburg Palace) and museums specializing in the antiquities, including the Ägyptisches Museum (Egyptian Museum) with the bust of Nefertiti. Finally, Berlin's newest museum area is in Tiergarten; still under construction, this region will eventually be the city's center for European art. Though not as important as the previously mentioned museum centers, Kreuzberg also has some unique and valuable museums.

It makes sense to cover Berlin section by section, not only because it saves time but also because it saves money. And it makes your planning easier. Most of the museum clusters, including most of those in Dahlem, several on Museumsinsel, and those in the Tiergarten, offer

> ### What's Special About Berlin
>
> **Museums**
> - The Pergamon Museum in eastern Berlin, with the Pergamon Altar, the Market Gate of Miletus, and the Babylonian Processional Street.
> - The Gemäldegalerie in Dahlem, with about 20 paintings by Rembrandt.
> - The Ägyptisches Museum, with the bust of Nefertiti.
> - The Neue Nationalgalerie and Nationalgalerie, with Berliner impressionist and expressionist artists.
> - Museums filled with art from around the world.
> - Museum Haus am Checkpoint Charlie, documenting the history of the Wall and nonviolent revolutions around the world.
> - Colorful neighborhoods, reflecting the ethnic/social mix: Kreuzberg with its large Turkish population, working-class Köpenick, and middle-class Dahlem.
>
> **Festivals**
> - International Film Festival, held every February.
> - Jazz-Fest Berlin in autumn, a colorful mix of avant-garde and classical jazz.
> - Weihnachtsmarkt, an annual Christmas market, held around the Ku'damm.

their own combination ticket (called a *Sammelkarte,* or *Tageskarte,* which literally translates as "day ticket"), allowing entrance to several museums in the same geographic area at a reduced rate. Also remember that most museums in Berlin are free on Sundays and holidays.

SUGGESTED ITINERARIES

To help you get the most out of your visit, here are some suggested itineraries to guide you to the most important attractions. Since the dining, nightlife, and sightseeing chapters are all arranged according to geographic locations, you can match your own choices in restaurants, attractions, and nightlife entertainment to the suggested itineraries. Have fun!

If You Have One Day

Berlin's most famous treasures are the Pergamon Altar and the bust of Nefertiti. If you wish to see both, get up early in the morning and head straight to the Ägyptisches Museum (closed on Friday) in Charlottenburg, where Berlin's most beautiful woman holds court: Nefertiti. Across the street is Schloss Charlottenburg, Berlin's most beautiful baroque building. If you have time, join a tour for a spin through its royal apartments, or at the very least visit the Knobelsdorff Flügel and the Schinkel Pavilion for a look at how Prussian royalty lived. Complete a tour of Charlottenburg with a stroll through the lovely gardens. For lunch, head to the nearby Luisen-Bräu for a beer and a typical German meal.

In the early afternoon, board bus 100 from Bahnhof Zoo for the Brandenburger Tor (Brandenburg Gate), built in the 1780s as the grand finishing touch to Berlin's most famous boulevard, Unter den Linden. After Berlin became a divided city, the gate and boulevard ended up under East Berlin's jurisdiction and were inaccessible to West Berliners—making the gate a poignant symbol of Germany's division. With the fall of the Wall, many Berliners gathered here at the gate to rejoice. Take a stroll down Unter den Linden, stopping for coffee at the famous Operncafé. By 4pm at the latest, you should be in the Pergamon Museum on Museumsinsel, with its incredible Pergamon Altar, Market Gate of Miletus, and Babylonian Processional Street leading to the Gate of Ishtar. Round out your eastern Berlin experience with a trip to the Museum Haus am Checkpoint Charlie (open to 10pm), established in 1961 to document the Berlin Wall and the many attempts of East Berliners to escape to the West. Today it's the best place in the city to gain an understanding of what Berlin was like during the decades of division.

Finish off the day with a leisurely evening stroll along the Ku'damm, Berlin's showcase avenue with many shops and restaurants. Relax over coffee at one of the area's many coffeehouses, or order a drink at one of the bars—if it's summer, try to get a seat outdoors. Dine at a traditional German restaurant. And then start planning your next trip to Berlin.

If You Have Two Days

Day 1 Devote your entire morning to Dahlem, first visiting the Gemäldegalerie with its masterpieces from the 13th to the 18th centuries, including works by Dürer, Brueghel, Botticelli, Raphael, Rubens, and Rembrandt. Add to it one or two of the other museums that most interest you—perhaps one of the fine museums of Asian art or the adjoining ethnological museum, one of the largest in the world. Nearby is the interesting Museum für Deutsche Volkskunde (Museum of German Ethnology), which boasts an excellent display of simple furniture and household items used by Germany's middle-class, peasants, and farmers. If you're still in Dahlem during lunchtime, you might dine on traditional German cuisine at Luise or enjoy a beer in its outdoor garden. If you're in a hurry, there's a thatched-roof *Imbiss* right across the street from the subway station, selling Würst, coffee, and beer.

In the afternoon, head for Charlottenburg, where your first stop should be Schloss Charlottenburg (Charlottenburg Palace) and its surrounding garden. At the palace itself, tour the royal quarters, the Knobelsdorff-Flügel (New Wing), and the Schinkel Pavilion. Across the street is the Ägyptisches Museum (Egyptian Museum), famous for its bust of Queen Nefertiti. Other museums here include the Museum of Greek and Roman Antiquities, the Museum of Primeval and Early

History, and, my favorite, the wonderful Bröhan Museum with its art deco and Jugendstil collection. Just southeast of the palace is the Luisen-Bräu brewery, a good spot for a meal or a beer. Finish the evening with a stroll down the Ku'damm.

Day 2 Go to Berlin-Mitte in eastside Berlin. Have a look at Brandenburger Tor and stroll down Unter den Linden. Then visit the outstanding Pergamon Museum on Museumsinsel. If you have time, add the Alte Nationalgalerie (Old National Gallery), the Bode Museum, or the Berliner Dom (Berlin Cathedral). Finish the afternoon with a walk to Alexanderplatz, once the heart of East Germany's capital and home of the towering TV tower, and the nearby Nikolai Quarter, a small neighborhood of restored buildings housing several pubs and restaurants.

At the end of the day, head for the Museum Haus am Checkpoint Charlie with its important collections documenting the history of the Berlin Wall. In the evening, try to attend a performance at the Deutsche Oper, Komische Oper, or the Philharmonie. Or, go to one of the half-price ticket booths (there's one on Alexanderplatz) to see what's available for that evening's performances at several venues around town.

If You Have Three Days

Days 1–2 Spend days 1 and 2 as outlined in "If You Have Two Days."

Day 3 On day 3, head for the Tiergarten museum complex (south of Tiergarten park); this is a recently developed center for European art, where you'll find the Neue Nationalgalerie (New National Gallery), which houses German and European artists of the 19th and 20th centuries. Nearby are the Kunstgewerbe Museum (Museum of Applied Arts), with its collections dating from the Middle Ages to the present day, the Musikinstrumenten Museum (Museum of Musical Instruments), and the Kupferstichkabinett (Collection of Prints and Drawings).

Spend the rest of the day indulging your own special interests. Good choices include the the Käthe-Kollwitz Museum (near the Ku'damm) with the artist's powerful drawings; the Bauhaus-Archiv and the Hansaviertel (Hansa Quarter) for architectural buffs; the Ku'damm and Wilmersdorfer Strasse for shopping. Be sure to visit KaDeWe department store's incredible food emporium on its top floor. If you're interested in German film, you might wish to tour the Babelsberg Studio near Potsdam.

In the evening, take advantage of Berlin's active nightlife scene. Watch a rock, jazz, or blues concert at a live-music house or enjoy an evening of pub crawling.

If You Have Five Days

Days 1–3 Spend days 1–3 as outlined above. In addition, if you're in Berlin on a Saturday or Sunday, be sure to schedule a trip to the flea market held every weekend on Strasse des 17. Juni near Tiergarten park. It offers antiques, junk, and curios, as well as arts and crafts from

Berlin's enterprising young artists. On a Tuesday or Friday afternoon, visit the fascinating Turkish Market in Kreuzberg.

Day 4 Pamper yourself with a day of relaxation. Take an excursion to Wannsee or Havel, where you can swim or board a pleasure boat. Alternatives include taking one of the suggested walking tours in the next chapter, heading for the Spreewald and a boat ride, or visiting all those other museums you haven't had time for.

Day 5 Head for the quaint old city of Potsdam with the palace and gardens of Sanssouci.

1 The Top Attractions

Since most of Berlin's top attractions are located near other worthwhile museums, be sure to read the next section, "More Attractions," to plan your day's itinerary. Under the same roof as the Gemäldegalerie in Dahlem, for example, are no fewer than five other museums, each important in its own right.

IN BERLIN-MITTE (EASTERN BERLIN)

✪ Pergamon Museum

Kupfergraben, Museumsinsel. ☎ **203 55**-**0**. Admission 4 DM ($2.65) adults, 2 DM ($1.35) students and children. Combination ticket 8 DM ($5.35) adults, 4 DM ($2.65) students and children. Free Sun and holidays. Tues–Sun 9am–5pm. Bus 100 to the Deutsche Staatsoper stop. S-Bahn: Hackescher Markt or Friedrichstrasse, each less than a 10-minute walk.

The Pergamon Museum houses Berlin's most valued cultural treasure, the Pergamon Altar. Essentially devoted to architecture, this museum was the first of its kind when it opened in 1930, and today ranks among the world's best for its collection of Greek, Roman, and Middle Eastern antiquities. It also contains Near Eastern and Asian art, Islamic art, and German folk art.

The Pergamon Altar, a magnificent masterpiece of Hellenistic art dating from 180 to 160 B.C., occupies a hall of its own. From a town in what is now Turkey, the altar was dedicated to Zeus and Athena and remains one of the architectural wonders of the ancient world. A seven-foot frieze along the base of the altar depicts the struggle of the Greek gods against the giants. Zeus and Athena are to be seen in the eastern frieze, across from the steps.

In the Roman Architecture Hall, you'll find the Market Gate of Miletus. Erected around A.D. 120, this two-story Roman gate provided access to a public market but was also large enough to contain a few shops as well. The museum's third architectural gem is the dazzling Babylonian Processional Street, which leads to the Gate of Ishtar. Originally 990 feet long and twice as wide as reconstructed here, the street was used for religious processionals during the reign of Nebuchadnezzar II (605–562 B.C.). It is bordered by walls decorated with lions in stride, against a striking blue background. The gate itself is of blue and ocher tiles, with fanciful bulls and dragons.

Upstairs are the collections of Asian and Islamic art, including Chinese porcelain from the Stone Age to the 20th century, and significant pieces of Chinese sculpture. The Japanese department contains ceramics and porcelain, lacquerware, and woodblock prints by one of Japan's foremost artists, Hokusai (1760–1849). The highlight of the Islamic art department is the Facade from Mschatta, a desert palace built in the 8th century but never completed. Note the intricate designs carved in its walls, not unlike the designs of an elaborate carpet. Carpets, too, are a part of the museum's collection, many from the 13th to 15th centuries.

Note that the museum is entered via a bridge off a lane called Kupfergraben, behind and to the left of Das Alte Museum. Near the entrance to the Pergamon is a small cafe where you can have a cup of coffee and snacks. Remember, if you plan on visiting other museums on Museumsinsel, be sure to purchase a combination ticket.

IN DAHLEM

✪ Gemäldegalerie (Picture Gallery)

Lanstrasse 8 or Arnimallee 23-27. ☎ **8301**-**216**. Dahlem complex combination ticket 4 DM ($2.65) adults, 2 DM ($1.35) students and children. Free Sun and holidays. Tues–Fri 9am–5pm, Sat–Sun 10am–5pm. Closed Jan 1; Tues after Easter and Whitsunday; May 1; Dec 24, 25, and 31. U-Bahn: Dahlem-Dorf.

Considered Berlin's top art museum, the Gemäldegalerie offers a comprehensive survey of European painting from the 13th to 18th century—possessing more than 1,500 works. Stemming from the royal court collection with works added through the years, it first opened to the public in 1830 in the Altes Museum on Museumsinsel. After World War II, during which 400 major works were destroyed, the collection was divided between East and West Berlin. Even so, only half of the Gemäldegalerie's present works can be displayed at one time; this will be remedied when the gallery moves into new and larger quarters in the Tiergarten at the end of the decade.

The museum's holdings are arranged historically and systematically, by schools and by periods. There are works by Dürer, Cranach, Holbein, Gainsborough, Brueghel, Titian, Botticelli, Raphael, Rubens, Vermeer, Murillo, El Greco, Goya, and Velázquez. It has an outstanding collection by Rubens, but the crowning achievement of the museum is probably its 20-some paintings by Rembrandt—one of the world's largest collections by this master. My personal favorite is his portrait of Hendrickje Stoffels and his common-law wife (note the intimacy of her gaze). The famous and striking *Man with the Golden Helmet,* though no longer attributed to Rembrandt but rather to one of his students, is nonetheless considered quite important.

Other must-see paintings include Botticelli's *Venus,* Dürer's portrait of a Nürnberg patrician, and Hans Holbein's portrait of merchant Georg Gisze. Brueghel the Elder's *The Netherlands Proverbs* illustrates more than 100 proverbs (How many can you find?). Lucas Cranach's *Fountain of Youth (Der Jungbrunnen)* depicts old women being led to the fountain, swimming through it, and then emerging youthful and beautiful. Note that apparently only women need the bath; men in the painting regain their youth through relations with younger women.

Since this museum is large, pick up a map and pamphlet; you may want to concentrate on a particular period or school. The ground floor is devoted to German, Netherlandish, and Italian art from the 13th through 16th centuries, as well as to French and English paintings of the 18th century. Sixteenth-century German art is especially well-represented, with works by Dürer, Altdorfer, and Baldung Grien.

The first floor has 17th- and 18th-century works, including Flemish, French, Dutch, and Spanish works, as well as baroque and rococo Italian paintings.

IN CHARLOTTENBURG

✪ Schloss Charlottenburg (Charlottenburg Palace)

Luisenplatz and Spandauer Damm. ☎ **32 09 11**. Combination ticket including guided tour, 8 DM ($5.35) adults, 3 DM ($2) students and children; Knobelsdorff Flügel only, 3 DM ($2) adults, 1.50 DM ($1) students and children; Schinkel Pavilion or Belvedere, 2.50 DM ($1.65) each adults, 1.50 DM ($1) students and children; Mausoleum, 1 DM (65¢) adults, 50 Pfennig (35¢) students and children; Galerie der Romantik, 4 DM ($2.65) adults, 2 DM ($1.35) students and children. Tues–Fri 9am–5pm, Sat–Sun 10am–5pm. Closed Mausoleum, Nov–Mar. Bus X26, 109, 110, or 145 to Charlottenburger Schloss. U-Bahn: Sophie-Charlotte-Platz or Richard-Wagner-Platz, each about a 10-minute walk.

Regarded as Berlin's most beautiful baroque building, Schloss Charlottenburg started out as something far less grand. First constructed in the 1690s as a small residence for Sophie Charlotte, wife of the future Prussian King Friedrich I, it was expanded in the 18th century into a palace fit for kings with extensions added by such renowned architects as Eosander von Göthe, Knobelsdorff, Schinkel, and Langhans. It served as the summer residence of almost all Prussian kings from Friedrich I to Friedrich Wilhelm IV, and as one of the few remaining castles of the Hohenzollern family still in existence, today it serves as a museum for objects from the baroque to Biedermeier periods.

The first thing that catches your eye as you approach the front of the palace is the equestrian statue of the Great Elector (*Grossen Kurfürsten*). Designed by Andreas Schlüter, it was cast in one piece in 1700 and originally stood on a famous bridge near the Berliner Schloss, which no longer exists. While being moved to a safe haven during World War II, it accidentally sank to the bottom of Tegel harbor, where it remained until the early 1950s when it was finally retrieved and placed here in 1952.

The central section of the palace, topped with a dome and a clock and known as the Nering-Eosander Building after the architects who designed it, is the oldest part of Charottenburg and contains the royal apartments (Historical Rooms). These served as the private summer quarters of Sophie Charlotte and her husband and are decorated with rich furnishings. Of these, the Porcelain Cabinet is the most striking, filled with about 2,000 pieces of porcelain and bordering on kitsch. Unfortunately, you must join a guided tour, conducted only in German, to visit this part of the palace, but if you have the time

I nevertheless highly recommend it. Before or after your tour, you are free to wander through some rooms upstairs which boast a collection of tapestries, goblets, swords, portraits and other royal possession. The stars of the collection are the royal Hohenzollern insignia and a stunning silver place setting completed in 1914 but never used by the royal family because of the outbreak of World War I. After being carted off to the United States as spoils of World War II and thereafter languishing in a Berlin bank vault, the priceless silver finally found a home in Charlottenburg in 1995.

To the right of the Nering-Eosander Building is the New Wing, better known as the Knobelsdorff-Flügel, where you can wander on your own through more royal living quarters charmingly decorated in the the Romantic and Biedermeier styles. Upstairs you'll find the Golden Gallery with its gold and green ornamentation, an impressive German rococo ballroom, and the state dining hall. If you're interested in German art, be sure, too, to walk through the Galerie der Romantik, a gallery of paintings from the German romantic period with works by C. D. Friedrich and Schinkel. Knobelsdorff-Flügel also contains Frederick the Great's art collection, including works by Watteau, Lancret, Pater, Chardin, Boucher, and Pesne.

Next, head for the Schinkel Pavilion, located on the far east end of the palace, behind the Knobelsdorff-Flügel. This delightful summer house, built in 1825, was designed by Karl Friedrich Schinkel, one of Berlin's most respected architects. Resembling an Italian villa, it contains a museum of arts and crafts and is decorated with sculptures, chandeliers, KPM porcelain, furniture, and paintings from the early 19th century, including some works by Schinkel, who was also an accomplished fine artist. Most interesting, in my opinion, are the paintings of old Berlin. Given a choice, I'd much prefer living in the small and cozy rooms here than in the more pretentious Schloss Charlottenburg.

The park that stretches behind the palace was first laid out in 1697 in French style, then transformed into an English garden early in the 19th century. It was destroyed in World War II and restored to its original baroque form. Besides the Schinkel Pavilion, the park contains two other important structures. The Mausoleum, located on the west end, contains the tombs of Queen Luise, King Friedrich Wilhelm III, Kaiser Wilhelm I, and Kaiserin Augusta. Designed by Schinkel and built in 1810, with its Doric columns it resembles an ancient temple. Belvedere, at the far end of the park near the Spree River, is a former teahouse that now contains Berlin porcelain of the 18th and 19th centuries, including some by KPM Berlin (Königliche Porzellan-Manufaktur).

✪ Ägyptisches Museum (Egyptian Museum)

Schlossstrasse 70. ☎ **32 09 11**. Admission 4 DM ($2.65) adults, 2 DM ($1.35) students and children. Combination ticket 8 DM ($5.35) adults, 4 DM ($2.65) students. Free Sun and holidays. Mon–Thurs 9am–5pm, Sat–Sun 10am–5pm. Closed: Jan 1; Maundy Thursday; May 1; Dec 24, 25, and 31. Bus X26, 109, 110, or 145 to Charlottenburger Schloss. U-Bahn: Sophie-Charlotte-Platz or Richard-Wagner-Platz, each about a 10-minute walk.

The Egyptian Museum is just across the street from Charlottenburg Palace in what was originally the barracks of the Royal Bodyguards. Here you'll find Berlin's most famous art object and probably the most well-known Egyptian artwork in the world: Queen Nefertiti (called *Königin Nofretete* in German). She's up on the first floor, in a dark room all to herself. Created more than 3,300 years ago, the bust never left the sculptor's studio and served only as a model for subsequent portraits of the queen. When the ancient city was later deserted, the bust was simply left on a shelf in the sculptor's studio. The studio eventually was buried and the bust protected for more than 3,000 years, until it was unearthed early in this century by a team of German archaeologists.

In adjoining rooms are smaller likenesses of her husband, King Ahkenaton, and her daughter, Princess Meritaton. Look also for Queen Tiyi, Akhenaton's mother, known for her shrewdness in politics. Also in this amazing museum are burial cult objects, a mummy and sarcophagi, a papyrus collection, everyday tools, and the Kalabasha Gate.

IN KREUZBERG

✪ Museum Haus am Checkpoint Charlie

Friedrichstrasse 44. ☎ **251 10 31**. Admission 7.50 DM ($5) adults, 4.50 DM ($3) students. Daily 9am–10pm. U-Bahn: Kochstrasse, a few minutes' walk.

Since the fall of the Wall, a visit to this significant museum is more important than ever, especially if this is your first trip to Berlin. Popularly known as the Museum of the Wall, it was established soon after the Wall went up in 1961, with the sole purpose of documenting the grisly events that were taking place because of the Wall. Located near what was once a major border check for foreigners entering East Berlin, Checkpoint Charlie, it manages to convey vividly what life was like during the grim decades of the Cold War, using photographs, items used in escapes and unsuccessful escape attempts (a hot-air balloon, cars with hidden compartments), and newspaper clippings. The museum also documents nonviolent revolutions that have taken place throughout the world, with information on Mahatma Gandhi, Lech Walesa, and the peaceful 1989 revolution in East Germany. A block farther north, on the original site of Checkpoint Charlie, is a continuation of the museum with an open-air exhibition that includes a guard tower, a section of the Wall, and other relics of the Cold War.

2 More Attractions

IN BERLIN-MITTE (EASTERN BERLIN)

The first three museums described here (and the Pergamon Museum under "The Top Attractions") are located in eastern Berlin on Museumsinsel, a museum complex that dates back to the 1820s when King Friedrich Wilhelm III decided to construct a home for art treasures collected through the ages by the royal family and make them available to the viewing public. During the next century—and particularly under the guidance of museum director Wilhelm von Bode—the museum collections grew with the express purpose of rivaling the other

❓ Did You Know?

- Berlin has more than 6,000 restaurants, as well as 6,500 pubs and bars.
- There is no official curfew in Berlin; some bars remain open all night.
- Each year, Berliners and their guests drink the equivalent of Wannsee—in beer.
- Berlin claims to have more local rock groups than any other city in Europe—about 1,000.
- Berlin claims to have more dogs than any city in the world—about 200,000.
- 80,000 Berliners lost their lives in World War II—50,000 of them Jewish.
- From 1949 until the Wall went up in 1961, approximately 3 million East Germans fled their country.
- From 1961 to 1989, 78 East Berliners died trying to escape to West Berlin; most were shot by East German border guards.
- City officials expect Berlin's population to double to about 6 million by the year 2005.
- Greater Berlin is larger than Munich, Stuttgart, and Frankfurt combined.
- Einstein developed his theory of relativity in Berlin.

great museums of Europe, including the Louvre and the museums of London, Madrid, and Vienna. German archaeologists combed the world for ancient artifacts, bringing back treasures from Persia, Greece, and Egypt. Paintings from Europe's old masters rounded out the outstanding collections.

After World War II, most of the collections housed here were divided between East and West; many works originally displayed here are now in Dahlem, Charlottenburg, and the Tiergarten. Museumsinsel, however, is still world-renowned for its ancient architectural and sculptural wonders, particularly the Pergamon Altar.

Note: A *Tageskarte*, or combination ticket valid for one day, is an economical way to see several museums in Berlin-Mitte. The ticket costs 8 DM ($5.35) for adults and 4 DM ($2.65) for students and children and allows entry to three museums on Museumsinsel—the Pergamon Museum, Bode Museum, and Alte Nationalgalerie, as well as the Friedrichswerdersche Kirche nearby.

Bode Museum

Bodestrasse 1-3 (entrance on Monbijoubrücke), Museumsinsel. ☎ **203 55-0**. Admission 4 DM ($2.65) adults, 2 DM ($1.35) students and children. Combination ticket available. Free Sun and holidays. Tues–Sun 10am–5pm. Bus 100 to Deutsche Staatsoper stop. S-Bahn: Hackescher Markt or Friedrichstrasse, each less than a 10-minute walk.

Named after the former director responsible for bringing great works of art and fame to Museum Island, this is actually several museums under one roof. Here you'll find the Egyptian Museum with its Papyrus Collection, the Early Christian and Byzantine Collection, the Sculpture Collection, the Picture Gallery with art from the 13th to 18th century, and the Coin Cabinet. The majority of what used to be here in the Picture Gallery, however, is now in the museum complex in Dahlem.

On the ground floor you'll find the Ägyptische Museum (Egyptian Museum)—considered one of the world's best—with a lively presentation of the life and times of the Pharaohs. The Early Christian and Byzantine Collection includes a valuable 6th-century mosaic from the church of San Michele in Ravenna, Byzantine and Italian medieval sculpture, and a collection of icons. The Picture Gallery—many of its masterpieces ended up in Dahlem—has German, Dutch, Flemish, French, English, and Italian works—ranging from the 13th to 18th centuries. The Coin Cabinet boasts more than a half million coins, medallions, notes, and seals—one of the largest collections in the world.

Alte Nationalgalerie (Old National Gallery)

Bodestrasse, Museumsinsel. ☎ **203 55-0** or **203 55-307**. Admission 4 DM ($2.65) adults, 2 DM ($1.35) students and children. Combination ticket available. Free Sun and holidays. Tues–Sun 10am–5pm. Bus 100 to Deutsche Staatsoper stop. S-Bahn: Hackescher Markt, about a 5-minute walk; Friedrichstrasse, about a 10-minute walk.

Built in the style of a Corinthian temple, the Alte Nationalgalerie is devoted to paintings and sculpture of the 19th century, by artists of Germany, France, and other European countries. Of special note are the works by German expressionists, the world's largest collection of Berlin artist Adolph von Menzel, and works by French impressionists. Since the museum is rather small, you can tour it in an hour or so—a must-see for art lovers.

Altes Museum (Old Museum)

Museumsinsel (entrance on Lustgarten). ☎ **203 55-0**. Admission varies according to exhibit. Tues–Sun 10am–5pm. Bus 100 to Deutsche Straatsoper stop. S-Bahn: Hackescher Markt, about a 5-minute walk; Friedrichstrasse, an 8-minute walk.

Built according to plans by Karl Friedrich Schinkel and considered one of his greatest works, this museum was the first one constructed on Museumsinsel. Easily recognized by its 18 Ionic columns and the first museum you see if you approach Museumsinsel from Unter den Linden, it offers changing exhibitions devoted mainly to ancient art. Refer to the monthly *Berlin Programm* for current exhibitions.

Berliner Dom

Lustgarten, on Museumsinsel. ☎ **246 91 35** or **246 91 19**. Free admission to cathedral; organ concerts 8 DM ($5.35) adults, 5 DM ($3.35) students and senior citizens, free to children under 14; crypt 3 DM ($2) adults, 1.50 DM ($1) students. Cathedral, Mon–Sat 9am–6:30pm, Sun 11:30am–6:30pm; worship service Sun 10–11:30am (English translation provided); organ concerts Mon–Sat 3pm, Sun 2pm. Bus 100 to Lustgarten stop.

The most striking and dominant structure on Museumsinsel, the Berlin Cathedral was constructed at the turn of the century in Italian

Berlin–Mitte Sights

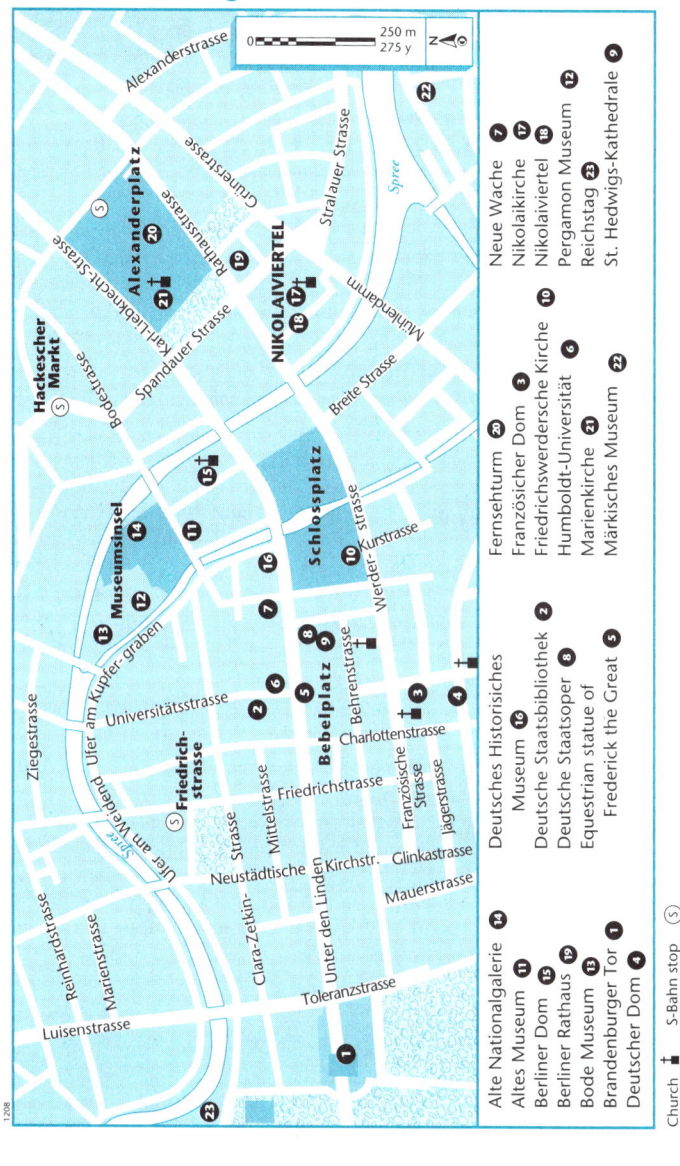

Alte Nationalgalerie **14**
Altes Museum **11**
Berliner Dom **15**
Berliner Rathaus **19**
Bode Museum **13**
Brandenburger Tor **1**
Deutscher Dom **4**
Deutsches Historisches Museum **16**
Deutsche Staatsbibliothek **2**
Deutsche Staatsoper **8**
Equestrian statue of Frederick the Great **5**
Fernsehturm **20**
Französicher Dom **3**
Friedrichswerdersche Kirche **6**
Humboldt-Universität **21**
Marienkirche **21**
Märkisches Museum **22**
Neue Wache **7**
Nikolaikirche **17**
Nikolaiviertel **18**
Pergamon Museum **12**
Reichstag **23**
St. Hedwigs-Kathedrale **9**

Church ✝ ■   S-Bahn stop Ⓢ

Renaissance style. It served as the central church for Prussian Protestants and as the court church and primary burial site of the Hohenzollern imperial family. Severely damaged during World War II and closed for decades, it finally reopened in 1993 after painstaking restoration. Of special note are the gilded wall altar of the 12 apostles designed by Schinkel; the impressive Sauer organ with more than 7,000 pipes and daily concerts; and the ornate coffins of the first Prussian royal couple,

King Friedrich I and his wife Sophie Charlotte, designed by Andreas Schlüter. The basement crypt holds more imperial coffins, but it's not worth the admission fee unless you're a real Hohenzollern fan.

Friedrichswerdersche Kirche

Werderstrasse. ☎ **208 13 23**. Admission 4 DM ($2.65) adults, 2 DM ($1.35) students and children. Combination ticket available. Free Sundays and holidays. Tues–Sun 9am–5pm. U-Bahn: Stadtmitte, or Französische Strasse.

Not far from Unter den Linden and Alexanderplatz, this church was built between 1824 and 1830 according to plans by Berlin's most famous architect, Karl Friedrich Schinkel. Today it houses the Schinkel Museum with sketches, models, and blueprints of his Berlin achievements, as well as sculpture from the first half of the 19th century.

Deutsches Historisches Museum

Unter den Linden 2. ☎ **215 02-0**. Admission varies according to exhibit. Thurs–Tues 10am–6pm. Bus 100 to Deutsche Staatsoper stop.

This rather austere-looking baroque building located on Berlin Mitte's most famous boulevard was built in the 17th century as an arsenal for the Prussian army. Its inner courtyard is famous for its 22 masks of dying soldiers designed by Schlüter. Serving as a museum of German history for East Berliners during the Communist regime (with a decidedly socialist bent), today it features changing exhibits related to German history, from photography to lives of the Hohenzollerns to Berlin of yore.

Märkisches Museum

Am Köllnischen Park 5. ☎ **301 66-0**. 3 DM ($2) adults, 1 DM (65¢) students and children. Tues–Sun 10am–6pm. U-Bahn: Märkisches Museum, a few minutes' walk.

This museum concentrates on the culture and history of Berlin from 1648 to 1815, depicted primarily through handicrafts and works of art. Displays include local archaeological finds beginning with the Stone Age; models of the city around 1500 when it was just the two villages of Berlin and Cölln; as well as paintings, glassware, porcelain (including KPM Berlin), wrought-iron furniture, and wares produced in the city through the centuries. A special section is dedicated to Berlin theater, with pictures of famous actors, actresses, and directors of the Berlin stage.

Reichstag (Parliament)

Platz der Republik. ☎ **39 77-0**. S-Bahn: Unter den Linden. Bus 100 to the Reichstag stop.

Although technically in western Berlin, the Reichstag is most easily combined with a sightseeing trip to Berlin-Mitte. Completed in 1894 in Neo-Renaissance style to serve the needs of Bismarck's newly united Germany, it is now being renovated for future use by Germany's parliament under the direction of British architect Sir Norman Foster. The Reichstag unfortunately is closed to the public; renovations should be completed by 1999. In 1995, the artists Christo and Jeanne-Claude brought international attention to the structure when they wrapped it in cloth. Behind the Reichstag are white crosses to memorialize the East Berliners who died trying to escape to West Berlin—the Wall used to run directly behind the Reichstag, with the Spree river and a manned watch tower on the other side.

Brandenburger Tor (Brandenburg Gate)
Unter den Linden. Free admission. Room of Silence, 11am–4pm daily. S-Bahn: Unter den Linden. Bus 100 to the Unter den Linden/Brandenburger Tor stop.

One of Berlin's best-known structures, the gate was built from 1788 to 1791 by Carl Gotthard Langhans as the grand western entrance into Unter den Linden. A Quadriga created by Johann Gottfried Schadow that shows the goddess of victory in a chariot pulled by four steeds tops the gate. During the decades of the Wall, the Brandenburger Tor stood in a no-man's land, marking the boundary of East and West Berlin and thus becoming the symbol of a divided Germany. After the November 1989 revolution and the fall of the Wall, many Berliners gathered here to rejoice and to dance together on top of the Wall. One of the gate's guardhouses serves as a Room of Silence, a place for silence and reflection; the other guardhouse is a branch of the Berlin tourist office, open daily from 10am to 6pm.

IN DAHLEM

You can reach the museums in Dahlem in about 20 minutes from the city center by taking U-Bahn 2 to Dahlem-Dorf station. At the station, there are signs pointing the direction to the various museums—most about a 5-minute walk. The Gemäldegalerie (described under "The Top Attractions") and museums for sculpture, ethnology, East Asian, Islamic, and Indian arts are all located in a huge sprawling complex with entrances on either Arnimallee and Lansstrasse.

Note: One admission price—4 DM ($2.65) for adults and 2 DM ($1.35) for students and children—allows entry to all museums in the entire complex. Museums in Dahlem are closed on Monday.

Several of the Dahlem museums may eventually find new homes in the Tiergarten by the end of the 1990s. The Kupferstichkabinett (Museum of Prints and Drawings), formerly in Dahlem, has already moved into new quarters in the Tiergarten. The Gemäldegalerie is scheduled to move to the Tiergarten in 1998, to be followed by the Skulpturengalerie at the turn of the century. That was the plan, at least, prior to reunification: Now that Berlin's state museums have come under one administration and museums may combine collections, the future of the Tiergarten is in question. Should the Gemäldegalerie and Skulpturengalerie move, the Tiergarten will become a new center for European art, while Dahlem will continue to house collections of non-European art.

Skulpturengalerie (Sculpture Gallery)
Arnimallee 23-27. ☎ **8301-252**. Admission 4 DM ($2.60) adults, 2 DM ($1.35) students and children. Free Sun and holidays. Tues–Fri 9am–5pm, Sat–Sun 10am–5pm. Closed Jan 1; Tues after Easter and Whitsunday; May 1; Dec 24, 25, and 31. U-Bahn: Dahlem-Dorf.

One of Germany's foremost sculpture collections, this gallery contains approximately 1,200 European works dating from the early Christian and Byzantine periods to the late 18th century. Most notable are the works from the Italian Renaissance and German Gothic periods, including carvings by one of Germany's most famous artists, Tilman Riemenschneider. Also on display in the two-story gallery are wooden religious figurines, ivories, marble reliefs, and bronzes.

Museum für Völkerkunde (Ethnological Museum)

Lansstrasse 8. ☎ **8301-226**. Admission 4 DM ($2.65) adults, 2 DM ($1.35) students and children. Free Sun and holidays. Tues–Fri 9am–5pm, Sat–Sun 10am–5pm. Closed Jan 1; Tues after Easter and Whitsunday; May 1; Dec 24, 25, and 31. U-Bahn: Dahlem-Dorf.

An engaging place for adults and children alike, this is one of the world's largest ethnological museums, with almost a half million objects from around the world in its possession. To me, most fascinating is its display of boats and water crafts from the Pacific region in the Oceania Department. There are also original dwellings and facades from the Pacific islands, including a men's clubhouse from Palau and a hut from New Guinea. Equally impressive is the museum's fine collection of pre-Columbian artifacts, especially its gold objects and Peruvian antiquities. Other departments center on religious life in China, the nomad cultures of Mongolia, shadow puppetry and marionette theaters of Asia, ceremonial masks, African sculpture, and musical instruments. In the Department of Music Ethnology, visitors can listen to recordings of folk music from around the world.

✪ Museum für Deutsche Volkskunde (Museum of German Ethnology)

Im Winkel 6-8. ☎ **839 01-01**. Admission 4 DM ($2.65) adults, 2 DM ($1.35) students and children. Free Sun and holidays. Tues–Fri 9am–5pm, Sat–Sun 10am–5pm. Closed Jan 1; Tues after Easter and Whitsunday; May 1; Dec 24, 25, and 31. U-Bahn: Dahlem-Dorf, a 5-minute walk.

This ethnological museum focuses on handcrafted objects of the German-speaking people in Central Europe, from the 16th century to the present day. With an emphasis on rural culture before and during the early stages of the Industrial Revolution, the museum displays farm machinery, furniture, costumes, jewelry, religious ceremonial objects, items of leisure, and household goods. This is an interesting contrast to the extravagance of Charlottenburg Palace.

Note: This museum is *not* part of the Dahlem museum complex containing the Gemäldegalerie; it charges its own separate admission.

Museum für Indische Kunst (Museum of Indian Art)

Lansstrasse 8. ☎ **8301-361**. Admission 4 DM ($2.65) adults, 2 DM ($1.35) students and children. Free Sun and holidays. Tues–Fri 9am–5pm, Sat–Sun 10am–5pm. Closed Jan 1; Tues after Easter and Whitsunday; May 1; Dec 24, 25, and 31. U-Bahn: Dahlem-Dorf.

Quite simply, this is the most significant collection of Indian art in Germany. Its displays, covering a period of almost 4,000 years, reflect the spread of Indian culture throughout Southeast and Central Asia. Objects range from prehistoric terra-cotta and stone sculptures of Buddhist, Jainist, and Hindu divinities, to finely crafted miniatures, ivories, and murals. Of special note is its Turfan Collection of frescoes from the 6th to 10th centuries, depicting Buddhist legends. The museum is also famous for its collection of art from Buddhist Dahlem Museumscave-monasteries from along the once legendary Silk Road. Not to be missed is the 9th-century stone sculpture of Shiva and his wife, considered a masterpiece of Nepalese art.

Museum für Islamische Kunst (Museum of Islamic Art)
Lansstrasse 8. ☎ **8301-1**. Admission 4 DM ($2.65) adults, 2 DM ($1.35) students and children. Free Sun and holidays. Tues–Fri 9am–5pm, Sat–Sun 10am–5pm. Closed Jan 1; Tues after Easter and Whitsunday; May 1; Dec 24, 25, and 31. U-Bahn: Dahlem-Dorf.

All Islamic countries are represented in this important collection of art from the 8th to 18th centuries, with carpets, sculptures, examples of Arabic script, pottery, glass, jewelry, miniatures, and other applied art on display. Highlights include a Koran parchment from the 9th century, enameled Syrian glassware, as well as Egyptian, Turkish, and Iranian carpets.

Museum für Ostasiatische Kunst (Museum of Far Eastern Art)
Lansstrasse 8. ☎ **8301-382**. Admission 4 DM ($2.65) adults, 2 DM ($1.35) students and children. Free Sun and holidays. Tues–Fri 9am–5pm, Sat–Sun 10am–5pm. Closed Jan 1; Tues after Easter and Whitsunday; May 1; Dec 24, 25, and 31. U-Bahn: Dahlem-Dorf.

The first of its kind in Germany when established in 1906, this museum offers a fine overview of Far Eastern decorative and religious art from 3,000 B.C. to the present. Of note are a lacquered Chinese imperial throne dating from the 17th century with mother-of-pearl inlays, the collection of Japanese woodblock prints, and Japanese and Chinese paintings and scrolls. Because the paintings and scrolls are fragile, displays are changed every three months and center on different themes. On one of my visits, a special exhibition featured 18th- and 19th-century woodblock prints depicting foreigners (who, despite their rounded eyes, still looked rather Asian).

Brücke-Museum
Bussardsteig 9. ☎ **831 20 29**. Admission 4 DM ($2.65) adults, 2 DM ($1.35) students and children. Wed–Mon 11am–5pm. U-Bahn: Dahlem-Dorf, about a 15-minute walk. Bus: No. 115.

This small but important museum is dedicated to members of Die Brücke (The Bridge), a group of painters from Dresden credited with introducing expressionism to Germany. Among the oil paintings, sculptures, watercolors, graphic prints, and other works on display, look for Heckel's *Mann in jungen Jahren* (Man in his Younger Years), Nolde's *Feriengäste* (Vacation Guests), Pechstein's *Fischerboot* (Fishing Boat), and Kirchner's *Berliner Strassenszene* (Berlin Street Scene).

Note: This museum is not part of the Dahlem museum complex; it charges its own admission.

IN CHARLOTTENBURG

The Charlottenburg precinct's top two attractions, Schloss Charlottenburg (Charlottenburg Palace) and the Ägyptisches Museum (Egyptian Museum), are described under "The Top Attractions." Near these two attractions are three other museums worth visiting: The

Antikenmuseum (Museum of Antiquities), Museum für Vor- und Frühgeschichte (Primeval and Early History Museum), and the Bröhan Museum.

Note: If you plan to visit several of these museums, consider purchasing a combination *Tageskarte* for 8 DM ($5.35), which allows entry to the Ägyptisches Museum, Antikenmuseum, Museum für Vor- und Frühgeschichte, and the Galerie der Romantik (located in Schloss Charlottenburg). The ticket is valid for one day. In addition, Charlottenburg Palace has its own combination ticket.

Antikenmuseum (Museum of Antiquities)

Schlossstrasse 1. ☎ **32 09 11**. Admission 4 DM ($2.65) adults, 2 DM ($1.35) student and children. Combination ticket available. Free Sun and holidays. Mon–Thurs 9am–5pm, Sat–Sun 10am–5pm. Closed Jan 1; Maundy Thursday; May 1; Dec 24, 25, and 31. Bus X26, 109, 110, or 145 to Charlottenburger Schloss. U-Bahn: Sophie-Charlotte-Platz or Richard-Wagner-Platz, each about a 10-minute walk.

Standing directly across from the Egyptian Museum, this museum, designed originally as barracks, contains ancient Greek, Etruscan, and Roman treasures, including pottery, ivory carvings, glassware, jewelry, wood and stone sarcophagi, and small marble statuettes. Particularly outstanding are the Attic red-figure vases of the 5th century, with depictions of everyday life and the world of the gods. Most impressive is the *Schatzkammer*, with its silver collection and its exquisite jewelry from about 2000 B.C. to late antiquity.

Museum für Vor- und Frühgeschichte (Primeval and Early History Museum)

Spandauer Damm. ☎ **32 09 11**. Admission 4 DM ($2.65) adults, 2 DM ($1.35) students and children. Combination ticket available. Free Sun and holidays. Mon–Thurs 9am–5pm, Sat–Sun 10am–5pm. Closed Jan 1; Maundy Thursday; May 1; Dec 24, 25, and 31. Bus X26, 109, 110, or 145 to Charlottenburger Schloss. U-Bahn: Sophie-Charlotte-Platz or Richard-Wagner-Platz, each about a 10-minute walk.

This museum is located in the west wing of Schloss Charlottenburg (to the left if you're facing the palace, outside the palace gate). It illustrates the history of humankind from the Stone Age through the Bronze Age and late Iron Age—with objects from prehistoric Europe and the Near East. Arranged in chronological order, the displays begin with Paleolithic cave paintings and idols, then continue with sections devoted to the creation of a written language, early agriculture, metalworking, Trojan antiquities, and items from the pre-Roman Iron Age and early Germanic tribes. Also included are archeological finds from the Spandau district of Berlin. Spandau, first settled in the 7th to 12th centuries by Slavic people, remains Berlin's most extensively researched archaeological site.

✪ Bröhan Museum

Schlossstrasse 1a. ☎ **321 40 29**. Admission 4 DM ($2.65) adults, 2 DM ($1.35) students and children. Tues–Sun 10am–6pm. Bus X26, 109, 110, or 145 to Charlottenburger Schloss. U-Bahn: Sophie-Charlotte-Platz or Richard-Wagner-Platz, each about a 10-minute walk.

This privately owned museum (located next to the Antikenmuseum) is named after Professor Karl Bröhan, who collected art nouveau

Sights Around Charlottenburg

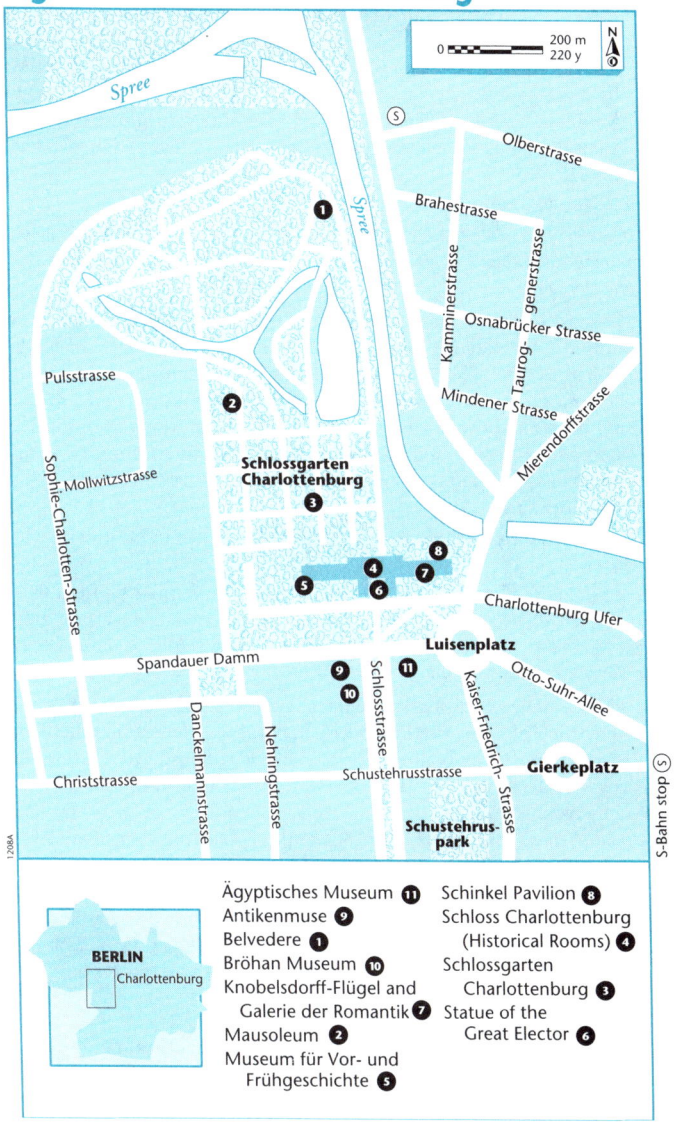

Ägyptisches Museum ⓫
Antikenmuse ❾
Belvedere ❶
Bröhan Museum ❿
Knobelsdorff-Flügel and Galerie der Romantik ❼
Mausoleum ❷
Museum für Vor- und Frühgeschichte ❺
Schinkel Pavilion ❽
Schloss Charlottenburg (Historical Rooms) ❹
Schlossgarten Charlottenburg ❸
Statue of the Great Elector ❻

BERLIN
Charlottenburg

(*Jugendstil* in German) and art deco pieces when others thought they were worthless and threw them away. Exquisite vases, glass, furniture, silver, sculptures, paintings, and other pieces dating from 1889 to 1939 are beautifully arranged to resemble a salon or home of the period rather than a museum. The porcelain collection is outstanding and includes KPM Berlin, Meissen, and Royal Copenhagen, as well as the turn-of-the-century buffet created by Hector Guimard (1867–1942), who also designed the cast-iron entranceways of the Paris Métro. There's also glass by Émile Gallé, Bohemian iridescent glass, paintings by a group of artists known as the Berlin Secession, silver objects by Viennese artist Josef Hoffmann, and magnificent furniture crafted by Jacques-Émile Ruhlmann. In short, the Brohan Museum is a joy; don't miss it.

✪ Käthe-Kollwitz Museum

Fasanenstrasse 24. ☎ **882 52 10**. Admission 6 DM ($4) adults, 3 DM ($2) children, students, and senior citizens. Wed–Mon 11am–6pm. U-Bahn: Uhlandstrasse, a 1-minute walk.

Located just a minute's walk south of the Ku'damm is this significant museum, displaying the powerful drawings and sketches of Käthe Kollwitz (1867–1945). This Berlin artist was a genius in capturing the emotions of her subjects, from the tenderness of mothers to the despair of poverty and the horrors of war. The museum covers four floors of an old villa; the top floor displays some of Kollwitz's sculptures. Don't miss the opportunity to see her works; their power will stay with you long afterward.

Kaiser-Wilhelm Gedächtniskirche (Kaiser-Wilhelm Memorial Church)

Breitscheidplatz. ☎ **24 50 23**. Free admission. Ruined church, Tues–Sat 10am–4pm; new church, daily 9am–7pm. Services Sun and holidays 10am and 6pm; short services Mon–Fri 1, 5:30, and 6pm. Organ concerts Sat 6pm. U-Bahn: Kurfürstendamm or Bahnhof Zoo, each a 1-minute walk.

This church, which marks the beginning of the Ku'damm, comes as something of a surprise in modern Berlin. First constructed in 1895, it was destroyed by bombs during World War II and was left in ruins as a visual reminder of the horrors of war. Underneath the skeletal remains of its war-damaged steeple is a small museum with displays related to war and destruction. Beside the Gedächtniskirche is a newer church, designed in the shape of an octagon by Professor Egon Eiermann and completed in 1961. A striking contrast to the ruined church beside it, it's made of blue glass plates from Chartres and includes a hexagonal tower. True to their style of nicknaming everything, Berliners refer to the new church as the "lipstick and powder puff."

IN TIERGARTEN

South of Tiergarten park is Berlin's newest cultural center, the Kulturforum—home of the Philharmonie, the Neue Nationalgalerie, the Kunstgewerbe Museum (Museum of Applied Arts), Musikinstrumenten Museum, and the Kupferstichkabinett. Originally planned by West Berlin city planners as a modern counterpart to East Berlin's Museumsinsel, this cultural area was to serve as a center for European art. Since reunification, however, the purpose of Tiergarten has been open to question. If plans continue as scheduled, Tiergarten will eventually house two museums now in Dahlem: the Gemäldegalerie and the Skulpturengalerie.

Sights Around the Tiergarten

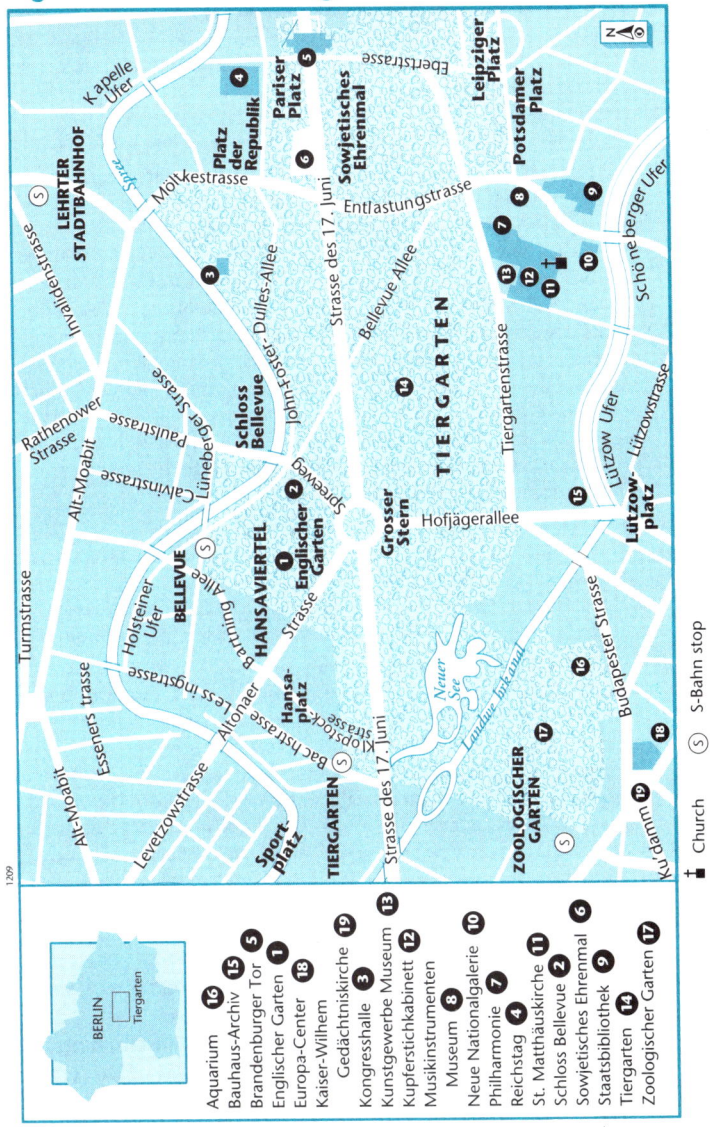

Aquarium **16**
Bauhaus-Archiv **15**
Brandenburger Tor **5**
Englischer Garten **1**
Europa-Center **18**
Kaiser-Wilhelm Gedächtniskirche **19**
Kongresshalle **3**
Kunstgewerbe Museum **13**
Kupferstichkabinett **12**
Musikinstrumenten Museum **8**
Neue Nationalgalerie **10**
Philharmonie **7**
Reichstag **4**
St. Matthäuskirche **11**
Schloss Bellevue **2**
Sowjetisches Ehrenmal **6**
Staatsbibliothek **9**
Tiergarten **14**
Zoologischer Garten **17**

Note: A combination ticket allowing entry to the Neue Nationalgalerie, Kunstgewerbe Museum, and Musikinstrumenten Museum is available for 8 DM ($5.35) adults and 4 DM ($2.65) students and children.

✪ Neue Nationalgalerie (New National Gallery)

Potsdamer Strasse 50. ☎ **266 26 62**. Admission to the permanent collection, 4 DM ($2.65) adults, 2 DM ($1.35) students and children. Combination ticket available. Free Sun and holidays. Temporary exhibits 4–10 DM ($2.65–$6.65). Tues–Fri 9am–5pm, Sat–Sun 10am–5pm. Closed Jan 1; Tues after Easter and Whitsunday; May 1; Dec 24, 25, and 31. Bus 129 from Ku'damm. U-Bahn: Kurfürstenstrasse, then bus 148 or 248.

The first museum to open in the Tiergarten cultural area, this starkly modern gallery was designed by architect Mies van der Rohe and built in the 1960s, set in a vast square surrounded by a sculpture garden. Called the New National Gallery to distinguish it from the much older Alte Nationalgalerie on Museumsinsel, it houses art of the 20th century and is therefore a chronological continuation of the 19th-century works displayed at the Alte Nationalgalerie. The ground floor is devoted to changing exhibitions, while the permanent collection in the basement shows works of Munch, Liebermann, Emil Nolde, and other members of the Die Brücke group, and internationally known artists such as Picasso, Ernst, Kokoschka, Dix, Klee, and Feininger. This bright and airy museum is one of my favorites in Berlin and is a good introduction to German artists of the past century.

✪ Kunstgewerbemuseum (Museum of Applied Arts)

Tiergartenstrasse 6. ☎ **266 29 11**. Admission 4 DM ($2.65) adults, 2 DM ($1.35) students and children. Combination ticket available. Free Sun and holidays. Tues–Fri 9am–5pm, Sat–Sun 10am–5pm. Closed Jan 1; Tues after Easter and Whitsunday; May 1; Dec 24, 25, and 31. U-Bahn: Kurfürstenstrasse, then bus 148 or 248. Bus 129 from Ku'damm.

Just a 5-minute walk from the Neue Nationalgalerie and next to the Philharmonie, this delightful museum, housed in a modern, redbrick building, displays European applied arts from the early Middle Ages to the present day. The oldest museum of its kind in Germany, it displays glassware, porcelain, beer steins, tableware, measuring instruments, and more. Particularly outstanding is its collection of medieval goldsmiths' works, including the *Guelph Cross* and the *Domed Reliquary*, considered among the richest ecclesiastical treasures in any German museum; an 8th-century *Burse-Reliquary*, associated with Charlemagne; and the baptism bowl of Emperor Barbarossa. Another priceless treasure is the *Lüneburg Town Hall Silver Plate*, which consists of 32 vessels and implements in gold-plated silver; it is regarded as one of the most valuable municipal treasures still in existence in Germany.

Musikinstrumenten Museum (Museum of Musical Instruments)

Tiergartenstrasse 1. ☎ **25 48 10**. Admission 4 DM ($2.65) adults, 2 DM ($1.35) students and children. Combination ticket available. Free Sun and holidays. Tues–Fri 9am–5pm, Sat–Sun 10am–5pm. Closed Jan 1; Tues after Easter and Whitsunday; May 1; Dec 24, 25, and 31. U-Bahn: Kurfürstenstrasse, then bus 148 or 248. Bus 129 from Ku'damm.

A small gray building overshadowed by the Philharmonie next door, the Musikinstrumenten Museum originated in 1888 but suffered greatly during World War II, losing more than 3,000 of its 4,000 pieces. Fortunately, the museum over the past decades has acquired many European musical instruments from the 16th century to the present day. On display are spinets, clavichords, violins, trumpets, flutes, alpenhorns, harps, zithers, guitars, and the now-forgotten glass harmonica, for which Mozart and others wrote compositions. Other highlights include the full family of Stradivarius instruments (Did you know it also includes guitars?), a Wurlitzer organ, and medieval instruments.

Kupferstichkabinett—Sammlung der Zeichnungen und Druckgraphik (Collection of Prints and Drawings)

Matthai-Kirchplatz 8. ☎ **266 20 02**. Admission free. Museum, Tues–Fri 9am–5pm, Sat–Sun 10am–5pm; Studien Sall, Tues–Fri 9am–4pm. U-Bahn: Kurfürstenstrasse, then bus 148 or 248. Bus 129 from Ku'damm.

This museum specializes in prints and drawings from the German masters, including important works by Albrecht Dürer, and more modern works by artists like Käthe Kollwitz, Schinkel, and Caspar David Friedrich. It is also a repository for architectural sketches from the late 15th century to the present, more than 40,000 photographs ranging from documentary to art, book illustrations, and poster and advertisement art. Works from the extensive collections are shown only on a temporary basis in themed exhibitions; if you wish to view specific prints or drawings, such as works by Dürer, you can do so at the Studien Saat (study hall).

IN KREUZBERG

Kreuzberg's most popular museum, Museum Haus am Checkpoint Charlie, is described in "The Top Attractions."

Martin-Gropius-Bau

Stresemannstrasse 110. ☎ **254 86-0**. Admission 8 DM ($5.35) adults; 4 DM ($2.65) children, senior citizens, and students. Temporary exhibits cost extra. Tues–Sun 10am–8pm. S-Bahn: Anhalter Bahnhof, about a 2-minute walk. Bus 129 from the Ku'damm to Stresemannstrasse stop, then a 3-minute walk.

Designed by architect Martin Gropius in 1881, the Renaissance-style Martin-Gropius-Bau is beautiful inside and out and houses two museums: the Berlinische Galerie and the Jewish department of the Berlin Museum. The Berlinische Galerie features modern art, photography, and architecture, with changing exhibitions and a permanent display, with an emphasis on art of the 20th century. Though most of its works are by contemporary Berlin artists, it also shows international art.

Topographie des Terrors

Stresemannstrasse 110. ☎ **245 86-703**. Admission free. Daily 10am–6pm. S-Bahn: Anhalter Bahnhof, about a 2-minute walk. Bus 129 from the Ku'damm to Stresemannstrasse stop, then a 3-minute walk.

Located beside the Martin-Gropius-Bau and easily overlooked, this museum documents Hitler's reign of terror and fittingly occupies what was once the site of Hitler's feared Gestapo headquarters. Here, the Third Reich's secret police held enemies of the state—Jews, Communists, Social Democrats, and members of resistance movements— for questioning and torture. Through photographs and explanations, the museum depicts Hitler's rise to power, the fate of Jews and gypsies sent to concentration camps, the role of the Gestapo, and other grim statistics of Hitler's Third Reich. Unfortunately, most of the explanations are in German only, but a booklet in English is available for a small fee. On the grounds beside the museum is a small hill, with diagrams showing where former Reich buildings stood. Along Niederkirchner Strasse, by the way, is a remnant of the Wall.

IN FRIEDRICHSHAIN

✪ East Side Gallery
Mühlenstrasse. S-Bahn: Hauptbahnhof, a 2-minute walk. U-Bahn: Schlesisches Tor, a 5-minute walk.

Formerly a part of East Berlin, Friedrichshain precinct bordered West Berlin, its western boundary marked by the Spree River and the Wall. In a surprise move, East German authorities decided in 1990 to leave a kilometer-long section of the Wall standing along Mühlenstrasse and invited artists from around the world to decorate it with murals (during a divided Germany, the East Berlin side of the Wall was always white and shiny; only in West Berlin could people approach it to paint). Since there is hardly any of the Wall remaining, this is bound to become a major tourist attraction. Look for my favorites: A Trabant (East German car) crashing through the Wall, and Brezhnev and Honecker kissing each other with the caption, "Will no one save me from this deadly love?" Unfortunately, graffiti artists have left their mark on the Wall here, just as they have on seemingly every flat surface in the city.

IN ZEHLENDORF

Museumsdorf Düppel
Clauertstrasse 11. ☎ **802 66 71**. Admission 3 DM ($2) adults, 1.50 DM ($1) children. May–Sept Sun and holidays 10am–5pm (enter before 4pm), Thurs 3–7pm (enter by 6pm). Bus 211 to Lindenthaler Allee/Ecke Clauertstrasse, or 118 or 115 to Potsdamer Chaussee/Ecke Lindenthaler Allee.

Open in summer only, this open-air reproduction of a medieval village that once occupied this site features thatched-roof houses and live demonstrations of woodworking, baking, weaving, plant cultivation, and other household and agricultural pursuits of medieval Germany. Explanations are in German only, but this is a pleasant trip in fine weather and a fun family outing, especially on Sundays when village "inhabitants" at their busiest.

IN KÖPENICK

Kunstgewerbemuseum (Museum of Applied Arts)
Schloss Köpenick, Schloss Insel. ☎ **657 26 51**. Admission 4 DM ($2.65) adults, 2 DM ($1.35) students and children. Free Sun and holidays. Tues–Sun 9am–5pm. S-Bahn: Spindlersfeld, then a 10-minute walk; or S-Bahn to Köpenick, then tram 62 or 68 to Schloss Insel stop.

There's been a fortress on this island in the river ever since the 12th century, with the present baroque palace completed in the mid-17th century. Today it holds the Kunstgewerbemuseum, with displays covering the last 10 centuries of European applied art, including glass, ceramics, jewelry, tapestries, furniture, and silver and gold objects. What makes the contemporary collection particularly interesting is the presence of artists from eastern Berlin, Dresden, Leipzig, Erfurt, Weimar, and other cities formerly of East Germany, providing insight into the DDR art scene. Another highlight is the ornate Wappensaal (Coat of Arms Hall). Above the fireplace is the coat of arms of the Prussian Brandenburg State. Be sure to stroll the palace garden.

IN ORANIENBURG

Gedenkstätte und Museum Sachsenhausen (Memorial and Museum Sachsenhausen)

Strasse der Nationen 22, Oranienburg. ☎ **03301/80 37 19** Admission free. Tues–Sun 8:30am–4:30pm. S-Bahn: Oranienburg.

Twenty-one miles north of Berlin but easily reached via a 45-minute ride on the S-Bahn with a normal transportation ticket, Oranienburg is an important destination for those who wish to know more about Hitler's death camps. In operation from 1936 to 1945, Sachsenhausen was one of the most infamous concentration camps, housing 220,000 prisoners from 22 countries, 100,000 of whom died here. Since 1961 its grounds have served as a memorial, containing original barracks and other camp structures and two museums complete with photographs. Documentary films and clips are shown in German and French only, but pictures speak louder than words. This sobering experience is not recommended for children under 12.

VIEWS

Fernsehturm TV Tower

Alexanderplatz. ☎ **242 33 33**. Admission 7 DM ($4.65) adults, 3 DM ($2) children. Observation platform daily 9am–midnight (enter by 11pm); Tele-Café daily 9am–10:45pm. Closed until 1pm second and fourth Tues of every month. S-Bahn or U-Bahn: Alexanderplatz, a 1-minute walk. Bus 100 to Alexanderplatz.

From the time the Fernsehturm was completed in 1969 until the fall of the Wall 20 years later, this towering structure was popular in East Berlin for its view of West Berlin far in the distance, especially on clear days when there's a 24-mile visibility (an update of the day's visibility is posted on the outside door). Elevators whisk visitors to the 670-feet-high observation platform in 35 seconds. More than 1,200 feet tall, the tower is Berlin's tallest edifice and contains the revolving Tele-Café, which makes a complete turn every hour. Come for a cup of coffee on a clear day; though costing a steep 7 to 10 DM ($4.65 to $6.65), it's worth it for the stunning views and the fun of locating all those Berlin's landmarks you've seen only from the ground up. *Note:* Rumors have it that the TV tower may close, perhaps during the lifetime of this book.

Rathaus Schöneberg

John F. Kennedy Platz. ☎ **7831**. Wed and Sun 10am–3:30pm. U-Bahn: Rathaus Schöneberg, a 1-minute walk.

From the steps of Rathaus Schöneberg, John F. Kennedy gave his famous "Ich bin ein Berliner" speech. Should you choose to climb the

Siegessäule (Victory Column)

Grosser Stern. ☎ **391 29 61**. Admission 1.50 DM ($1) adults, 1 DM (65¢) children. Mon 1–6pm, Tues–Sun 9am–6pm (enter by 5:30pm). Closed during icy weather conditions. Bus 100 to Grosser Stern stop.

Located in Tiergarten park in the middle of a traffic circle, the Siegessäule was dedicated in 1873 to commemorate three victorious wars. More than 220 feet high, it's topped by a gilded goddess of victory, as well as a 157-feet high observation platform, reached via 290 steps of a spiral staircase.

3 Parks & Gardens (and a Zoo, Too)

Most visitors to Berlin are surprised to learn that the city limits encompass a large area of woods and lakes. During the decades when West Berlin was surrounded by East Germany and the Wall, its green spaces and water, accounting for a full 30% of its total 190 square miles, served as an important emotional escape valve for city dwellers in need of nature.

THE TIERGARTEN

Berlin's most convenient park, as well as the city's largest, is Tiergarten park. About two miles long and a half-mile wide, it stretches east from Bahnhof Zoo all the way to Brandenburger Tor. Originally used as a hunting reserve and then as the elector's private park, Tiergarten was opened to the public at the end of the 19th century. Like the rest of the city, the park suffered extensive damage during World War II, and

---

Time for a Picnic

Want to picnic? You can buy everything from cheese, bread, fruit, and wine to Leberkäs, grilled chicken, and casseroles at any department store's food department. Two of the largest are **KaDeWe** (Kaufhaus des Westens), on Wittenbergplatz (☎ 212 10), with a huge food department on the sixth floor; and **Hertie bei Wertheim,** Kurfürstendamm 231 (☎ 88 20 61), with a food section in the basement. In addition, some restaurants listed in Chapter 6, "Where to Eat," sell take-out foods that may be perfect for an afternoon picnic.

And where to enjoy your goodies? The largest and most convenient green space in the center of Berlin is the Tiergarten, just northwest of Bahnhof Zoo. This park stretches all the way to Brandenburger Tor, with ponds, woods, meadows, and trails throughout. If you don't feel like walking far from the Ku'damm, there are public benches on Breitscheidplatz in the shade of the Kaiser-Wilhelm Gedächtniskirche, from which you can watch the never-ending parade of people on Berlin's most fashionble boulevard.

then lost all its trees when freezing Berliners cut them down to use as firewood during the long postwar winters. Today trees have been replanted, and it's one of the most popular places in the city for picnics, jogging, sunbathing, and strolling. The park is filled with ponds, streams, a rose garden, an English-style garden, and several restaurants.

✪ Zoologischer Garten (Berlin Zoo)

Budapester Strasse 32 and Hardenbergplatz 8. ☎ **25 40 10**. Combination ticket to zoo and aquarium, 15 DM ($10) adults, 12 DM ($8) students, 7.50 DM ($5) children; zoo only, 10 DM ($6.65) adults, 8 DM ($5.35) students, 5 DM ($3.35) children. Summer daily 9am–6:30pm; winter daily 9am–5pm. U-Bahn: Bahnhof Zoo, a 1-minute walk.

Founded in 1841 and opened to the public in 1844, this is Germany's oldest and one of Europe's best zoos, with beautifully designed grounds. Located just a short walk from the Ku'damm or Bahnhof Zoo, it is home to more than 14,000 animals of almost 2,000 species. Probably the best-known and most-beloved resident is BaoBao, Germany's only panda. Also popular are the camels, kangaroos, antelopes, lions, tigers, and monkeys. There's a birdhouse (Europe's largest) with 720 species, and a nocturnal house. The adjacent aquarium, built in 1913, has a collection of more than 6,000 fish, reptiles, and amphibians, including an impressive crocodile hall, and sea turtles, sharks, and snakes. In the Tiergarten's southwest corner, the zoo is a great escape from Berlin city life.

Botanischer Garten (Botanical Garden)

Located in Dahlem at Königin-Luise-Strasse 6-8, Berlin's Botanischer Garten (☎ 83 00 60) was laid out at the turn of the century and boasts 104 acres with 18,000 species of plants. Its 16 greenhouses contain plants from all the continents—from rain forests to deserts. Especially recommended are the great Tropenhaus, constructed in 1907 and one of the largest greenhouses in the world, and the orchid collection. Outdoor beds are arranged geographically so that visitors can wander through landscapes that resemble the Alps, Japan, the Himalayas, South Africa, North America, and other regions. There's also a garden of medicinal plants, as well as a garden for the visually handicapped, where visitors can smell and touch the plants. The small Botanisches Museum displays the history and usage of various plants, but only in German.

Admission to the Botanischer Garten costs 4 DM ($2.65)for adults, 2 DM ($1.35) students. It's free for children under 14 and people with disabilities. There's free admission to the Botanisches Museum. The Botanischer Garten is open daily from 9am to 4 pm from November through February. In March and October, it's open from 9am to 5pm; in April and September, 9am to 7pm; from May to August, 9am to 8pm. The greenhouses are open daily from November through February from 10am to 3:15pm; in March and October from 9am to 4:15pm; from April through September from 9am to 5:15pm. The Botanisches Museum is open Tuesday through Sunday from 10am to 5pm. Take the S-Bahn to Botanischer Garten; then it's a 5-minute walk.

Pfaueninsel and Schloss Pfaueninsel (Peacock Island)

With an area of 185 acres, Pfaueninsel (☎ 805 30 42) is the largest island in the Havel and has long been a popular destination for day-trippers. A nature reserve with many rare trees and birds, the island gets its name from a flock of 60 or so peacocks that has roamed here freely since 1795. But most famous on the island is Schloss Pfaueninsel, an artificial ruin built in the 1790s by Friedrich Wilhelm II for his mistress, the Countess Lichtenau. In contrast to his uncle, Frederick the Great—who spent much of his life waging wars and building empires—Friedrich Wilhelm II apparently preferred to spend his time building architectural fantasies. Schloss Pfaueninsel, later used by Friedrich Wilhelm III and Queen Luise as a summer residence, now contains a small museum with furnishings and artworks dating from 1795 to 1830.

As for the island itself, it's a great place to relax and escape from the hustle and bustle of the city—cars, dogs, portable radios, and smoking are forbidden. You can walk around the island in about an hour or two, though you'll probably want to make several stops along the way. Many rare trees and shrubs were planted here, including Weymouth and Arolla pines, sequoias, gingkos, and cedars. Other items of interest include the Schweizerhaus (Swiss Cottage), designed by Karl Friedrich Schinkel in 1825; the Kavaliershaus, built in 1804 and renovated by Schinkel in 1826, when he added the facade of a late-Gothic patrician home from Danzig; and the Meierei (Dairy Farm), located on the north end of the island and also built in the style of a ruin.

Admission to Schloss Pfaueninsel costs 4 DM ($2.65) adults, 2 DM ($1.35) students and children. Pfaueninsel is open daily during the summer from 8am to 8pm, in the winter daily from 10am to 4pm. Schloss Pfaueninsel is open Tuesday through Sundays from April through October from 10am to 5pm. To get there, take bus 116 or 216 to Pfaueninselchaussee, then walk to Nikolskoer Weg, and then take the ferry, which costs 2 DM ($1.35) one way.

4 Especially for Kids

MUSEUMS

Museum für Verkehr und Technic (Museum for Transport and Technology), Trebbiner Strasse 9, in Kreuzberg (☎ 254 84 0), is a good diversion for older children, especially on rainy days. The main building contains old model cars, trains, boats, and displays relating to the information age, from printing technology to computers, with most explanations unfortunately only in German. Of most interest to children from around the world, therefore, is probably the nearby Spectrum building, with four floors of hands-on displays, experiments, and models, including pulleys, pendulums, trick mirrors, optical illusions, electrical experiments, and more. It's open Tuesday to Friday from 9am to 5:30pm and Saturday and Sunday from 10am to 6pm; admission is 4 DM ($2.65) for adults and 2 DM ($1.35) for children and students. Take the U-Bahn to Gleisdreieck or Möckernbrücke.

Museum für Völkerkunde (Ethnological Museum) *(see p. 130)* One of the largest ethnological museums in the world, with a fascinating display of boats, canoes, masks, dwellings, weapons, clothing, and other objects. It's fun and educational.

Museum Haus am Checkpoint Charlie *(see p. 124)* Older children will find this museum documenting the decades of the Berlin Wall fascinating. On display are vehicles used in daring escapes, including cars with hidden compartments and a hot-air balloon. With its many photographs, it is one of the best places to show your children what Berlin was like during the Cold War.

Museumsdorf Düppel *(see p. 138)* This re-created medieval village, complete with thatched-roof houses and live demonstrations of woodworking, baking, weaving, and other old-time pursuits, is fun for a family outing.

PARKS, THE ZOO & OUTDOOR ACTIVITIES

BLUB *(see p. 148)* This is Berlin's bathing paradise, a complex of indoor and outdoor pools, including a wave pool, a 396-foot super slide, a children's pool, and an outdoor heated pool open year-round.

Boat Trips *(see p. 147)* Fleets of ships await passengers wishing to travel the Spree River, the Wannsee, and other waterways of Berlin.

Botanischer Garten *(see p. 141)* Show your child that cocoa grows on trees and that there are such things as insect-eating plants. It has a special area where visually impaired visitors are encouraged to touch and smell the plants.

Tiergarten *(see p. 140)* Berlin's largest park, located in the heart of Berlin, is another good spot for an outing and picnic.

Wannsee Beach *(see p. 148)* A day at the beach is always fun; kids enjoy the playground with slides.

Zoologischer Garten and Aquarium *(see p. 141)* Who can resist BaoBao the panda, as well as the monkeys, lions, and camels? The Berlin Zoo, with more than 14,000 animals, and the adjacent aquarium with over 6,000 fish, are only minutes from the Ku'damm.

ENTERTAINMENT

Grips (Altonaer Strasse 22; ☎ 391 40 04) This is the undisputed champion of children's theater in Berlin, with shows that appeal to kids ages 7 to 100. If your child doesn't understand German, attend a production designed for a young age group—there's lots of action, and the plot is easy to follow. There are performances throughout the year, usually at 10am or 3pm, with tickets averaging 10 DM ($6.65) for children and 15 DM ($10) for adults. It's located only a minute's walk from Hansaplatz U-Bahn station.

Puppen-Traum-Bühne (Siegfriedstrasse 192a; ☎ 55 89 87 3) Puppet plays for children of all ages are staged here, with performances held most week days at 10am and 2pm and Sundays at 4pm. Admission is usually 7 DM ($4.65) for children and 10 DM ($6.65) for adults, and it's about a 10-minute walk from the Lichtenberg S- and U-Bahn station.

5 Special-Interest Sightseeing

FOR THE ARCHITECTURE LOVER Because Berlin suffered widespread destruction during World War II, the city is conspicuously devoid of the architectural gems that grace many other European cities. One notable exception is Schloss Charlottenburg, Berlin's most beautiful baroque structure, described under "Top Attractions."

In addition, some buildings remain that were designed by Karl Friedrich Schinkel (1781–1841), one of Berlin's best-known architects. Among his surviving works are the **Schinkel Pavilion** on the grounds of Schloss Charlottenburg, the **Altes Museum** on Museum Island, and the **Schlossbrücke** that bridges Unter den Linden and the Lustgarten.

Most of Berlin's architecture is only a few decades old. The most famous postmodern buildings are those in the **Hansaviertel** (Hansa Quarter), which stretches along the northern border of Tiergarten park. It consists primarily of housing projects, from one-family dwellings to apartment buildings, along with two churches, a library, and a school. The Hansaviertel is the result of an international gathering in 1957 by 48 leading architects from 13 countries, who were asked to design a community for Berliners still homeless as a result of World War II. Famous architects who participated include Walter Gropius, Alvar Aalto, Pierre Vago, Oscar Niemeyer, and Werner Düttmann. The closest subway stop is Hansaplatz station. For orientation, be sure to consult the outdoor map of the Hansaviertel, which lists each building and its architect. Incidentally, Le Corbusier's design turned out to be so large that it was built in the western end of the city near the Olympic Stadium. It's Berlin's largest housing project, with 530 apartments.

And of course, with Berlin as capital, a flurry of new buildings are being built throughout the city, particularly in Potsdamer Platz and in Berlin-Mitte. One particularly noticeable architectural addition to the city is an office building on the corner of Kantstrasse and Fasanenstrasse, not far from Bahnhof Zoo, topped with a gigantic weather vane that weighs 34 tons and actually turns in strong winds. Berliners have yet to give it a nickname, though "shark's fin" wouldn't be far off the mark.

Another place of interest to architecture fans is the **Bauhaus-Archiv,** Klingelhöferstrasse 13-14 (☎ **2540 02-0**). Located in a light, airy building constructed from plans designed by Walter Gropius, it is dedicated to preserving both the ideals and artifacts relating to the Bauhaus school of design. The Bauhaus, founded by Walter Gropius in Weimar in 1919 and disbanded in Berlin in 1933, revolutionized the teaching of architecture and industrial design, influencing modern design so greatly that its emphasis on aesthetics is still reflected in designs throughout the world.

The Bauhaus-Archiv contains a small museum, an extensive collection of documents, and a library, and it stages special exhibitions and seminars throughout the year. The museum's collections, shown on a rotating basis, include architectural models, designs, paintings, drawings, and applied arts that adhere to Bauhaus principles, including architectural models and designs by Gropius, Hannes Meyer,

Special-Interest Sightseeing 145

Ludwig Mies van der Rohe, Marcel Breuer, and Ludwig Hilberseimer. In addition, paintings and drawings by Herbert Bayer, Lyonel Feininger, Johannes Itten, Wassily Kandinsky, Paul Klee, László Moholy-Nagy, Georg Muche, and Oskar Schlemmer are also sometimes on display. Note, however, that the small permanent display is sometimes removed to make way for temporary special exhibitions, which nevertheless also relate to the Bauhaus.

The Bauhaus-Archiv, which can be reached by taking bus 100, 109, 129, or 341 to Lützowplatz, is open Wednesday to Monday from 10am to 5pm. Admission is 4 DM ($2.65) for adults and 2 DM ($1.35) for students. On Monday, admission is free.

And finally, the gallery **Aedes** in S-Bahn Bogen 66 at Savignyplatz regularly displays exhibits relating to architectural projects. There are also architectural exhibits at the Berlin Pavilion on Strasse des 17. Juni near the Tiergarten S-Bahn station, staged by the Berlin department for construction and housing and constantly updated with new architectural developments in Berlin.

FOR FILM BUFFS Home of Marlene Dietrich and the acclaimed Berlin International Film Festival held in February, Berlin also boasts **Babelsberg Studios** (☎ 0331-721 27 55), located just south of the city near Potsdam. First founded in 1912 and formerly known as UFA and then DEFA studios, it produced such early classics as *The Song of the Nibelungen* (1922–24) by Fritz Lang, *Metropolis* (1925–26), and *The Blue Angel* (1930), the film that launched Dietrich's career to international fame. After reunification and the call for privatization of East German companies, Babelsberg was bought by a French firm, with German director Volker Schlöndorff named director of the historic studios. With major TV studios expected to relocate here following extensive renovation and expansion of existing facilities, studio employees have continued to support themselves by opening the studios to the public since 1992. Today the Babelsberg Studiotour includes a theme park, cavernous halls housing one of the world's largest collections of film props (including models, masks, and creatures used in decades of filmmaking), movie sets (including one from the *Never-Ending Story III*), a stunt show, a special-effects display, screens throughout playing films produced here, and tours of the studio grounds, including a stop at the Marlene Dietrich Hall where *The Blue Angel* was filmed. This is not a slick Hollywood production; indeed, buildings are run-down, the mud on the pathway is real, and those running the tours are not professional tour guides but professional film people. A must for fans of German classic films; allow at least three hours for a tour of the grounds. Admission is 18 DM ($12) for adults and 14 DM for senior citizens, students and children four and older. It's open March through October daily from 10am to 6pm and November through February from 10am to 4pm. To get there, take the S-Bahn 3 or 7 to Babelsberg station and then bus 690 to Grünstrasse.

For more on German film, visit the **Filmmuseum**, located in Potsdam at Marstall (☎ 0331/29 36 75). Housed in an attractive baroque building originally constructed as an orangerie and then converted into a stable for the royal horses, it contains an outstanding exhibition depicting the history of the UFA/DEFA studios in Babelsberg, including photographs, TV screens showing classic films produced there, and an interesting display of films produced there during the Communist regime (including, interestingly enough, 12 Indian movies of the American Old West produced between 1966 and 1983). One room lists the 1,532 actors and actresses, directors, and others working in the film industry who fled Germany under the Nazis, including Marlene Dietrich and Fritz Lang. Unfortunately, displays are in German only, but those interested in the history of German film will find the museum worthwhile. A cinema at the museum screens German and foreign classic and artistic modern films. The museum is open Tuesday to Friday from 10am to 5pm and Saturday and Sunday from 10am to 6pm. Admission is 4 DM ($2.65) for adults and 2 DM ($1.35) for students, children and senior citizens. It's located about a 5-minute walk from the Potsdam-Stadt S-Bahn station.

FOR VISITING AMERICANS   More than 100 streets, boulevards, and squares are named after Americans—testimonial to the close tie with the United States. Most famous is probably **John F. Kennedy Platz,** the square in front of **Rathaus Schöneberg** (☎ 7831). Here Kennedy delivered his famous "Ich bin ein Berliner" speech on June 26, 1963, just months before he was assassinated. Of interest at the Rathaus is the huge Freedom Bell, given to Berlin by the American people in 1950. Located in a tower and modeled after the U.S. Liberty Bell, it's open for viewing, free, on Wednesday and Sunday only from 10am to 3:30pm (follow the signs that say "Zum Turm"). In the tower are some display cases on the history of the bell, including some signatures of Americans who pledged their support to Berlin by signing a "Declaration of Freedom." Altogether, there are 16 million American signatures, which are kept in a vault in the tower. To reach the tower, you have to climb a lot of steps, but the view is grand. To reach Rathaus Schöneberg, take U-4 to the U-Bahn station of the same name, from which it's a minute's walk.

Other streets and places named after Americans include **Truman Plaza**, **Clayallee** (named in honor of Gen. Lucius Clay for initiating the airlift of 1948–49), and the **John F. Kennedy School** (part of the Berlin school system but staffed by both American and German teachers). Americans who are Beatles fans will be pleased to know that a school in Berlin-Mitte was recently renamed the **John-Lennon-Gymnasium**.

6 Organized Tours

In light of the many changes taking place in Berlin since reunification, companies are redesigning their tours. In particular, tours to the surrounding environs of Berlin have increased greatly, so be sure to inquire for an update on tour offerings.

BUS TOURS   Using this book, you don't have to spend money for a bus tour. However, you may wish to take one for orientation purposes and to see the city's highlights. You can then return to the sights that interest you and visit them at your leisure.

There are a number of tour companies in Berlin, with most buses departing from the Ku'damm area. The biggest is **Severin + Kuhn,** Kurfürstendamm 216 (☎ 883 10 15), which is open daily from 9am to 6pm. Its 2-hour tour of Berlin costs 30 DM ($20), while a 4-hour tour, with a stop at the Pergamon Museum on Museumsinsel, costs 45 DM ($30).

If you're in Berlin for several days, you may wish to take Severin + Kuhn's 4-hour trip to Potsdam, where you'll see Frederick the Great's rococo palace, Sanssouci, and its surrounding gardens; it costs 54 DM ($36) for adults and 44 DM ($29.35) for children. From April through September, Severin + Kuhn offers a $6^{1}/_{2}$-hour trip to the Spreewald, including a boat ride, for 54 DM ($36). Another tour worth considering is its 10-hour trip to Dresden for 99 DM ($66). For more information, contact Severin + Kuhn.

Other tour companies include **Berolina,** with buses departing from the corner of Kurfürstendamm and Meinekestrasse (☎ 882 20 91), and **Berliner Bären Stadtrundfahrt,** Rankestrasse 35 (☎ 213 40 77). With prices similar to Severin + Kuhn, they also offer tours of the city, as well as tours of Potsdam, the Spreewald, and Dresden.

BOAT TRIPS If you're in Berlin from April to the end of October, you can climb aboard one of the many pleasure boats plying the River Spree and Havel and Wannsee lakes. **Stern and Kreisschiffahrt** is the largest company, offering more than a dozen different trips in Berlin and beyond. City boat tours along the Spree are offered daily from April through October, with departures from either Schlossbrücke near Schloss Charlottenburg (Charlottenburg Palace) or from Jannowitzbrücke in eastern Berlin. Trips last approximately 3 hours and cost 20 DM ($13.35).

On the outskirts of Berlin, one of the most popular trips is from Wannsee (near the U-Bahn station) to Glienicker Brücke bridge and Pfaueninsel and back, which takes approximately two hours and costs 12.50 DM ($8.35). In eastside Berlin, Stern and Kreisschiffahrt operates a $3^{1}/_{2}$-hour boat trip from Treptow to Müggelsee, Berlin's largest lake. The round-trip excursion runs through Köpenick, past the Altstadt (Old City) and Schloss Köpenick, to Friedrichshagen, a peaceful suburb, and then onto Müggelsee. The trip costs 15 DM ($10). For more information, contact Stern and Kreisschiffahrt (☎ 61 73 90-0) or drop by the Berlin tourist office.

WALKING TOURS If you're interested in Berlin's dark past—a subject all but ignored by other tour companies—you might wish to join one of several guided walking tours offered in English by **Berlin Walks**. "Infamous Third Reich Sites" takes visitors past buildings that once served as the nucleus of Hitler's regime, including the former location of Hitler's bunker, the headquarters of the Gestapo, Goebbel's propaganda ministry, and Speer's Reich Chancellery. "Where the Wall Was" traces the former boundary of the Wall, tells of extraordinary escape attempts, shows some remaining sections of the Wall, and ends with the remarkable story of its collapse. Others tours include an introductory "Discover Berlin" tour and "Jewish Berlin." Tours last approximately 1½ to 2 hours, take place daily from April through October, and cost 15 DM ($10) for adults, 10 DM ($6.65) for those 26 and under. For more information, call Berlin Walks (☎ 211 6663).

7 Swimming

With approximately 6,000 sports grounds, 70 gyms, 60 indoor and outdoor public swimming pools, as well as numerous bowling alleys, tennis courts, and other sports facilities, Berlin offers a wide range of activities for the sports-minded visitor. If you'd rather watch sports than participate, check *Berlin Programm* for a day-by-day account of spectator events, from ice hockey and soccer to basketball and table tennis.

Berlin may be landlocked, yet swimming is among the city's most popular summer recreations. Berliners and visitors alike flock to **Wannsee,** which boasts Europe's largest lake beach. On a warm sunny day, as many as 20,000 people will take advantage of its facilities, which includes a children's playground, slides, and a terrace with shops and restaurants. If you wish, you can rent one of those huge basketlike beach chairs common to northern Germany, which help shield against winds as well as the sun. The beach, open daily May through September from 7am to 8pm, costs 4 DM ($2.65) for adults and 2 DM ($1.35) for children. To reach it, take the S-Bahn to Nikolassee. Incidentally, don't be surprised to see topless bathing. Wannsee even has a section devoted to bathing au naturel.

If it's winter or you prefer swimming pools, you might try **BLUB,** Buschkrugallee 64, in Britz (☎ 606 60 60). This is a huge bathing-entertainment leisure complex, which contains a pool with 3-feet-high artificial waves, a 396-foot-long water slide (Europe's longest), bathing grottoes complete with mist and music, saunas, steam baths, and a heated outdoor pool open year round. There's also a children's area, two restaurants, and a bar. Admission is 21 DM ($14) for adults, 18 DM ($12) for students, and 16 DM ($10.65) for children, with a 4-hour limit. It's open Monday to Saturday from 10am to 11pm and Sunday from 9am to 11pm. The nearest U-Bahn station is Grenzalee.

Although it's expensive, you may wish to indulge in the hot baths and saunas of the **Thermen,** located in the Europa-Center but with its own entryway at Nürnberger Strasse 7 (☎ 261 60 31 or 261 60 32). Open Monday to Saturday from 10am to midnight, and on Sunday from 10am to 9pm, it charges 30 DM ($20) for 3 hours, which includes use of a thermal swimming pool with an outdoor lane, saunas, steam room, fitness room, TV room, table-tennis room, and a sunning terrace with 150 lounge chairs. If you wish to really pamper yourself and hang out all day, the cost is 34 DM ($22.65). Also available is a solarium, massage, and even a restaurant. Again, bathing is mixed, and in European style, visitors are required to go in the buff.

8

City Strolls

Even though Berlin is a large city, most of its sights, shops, restaurants, and attractions are concentrated in specific neighborhoods—making the city easy to explore on foot. From my experience, visitors usually prefer walking wherever possible, simply because it's sometimes easier than figuring out which bus to take and it allows them to see something of the city en route. Natives, more likely to jump on the subway or bus, are often astounded at the great distances visitors are prepared to walk. How often have you been told by a native, "It's too far to walk," only to discover that it's actually only a 10- or 20-minute hike?

WALKING TOUR 1
ALONG THE KU'DAMM

Start: The Europa-Center on Tauentzienstrasse.
Finish: Wittenbergplatz.
Time: Allow approximately 3 hours, not including stops at museums, shops, and the zoo.
Best Times: Weekdays, when shops are open, or the first Saturday of the month, when shops stay open until 6pm in winter and 4pm in summer.
Worst Times: Tuesday, when the Käthe-Kollwitz Museum is closed, or Sunday, when all shops are closed.

The Kurfürstendamm is Berlin's most famous boulevard, home to the city's most expensive shops, hotels, restaurants, bars, and nightclubs. No visit to Berlin would be complete without at least one stroll down the Kurfürstendamm, affectionately called the Ku'damm by Berliners—who in the same breath are also apt to complain about their beloved boulevard. It's too crowded with tourists, they say, and there are too many bad restaurants out to make a buck. But that doesn't stop them from coming here, especially when the weather's warm and they can sit at one of the outdoor cafes to watch the passing parade. And what a parade it is: tourists from around the world, street performers, shoppers, punks, bejeweled women. There's never a dull moment on the Ku'damm.

By the way, the Ku'damm stretches 2½ miles, but don't worry, we'll cover only the more important eastern half of it, with excursions down the most interesting side streets along the way. It's a loop stroll, ending up at nearby Wittenbergplatz, home of the largest department store on the continent, KaDeWe.

From The Europa-Center to Savignyplatz

1. **The Europa-Center**, easy to spot from far away because of the Mercedes-Benz logo at its top, is 22 stories high and contains offices, a hotel, more than 100 shops and restaurants, a movie theater, cabarets, and a casino. In the main atrium on the ground floor is a strange-looking contraption 42 feet high. It's a clock, showing the time by way of colored water passing through pipes, and is known as the *Fliessenden Uhr* (the "Running Clock"). At the Tauentzien-Strasse exit is a section of the Berlin Wall. Be sure to stop at the Berlin tourist office, located in the Europa-Center but with its own separate entryway on Budapester Strasse, for maps and brochures. Also on Budapester Strasse, down the street from the tourist office, is the:

2. **Zoologischer Garten (Berlin Zoo) and Aquarium**, Budapester Strasse 32. Founded in 1844, it boasts more than 14,000 animals, including a panda. Since you'll probably want to spend at least 3 hours here, you might consider returning to this urban oasis another day.

   It would be hard to miss the:

3. **Kaiser-Wilhelm Gedächtniskirche**, located on Breitscheidplatz next to the Europa-Center. This ruined church looks so out of place beside the modern highrises that surround it. Left as a reminder of World War II and containing a small museum, it marks the beginning of the Ku'damm. Next to it is a colorful church and hexagonal tower, completed in 1961.

   West of the Gedächtniskirche on Breitscheidplatz you might want to:

   TAKE A BREAK At the **Tschibo coffee shop**, you can drink a cup of coffee standing at one of its chest-high counters for 1.95 DM ($1.30) a cup, a real bargain. You'll find this chain, together with the chain Eduscho, at many locations throughout Berlin.

   Follow Ku'damm to:

4. **KPM**, no. 26a, a shop that deals in the exquisite porcelain of the Königliche Porzellan-Manufaktur, one of Berlin's most famous products with a history dating back more than 200 years. It doesn't cost anything to window shop (see Chapter 9, "Shopping").

   The next intersection is Fasanenstrasse, and if you turn right here and walk past the Bristol Hotel Kempinksi, within a minute you'll come to:

5. **Zille Hof**, Fasanenstrasse 14, on your left, a jumble of junk stalls underneath the S-Bahn tracks. Who knows? You might find a treasure here among the crowded and dusty shelves laden with plates, glasses, pots and pans, books, old postcards, clothing, and odds and

ends (see Chapter 9, "Shopping," for more information). If nothing else, its entryway is worth a photograph.

Back on the Ku'damm, continue heading west one block to the corner of Uhlandstrasse. Here, in the median that runs in the middle of the Ku'damm, you'll notice a futuristic-looking row of lights. Believe it or not, it's a:

6. Clock, and here's how it works. Every light of the top row represents 5 hours; the lights beneath it each represent 1 hour; the third row stands for 5 minutes, and the bottom-row lights each represent 1 minute. If you count them all together, they'll tell you the exact time. Thus, if you had two lights on the top row, followed by one light in the next row, three lights on the third, and then two, it would be 11:17am. Berliners consider this a child's game.

☕ **TAKE A BREAK** One of my favorite restaurants on the Ku'damm for a reasonably priced, diverse, and quick meal is **Restaurant Marché Mövenpick,** Ku'damm 14-15, a cafeteria that imitates the neighborhood market with stands offering salads, soups, pasta, daily specials, and desserts. You can linger over a cup of coffee and watch the human parade at a few outside tables. Nearby is **Café Kranzler,** Ku'damm 18, more expensive but oh-so-famous and the boulevard's best-known spot for people-watching. Even if you only order coffee, you can sit at a table here.

Continue walking west along the Ku'damm to Knesebeckstrasse, where you should turn right. Within a couple minutes you'll find yourself on:

7. Savignyplatz, a grassy square lined with restaurants, bars, and turn-of-the-century apartment buildings. Here you'll find some of Berlin's interesting nightlife, including trendy bars and restaurants, so you might want to return here after dark (see Chapter 10, "Berlin After Dark").

North of Savignyplatz is the very special:

8. Berliner Zinnfiguren, Knesebeckstrasse 88, a small family-owned operation that has been producing and selling handcrafted pewter figurines since 1934. Of the approximately 10,000 figures for sale, the most popular are characters of Berlin, including the Potsdamer Soldat (Potsdam soldier), the Blumenfrau (flower vendor), and Frederick the Great playing a flute. Flat unpainted figures begin at a modest 1.50 DM ($1) and make a great and inexpensive souvenir.

From Savignyplatz to Wilmersdorfer Strasse Begin from Savignyplatz's southwest corner, where you'll find the overhead tracks of the S-Bahn. Beneath the arches are a few interesting shops, bars, and restaurants, including a boutique devoted to lamps, gift shops, and an inexpensive Chinese eatery. At the end of the passage is Bleibtreustrasse, home to some interesting and trendy shops. You'll reach the first of these by making a left at Bleibtreustrasse, where you'll soon find on your left:

9. **7 up's,** Bleibtreustrasse 48, a fun women's clothing store specializing in the creations of young Berlin designers working on commission.

    Adjacent to this store is:

10. **Kaufhaus Schrill,** Bleibtreustrasse 46, a wacky clothing store that sells costume jewelry, clothing, and hundreds—if not thousands—of unusual ties (not the kind you'd wear to impress an important business client). There are two parts to this store, with separate entrances side by side.

    If you backtrack and walk farther north on Bleibtreustrasse, within a minute you'll come to:

11. **Astoria** on your right at Bleibtreustrasse 50, which deals in lamps, statues, jewelry, and some furniture, including antiques and reproductions.

    You're now on the corner of Bleibtreustrasse and Kantstrasse. Turn left and head west on Kantstrasse, passing a number of Asian and Middle Eastern restaurants, grocery stores, and shops selling ethnic souvenirs and goods. After approximately 10 minutes you'll reach:

12. **Wilmersdorfer Strasse,** Berlin's main pedestrian shopping lane, where in quick succession you'll find such large department stores as Karstadt, C&A, and Hertie. There are also a number of smaller shops and boutiques, as well as several restaurants. Just west of Wilmersdorfer Strasse is one of Berlin's most endearing institutions:

13. **Harry Lehmann,** Kantstrasse 106. This tiny, family-owned shop has been selling its own perfumes since 1926, using flowers, leaves, and grasses. A vial of perfume makes an inexpensive gift (see Chapter 9, "Shopping," for details).

    If you're tired or decide to spend the rest of the day shopping, you can return to your hotel by taking the subway from Wilmersdorfer Strasse station. Otherwise, take advantage of the many fast-food restaurants in the area, or head back down to the Ku'damm.

> ☕ **TAKE A BREAK** Along Wilmersdorfer Strasse are a number of inexpensive eateries, including cafeterias and restaurants in the two department stores listed above. For a quick stand-up meal, try **Joseph Langer** at Wilmersdorfer Strasse 118, a butcher shop that also sells simple meals and Würste. Across the street is **Nordsee,** Wilmersdorfer Strasse 58, a fast-food fish restaurant.
>
> If you prefer a more relaxed and less hectic environment where you can linger over a meal or drink, head to **Udagawa Japan Imbiss,** Kantstrasse 118, an informal Japanese restaurant serving everything from teriyaki and fried noodles to stews and tempura. **Athener Grill,** Ku'damm 156, near Adenauerplatz, is a cafeteria selling both Greek and Italian food, from moussaka to pizza. Next door is **Ciao Ciao,** a popular Italian restaurant with outdoor seating.

Along the Ku'damm

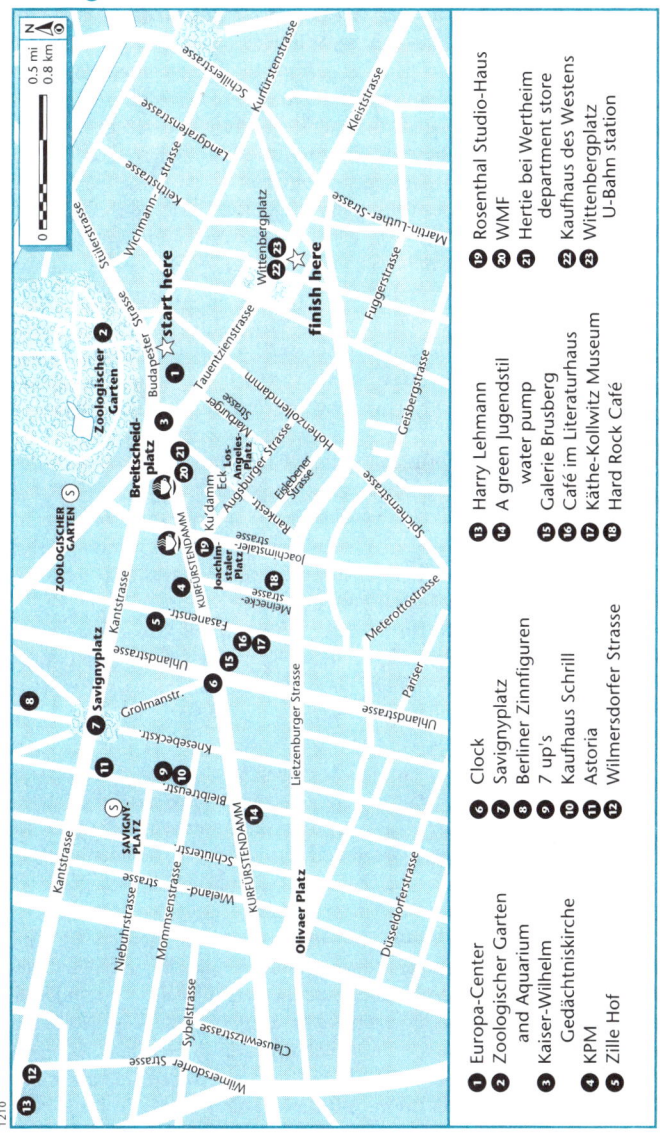

1. Europa-Center
2. Zoologischer Garten and Aquarium
3. Kaiser-Wilhelm Gedächtniskirche
4. KPM
5. Zille Hof
6. Clock
7. Savignyplatz
8. Berliner Zinnfiguren
9. 7 up's
10. Kaufhaus Schrill
11. Astoria
12. Wilmersdorfer Strasse
13. Harry Lehmann
14. A green Jugendstil water pump
15. Galerie Brusberg
16. Café im Literaturhaus
17. Käthe-Kollwitz Museum
18. Hard Rock Café
19. Rosenthal Studio-Haus
20. WMF
21. Hertie bei Wertheim department store
22. Kaufhaus des Westens
23. Wittenbergplatz U-Bahn station

Ⓢ S-Bahn stop

· A popular watering hole in the area is **New York**, Olivaer Platz 15, where Berlin's trendy youth gather throughout the day and late into the evening.

From Wilmersdorfer Strasse to Rankestrasse on the Ku'damm Walk south on Wilmersdorfer Strasse, cross the Ku'damm, and then turn left heading back in the direction of the Gedächtniskirche, this time on the south side of the Ku'damm. You'll pass a number of designer shops on this stretch of the boulevard, including those for Gianni Versace, Jil Sander, Sonia Rykiel, Yves Saint Laurent, and Jean Paul Gaultier. Note the many freestanding display cases along the sidewalk, advertising the wares of nearby shops. During the evening, wares of a different sort are peddled, as the Ku'damm has long been a hot spot for the ladies of the night (prostitution, by the way, is legal in Germany). You'll also pass several Litfassäulen—cylindrical green pillars plastered with posters. A Berlin institution, they were invented in the mid-1800s by a printer named Ernst Litfass as a way to display public notices. Today they carry advertisements for concerts, exhibits, and other events.

On the corner of Bleibtreustrasse and the Ku'damm is another vestige of Berlin's past:

14. **A green Jugendstil water pump** with an ornate handle and dragon spout. Such pumps were installed around 1900 throughout Berlin to keep roads clean (horses being the biggest culprits).

Our first stop on this leg of our journey is the:

15. **Galerie Brusberg,** located on the corner of Uhlandstrasse at Ku'damm 213. The gallery, located up on the first floor of a beautiful century-old patrician home, represents famous artists such as Salvador Dalí, Bernhard Dörries, Max Ernst, Joan Miró, and Picasso, in a setting as good as any museum. Entry is free, so it's worth a spin through to see the current exhibition (see Chapter 9, "Shopping," for hours).

A block farther east on the Ku'damm brings you to Fasanenstrasse, where you should turn right. This wonderful street is lined with turn-of-the-century villas embellished with graceful, ornate facades. On your right you'll see:

16. **Café im Literaturhaus,** surrounded by a lush garden. On the ground floor is an interesting bookstore specializing in biographies of writers and artists and novels in German; upstairs is a wonderful coffee shop. This is a great place for a cup of coffee in the outdoor garden, or, in winter, in its greenhouse. Beside the cafe is:

17. **Käthe-Kollwitz Museum,** located at Fasanenstrasse 24, one of my favorite museums in Berlin. A Berliner, Kollwitz was a genius in capturing human emotions in her portraits. I feel she deserves more worldwide recognition, and the works you see here will stay with you long after you've left Berlin. (See "More Attractions" in Chapter 7, "What to See & Do," for details.)

Returning to the Ku'damm and walking one block farther east brings you to the next side street, Meinekestrasse, where you should turn left to find the:

18. **Hard Rock Café**, Meinekestrasse 21, a worldwide chain featuring rock 'n roll memorabilia and burgers and beer. Prices are a bit high, so stop here to buy your T-shirt and then move on to:
19. **Rosenthal Studio-Haus** at Ku'damm 226, which sells porcelain, Boda crystal, Rosenthal porcelain, and, in the adjoining shop, kitchenware. This is a good place to shop for a wedding gift. Ordinary and not-so-ordinary cookware and tableware is featured at:
20. **WMF**, Ku'damm 229, a well-known chain throughout Germany. (See Chapter 9, "Shopping," for details.) Next door is:
21. **Hertie bei Wertheim department store**, Ku'damm 231, convenient for stocking up on sundry items, film, or a souvenir of Berlin.

    TAKE A BREAK Down in the basement of Wertheim department store—next to the grocery section—is an informal **cafeteria** with various counters devoted to different foods ranging from salads and stews to chicken and beer. Just around the corner from Wertheim is **Eierschale,** Rankestrasse 1, a popular bar open throughout the day and featuring live jazz in the evenings.

    From Rankestrasse to Wittenbergplatz Tauentzienstrasse continues where the Ku'damm ends, running from the Europa-Center to Wittenbergplatz. It's lined with a number of inexpensive and expensive clothing stores, appealing to shoppers of all ages. Since many of the shops are open-fronted, it may be difficult to refrain from the temptation of giving the sales racks a once-over. If you can resist, however, within minutes you'll find yourself at Wittenbergplatz, home of:

22. **Kaufhaus des Westens**, popularly called KaDeWe. It's the star of this walk, and not to be missed is its food department on the sixth floor. It's lavishly stocked with gourmet foods; there are more than 1,000 different kinds of sausages alone. This is a true culinary adventure. (See Chapter 9, "Shopping," for more information.) Also on Wittenbergplatz is the:
23. **Wittenbergplatz U-Bahn Station**, one of Berlin's most beautiful stations, with art nouveau grillwork and oak ticket booths. In front of the station is a large black-and-gold sign that lists "Places of terror we should never be allowed to forget," including Auschwitz, Dachau, and Bergen-Belsen, all World War II concentration camps. It's a strange place for a memorial, as commuters and shoppers rush by, seemingly oblivious to the sign and its message.

    Inside the station you'll find an odd electromechanical scale, one of 55 such mechanical treasures dating from the 1920s still in operation in Berlin's subways. It's on Bahnsteig (platform) I, down the escalator (you need a valid subway ticket to enter the platform). By inserting a 10-Pfennig coin and stepping onto the weighing platform, you'll receive a card printed with your weight in kilos and the date.

156 City Strolls

WINDING DOWN The **KaDeWe's food emporium** on the sixth floor is a good place to dine as well as shop. There are separate counters with stools spread throughout, each specializing in a different food or drink: Choose from pasta, salads, grilled chicken, wines, and much more. You can order take-out and eat your goodies on one of the benches on Wittenbergplatz. Another good place for take-out food—especially if you're vegetarian—is **Einhorn,** Wittenbergplatz 5-6, on the opposite end of the square from KaDeWe. A natural foods shop, it offers daily specials such as vegetarian lasagna, spinach casserole, and vegetarian moussaka.

WALKING TOUR 2
BERLIN-MITTE (EASTERN BERLIN)

Start: Unter den Linden at Brandenburger Tor.
Finish: Nikolaiviertel.
Time: Allow approximately 3 hours, not including stops along the way.
Best Times: Weekdays when museums aren't as crowded, or Sunday when they're free.
Worst Times: Monday when museums are closed, or Tuesday, when the Berlin Antique and Flea Market is closed.

This stroll brings you through what used to be the heart of old Berlin before World War II, later serving as East Germany's capital. From the historic boulevard Unter den Linden, you'll pass Museumsinsel and end your tour at the Nikolaiviertel (Nikolai Quarter), a restored neighborhood of restaurants and pubs.

From Brandenburger Tor to Schlossbrücke The easiest way to get to Brandenburger Tor is via S-Bahn to Unter den Linden station. A more picturesque way to get there is to take bus 100 from Bahnhof Zoo to the Brandenburger Tor stop. In any case, the first stop on our tour is one of Berlin's most famous and most photographed structures:

1. Brandenburger Tor. Modeled after the Ppropylaea in Athens, the gate was built by Carl Gotthard Langhans in 1788–91 as the west entrance into Under den Linden. The only remaining city gate of 14, it is topped by a Quadriga created by Johann Gottfried Schadow, which consists of the goddess of victory in a chariot pulled by four steeds. After Napoléon's triumph over Prussia, the Quadriga was carted off to Paris by the French in 1806, where it remained until Marshal Blücher retrieved it in 1814. It was severely damaged in the war but has since been restored.

After the Wall went up in 1961, the Brandenburger Tor became inaccessible from West Berlin, making it a symbol of a divided Berlin. After the November 1989 revolution, many Berliners, from both East and West, gathered here to rejoice and to dance together on top of the Wall. I myself witnessed part of the celebration in the months that followed, as people from around the world chiseled at the Wall for a piece of history. At the end of February 1990, the East German government began tearing down the Wall in anticipation of a united Germany. Finally, for the first time in decades, people could pass freely from Strasse des 17. Juni through Brandenburger Tor to Unter den Linden in East Berlin.

Brandenburger Tor is flanked by two guardhouses, one serving as a branch of the Berlin tourist office and open daily from 10am to 6pm, and the other housing a "Room of Silence," open daily from 11am to 4pm for quiet reflection for people of all nationalities and beliefs. If you face west, you can see the Siegessäule (Victory Column) far in the distance, erected in the 1870s to commemorate three victorious wars and topped with the gilded goddess of victory. North of Brandenburger Tor is a large, solemn-looking building:

2. **The Reichstag** (Parliament). Completed in 1894 in Neo-Renaissance style to serve the needs of Bismarck's united Germany, it had its darkest hour on the night of February 17, 1933, when a mysterious fire broke out. The Nazi government blamed the German Communist party for setting the blaze, and used the incident as a reason for arresting Communist party members and other opponents, thus abolishing such basic democratic rights as personal liberty and freedom of the press. Damaged in World War II, the Reichstag was restored with the exception of its dome. On October 3, 1990, Germany's official ceremony of unification took place in front of the Reichstag, followed the next day by a meeting of the German parliament (both East and West), the first joint session held in the Reichstag after more than four decades of separation. The Reichstag is now closed to the public, undergoing extensive renovation according to plans by British architect Sir Norman Foster in preparation of the German parliament's move from Bonn to Berlin by the turn of the century. In 1995, the Reichstag became the center of international attention when artists Christo and Jeanne-Claude wrapped the historic building in silver fabric.

The square that stretches east of Brandenburger Tor is:

3. **Pariser Platz**, once a pretty plaza with formal gardens and fountains. Plans call for restoring the square to its former grandeur and reconstructing the American Embassy and Adlon Hotel, both of which once faced the square. How different the land you now see surrounding Pariser Platz, barren after the removal of the Wall, will look in 10 years' time. For now, Pariser Platz is filled mostly with tourists, sausage stands, and vendors from eastern European countries selling souvenir pieces of the Wall (or, most likely, bogus chunks from elsewhere), Russian watches, dolls, postcards, helmets, and military insignia of former East European regimes.

Walk through Pariser Platz, passing on your left what may be Berlin's most attractive public rest room, built to resemble a Litfassäule. You are now on Berlin's most historic boulevard:

Berlin-Mitte

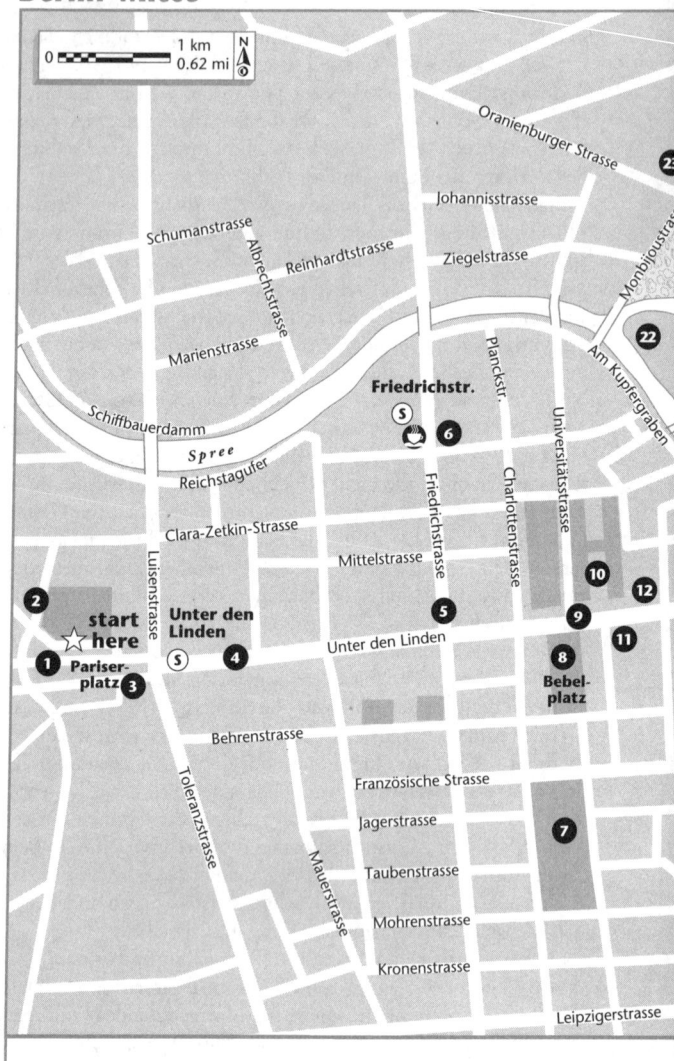

1. Brandenburger Tor
2. Reichstag
3. Pariser Platz
4. Unter den Linden
5. Friedrichstrasse
6. Berliner Antik- und Flohmarkt
7. Gendarmenmarkt
8. Bebelplatz
9. Equestrian statue of Frederick the Great
10. Humboldt Universität
11. Deutsche Staatsoper
12. Neue Wache
13. Zeughaus
14. Schlossbrücke
15. Schlossplatz

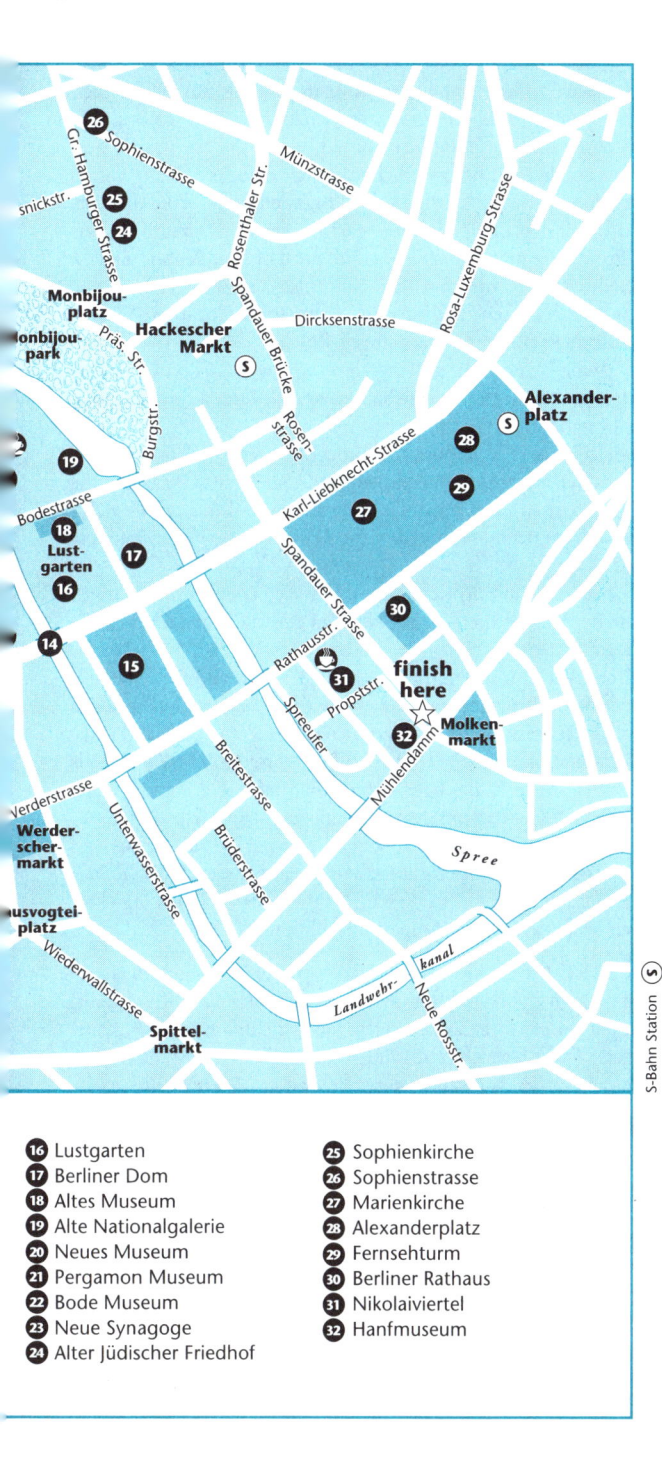

- **16** Lustgarten
- **17** Berliner Dom
- **18** Altes Museum
- **19** Alte Nationalgalerie
- **20** Neues Museum
- **21** Pergamon Museum
- **22** Bode Museum
- **23** Neue Synagoge
- **24** Alter Jüdischer Friedhof
- **25** Sophienkirche
- **26** Sophienstrasse
- **27** Marienkirche
- **28** Alexanderplatz
- **29** Fernsehturm
- **30** Berliner Rathaus
- **31** Nikolaiviertel
- **32** Hanfmuseum

4. **Unter den Linden.** The Elector used to pass this way to the Tiergarten to hunt, and by 1675 this was a paved road. In the centuries that followed, it was the lifeline of old Berlin: the city's most fashionable and liveliest boulevard. Today, after decades of being cut off from western Berlin by the Wall at Brandenburger Tor, the tree-lined Unter den Linden is once again the center of a reunited Berlin. From here you have a view of the front of Brandenburger Tor, topped by the quadriga. Unter den Linden is 200 feet wide and stretches seven-tenths of a mile, from Brandenburger Tor to Schlossbrücke (formerly Marx-Engels-Brücke).

With the Brandenburger Tor behind you, walk east on Unter den Linden (which means "under the lime trees"). After a couple blocks, you'll reach:

5. **Friedrichstrasse**, an important thoroughfare. Before World War II, this was Berlin's busiest intersection, and Café Kranzler, now on the Ku'damm, used to sit on this corner. At this point, Berlin's grand old buildings begin—most from the 1800s and now painstakingly restored.

Take a left onto Friedrichstrasse, and walk a couple minutes north to the overpass of the S-Bahn. Here, underneath the arches of the track to the right, is the:

6. **Berliner Antik- und Flohmarkt** (Berlin Antique and Flea Market), where about 60 vendors sell everything from glassware and lamps to porcelain, jewelry, books, pocketwatches, canes, and odds and ends. Prices aren't cheap, but it's fun walking through. (The market is open Wed–Mon 11am–6pm.) Here, too, inside the market, is the **Heinrich-Zille-Museum,** featuring drawings and personal items of one of Berlin's most well-known and beloved graphic artists and caricaturists. A chronicler of turn-of-the-century Berlin life, Zille is particularly known for his sketches of the poor and working class, which he depicted with compassionate humor.

☕ TAKE A BREAK On Friedrichstrasse, just before the overhead S-Bahn tracks and station, a handful of **Imbisse** (food stalls) selling a variety of inexpensive fast food, including Würste, hamburgers, Turkish snacks, fish, and Chinese dishes. Since many have tables and chairs, you can sit down here and eat your purchase.

Back on Unter den Linden, continue walking one block east, taking a right onto Charlottenstrasse. After a few short blocks, you'll soon find yourself at the historic:

7. **Gendarmenmarkt**, once considered one of Berlin's most attractive squares and formerly the site of Berlin's main market. Totally destroyed during World War II, it has been painstakingly restored and features three neoclassical buildings. Most important is the Schauspielhaus in the middle, designed by Karl Friedrich Schinkel in 1821 and now a concert house that is flanked by the German and French cathedrals. The German cathedral, which suffered damage from a fire in 1994 and is presently being restored yet again, will

eventually hold an exhibition relating to German history formerly housed in the Reichstag.

The French cathedral, located on the north end of Gendarmenmarkt, is home of a Hugenottenmuseum (Huguenot Museum), as well as a carillon that features free concerts every second and fourth Saturday at 3pm. Most interesting for us, however, is the fact that you can walk up the winding stairs to the top of the dome, where there's an outside balustrade offering an unparalleled view of Berlin-Mitte—and more construction cranes than you've probably ever seen concentrated in one spot. Entrance to the observation platform is free, and it's open daily in winter from 10am to 4pm (closed during inclement weather) and in summer from 10am to 6pm.

Take a left onto Markgrafenstrasse, which runs in front of the Schauspielhaus, and a right at Behrenstrasse, which brings you to:

8. **Bebelplatz**, dominated by St.-Hedwigs-Kathedrale. On May 10, 1933, the Nazis staged a massive book-burning here, destroying books deemed offensive to the regime, including works by Thomas Mann, Sigmund Freud, Karl Marx, Albert Einstein, Kafka, Jack London, and Ernest Hemingway.

In front of Bebelplatz, in the median on Unter den Linden, is an:

9. **Equestrian statue of Frederick the Great**, the ruler responsible for much of Berlin's Prussian grandeur, depicted here surveying his domain. On the other side of the street is:

10. **Humboldt-Universität** (Humboldt University), where Hegel, Marx, and the Brothers Grimm taught. Take a right onto Unter den Linden and walk east (with your back toward Brandenburg Tor), and soon on your right just past Bebelplatz you'll see a building that looks like a Corinthian temple. It's the:

11. **Deutsche Staatsoper**, designed by Georg Wenzeslaus von Knobelsdorff in the 1740s and rebuilt after the war. Today it serves as a venue for opera, ballet, and concerts. Next on Unter den Linden, to your left, is the:

12. **Neue Wache** (New Guardhouse). Easy to spot with its columns resembling a Greek temple, it was built from 1816 to 1818 according to plans designed by architect Karl Friedrich Schinkel. In 1931 it became a memorial to German soldiers killed in World War II; in 1960 it became a memorial to victims of fascism and militarism, with an eternal flame burning for the Unknown Soldier and Unknown Resistance Fighter. Its purpose was changed once again in 1993, when it became Germany's primary memorial for all victims of war and totalitarianism. The eternal flame lit by the East German Communists was extinguished forever, and in its place is a life-sized version of Käthe Kollwitz's sculpture *Mother with Dead Son.*

Beside the Neue Wache is the baroque:

13. **Zeughaus** (Arsenal) at Unter den Linden 2. Built in the 17th century as an arsenal for the Prussian army, it—together with Charlottenburg Palace—is considered a pinnacle of baroque

construction in Berlin. Of special note are the 22 sculpted masks of dying warriors by Andreas Schlüter above the windows of the inner courtyard. After World War II, the Zeughaus served as East Germany's Museum of German History, with a decidedly socialist slant. Today it holds special changing exhibitions relating to German history.

TAKE A BREAK Across the street from the Neue Wache and Zeughaus is the equally famous **Opernpalais** (Unter den Linden 5), which contains several eating establishments under one roof. Occupying part of a palace originally built in 1733 and faithfully restored after World War II, it is best known for the ground-floor **Operncafé,** a coffeehouse offering more than 50 varieties of tortes and with indoor dining or outdoor seating in a pretty square. There's also an outdoor Imbiss (food stall) here serving snacks and drinks. Another good place for budget dining is the **Casino** in the Staatsbibliothek (Unter den Linden 8). This inexpensive cafeteria, located in the National Library, offers a limited number of soups, salads, and daily specials.

Unter den Linden terminates at the:
14. Schlossbrücke (Palace Bridge), designed by Schinkel. Its eight statues, also by Schinkel, are goddesses and warriors from Greek mythology. At the base of the bridge, to the left, is one of several companies offering 1-hour sightseeing tours of Berlin by boat. (See "Organized Tours" in Chapter 7, "What to See & Do," for more information on boat trips.)

Museumsinsel After crossing the Schlossbrücke, you will find yourself on Museumsinsel, named for the several important museums located on this island in the middle of the Spree. To your right you will see a rather unimpressive square:
15. Schlossplatz (formerly Marx-Engels-Platz), filled with drab socialist architecture. The most conspicuous building here is the Palast der Republic, once popular in East Berlin for its various concert halls and restaurants. Insulated with asbestos, it is now closed and will soon be demolished, to be replaced with a new conference center. It occupies the former site of Berlin's royal palace, once the largest baroque structure north of the Alps. Although what remained after World War II could have been salvaged, the Politbüro dynamited it in 1950 as a symbol of "Prussian imperialism."

Now turn your attention to the tree-lined square at the left, the:
16. Lustgarten (Pleasure Garden), once the site of the royal palace's botanical garden but paved by the Nazis for parades and rallies.

Facing the Lustgarten to rhe right is the most striking building here, the:
17. Berliner Dom (Berlin Cathedral), erected at the turn of the century in Italian Renaissance style to serve as the court church of

Hohenzollerns. After decades of restoration following massive World War II destruction, it reopened in 1994 and contains the tombs of Queen Sophie Charlotte and her husband, Friedrich I, both designed by Andreas Schlüter. Also facing the Lustgarten is the:

18. **Altes Museum** (Old Museum), which stages changing exhibitions devoted to art and objects of ancient times. The first museum constructed on Museumsinsel and built from plans by Schinkel, it features 18 Ionic columns and resembles a Greek temple. You can go inside and take a look at its famous rotunda for free.

    Behind the Altes Museum, to the right, is the:

19. **Alte Nationalgalerie** (Old National Gallery), which features art from the 19th century, including French impressionists and early German expressionists. (See "More Attractions" in Chapter 7.)

    From the Alte Nationalgalerie, turn right onto Bodestrasse and walk west, crossing the bridge over the Spree and turning right onto Kupfergraben. As you walk north, you will see across the Spree to your right the:

20. **Neues Museum** (New Museum), constructed in the 1840s but closed since World War II. Under restoration for decades, it will someday house the combined collections of east and west Berlin's Egyptian museums. Just past the Neues Museum is the star of this walk, the:

21. **Pergamon Museum**, the most important and famous museum on Museumsinsel. Named after its most prized treasure, the Pergamon Altar (160–180 B.C.), this museum of architectural wonders also contains art from Asia, the Near East, the Middle East, and German folk art. Don't miss it. (See "The Top Attractions" in Chapter 7, "What to See & Do," for details.) Past the Pergamon to the north you'll find the:

22. **Bode Museum**, which contains the Egyptian Museum, the Early Christian and Byzantine Collection, Museum for Primeval and Early History, the Sculpture Collection, and the Picture Gallery with art from the 14th to 18th century. (See "More Attractions" in Chapter 7 for details.)

    TAKE A BREAK There are two **cafeterias** on Museumsinsel, in the Altes Museum and in the Pergamon Museum—and since they have their own entrances you don't have pay museum admission fees to enjoy a drink or snack here. For more substantial dining, just a minute's walk west of the Pergamon Museum is **Lucky Strike,** Georgenstrasse 5, underneath the arches of the elevated S-Bahn tracks. It features American food ranging from burgers to gumbo. On the opposite side of Museumsinsel, behind the Berliner Dom across the Spree river, is the popular **T.G.I. Fridays**, Karl-Liebknecht-Strasse 5, an American chain serving a wide variety of American favorites. A plus is the outdoor dining in summer—or perhaps it's the 400 or so cocktails offered by the restaurant's bar. Another great choice in dining is **Oren**, Oranienburger Strasse 28, located next to the Neue Synagoge (described below). It offers an intriguing menu of Middle Eastern, Jewish, and international vegetarian dishes at reasonable prices.

From Museumsinsel to Alexanderplatz Make a right out of the Bode Museum, cross the bridge, and walk along Monbijoustrasse to Oranienburger Strasse. Across the street to the left is the gold-domed:

23. **Neue Synagoge—Centrum Judaicum** (New Synagogue), first built in the 1860s after designs by Eduard Knoblauch and August Stüler, both pupils of Schinkel, with Byzantine and Moorish influences. Only slightly damaged in the Kristallnacht Nazi rampage against Jews in 1938, it was later bombed in 1943 and destroyed by fire. After extensive renovation, it reopened in 1995 and houses an exhibit chronicling its long history and the Jewish community in Berlin.

Monbijoustrasse stops at Oranienburger Strasse, continuing on the other side as Krausnickstrasse. In marked contrast to the pomposity of Unter den Linden, this street still has buildings that look like World War II ended only yesterday, with crumbling facades pockmarked with shrapnel. This was once a major Jewish settlement, and since the fall of the Wall, has become a popular address for young artists in search of inexpensive rents for galleries and shops.

Take a right at the next street, Grosse Hamburger Strasse, where almost immediately on your left you will find another landmark from the neighborhood's Jewish past, the:

24. **Alter Jüdischer Friedhof** (Old Jewish Cemetery). Near the entrance are statues of concentration camp inmates, marking the spot of a former Jewish old people's home that was used by the Nazis as a gathering spot for Jews being shipped to Auschwitz and Theresienstadt. Behind the memorial is an open, grassy meadow, which served from 1672 to 1827 as Berlin's oldest Jewish cemetery. In 1943 it was desecrated and levelled by Nazis but still contains the tombstone of Moses Mendelssohn (1729–86), a noted philosopher and Jewish community leader. Quiet and peaceful, the empty cemetery is a powerful commentary of Jewish persecution and a nation gone mad. Future plans call for the construction of a Jewish school next to the cemetery.

Just north of the cemetery is the:

25. **Sophienkirche,** built in 1712 and renovated in neo-baroque style in 1892. Walk north on Grosse Hamburger Strasse past Sophienkirche, taking the next right onto:

26. **Sophienstrasse,** lined with tenements dating from the 18th and 19th centuries. In marked contrast to the neglected Krausnickstrasse, the buildings here were restored under the Communists as a kind of glorification of working-class life. About halfway down the street is the Heimatmuseum Berlin-Mitte, Sophienstrasse 23, which documents the history of Berlin's most important precinct with photographs, models, and memorabilia. Entrance is free.

At the south end of Sophienstrasse, take a right onto Rosenthaler Strasse, turning left at the stop light and walking under the S-Bahn tracks in the direction of the TV tower. Underneath the tracks is an indoor flea market, open every day except Mondays. Continue walking along the street as it makes an S-curve into An der Spandauer Brücke and Spandauer Strasse, ending at Karl-Liebknecht-Strasse. Across the street is a small brick church, looking rather out of place here with the huge TV Tower rising behind it. This is the:

27. Marienkirche (Church of St. Mary), the second-oldest church in Berlin. First constructed in the 13th century and then added to through the centuries, it's noted for its marble baroque pulpit by Andreas Schlüter. Take a look at the *Dance of Death* mural in its tower hall at the back of the church. Painted in the 15th century, the mural was subsequently covered up until it was rediscovered in 1860. The church is open Monday through Thursday from 10am to noon and 1 to 5pm and on Saturday from noon to 5pm.

Behind the church sprawls:

28. Alexanderplatz. Named after Czar Alexander I, it served as an oxen market and an exercise field in Berlin's early days, becoming the center of East Berlin during the decades of Communist rule. Future plans call for the construction of a huge office-and-shopping complex, complete with 40-story skyscrapers. In the meantime, its landmark building is the towering:

29. Fernsehturm. Rising 1,200 feet, this television tower is Berlin's tallest structure and contains an observation platform and a revolving restaurant. Before the Wall fell, of course, this was one of the few places East Germans could go for a panoramic glimpse of the West—and it's still a popular attraction. If the sky is clear, the view is stupendous. (See "More Attractions" in Chapter 7 for information.) If you wish to end your tour here, you can take the S-Bahn from Alexanderplatz to Bahnhof Zoo and beyond.

TAKE A BREAK The **Tele-Café,** a revolving cafe 650 feet above ground in the Fernsehturm, is a great—though slightly expensive—place for a snack. Making a complete turn every hour, it offers unparalleled views of Berlin and a limited menu of coffee, cakes, ice cream, beer, wine, and warm and cold dishes. More affordable are the fast-food outlets at **Die Berliner Markthalle** on the north end of Alexanderplatz, an indoor shopping complex. McDonald's, Ihre Frish-Backstübe (good for sandwiches and pastries), Nordsee (serving fish), and AlexanderBräu (a microbrewery serving German specialties) are open seven days a week.

From Alexanderplatz through the Nikolaiviertel At the southwestern end of Alexanderplatz, on the corner of Rathausstrasse and Spandauer Strasse, is an imposing red-brick building topped with a tower. This is the:

166 City Strolls

30. Berliner Rathaus (City Hall). Built in the 1860s, it served as the seat of Berlin's municipal administration—and since reunification has the same function. Note the frieze around the entire building: It's a stone chronicle of the history of Berlin.

Walk past the front facade of the Rathaus, cross Spandauer Strasse, and to your left you'll see a small side street, Am Nussbaum, leading to church spires. This is the beginning of the:

31. Nikolaiviertel (Nikolai Quarter), a re-created neighborhood of Berlin as it was centuries ago. In the center is the Nikolaikirche (St. Nicholas' Church), regarded as Berlin's oldest church even though it was destroyed during World War II and was for the most part rebuilt. It dates back to 1230 but its architectural style has changed several times since then. In fact, all the buildings you see around the church are new—many built by craftspeople according to plans of earlier buildings that existed elsewhere. Facing the church, walk around it to the right, where you'll see several shops selling handcrafted items. A block farther behind the church is a busy street called Mühlendamm, where, at Mühlendamm 5, you'll find one of Berlin's more surprising museums, the:

32. Hanfmuseum (Hemp Museum), striking confirmation that eastern Berlin is no longer the city it was. Very alternative, the small exhibition takes a semi-scientific approach in documenting the history and use of this controversial weed, with products made of hemp (the hemp wig looks like a real winner), plants (accompanied by a note of official permission), displays showing medicinal uses of the drug, a shop selling hemp products and books, and a basement cafe with literature, including the grandfather of them all, *High Times*. Opened in 1995, it's doubtful whether the museum will pull in enough visitors to survive, but its existence in this location certainly is an anomaly.

As the Nikolaiviertel is a small district of mostly apartments and bars, explore it at your leisure, stopping off for a meal or a beer at one of the places below.

WINDING DOWN   Among the best-known *Gaststätte* in the Nikolaiviertel are **Zum Nussbaum**, Am Nussbaum 3, modeled after a 16th-century pub, and **GeorgBrau**, Spree Ufer 4, a microbrewery beside the Spree river with outdoor seating. A five-minute walk away is one of Berlin's most famous restaurants, **Zur Letzten Instanz**, Waisenstrasse 14-16, open since 1621 and claiming to be Berlin's oldest eating establishment. It serves Berlin specialties.

WALKING TOUR 3
PRENZLAUER BERG

Start: Senefelderplatz U-Bahn station, Saarbrücker Strasse exit.
Finish: Eberswalder Strasse U-Bahn station.

Time: Approximately 2 hours, not including stops along the way.
Best Times: Tuesday through Friday, when everything is open.
Worst Times: Monday, when the Museum of Berlin Working-Class Life is closed; Saturday or Sunday, when the Jewish cemetery is closed.

Located just north of Berlin-Mitte, Prenzlauer Berg has been the domain of the working class ever since the 19th century, when five-story tenements were built to house as many people as possible, often in miserable conditions. Families of 10 shared 2-room flats; the poorest lived in damp cellars. Little wonder that artist Käthe Kollwitz (1867–1945), who lived in Prenzlauer Berg for more than 50 years, became Berlin's best graphic commentator on the working class, capturing despair and abject poverty and also moments of tenderness in powerful sketches and sculpture.

During the years of Communist rule, Prenzlauer Berg was as alternative as the system allowed, a place for dissidents, rebels, and political activists. Of course, in Prenzlauer Berg rebellion was forced to take a subtle and underground form, expressing itself in secret meetings and unadvertised, spontaneous cultural events. In 1989, Prenzlauer Berg's Gethsemanekirche became the meeting place for a group of dissidents who led the uprising against the East German regime, providing protection for protesters, serving as a forum for debate, and disseminating information.

Today, Prenzlauer Berg has remained faithful to its working-class origins. Its spirit of resistance is still directed at the unified German government, as the residents of Prenzlauer Berg try to preserve some aspects of socialism and ward off the more onerous aspects of capitalism. It has become one of Berlin's most hip addresses for alternative living, and although some buildings have been renovated (forcing occupants to seek cheaper rents elsewhere), many 19th-century tenements remain derelict and crumbling, neglected since World War II. There are also postwar housing blocks, nondescript and impersonal legacies of Communist rule. If you want to know what Berlin was like around 1900, or even in the 1980s, head for Prenzlauer Berg. This is the old Berlin, unadorned, simple, and proud.

From Senefelderplatz to Kollwitzplatz After emerging from the Saarbrücker Strasse exit of the Senefelderplatz U-Bahn station, look across the street for:

1. **Pfefferberg,** a former brewery that is now one of Prenzlauer Berg's main alternative venues for concerts, theater, art exhibitions, film showings, and other events. It was one of many empty buildings in Prenzlauer Berg seized by squatters following the fall of the Wall. In an attempt to curb what could become epidemic, German authorities banned all future house occupations and sought to regulate most of the existing squats. Pfefferberg, occupied by artists and musicians, was allowed to survive and is still going strong. This area, by the way, was once famous for its breweries and beer gardens, which served as social centers for the working class.

Walking uphill on Schönhauser Allee, you immediately reach:

2. **Senefelderplatz,** first laid out in 1880 and named after Alois Senefelder (1771–1834), inventor of lithography and whose statue graces the square. Plans call for the square to be restored to its former glory, complete with a historic pissoir that was torn down in 1983 due to its neglected state.

Continue walking on Schönhauser Alle in the same direction, passing Senefelderplatz and crossing Metzer Strasse. On your right, at Schönhauser Allee 22, is a yellow brick building dating from the 1800s that once served as a:

3. **Jewish old age home.** Its occupants had to be at least 60 years old and had to have lived in Berlin at least 15 years. During the Nazi regime, it was used as a gathering spot for transport of Jews to concentration camps. Ukranian girls lived in its basement, forced into labor for Telefunken AG and working secretly in the cellars of the Schultheiss brewery. Today the building serves as a police station.

Just past the police station is the old:

4. **Jüdischer Friedhof** (Jewish cemetery), testimony to the fact that Jews were among the first people to settle Prenzlauer Berg. Laid out in 1827 after the older Jewish cemetery in Berlin-Mitte (covered in the previous walking tour) reached capacity, it became the final resting place of many prominent citizens, including composer Giacomo Meyerbeer (1791–1864), publisher Leopold Ullstein (1826–1899), and painter Max Liebermann (1847–1935). Closed by the Nazis in 1942 and subsequently vandalized, today it is a peaceful place, with gravestones shielded by a canopy of birch trees. You'll notice that, in accordance with Jewish tradition, stones rather than flowers adorn the graves. An inscription at the entrance admonishes guests: "Here you stand in silence, but when you turn away, do not remain silent." Another sign advises that men must cover their heads before entering the cemetery. It's open Monday through Thursday from 8am to 4pm and Friday from 8am to 1pm.

Retrace your steps back south on Schönhauser Allee, turn left at the first street, Metzer Strasse, and then make an immediate left onto:

5. **Kollwitzstrasse,** named after the famous artist Käthe Kollwitz who used to live on this street. This street, in my opinion, epitomizes working-class Prenzlauer Berg, with the sounds of children's laughter, the five-story tenements with crumbling stucco facades (contrasting sharply with the brightly painted facades of those that have been recently renovated), and couples pushing baby carriages along the tree-lined street. Just a couple of years ago there used to be Trabant and Wartburg parked here as well, but strict automobile regulations have weeded out most of these.

When you reach Knaackstrasse you'll want to turn right. First, however, look across the street for the small statue at Kollwitzstrasse 59 of a mother trying to shield her child from the death and

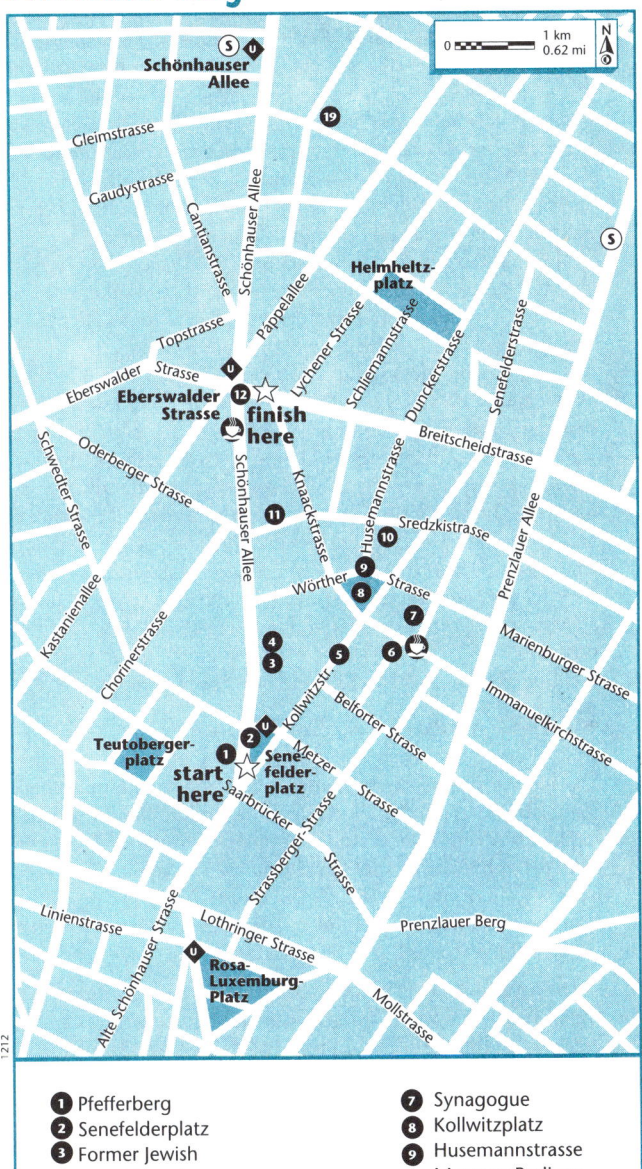

Prenzlauer Berg

1. Pfefferberg
2. Senefelderplatz
3. Former Jewish old age home
4. Jüdischer Friedhof
5. Kollwitzstrasse
6. Wasserturm
7. Synagogue
8. Kollwitzplatz
9. Husemannstrasse
10. Museum Berliner Arbeiterleben
11. Schultheiss-Brauerei
12. Eberswalder Strasse U-Bahn station

destruction of World War II. Titled *Die Mutter* ("The Mother"), it's the work of Käthe Kollwitz, who lived at this site from 1891 to 1943, together with her physican husband who served the needs of the poor. The house was destroyed in World War II; now the site is a vacant lot. To view more of the artist's work, visit the Käthe-Kollwitz Museum near the Ku'damm (covered in Walking Tour 1, above), housed—incongruously, it seems, after you've visited her old neighborhood—in a beautiful turn-of-the-century villa.

Now back to Knaackstrasse. See those bell-shaped containers up ahead? They're recycling bins for glass, paper, and other reusable materials. Usually painted green or white, they're found all over the city. Germany has long been a proponent of recycling.

To your right just past the bins is the:

6. Wasserturm (Water Tower), Knaackstrasse 23, a round, brick building. Constructed in the mid-1800s, it was part of the city's first waterworks, built after an epidemic of cholera swept the city. Until the tower's construction, residents took water directly from the Spree river or from wells. Capitalizing on its height and the force of gravity to conduct water to the lower, surrounding houses, the tower fell into disuse in 1915 after the introduction of mechanical pumps. In 1933 the Nazis found another use for the tower, turning it into a secret concentration camp and murdering several dozen political prisoners in its cellar. Today it serves as a rather unique apartment building, complete with a children's outdoor playground.

☕ **TAKE A BREAK** Across the street from the water tower are two new enterprising restaurants catering primarly to a youthful clientele drawn to Prenzlauer Berg's bohemian atmosphere. **Tantalus**, Knaackstrasse 24, occupies the ground floor of a decaying building and boasts an indoor mural and ornate ceiling dating from the turn of the century. A cafe/bar, it opens at 2pm daily. Next door is **Café Anita Wronski**, Knaackstrasse 26-28, a pleasant and relaxing split-level cafe. Opening at 10am daily, it offers a tempting breakfast buffet, as well as daily specials.

From the tower walk north on Rykestrasse, where immediately to your left at no. 53 is an attractive brick building with an arched entryway and star of David on its gate. This is a:

7. Synagogue, built shortly after 1900. It was one of the few not destroyed during the Kristallnacht pogrom in 1938 but was later closed down by the Nazis. It is still a synagogue (and therefore has the telltale policemen keeping guard outside to prevent vandalism and terrorism) and in fact was the only synagogue in operation in former East Berlin. It shares quarters with Volkssolidärität, a workers' union.

As you walk along Rykestrasse, it's hard not to notice the marked difference between tenements that have been renovated and painted and those that are in acute disrepair. Some balconies look so precarious that you hate to tempt fate by walking beneath them. Make a left onto Wörther Strasse, which brings you to the spiritual and cultural heart of Prenzlauer Berg:

8. Kollwitzplatz. An expanse of green with a playground, it also contains the Käthe-Kollwitz Memorial, a statue of the artist in her seventies. As a long-time resident of this working-class neighborhood, Kollwitz was a genius at portraying the poverty, misery, despair, and fear of the people around her, as well as emotions like love and tenderness. Mothers with children were especially favorite subjects, like the one you saw earlier. Sadly, her statue here was marred by graffiti the last time I saw it. Being who she was, Kollwitz would have probably sympathized with the youths who did it and may have even captured their actions in one of her powerful drawings.

Kollwitzplatz is surrounded by a few alternative establishments, including a neighborhood theater, several bars, and galleries. At the north end of Kollwitzplatz is:

9. Husemannstrasse, singled out by the old East German regime to showcase proletariat life in Prenzlauer Berg at the turn of the century. In 1987, as part of the city's 750th birthday celebrations, Husemannstrasse was renovated into a sort of open-air museum of a working-class neighborhood, but in Hollywood-like fashion with scrubbed, painted facades, picturesque street lamps and signs, and quaint shops. Prenzlauer Berg never looked so good. After the fall of the Wall, more pressing problems in the city pushed Husemannstrasse back into obscurity, and neglect has left its mark here just like in much of the district.

Head north on Husemannstrasse. On your right will soon be the:

10. Museum Berliner Arbeiterleben (Museum of Berlin Working-Class Life), Husemannstrasse 12. Occupying the ground floor of a 19th-century tenement, this small museum documents working-class life at the turn of the century with photographs, furniture, household items, and a two-room flat decorated as it might have looked in 1900. In a typical living arrangement, better-off families lived on the first few floors of the main building facing the street, while poorer families were relegated to the crowded buildings in inner courtyards, many of which received hardly any sunlight. The poorest lived in tiny attics or, worse yet, in dark and damp cellars (in the late 1800s, one-tenth of Berlin's population lived in basements). As many as 10 people shared two-room flats consisting of a kitchen and a living/sleeping room, including the married couple of the household, their children, perhaps their extended family, and even single workers who paid rent to sleep on the kitchen floor. As the only heated room, the kitchen was the center of family life, where meals were cooked, clothes washed, and cottage industries pursued. The museum heralds these workers and is open every day except Monday from 10am to 6pm.

Back to the real world, turn left onto Sredzkistrasse. That brick building on the right is the:

11. Schultheiss-Brauerei, a Jugendstil structure built in 1890 and formerly the city's largest brewery. It's a rare example of late-19th-century brewery constuction but today serves as a furniture store. At the corner of the former brewery is a tower, today serving as a youth club and cultural center.

Take a right onto Schönhauser Allee. Note how the U-Bahn rises slowly above ground here, becoming elevated at the:

12. Eberswalder Strasse U-Bahn station. Opened in 1913 and nicknamed *Magistratsschirm* ("magistrate's umbrella"), the elevated track serves as a shelter on inclement days for people walking along Schönhauser Allee.

WINDING DOWN For a quick meal or snack, stop by the **Konnopkes Imbiss** food stall, located underneath the elevated U-Bahn tracks just before Eberswalder Strasse station. Operated by the Konnopke family since 1930, it's famous for its currywurst, sausage smothered in a curry sauce. Order a beer to wash it down, and sit at the outdoor table. It's open Monday to Friday from 5am to 7pm.

9

Shopping

If it exists, you can find it in Berlin. You may not find it at bargain rates, however, especially with today's dollar exchange rate. Germany is not a shopper's paradise for travelers on a budget, but that doesn't mean you won't find a few treasures here and there. It just means you have to search for them, and recognize them when you see them.

But even if you don't buy anything, looking is half the fun. Window-shopping on the Ku'damm is a favorite Berliner pastime, and who could resist a whirl through the KaDeWe department store? You can also lose yourself for hours or day browsing in markets, specialty shops, clothing boutiques, art galleries, and antique shops.

1 The Shopping Scene

Only you can judge whether a purchase is a true bargain, but if you're making a major purchase, be sure to comparison shop. Many European products, including clothing, kitchenware, and linen, are now readily available in U.S. stores. It may not be worth it to buy that German comforter, for example, and pay for shipping it home, only to find you've saved all of $5 for your efforts.

BEST BUYS Products unique to Berlin that don't cost an arm and a leg include small etchings, mostly of famous buildings and streets in the city, fragments of the Wall, pewter figurines from the family-owned Berliner Zinnfiguren shop, and perfume from the Harry Lehmann shop, which has been selling its own scents for 70 years. If souvenirs make your heart beat faster, you'll delight in porcelain freedom bells (fashioned after the one hanging in Schöneberg Rathaus), T-shirts, mugs, ashtrays illustrated with Brandenburger Tor, and the *Berliner Bär* (the Berlin Bear), the city's mascot. If kitsch doesn't appeal to you, Germany is known for well-made kitchen gadgets and cutlery, linens, those luxuriously fluffy *Federbetten* (literally "feather beds," or down comforters), binoculars and telescopes, cameras, and toys (including model trains and building blocks). If you like porcelain, look for Rosenthal, antique Meissen, and Berlin's own Königliche Porzellan-Manufaktur—assuming, of course, you have a Swiss bank account.

Another good purchase in Berlin is original artwork. There are so many galleries in the city that you could easily spend an entire lifetime making the rounds of changing exhibits. A good place to look for handmade arts and crafts is the weekend fleamarket on Strasse des 17.

Juni, where young Berliners hawk their wares, including jewelry, sketches, and clothing.

For clothing, there's everything from designer fashions to punk, funk, and the ordinary. Finally, antiques are also in abundant supply in Berlin, evident by the city's several antique flea markets.

GREAT SHOPPING STREETS Berlin and the Kurfürstendamm are synonymous. Two-and-a-half miles long, the Kurfürstendamm, called Ku'damm by the locals, is the city's showcase—quite literally. Up and down the sidewalks are freestanding display cases containing goods of surrounding stores, just a little something to whet your shopping appetite. Along the boulevard are boutiques and shops selling clothing, accessories, porcelain, kitchenware, eyeglasses, and art. But don't neglect the side streets, since they're virtual treasure troves of antique shops, more art galleries, bookstores, and clothing shops. North of the Ku'damm, for example, are a number of shops specializing in art deco. Tauentzienstrasse is good for inexpensive and fun fashions.

The other big name in shopping streets is Wilmersdorfer Strasse, a pedestrian-only lane lined with department stores, boutiques, and restaurants. The locals come to shop here, both for essentials and such nonessential essentials as yet another skirt. Since shops are concentrated along this street, you can cover a lot of ground in a short amount of time; simply take the U-Bahn to Wilmersdorfer Strasse.

Other places for a concentrated shopping effort include the Europa-Center, department stores, and markets, described in the next sections. In fact, probably the best place to begin your shopping expedition is KaDeWe, the largest department store on the European continent. Come here for everything from bedsheets, comforters, fabrics, and clothing to souvenirs and even sausages. After that it's an easy walk to the Ku'damm.

HOURS, TAXES & SHIPPING Most shops and businesses are open Monday through Friday from 9:30 or 10am to 6 or 6:30pm and on Saturday from 9am to 2pm. On the first Saturday of the month (called *langer Samstag*), shops remain open until 6pm in winter (October through March) and until 4pm in summer. In addition, many shops remain open longer on Thursday, until 8:30pm. *Note:* Some smaller shops, especially art galleries and antique shops, are open only in the afternoons. Be sure to check individual listings or call.

If you purchase more than 60 DM ($40) worth of goods from any one store and you're taking your purchases out of the country, you're entitled to partial recovery of the Value-Added Tax (VAT), which is 15% in Germany and is called the *Mehrwertsteuer*. You will not receive the total 15% refund; rather, depending on the item you purchased, you will receive a refund of 6% to 11% of the purchase price. If you've purchased an object of considerable worth, even this can add up to a savings. When shopping, look for shops that display the "Tax-Free" sticker.

In any case, the procedure for obtaining the VAT refund is the same. All department stores and most major shops will issue a Tax Refund Cheque (along with a Tax-Free Envelope) at the time of your purchase. Simply fill in the reverse side, and upon leaving the *last* European Union country you visit before heading home, present the Tax Refund

Shopping Along the Ku'damm

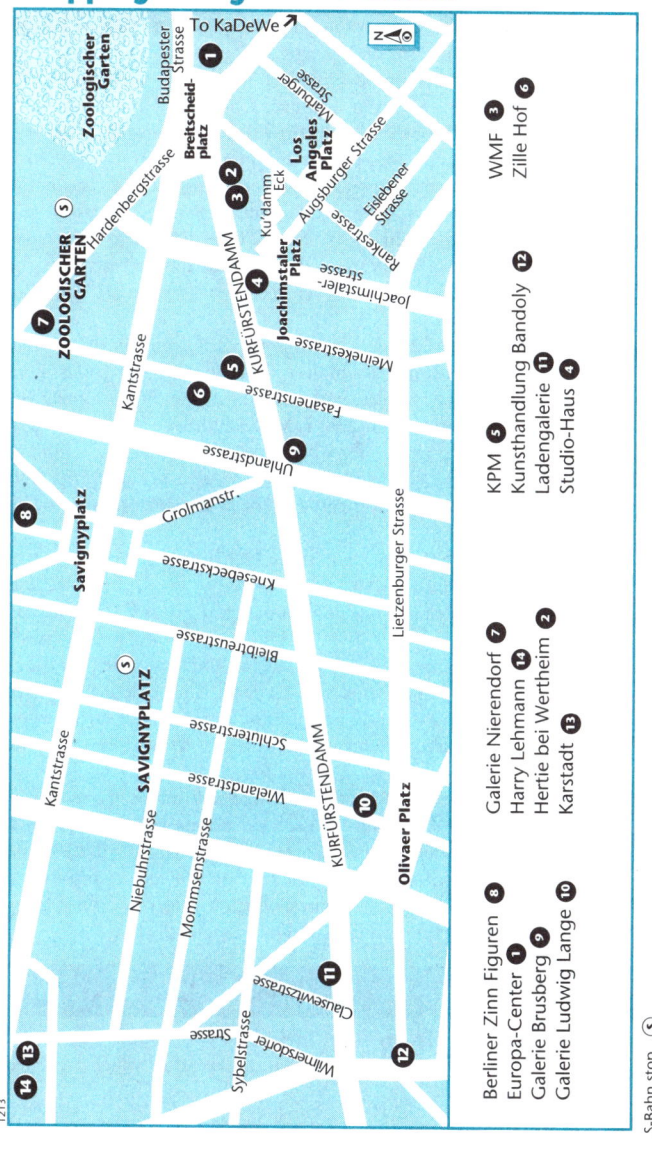

WMF ❸	Zille Hof ❻
KPM ❺	Kunsthandlung Bandoly ❿❷
Ladengalerie ⓫	Studio-Haus ❹
Galerie Nierendorf ❼	Harry Lehmann ⓮
Hertie bei Wertheim ❷	Karstadt ⓭
Berliner Zinn Figuren ❽	Europa-Center ❶
Galerie Brusberg ❾	Galerie Ludwig Lange ❿

S-Bahn stop Ⓢ

Cheque, the receipt from the store, and the purchased articles (which cannot be used prior to departure) to the German Customs official, who will stamp your check. If Germany is your last stop in departing the European Union and you're leaving from Berlin's Tegel Airport, you can receive your cash refund immediately at the Berliner Bank counter in the Main Hall, in German or U.S. currency. In Frankfurt, you can receive an immediate tax refund at the International

Departure Hall. Since Customs may ask to see your purchases, be sure to pack them in the carry-on luggage. If you're leaving Germany by train, ask the Customs official who comes into your train to stamp your check. You can then mail your Tax-Free Cheque back to the country of purchase in a Tax-Free Envelope provided by the store.

You may wish to ship your purchases home, especially if you've gone overboard and can no longer carry everything with a reasonable semblance of dignity. Most shops used to dealing with tourists will ship your purchases home, which may be the easiest route to take. Your Tax-Free Cheque will indicate that the goods have already left the country; in some cases you may even receive an immediate refund of the VAT at the store.

If you wish to send home a package yourself, you can do so at all major post offices. All you have to do is show up with your goods, since post offices sell boxes complete with string and tape. Boxes come in six sizes and range in price from 2.90 DM ($1.95) to 5.50 DM ($3.65). If you're sending a purchase for which you are entitled to a refund of the VAT, be sure to have an official at the post office stamp your Tax-Free Cheque (which you can present at the airport later for an immediate refund).

Keep in mind, however, that there is a limit to the amount of duty-free goods you can bring back with you to the United States. If you're sending a package, it will automatically go to Customs upon arrival in the United States. If the total value of the goods acquired from abroad is less than $50, the package is sent on to the post office and is delivered to you by your mail carrier. If the value is more than $50, the amount you owe will be collected by your mail carrier upon delivery of your package. Note that it is illegal to mail liquor to the United States.

As for hand-carried items, you are allowed to bring back free of duty $400 worth of personal and household goods obtained abroad. Anything above this $400 personal exemption is charged a flat 10% on the next $1,000. Unfortunately, you are not allowed to import any meat products into the United States, which means you cannot bring any of those wonderful German sausages home with you.

2 Shopping A to Z

In addition to the specialty stores listed below, the single best source for most needs is a large department store, several of which are listed here.

ANTIQUES

The best place to search for antiques and curios is at one of Berlin's several **flea markets.** Not only is the atmosphere festive, but the range of goods offered by the various vendors is usually much more extensive—and cheaper—than that offered by a single store. The most easily accessible and my favorite is the flea market held every Saturday and Sunday on Strasse des 17. Juni, where vendors sell porcelain, coffee grinders, glassware, brass, door knockers, lamps, clothing, books, and a seemingly endless supply of junk, as well as handmade arts and crafts. More upscale is the Berliner Antik- und Flohmarkt, an indoor market open six days a week at the Friedrichstrasse S-Bahn station. Check the "Markets" section for more information.

Zille Hof
Fasanenstrasse 14. ☎ **881 95 09**. U-Bahn: Uhlandstrasse, a 1-minute walk.

Hard to believe that this quirky place exists in the middle of Berlin near the exclusive Bristol Hotel Kempinski just off the Ku'damm—it looks like an abandoned junkyard. Occupying a little courtyard that spreads beside and under the elevated tracks of the S-Bahn, this is a good place to browse through shelves of plates, glasses, rusted pots and pans, furniture, dusty books, old postcards, secondhand clothing, and piles upon piles of junk. If nothing else, this place is worth a photograph. It's open Monday through Friday 8:30am to 5:30pm, Saturday 8:30am to 1pm.

ART GALLERIES

There are so many art galleries in Berlin—estimates range from 125 to nearly 250—that it's almost an epidemic, albeit a very nice one. Since it doesn't cost anything to look, you might like to wander through some.

Within easy walking distance of the Ku'damm are several galleries that offer a varied assortment of contemporary art from established artists. At Ku'damm 213 on the corner of Uhlandstrasse is **Galerie Brusberg** (☎ 882 76 82), one of Berlin's best-known galleries. **Ladengalerie** (☎ 881 42 14) at Ku'damm 64, features contemporary German artists. For the works of German expressionists, stop by the **Galerie Nierendorf** (☎ 832 50 13), at Hardenbergstrasse 18. **Galerie Ludwig Lange** (☎ 881 29 26), at Wielandstrasse 26, has a charming sculpture garden.

For more off-the-wall and avant-garde art, the hottest address at the moment is the area around Oranienburger Strasse in Berlin-Mitte. I recommend **Kunst-Werke Berlin** (☎ 281 73 25), at Auguststrasse 69, and **Galerie Wohnmaschine** (☎ 282 07 95), at Tucholskystrasse 34-36. Be sure to check *zitty* for a more complete listing.

CRAFTS

For handmade arts and crafts, the best place to look is the **weekend market held on Strasse des 17. Juni** just west of the Tiergarten S-Bahn station. Many young entrepreneurs and artisans set up shop here, selling sketches, jewelry, batik clothing, toys, and other items they've made themselves. In addition, check with the Berlin tourist office to see whether any other special crafts fairs are being held.

DEPARTMENT STORES & MALLS
THE EUROPA-CENTER AREA

Europa-Center
Tauentzienstrasse and Budapester Strasse. U-Bahn: Kurfürstendamm or Bahnhof Zoo, each a 2-minute walk.

This is Berlin's largest indoor shopping center, with approximately 70 shops on its first 3 floors. Located near the Ku'damm and Bahnhof Zoo, it's a good place to explore on a cold or rainy day, where you can shop for everything from records and cassettes to clothing, shoes, and accessories. There are also plenty of cafes, restaurants, and bars where you can stop for refreshment. Shops are open Monday through Friday 10am to 6pm, Saturday 10am to 2pm (first Saturday hours); the Europa-Center is open until 3am.

✪ KaDeWe
Wittenbergplatz. ☎ **21210**. U-Bahn: Wittenbergplatz, a 1-minute walk.

The KaDeWe rates as one of Berlin's major tourist attractions and is worth the trip, even if you don't plan on buying anything. The largest department store on the European continent, it occupies 51,600 square yards of selling space with an inventory of 250,000 items and employs a staff of 3,000. In addition to shopping its seven floors, customers can eat, buy theater tickets, have their shoes repaired, their marriages and vacations planned, their hair done, their dogs shampooed, their money exchanged, their purchases wrapped and shipped abroad, their pictures taken, and—if necessary after all that—have first aid administered.

Officially known as Kaufhaus des Westens (which means "department store of the West") but popularly referred to as KaDeWe, it sells about anything you might imagine, including perfume, cosmetics, jewelry, watches, shoes, gloves, hats, luggage, umbrellas, housewares, carpets, office supplies, toys, leather goods, musical instruments, furs, wigs, porcelain, glassware, antiques, and much more. Souvenirs of Berlin are sold on the fourth floor, including beer steins and ashtrays stamped with the Berliner Bär.

But by far the biggest attraction of KaDeWe is its sixth-floor food emporium. There are 1,000 different sorts of sausage, 500 different kinds of bread, 1,500 different types of cheese, and gourmet items from around the world. There are exotic teas, coffees, liquors, wines, jams, sweets, vegetables, fruits, spices, canned goods, and fresh seafood, including eels, lobster, and fish still swimming around in tanks. Since few people eat as much pork in so many different ways as the Germans, it's no wonder that KaDeWe's pork section is one of the world's largest. If all this food makes you hungry, you can dine at one of the many counters spread throughout the sixth floor, offering everything from soups and salads to fresh seafood. You could easily get lost and spend the rest of your days here—but there are certainly worse things in life. The KaDeWe is located just a 5-minute walk from the Ku'damm and the Gedächtniskirche. It's open Monday through Wednesday and Friday from 9:30am to 6:30pm, Thursday from 9:30am to 8:30pm, Saturday 9am to 2pm (first Saturday hours).

Hertie Bei Wertheim
Kurfürstendamm 231. ☎ **88 20 61**. U-Bahn: Kurfürstendamm, a 1-minute walk.

This department store is conveniently located at the eastern end of the Ku'damm, across from the Gedächtniskirche. It's good for basic needs such as shampoo, film, or picnic supplies. It also has good souvenir, clothing, porcelain, and housewares departments. It's open Monday through Wednesday and Friday from 9:30am to 6:30pm, Thursday 9:30am to 8:30pm, Saturday 9am to 2pm (first Saturday hours).

On Wilmersdorfer Strasse

Hertie
Wilmersdorfer Strasse 118-119. ☎ **311 050**. U-Bahn: Wilmersdorfer Strasse, a 1-minute walk.

Hertie department store is a good medium-price store, serving the basic needs of families. Stop here for those traveling necessities. It's open Monday through Wednesday and Friday from 9:30am to 6:30pm, Thursday 9:30am to 8:30pm, Saturday 9am to 2pm (first Saturday hours).

Karstadt
Wilmersdorfer Strasse 109-111. ☎ **31 891**. U-Bahn: Wilmersdorfer Strasse, less than a 1-minute walk.

Located at the corner of Kantstrasse and Wilmersdorfer Strasse, this large department store chain can be found all over Germany and is slightly more upper-scale than other competing chains. A good place to look for clothing and accessories. It's open Monday through Wednesday and Friday from 9:30am to 6:30pm, Thursday 9:30am to 8:30pm, Saturday 9am to 2pm (first Saturday hours).

In Berlin-Mitte (Eastern Berlin)

Kaufhof
Alexanderplatz. ☎ **21 64 000**. U- and S-Bahn: Alexanderplatz.

Occupying the former East German Centrum department store (where there was very little offered that tempted Western shoppers), this German chain offers the usual goods and services, including toys, clothing, household goods, food, and shoe repair. It's open Monday through Wednesday and Friday 9am to 6:30pm, Thursday 9am to 8:30pm, Saturday 9am to 2pm (first Saturday hours).

FASHION

The best places to check for clothing and accessories are the department stores listed above. In addition, there are many boutiques in the Europa-Center, as well as open-fronted shops along the Ku'damm, Tauentzienstrasse, Bleibtreustrasse, and Wilmersdorfer Strasse, selling young, fun fashions at inexpensive prices. Finally, clothing is also sold at the weekend market on Strasse des 17. Juni, including ethnic clothing from Bali; batik scarves and shirts; and original, handmade jackets, hats, and accessories.

FOOD

Almost all German department stores have food departments, usually in their basements. In Berlin the ultimate in food emporiums is the sixth floor of the KaDeWe department store on Wittenbergplatz, with an incredible stockpile of gourmet foods (see "Department Stores & Malls," above). If it's to be found anywhere in Berlin, KaDeWe is the place.

If your tastes run more towards natural foods, across the square from KaDeWe is a small shop called **Einhorn**, Wittenbergplatz 5-6 (☎ 24 63 47). In addition to ready-made vegetarian dishes, the shop also sells *Müsli,* breads, jams, juices, organic fruits and vegetables, nuts, and more. It's open Monday through Friday from 9am to 6pm and on Saturday from 10am to 1:30pm. **Higher Taste,** Kurfürstendamm 157-158, is a vegetarian health-food store run by the Hare Krishna organization. See Chapter 6 for more information.

GIFTS/SOUVENIRS

The largest selection of gifts and souvenirs can be found in Berlin's department stores, particularly KaDeWe and Hertie bei Wertheim, which are used to a steady flow of tourist traffic. Other places to look for unique gifts include the weekend crafts market on Strasse des 17. Juni, where young entrepreneurs sell their creations; Harry Lehmann, listed below, which has been selling perfume for 70 years; and Studio-Haus and WMF, described below under "Kitchenwares."

Berlin-Grafik

Schlossstrasse 60. ☎ **341 50 68**. U-Bahn: Sophie Charlotte-Platz, about a 5-minute walk.

Located about a five-minute walk from Charlottenburg Palace, this shop sells original drawings and reproductions, many of famous Berlin architecture. Engravings of Berlin begin at 20 DM ($13.35) framed, 10 DM ($6.65) unframed. It also sells postcards and books, primarily books on Berlin written in German. It's open Monday through Friday from 11am to 6pm, Saturday 11am to 2pm.

Berliner Zinnfiguren

Knesebeckstrasse 88. ☎ **313 08 02**. S-Bahn: Savignyplatz, about a 4-minute walk.

This small family-owned shop, located just north of Savignyplatz, has been producing and selling handcrafted pewter figures since 1934. Approximately 10,000 various figures are for sale, including more than 1,000 animals alone. Some are collectors items; others are appropriate as toys. Most popular are characters of Berlin, including the Potsdamer Soldat (soldier), the Blumenfrau (Flower Vendor), and Frederick the Great playing the flute. Flat, unpainted figures begin at only 1.50 DM ($1), a great souvenir of Berlin. It's open Monday through Friday from 10am to noon and 1 to 6pm, Saturday 10am to 1pm.

Kunsthandlung Bandoly

Brandenburgische Strasse 27. ☎ **881 49 10**. U-Bahn: Adenauerplatz, a 3-minute walk.

This shop deals in reproductions of famous paintings, small etchings of Berlin, and copperplate prints. Many of its copperplate prints depict the architecture of old Berlin, while small etchings of such sights as the Brandenburger Tor can be purchased for as little as 15 DM ($10) framed, 12 DM ($8) unframed. It's a good place to purchase a small souvenir of Berlin. It's open Monday through Friday from 10am to 1pm, and 3 to 6pm, Saturday 10am to 1pm.

Berlin Souvenirs

Hertie bei Wertheim, Kurfürstendamm 231. ☎ **88 20 61**. U-Bahn: Kurfürstendamm, a 1-minute walk.

This is the easiest place to shop for a souvenir of Berlin. With its own sidewalk entrance, it's located in the Hertie bei Wertheim department

KITCHENWARES

Studio-Haus

Kurfürstendamm 226. ☎ **881 7051**. U-Bahn: Kurfürstendamm, less than a 1-minute walk.

This smart-looking shop sells a wide range of decorative and functional items for the home, including Rosenthal porcelain, Boda glass, tableware, and chrome kitchenware. Prices are high, but if you're looking for a wedding gift, this is a good place to start. The adjoining In-Shop sells more items for the kitchen and table. It's open Monday to Wednesday and Friday from 9:30am to 6:30pm, Thursday 9:30am to 8:30pm, Saturday 9:30am to 2pm (first Saturday hours).

WMF

Kurfürstendamm 229. ☎ **882 39 41**. U-Bahn: Kurfürstendamm, a 1-minute walk.

WMF, a chain found all over Germany, specializes in both tableware and cookingware, from chrome eggcups and coffee-pot warmers to pots and pans—sleek, functional, and sturdy. If you're looking for something inexpensive and easily transportable, you might check the store's wonderful kitchen gadgets, ranging from bottle stoppers and can openers to hardboiled-egg slicers. It's open Monday through Wednesday and Friday from 9:30am to 6:30pm, Thursday 9:30am to 8:30pm, Saturday 9am to 2pm (first Saturday hours).

MARKETS

Some of Berlin's best buys can be found at its many antique and flea markets. Some are indoor and are held almost daily. Others are outdoors and are open only 1 or 2 days a week. Altogether there are more than 70 weekly markets (mostly neighborhood produce markets), a handful of market halls, and more than a dozen flea markets spread throughout the city. Below are a few of the best; for information on other markets, drop by the Berlin Verkehrsamt in the Europa-Center.

✪ Market at Strasse des 17. Juni

Strasse des 17. Juni. ☎ **322 81 99**. S-Bahn: Ernst-Reuter-Platz, a five-minute walk (*Note:* The Tiergarten S-Bahn station is a minute away, but it's closed for renovations until 1997.)

This is my favorite market, and one I never miss when I'm in Berlin. Stretching just west of the Tiergarten S-Bahn station, this weekend market offers a staggering variety of antiques, including silverware, books, china, glass, jewelry, clothing, kitchenware, and junk. Don't overlook the second half of the market (past the stone portal and on the other side of the bridge); it features original arts and crafts, including funky and ethnic jewelry, clothing, hats, sketches, and innovative artwork. It's a good place to hunt for gifts, and prices are very reasonable. The market is open Saturday and Sunday from 10am to 5pm.

Shopping

Berliner Antik- und Flohmarkt Berlin Antique and Flea Market.
Georgenstrasse, Friedrichstrasse S-Bahn Station. ☎ **215 02 129**. S-Bahn: Friedrichstrasse, less than a minute away.

Located at the eastern end of Friedrichstrasse S-Bahn station, under the arches of the elevated track, this upscale market features more than 60 vendors selling antiques and curios, including jewelry, porcelain, glassware, pocketwatches, canes, books, lamps, and odds and ends. It's Berlin's largest permanent flea market, and during warm weather additional vendors open shop outside along Georgenstrasse. Prices are relatively high, but bargains can be found. For refreshment, drop by Zur Nolle, a pub decorated in the style of 1920s Berlin. The market is open Wednesday through Monday from 11am to 6pm.

✪ Turkish Market
Bank of Maybachufer, Kreuzberg. ☎ **6809 29 26**. U-Bahn: Kottbusser Tor, about a 5-minute walk.

Kreuzberg is home to much of the city's Turkish population, so little wonder that here you'll find Berlin's best Turkish market. Spread along the bank of a canal, this market offers a taste of the exotic, with both German and Turkish vendors selling vegetables, sheep's cheese, pita bread, olives, beans, rice, noodles, spices, and clothing. If you like color, activity, the smell of spices, and being outdoors, you'll love this place. Friday's markets are livelier, with more vendors. It's open Tuesday and Friday from noon to 6:30pm.

Weihnachtsmarkt
Breitscheidplatz and from Nürnberger Strasse to Joachimstaler Strasse. U-Bahn: Kurfürstendamm, Bahnhof Zoo, or Wittenbergplatz.

Every December from the beginning of the month to Christmas Eve, there's a traditional Christmas market in the inner city. It radiates out from the Gedächtniskirche on Breitscheidplatz to Wittenbergplatz, particularly on Nürnberger Strasse and Joachimstaler Strasse. Colorful stalls sell wonderful German Christmas ornaments, candies, cookies, sausages, and other goodies, including *Glühwein* (spiced mulled wine). Incidentally, there are also other Christmas markets in Berlin, including Spandau's Altstadt (Old City), known for its traditional ambience and handmade decorations, and on Schlossplatz in Berlin-Mitte, complete with a fun fair and rides for the kids. This one is open daily December 1 through December 24 from 11am to 9pm.

Winterfeldplatz Market
Winterfeldplatz, Schöneberg. U-Bahn: Nollendorfplatz, a 5-minute walk.

Founded more than 80 years ago, Berlin's largest weekly market—selling fruits, vegetables, meat, flowers, clothing, and accessories—is lively with vendors hawking their wares at the top of their lungs. On a pretty square lined with old Berlin buildings, it is where Berliners come to do their shopping, whether it's for cabbage, olives, basil, mozzarella, or flowers. And of course, they also come to meet their friends and exchange the latest gossip. After making their purchases, many of the younger shoppers retire to Slumberland or Café Sidney, two bars on Winterfeldplatz. Saturday is the busier day. It's open Wednesday and Saturday from dawn to 1pm.

A R T

Accessoires &
Designer- und Modeschmuck
Bentin

22-10-07   ABSE6009
LOG 1/pos   *29.90

ZW-SUMME   *29.90

TOTAL   *29.90
ZAHLGELD   *40.00
RUECKGELD   *10.10

11:45 0004

A R T
Accessiores
Designer-und Modeschmuck
Berlin

22-01-97	KASSE0000
WGR 1	*29.90
ZW-SUMME	*29.90
TOTAL	*29.90
ZAHLGELD	*40.00
RÜCKGELD	*10.10

— 1 —   11-45 0004

PERFUME

For the big names in perfume from around the world, head for the ground floor of KaDeWe. However, if you're looking for a scent unique to Berlin or an inexpensive and unusual gift, try **Harry Lehmann,** Kantstrasse 106 (☎ 324 35 82). It's a 2-minute walk from the Wilmersdorfer Strasse U-Bahn stop. This tiny family-owned shop has been selling its own concoctions of scents since 1926, with approximately 50 scents now available made from flowers, leaves, and grasses. Scents, ranging from lavender and jasmine to magnolia, are sold by the weight, starting at 4.50 DM ($3) for 10 grams. Customers can either bring their own perfume bottle or purchase one of the inexpensive vials starting at 1.50 DM ($1), a concept begun by Harry Lehmann in 1926 when he decided it was a shame that pretty bottles had to be discarded when the perfume ran out. In addition to its scents, the shop, now in its third generation of owners, also sells Kölnisch Wasser and other colognes, as well as after-shave lotion for men. Don't be put off by the fake flowers in the shop; just one of the idiosyncrasies of this charming little establishment, they're available scented with the real thing. How about a fragrant bouquet of fake roses? This shop is located a stone's throw west of the Wilmersdorfer Strasse pedestrian lane. It's open Monday through Friday from 9am to 6:30pm, Saturday from 9am to 2pm (first Saturday hours).

PORCELAIN

KPM

Kurfürstendamm 26a. ☎ **881 18 02**. U-Bahn for Ku'damm branch: Uhlandstrasse, a 1-minute walk. S-Bahn for main shop: Tiergarten, a 1-minute walk.

The Königliche Porzellan-Manufaktur (KPM) is a Berlin tradition, with a history stretching back more than 225 years. In 1763, Frederick the Great acquired a preexisting porcelain company, renamed it the Königliche Porzellan-Manufaktur, and made it the royal porcelain manufacturer for his Prussian government. Since then, monarchs and heads of state from around the world have been owners of KPM pieces, including Catherine II of Russia, Louis XVI of France, Elizabeth II of England, Margaret Thatcher, and Henry Kissinger. Although the official name was changed in 1918 to Staatliche Porzellan-Manufaktur, pieces are still identified with the KPM mark, and everyone simply calls it KPM.

KPM pieces today include table settings, vases, baskets, figurines, and art pieces. All decorations and floral designs are handpainted. For tourists, the most popular KPM pieces include reproductions of the Liberty Bell in Rathaus Schöneberg, white statues of the Berliner Bär, and Christmas plates issued each year.

The Ku'damm branch is open Monday through Friday from 10am to 6:30pm, Saturday 10am to 2pm (first Saturday hours). Although not as centrally located, the main shop of KPM is at Wegelystrasse 1 (☎ 39 00 90) and is open Monday through Friday from 9am to 6pm, Saturday 9am to 2pm (first Saturday hours).

10

Berlin After Dark

Berlin has no mandatory closing hours for nightclubs, bars, and discos, so many of these places stay open all night—making it the most popular German city with Europe's younger set of travelers. As one native told me, "The reason everyone comes to Berlin is its nightlife." When I pointed out that it could also be Berlin's wealth of museums, it seemed a possibility he hadn't considered. The action starts late; some travelers—those who are in bed each night by 11pm—may remain unaware of the city's garish nighttime transformation. Perhaps blissfully so: There's something to be said for early curfews.

Yet it would be difficult to remain completely ignorant of the city's after-dark activities. Signs of it are everywhere: The wicked exists beside the innocent; the tawdry beside the deluxe. On a street off the Ku'damm, a first-class hotel and a haute cuisine French restaurant may sit next to or be near a strip joint, peep show, and porn shop. At night even the elite boulevard itself is the domain of dolled-up hookers. It's this juxtaposition that makes Berlin fascinating; and it's this tolerance that makes the city what it is today.

You don't have to be a night owl to enjoy evenings in Berlin. There are cabarets, wine cellars, live music houses, and gambling casinos, as well as opera, chamber music, two world-renowned orchestras, and classical and contemporary theater.

To find out what's going on in the traditional performing arts, pick up a copy of *Berlin Programm,* a booklet published monthly and available at the Berlin tourist office and newsstands. It gives a daily schedule of events in all the city's opera, theater, and concert halls. Rock concerts, experimental theater, and avant-garde happenings are covered in more detail in city magazines *tip* and *zitty* (but these are printed only in German).

If you don't mind taking a chance on what's available on any given night, the best bargain in last-minute tickets is at **Hekticket**, with two convenient locations: Kurfürstendamm 14 and Rathausstrasse 1 on Alexanderplatz (☎ 242 67 09). Unsold tickets for that evening's performances are available for more than 80 venues throughout Berlin, including the Deutsche Staatsoper, Komische Oper, classical music concerts, pop performances, and cabaret, most at a 50% reduction off the normal ticket price. Both ticket booths are open Tuesday to Thursday from 4 to 7:30pm, Friday and Saturday from 4 to 8pm, Sunday from 4 to 7:30pm, and Monday from 5 to 7:30pm. If you wish to know beforehand whether tickets for a specific performance are still available, you can even call earlier in the day to reserve your ticket.

Otherwise, if your heart is set on seeing a particular performance and you don't mind paying a commission, convenient ticket outlets can be found at **Centrum**, Meinekestrasse 25 (☎ 882 76 11); **City Center**, Kurfürstendamm 16 (☎ 882 65 63); the **Europa-Center**, Tauentzienstrasse 9 (☎ 264 11 38); **KaDeWe** department store, Wittenbergplatz (☎ 218 10 28); and **Hertie bei Wertheim** department store, Kurfürstendamm 231 (☎ 882 53 54).

You'll save money, however, by buying your ticket directly from the theater or concert hall during box-office hours or an hour before the performance begins.

1 The Performing Arts

CLASSICAL MUSIC

✪ Philharmonie

Mattäikirchplatz 1. ☎ **254 88-0**. Tickets 13–100 DM ($8.65–$66.65) for Berlin Philharmonic Orchestra. Bus 129, 148, or 248.

This is Berlin's most famous concert hall, home of the world-renowned **Berlin Philharmonic Orchestra**. Located on the southern edge of the Tiergarten district and designed by architect Hans Scharoun in 1963, the Philharmonie is an asymmetric structure with a tentlike roof. Its main hall seats more than 2,200—with the conductor and orchestra placed in the very center—and no concertgoer is more than 100 feet from the podium. The acoustics are said to be nearly perfect.

Founded in 1882, the Berlin Philharmonic Orchestra has been led by some of the world's greatest conductors. It gained acclaim under the baton of the late Herbert von Karajan—acclaim that continues unabated under the skillful direction of conductor Claudio Abbado. Leading guest conductors and soloists regularly join the Berlin Philharmonic, including such notables as Daniel Barenboim, Zubin Mehta, Christoph von Dohnányi, and Seiji Ozawa.

The Philharmonic performs approximately 100 times in Berlin during its August-through-June season, attracting more than 220,000 people annually. It also performs 20 to 30 concerts around the world each year. Because the Berlin Philharmonic is so popular, tickets often sell out 2 months in advance. If you're able to procure one, consider yourself very lucky.

The Philharmonie is also the venue of the Sinfonie Orchester Berlin, Deutsches Symphonie-Orchester Berlin**,** and Berliner Barock-Orchester**.** Visiting orchestras perform here as well. In addition to the main hall, there's also a smaller Kammermusiksaal (Chamber Music Hall). The box office is open Monday through Friday from 3:30 to 6pm, and Saturday, Sunday, and holidays from 11am to 2pm.

Konzerthaus Berlin

Schauspielhaus am Gendarmenmarkt, Berlin-Mitte. ☎ **20 309-0** (information), **20 309-2100** (tickets). Tickets 10–70 DM ($6.65–$46.65). U-Bahn: Französische Strasse, Hausvogteiplatz, or Stadtmitte. Bus 100.

> ## Church Music
>
> Churches are one of the least expensive places to hear music in Berlin. At the Kaiser-Wilhelm Gedächtniskirche on Breitscheidplatz off the Ku'damm free organ concerts are held most Saturdays at 6pm, as well as choirs, soloists, and other performances throughout the month. The Berliner Dom on Museumsinsel in Berlin-Mitte features organ concerts Monday to Saturday at 3pm and Sunday at 2pm; admission is 8 DM ($5.35) for adults and 5 DM ($3.35) for students and senior citizens. In addition, organ concerts, choirs, and instrumental classical music concerts are held most weekends, usually on Saturday at 6pm and Sunday at 4pm. Prices for these are generally 5 to 12 DM ($3.35–$8). For more information on church music throughout the city, call 784 30 61 for concerts in Catholic churches and 229 17 14 for concerts in Protestant churches.

Located on the historic Gendarmenmarkt, this was originally a theater house, designed by Schinkel in 1819–1821 and restored after World War II. Now used for concerts, it was here that the late Leonard Bernstein conducted a performance of Beethoven's Ninth Symphony in celebration of the fall of the Wall. It features concerts by the Berliner Sinfonie-Orchester, Rundfunk-Sinfonieorchester Berlin (Radio Symphony Orchestra), and guest orchestras and ensembles. It has both a large music hall and a chamber-music hall. The box office is open Tuesday through Saturday from 2 to 6pm.

OPERA, OPERETTA & BALLET

Deutsche Oper Berlin

Bismarckstrasse 35, Charlottenburg. ☎ **34 381** (information), **341 02 49** (tickets). Tickets 15–135 DM ($10–$90); 50% reductions for students and for "last-minute tickets," unsold tickets for that evening's performance. U-Bahn: Deutsche Oper.

Whereas most of Europe's opera houses are grand edifices from another era—the Deutsche Oper Berlin, rebuilt after World War II, is intentionally plain and modern with a stark streetside wall designed to shut out traffic noise. Seating 1,900, it features performances of opera or ballet almost every night. The Deutsche Oper Berlin attained worldwide success in the 1920s under such great conductors as Richard Strauss, Bruno Walter, Leo Blech, Wilhelm Furtwängler, Erich Kleiber, and Otto Klemperer. The box office is open Monday through Saturday from 11am to 7pm, Sunday 10am to 2pm; performances usually begin at 7 or 8pm.

Deutsche Staatsoper

Unter den Linden 7, Berlin-Mitte. ☎ **200 47 62** (information), **200 43 15** (tickets). Tickets 6–150 DM ($4–$100); 50% reductions for students on unsold tickets on evening of performance. U- and S-Bahn: Friedrichstrasse or Französische Strasse. Bus 100 to Deutsche Staatsoper stop.

The German State Opera—located on the famous Unter den Linden boulevard in Berlin-Mitte—has long been one of Berlin's most famous opera houses. Although its present building dates only from the 1950s, its facade is a faithful copy of a pre-existing structure first erected in the 1740s by Knobelsdorff and then renovated in 1927. Now under the musical direction of Israeli conductor Daniel Barenboim, it features opera, ballet, and concerts, with an emphasis on classical German operas and German operas of the 20th century. The box office is open Monday through Saturday from noon to 6pm, Sunday and holidays 2 to 6pm; performances usually begin at 7 or 8pm.

Komische Oper
Behrenstrasse 55-57, Berlin-Mitte. ☎ **229 26 03** (information), **229 25 55** (tickets). Tickets 10–75 DM ($6.65–$50). U-Bahn: Französische Strasse. S-Bahn: Unter den Linden. Bus 100.

Although Komische Oper translates as "comic opera," this innovative opera company serves as an alternative to the grander, more mainstream productions of Berlin's two other opera houses (see above). It's known for its innovative and avant-garde performances; it also stages light opera, operetta, and ballet. The box office at Unter den Linden 41 is open Monday through Saturday from 11am to 7pm, Sunday 1pm until 90 minutes before the performance begins; performances usually start at 7 or 8pm.

THEATER

With a long tradition behind it, Berlin has played a leading role in the history and development of German theater. Hauptmann, Ibsen, Strindberg, and Brecht all left their mark on Berlin's stages, as did such well-known directors as Max Reinhardt, Erwin Piscator, and Gustaf Gründgens.

Unfortunately, several theaters were forced to close following unification, but a few remain. You'll be at a disadvantage if you don't speak German, but if you do, you're in for a treat.

Deutsches Theater Berlin
Schumannstrasse 13, Berlin-Mitte. ☎ **284 41-225**. Tickets 10–52 DM ($6.65–$34.65). U- or S-Bahn: Friedrichstrasse.

This East Berlin theater stages both modern and classic plays, including adaptations of English-language plays produced in German. The box office is open Monday through Saturday from noon to 6pm, Sunday 3 to 6pm; performances most evenings start at 7:30pm.

Schiller Theater
Bismarckstrasse 110, Charlottenburg. ☎ **312 65 05**. Tickets 46–96 DM ($30.65–$64); 50% reduction for students on unsold tickets, available 30 minutes before that night's performance. U-Bahn: Ernst-Reuter-Platz.

> **Impressions**
>
> *He said that in Berlin, if you wanted to make a scandal in the theatre, you had to have a mother committing incest with two sons; one wasn't enough.*
>   —Arnold Bennett, quoting Rudolf Kommer, 1925

Of Berlin's many theater houses, this is one of the best known. Built in 1951 from the ruins of an older theater destroyed in World War II, it was known throughout Germany for its playfully light interpretations of classical productions and was almost closed down for good following unification. It has now been resurrected as a venue for musicals. The box office is open daily from 9:30am; performances are Tuesday through Friday at 8pm, Saturday at 4 and 9pm, Sunday at 3 and 8pm.

Schaubühne am Lehniner Platz
Kurfürstendamm 153, Wilmersdorf. ☎ **89 00 23**. Tickets 15–50 DM ($10–$33.35); dress rehearsals 25 DM ($16.65). U-Bahn: Adenauerplatz. Bus 119, 129, 219.

Located on the Ku'damm near Lehniner Platz, this is one of Berlin's leading venues for drama and experimental theater. Although the original art deco facade from the 1920s has been preserved, inside is the latest in modern theatrical technology and three stages where plays can be given simultaneously. The box office is open Monday through Saturday from 11am to 6:30pm, Sunday and holidays from 3 to 6:30pm.

Berliner Ensemble
Am Bertolt-Brecht-Platz, Berlin-Mitte. ☎ **282 31 60**. Tickets 40 DM ($26.65). S-Bahn: Friedrichstrasse.

Bertolt Brecht and Helene Weigel founded this remarkable theater in 1949, and even when the Wall cut off the Berliner Ensemble from Western eyes, it maintained an estimable reputation in West Germany. It used to stage almost exclusively the works of Brecht but has now branched out to include guest playwrights, from Shakespeare to Ibsen. The box office is open Monday through Saturday from 11am to 6:30pm, Sunday and holidays from 3 to 6:30pm; performances most nights begin at 7:30pm.

Theater des Westens
Kantstrasse 12, Charlottenburg. ☎ **882 28 88**. Tickets 18–86 DM ($12–$57.35). S-Bahn or U-Bahn: Bahnhof Zoo.

Built in 1896 and occupying a prime spot near the Ku'damm and Bahnhof Zoo, this is the place to go for popular productions, musicals, spirited revues, and frivolous comedies. The box office is open Tuesday through Saturday from noon to 6pm, Sunday and holidays 2 to 4pm; performances start at 8pm Tuesday through Sunday.

2 The Club & Music Scene

CABARET & REVUES

Liza Minnelli sang to her old chums that life is very much like a cabaret, and nowhere is this more true than in Berlin. Granted, the old days of stinging political satires are long gone; understanding those required an excellent command of German. Some nightclubs do offer political commentary, but mostly you'll find music and dance, including transvestite shows.

Die Stachelschweine

Basement of Europa-Center, Tauentzienstrasse and Budapester Strasse, Charlottenburg. ☎ **261 47 95**. Tickets 22–38 DM ($14.65–$25.35). S- and U-Bahn: Bahnhof Zoo or Kurfürstendamm, each less than a 2-minute walk.

This is one of Berlin's old-timers, a cabaret with more than 40 years under its belt. Its name means "Porcupine," and it continues to make barbed political commentaries, so you'll need a good understanding of German to appreciate it. Tickets sell out quickly, so come here immediately upon arrival in Berlin to procure a ticket. The box office is open Monday through Friday from 10:30am to 12:30pm, Tuesday through Friday from 4 to 7pm, Saturday and Sunday 5 to 6pm; performances start around 7:30pm from Monday through Saturday.

Chez Nous

Marburger Strasse 14, Charlottenburg. ☎ **213 18 10**. Admission 15 DM ($10); plus a 25 DM ($16.65) drink minimum per person at the bar, 35 DM ($23.35) at a table. U-Bahn: Kurfürstendamm or Augsburger, a 4-minute walk.

This is a cabaret of a different sort: With a bevy of transvestites, the shows here have been titillating audiences for more than 30 years. The elaborate costumes and the song-and-dance numbers make this a Berlin institution; it offers two shows nightly and is located just a minute's walk from the Europa-Center. But an evening here will definitely be a splurge; mixed drinks average 25 DM ($16.65). You'll save money standing at the bar rather than sitting at a table.

ROCK CONCERTS & OTHER SHOWS

If you buy tickets to one of Berlin's premier rock concerts, you'll probably be heading toward one of these major concert halls. For local bands and live music houses that offer nightly entertainment, refer to the section that follows, "Live Music Houses." Also, check *tip* or *zitty* for the latest concert information.

✪ Metropol

Nollendorfplatz 5, Schöneberg. ☎ **216 41 22**. U-Bahn: Nollendorfplatz.

A disco on weekends, the Metropol offers some of the best in contemporary music on weekday evenings. Since it's not large enough to accommodate the big names, you can catch your favorite lesser-known artists here before they make it big. Paul Young, David Sanborn, Ziggy Marley, and Johnny Clegg & Savuka have played here. There's a smaller, separate stage in Metropol called Loft, which features punk rock to rhythm and blues in a more intimate setting (see "Live Music Houses"). The box office is open Monday through Friday from 11am to 6pm.

Waldbühne

Ruhleben, Charlottenburg. ☎ **852 40 80**. U-Bahn: Ruhleben, then a 20-minute walk through a park, or Olympiastadion.

Beautifully situated in a wooded ravine near the Olympiastadion (Olympic Stadium), the Waldbühne is Germany's largest open-air arena. It's Berlin's best-loved spot for rock, pop, and folklore concerts held in summer. Although concerts usually feature big-name rock-and-roll performers, the Berlin Philharmonic Orchestra has been known to give concerts here as well. Be sure to pack a picnic and a warm blanket, and rain gear just in case. Performances run May through October.

Deutschlandhalle
Messedamm 26. ☎ **303 81**. U-Bahn: Kaiserdamm. S-Bahn: Westkreuz. Bus 219, 149.

With 14,000 seats, this is Berlin's largest arena. In addition to occasional rock concerts, it is also used for conventions, horse shows, some sporting events, and other events with mass attendance. It's located on the grounds of the city's largest conference and convention center, near the International Congress Centrum (ICC) and Radio Tower. The box office is open Monday through Friday from noon to 6pm, Saturday from 10am to 2pm.

Internationales Congress-Centrum (ICC)
Am Messedamm. ☎ **3038-0** or **3038-44 44**. Bus 104, 105, 110, 149, or 219.

Opened in 1979, the ICC Berlin, right next to the Radio Tower, is massive, with 80 lecture halls, conference and meeting rooms, as well as 2 main halls (one with 2,000 seats, the other with 5,000 seats) used for both conferences and concerts of jazz, country, and rock music. The box office is open Monday through Friday from noon to 6pm, Saturday 10am to 2pm.

LIVE MUSIC HOUSES

In addition to the venues listed here, be on the lookout for occasional concerts and jam sessions, sometimes free, at bars throughout town. For example, **Yorckschlösschen** at Yorckstrasse 15, offers live music Wednesdays from 9pm to 1am in winter only, from October to March, and there's no admission charge, but drinks cost 50 Pfennig (35¢) more. It also offers live Dixieland jazz Sundays throughout the year from 2 to 6pm.

A-Trane
Bleibtreustrasse 1, Charlottenburg. ☎ **313 25 50**. Cover usually 15 DM ($10); 10 DM ($6.65) for students. Free Tues and Wed. S-Bahn: Savignyplatz, a 2-minute walk.

Located on the corner of Bleibtreustrasse and Pestalozzistrasse not far from Savignyplatz, this classy jazz venue opened in 1992, with the aim of putting Berlin on the map as a city offering first-rate jazz. Featuring local and international talent, it opens its doors 9pm Tuesday through Saturday, with music beginning at 10pm. A glass of wine begins at 5.50 DM ($3.65) for an eighth of a liter; a .4-liter beer is also 5.50 DM ($3.65).

Eierschale an der Gedächtniskirche
Rankestrasse 1, Charlottenburg. ☎ **882 53 05**. Cover 4 DM ($2.65) if live music, applied toward first drink. U-Bahn: Kurfürstendamm, a 1-minute walk.

Conveniently located just off the Ku'damm across the street from the Gedächtniskirche, this popular music house and bar offers live music nightly starting at 8:30 or 9pm—everything from traditional jazz and blues to oldies, rock and roll, country western, and popular music. With outdoor sidewalk seating in the summer, it's also a good place to come for breakfast, especially on Sunday when there's live music all day long. Breakfast is served daily from 8am to 2pm and costs from

5.90 DM ($3.95) to an 11.90 DM ($7.95) fixed-price brunch. A half-liter of beer costs 4.90 DM ($3.25) when there isn't a band, rising to 6.30 DM ($4.20) when there's live entertainment.

Ewige Lampe

Niebuhrstrasse 11a, Charlottenburg. ☎ **324 39 18**. Cover 10 DM ($6.65), occasionally more for big names. S-Bahn: Savignyplatz, a 2-minute walk.

This small and popular jazz bar features bands primarily from the United States, Germany, and Holland and can get pretty crowded. Either buy your ticket in advance or get there early. It's open Wednesday to Sunday from 8pm to at least 2am; the music begins at 9pm. A half-liter of beer costs 5.50 DM ($3.65).

Loft

Nollendorfplatz 5, Schöneberg. ☎ **216 10 20**. Cover 10–20 DM ($6.65–$13.35) depending on the group. U-Bahn: Nollendorfplatz, a 1-minute walk.

Located in the massive building that houses the Metropol disco, the Loft serves as a smaller arena for everything from punk rock to rhythm and blues, with concerts held two to four times a week. It features musicians from around the world and bands from the United States and Great Britain; if there's an opening act, it's likely to be one of Berlin's own.

Lucky Strike Originals

Georgenstrasse, S-Bahnbögen 177-180, Berlin-Mitte. ☎ **201 774 22**. Cover 5–10 DM ($3.35–$6.65) Mon–Sat, Sun free.

This American-style restaurant-bar, located under the elevated tracks of the S-Bahn just a stone's throw from the famous Pergamon Museum, has an adjacent small club with live music nightly, ranging from latin to jazz, swing to soul, blues to funk. The doors open at 8pm; music begins at 9pm Friday and Saturday and at 9:45pm Sunday through Thursday. The house band plays every Sunday evening (no cover), or come for Sunday brunch with live jazz starting at 10am.

✪ Quasimodo

Kantstrasse 12a, Charlottenburg. ☎ **312 80 86**. Cover 10–25 DM ($6.65–$16.65), depends on band. U-Bahn: Bahnhof Zoo.

This basement establishment—in a small building dwarfed by the large Theater des Westens next door—features contemporary jazz and rock groups and is considered one of the best places in town to hear live music. Performances begin at 10pm, doors open at 9pm; check *tip* or *zitty* for concert information. There's a ground-floor cafe, a convenient place to hang out until the music begins. A beer costs 5.50 DM ($3.65).

DANCE CLUBS & DISCOS

Big Eden

Kurfürstendamm 202, Charlottenburg. ☎ **882 61 20**. No cover Sun–Thurs or for unaccompanied women; Fri–Sat 10 DM ($6.65), including a ticket toward 2 DM ($1.35) worth of drinks. U-Bahn: Uhlandstrasse, about a 3-minute walk.

Right on the Ku'damm, this disco opened in 1968 and proudly displays photographs of celebrities who came here in the golden ages—

Klaus Kinski, Roman Polanski, Telly Savalas, and a very young Paul McCartney. Its days of being the hottest thing in town have long gone, but the Big Eden still attracts young visitors of every nationality. Teenagers crowd the dance floor until midnight; after the teens catch the last subway home, revelers in their 20s and 30s take over. In addition to a large dance floor, the place has pool tables and pinball machines. It maintains a strict front-door policy and won't admit anyone who even looks like they're drunk. Opening nightly at 8pm, it closes at 4am Sunday to Thursday, at 6am Friday and Saturday. Beer costs 5 DM ($3.35) until 10pm, from 8 DM ($5.35) thereafter.

Café Keese
Bismarckstrasse 108, Charlottenburg. ☎ **312 91 11**. Free, but there's a minimum drink charge of 8 DM ($5.35) Sun–Thurs, 16 DM ($10.65) Fri–Sat and holidays. U-Bahn: Ernst-Reuter-Platz.

A unique Berlin institution, it's the women who ask the men to dance here (except for the hourly "Men's Choice," when the green light goes on). Seating 700, it's popular with the middle-aged set, though there are some curious 20- and 30-year-olds. It opened in 1966, a companion to one in Hamburg since 1948. Both claim that in the past 40-some years, more than 95,000 couples have met on their dance floors and married. No jeans or tennis shoes are allowed; most men are in jacket and tie, and women are dressed up. If you're over 30, you'll probably get a kick out of this place. It's open Monday to Thursday from 8pm to 3am, Friday and Saturday from 8pm to 4am, and Sunday from 4pm to 1am. A live band plays most evenings. It's located about a 15-minute walk north of the Ku'damm.

Clärchen's Ballhaus
Auguststrasse 24/25, Berlin-Mitte. ☎ **282 92 95**. Cover Tues 4.60 DM ($3.05); Wed and Fri–Sat 6.40 DM ($4.25). U-Bahn: Rosenthaler Platz.

This dance hall is a relic of a more innocent age, when neighborhood establishments such as this dotted prewar Berlin. Founded by Clärchen in 1913 and now run by her grandson, this modest and casual dance hall is popular with middle and older generations, both married and single. A live band serenades those on the dance floor, and on Wednesdays it's ladies' choice—and it's considered extremely bad taste for men to say no. I get a kick here watching everyone have a good time. It's open Tuesday, Wednesday, Friday and Saturday evenings beginning at 7:30pm, closing when management decides to call it quits. A fifth-liter of beer is 2.10 DM ($1.40).

✪ Far Out
Kurfürstendamm 156, Charlottenburg. ☎ **320 007 24**. Cover Sun, Tues–Thurs 6 DM ($4); Fri–Sat 10 DM ($6.65). U-Bahn: Adenauerplatz, a couple minutes' walk.

This disco has several things going for it. For one thing, it's easy to reach, on the side street between Ciao Ciao restaurant and the Schaubühne am Lehniner Platz theater, toward the western end of the Ku'damm. It's also modern, spacious, clean, and laid-back, featuring rock and roll from the 1970s and 1980s and catering to a sophisticated crowd in their 20s and 30s. And wonder of wonders, it features a no-smoking night Tuesday evenings. If you want to see it at its roaring best, don't even think about showing up before midnight. Opening at 10pm, it closes at 4am weekdays and at 6am Friday and Saturday. Beer starts at 4.50 DM ($3).

✪ Metropol
Nollendorfplatz 5, Schöneberg. ☎ **216 41 22**. Cover 12 DM ($8), 3 DM ($2) applied to first drink. U-Bahn: Nollendorfplatz, a 1-minute walk.

Housed in a colossal and striking building that once was a theater, the Metropol has been one of the most popular and innovative establishments on the Berlin scene for years. Staging live concerts on weekdays, it serves as a disco every Friday and Saturday, from 9pm to 6am. It's a massive place, with three different dancing areas and eight bars, each with its own theme and design scheme, giving customers the illusion of moving from one locale to the next as they move through the club. The first floor boasts the largest bar, complete with video and a glazed facade overlooking the traffic of Nollendorfplatz. The main disco upstairs, with all the latest in laser and electric technology, is dominated by a spectacular lighting system and has a Japanese-theme bar.

3 The Bar & Cafe Scene
ON OR NEAR THE KU'DAMM

Aschinger
Kurfürstendamm 26. ☎ **882 55 58**. U-Bahn: Kurfürstendamm.

One of the most civilized places for a beer on the Ku'damm, this basement establishment with vaulted cellar rooms and subdued lighting is actually a brewery, featuring everything from its dark and heavy Bock Bier to a more light and thirst-quenching pilsner. German food is available "*Imbiss*-style" —simply go up to the food counter and choose what looks good. Sidewalk seating in summer. A fifth-liter of beer is 2.80 DM ($1.85). Open daily at 11am, it closes at 1am Sunday through Thursday and at 2am Friday and Saturday.

Ax Bax
Leibnizstrasse 34. ☎ **313 85 94**. S-Bahn: Savignyplatz, less than a 4-minute walk.

For a thirtysomething Berliner out on the town, Ax Bax is likely to be on the evening's agenda. This popular watering hole is frequented by writers and personalities in the film industry. A combination restaurant-bar, it offers a changing selection of Viennese specialties, which may include a meat-and-vegetable strudel, or marinated beef. Earlier in the evening people come to eat; after 10pm they usually come to drink, though food is served until a late 1am. Beer prices start at 5.50 DM ($3.65) for .4 liter. Open daily from 6pm to 3am, it's located a few minutes' walk west of Savignyplatz, off Kantstrasse.

Café am Arsenal
Fuggerstrasse 35. ☎ **213 58 26**. U-Bahn: Wittenbergplatz, less than a 5-minute walk.

The Berlin night crowd is rather fickle—patronizing the latest hot spot in droves, abandoning it the next week in pursuit of the newest craze. One of the streets of the moment is Fuggerstrasse, south of

Wittenbergplatz off Lietzenburger Strasse, lined with bars and restaurants. It's especially hopping in summer, when establishments take over sidewalks with their sprawls of tables and chairs. This unpretentious cafe is one of my favorites and one of the few establishments on the street open throughout the day, from 9am to 1am daily. It serves breakfast until 4pm and also offers more than a dozen choices of baguettes. A .4-liter beer is 4.50 DM ($3).

Café Bleibtreu
Bleibtreustrasse 45. ☎ **881 47 56**. S-Bahn: Savignyplatz, a 1-minute walk.

Located a short walk north of the Ku'damm on a side street noted for its bars and restaurants, this is one of my favorite cafes, day or night. One of the first so-called cafe/bars to open in Berlin, it has a cordial atmosphere and sidewalk seating in summer. It's popular with the 30-ish crowd and serves breakfast until 2pm. A glass of wine is 5.50 DM ($3.65), beer starts at 4.70 DM ($3.15) for .4 liter. It opens daily at 9:30am, closing at 1am Sunday to Thursday, and stays open until 2:30am Friday and Saturday.

Cour Carrée
Savignyplatz 5. ☎ **312 52 38**. S-Bahn: Savignyplatz, about a 2-minute walk.

One of several bars clustered around Savignyplatz, a small square just a 5-minute walk north of the Ku'damm, Cour Carrée offers outdoor seating beneath a canopy of spreading vines. Come in the summertime, and watch the world go by. Beer prices start at 5.50 DM ($2.80) for .4 liter. It's open daily from noon to 2am.

Dicke Wirtin
Carmerstrasse 9. ☎ **312 49 52**. S-Bahn: Savignyplatz, about a 3-minute walk.

Dicke Wirtin is named for the "fat barmaid" who used to run this place, but she's long gone, and so are the days when this was the hottest bar around. Still, it's one of the old-timers near Savignyplatz and continues to draw a faithful clientele. I've never been here in the wee hours of the night, but judging from the serious beer drinkers who are already here by early evening, things can only get rowdier. This old-style German pub, known for its stews, occupies part of the ground floor of a beautiful but neglected and bullet-ridden building, recently earmarked for renovation (from the looks of things, it could take years). Stews start at 4.50 DM ($3); beer at 3.90 DM ($2.60). It's open daily from noon to a late 4am.

Diener
Grolmanstrasse 47. ☎ **881 53 29**. S-Bahn or U-Bahn: Savignyplatz or Uhlandstrasse, both about a 3-minute walk.

This is a typical German *Kneipe*, or bar, but it's been here for decades and is named after a former champion boxer named Franz Diener. On the walls are photographs of famous people who have dropped in, including theater and film stars. Otherwise it's an unpretentious-looking place, the service is friendly, and it serves German soups and snacks. A good place for a bit of old Germany away from the glitz of the Ku'damm. It's open daily from 6pm to 1am and serves beer starting at 4.80 DM ($3.20) a glass.

Hard Rock Café

Meinekestrasse 21. ☎ **884 62 20**. U-Bahn: Kurfürstendamm, a couple minutes' walk.

You know Berlin is in when a Hard Rock Café moves to town. Opened in 1992, this worldwide chain features the usual rock 'n' roll memorabilia, T-shirts for sale, hamburgers, and beer. Be forewarned, however, that the music is loud and prices for food are high; a burger is 13.90 DM ($9.25). If you must, come for a beer, which starts at 4.50 DM ($3) for .3 liter, and a T-shirt. Located just south of the Ku'damm, it's open daily from noon to 2am.

Klo

Leibnizstrasse 57 (a few minutes' walk north of the Ku'damm). ☎ **324 22 99**.

I walked past this bar many years before finally being tempted to enter its doors. After all, its name is low-class slang for the word "toilet," the place is obviously tourist oriented, and, furthermore, to enter its doors one has to insert a mark, just like a stall in a public restroom. But while I can't recommend Klo as a must-see, it certainly is unique, and might be worth a laugh on a midnight prowl around the Ku'damm. Opened more than 25 years ago, it reminds me of a fun-fair spook house, except its theme is taken from that smallest room of the house and is packed full with weird statues, rolls of toilet paper, toilet lids, toilet brushes, bedpans, and, for some reason, bras. Gimmicks include a table that goes up and down (woe to the unsuspecting, slightly inebriated victims sitting here), a ceiling that rises and descends, sprays of mist throughout, and a surprise for women who use the first-class pay toilet. The owner certainly had fun here. A .3-liter mug of beer starts at 5 DM ($3.35), costing slightly more when there's occasional live music or disco. It opens at 7pm on weekdays and 6pm weekends, closing in the wee hours of the morning.

Ku'dorf

Joachimstaler Strasse 15. ☎ **883 66 66**. U-Bahn: Kurfürstendamm, about a 2-minute walk.

Located in a basement, the Ku'Dorf is a sprawling underground "village," which consists of several "lanes" lined with one tiny bar after another. In fact, there are 18 bars here, each with a different theme. At one end of the village is a disco; at the other, the Carrousel, popular with a middle-aged crowd and featuring music of the 1950s through the 1970s. Everybody in the Ku'Dorf is likely to be a tourist, the majority still in their teens; if you want to be among Berliners, go someplace else. There's a cover charge of 5 DM ($3.35), and a half liter of beer costs 7.50 DM ($4.65). Look for specials—during my last visit, beer was half-price on Wednesdays. Closed on Sunday, it opens the rest of the week at 8pm, staying open until 2am weekdays and a late 4am on weekends.

New York

Olivaer Platz 15. ☎ **883 62 58**. U-Bahn: Adenauerplatz.

Casual and trendy, this is one of the "in" places for people in their 20s and 30s. Even in the middle of the day people hang out here, read the newspaper, and bask in the sun at an outdoor table. A cafe by day, by midnight it looks more like a bar, and food specialties are breakfasts and American food. Located on a square south of the Ku'damm near Adenauerplatz, it opens at 9:30am, closing at 2am Sunday through Thursday, and 4am on the weekends. Beer starts at 4.50 DM ($3) for .3 liter, while a cup of coffee is 3.50 DM ($2.35).

Schwarzes Café
Kantstrasse 148. ☎ **313 80 38**. S-Bahn or U-Bahn: Savignyplatz or Uhlandstrasse, each about a 3-minute walk.

Schwarz means "black," and true to its name, the front room of this unconventional cafe is painted black. If you find black rooms depressing, head upstairs to a more cheerful surrounding, where the only black in sight is the furniture. Breakfast is the specialty, available anytime, ranging from 7 DM ($4.65) for a continental to 30 DM ($20) for the works. There's also a large selection of coffees, including spiked coffees starting at 8 DM ($5.35). A simple cup of coffee is 3 DM ($2). It's open round the clock, except Tuesdays from 3am to noon.

Wirtshaus Wuppke
Schlüterstrasse 21. ☎ **313 81 62**. S-Bahn: Savignyplatz, about a 2-minute walk.

This is a working man's neighborhood pub—plain, unrefined, and blackened from years of cigarette smoke. Most people come to drink, but there are also daily specials written on a blackboard, including hearty stews and salads. For entertainment, there's a pinball machine. Beer starts at 3.80 DM ($2.55) for .4 liter. It's open daily from 10am to 3am (in winter from noon to 3am).

Wirtshaus Zum Löwen
Hardenbergstrasse 29. ☎ **262 10 20**. U-Bahn: Kurfürstendamm or Bahnhof Zoo, each just a 1-minute walk.

Located between the Gedächtniskirche and Bahnhof Zoo and tucked behind a plaza, this beer hall is reminiscent of those in Munich. There's outdoor seating in summer, but even in winter you feel as if you're in a beer garden: the interior resembles a tree-filled Bavarian plaza. As with most beer halls, hearty platters of German food are available, and there's live music beginning at 7pm. Predictably, the clientele is almost exclusively tourists, but it's convenient if waiting for a train. A half-liter of beer costs 5.90 DM ($3.95) during the day, increasing to 6.90 DM ($4.60) in the evenings. It's open Sunday to Thursday from 10am to midnight, Friday and Saturday from 10am to 2am.

Zillemarkt
Bleibtreustrasse 48a. ☎ **881 70 40**. S-Bahn: Savignyplatz, a 1-minute walk.

This pleasant and airy establishment is named for the antique and curio market that used to be housed here. The building is from the turn of the century and features a brick floor and grillwork. In summer, there's a garden out back with seating, as well as sidewalk seating. Open daily from 10am to midnight, it serves breakfast until a late 4pm. Beer starts at 5.50 DM ($3.65) for a half-liter, while a Berliner Weisse is 6.50 DM ($4.35).

Zwiebelfisch

Savignyplatz 7-8. ☎ **312 73 63**. S-Bahn: Savignyplatz, a 2-minute walk.

This bar, with tables outside, has been around for more than 25 years and still enjoys great popularity. Because it stays open later than others in the area, this is where everyone ends up. Open daily from noon to 6am, usually most crowded at 4am. Beer starts at 5 DM ($3.35) for .4 liter, a .2-liter glass of wine is 5.50 DM ($3.65).

BERLIN-MITTE (EASTERN BERLIN)

The first few bars listed below are near Alexanderplatz, in the reconstructed neighborhood known as the Nikolaiviertel. The rest are found on or near Oranienburger Strasse, located near the S-Bahn station of the same name. One of Berlin's newest alternative nightlife meccas, Oranienburger Strasse has several weird and wonderful bars and also is the working street of prostitutes in search of customers in cars. It's a very strange mix.

Georg Brau

Spreeufer 4, Nikolaiviertel. ☎ **242 42 44** or **242 34 15**. U-Bahn: Alexanderplatz or Klosterstrasse.

Located on the banks of the Spree in the heart of the renovated Nikolai Quarter not far from Alexanderplatz, this microbrewery features spacious indoor seating and outdoor tables beside the Spree. It serves beer only in small fifth-liter glasses to keep it at its freshest, priced at 2.80 DM ($1.85), but if that's too much of a bother you can order the 1-meter-long "Georg-Pils," which is a meter-long board with 12 small glasses of beer for 28.20 DM ($18.80). The best time to come is on Saturday or Sunday from 10am to 1pm, when there's live music and a glass of beer is half-price. A limited menu offers German specialties. It's open daily in summer from 10am to midnight and in winter Monday to Friday from noon to midnight and Saturday and Sunday from 10am to midnight.

Zum Nussbaum

Propstrasse, Nikolaiviertel. ☎ **242 30 95**. U-Bahn: Alexanderplatz or Klosterstrasse, about 5-minute walk.

A reconstruction of a famous inn built in 1571 but destroyed during World War II, Zum Nussbaum is a cozy bar with wood-paneled walls, low-ceilings, and minuscule rooms. It was a favorite hangout of Heinrich Zille, a famous Berliner artist. A few outside tables, under a walnut tree, offer a view of the Nikolaikirche. It's open daily from noon to 2am, with beer prices starting at 5 DM ($3.35) for a half-liter.

Obst & Gemüse

Oranienburger Strasse 48. ☎ **282 96 47**. S-Bahn: Oranienburger Strasse, about a 1-minute walk. U-Bahn: Oranienburger Tor, a 1-minute walk.

One of the most "normal"-looking bars on Berlin-Mitte's most active nightlife strip, this small establishment takes its name from the fruit and vegetable store that used to occupy this spot. First opened in 1992, it was forced to shut down shortly thereafter, when neighbors complained of the loud music and the equally loud patrons. It reopened with insulation installed in its walls and ceiling, and has been happily loud ever since. The bar-hoppers here are mostly in their mid- to late-20s, and, according to one of its regular customers, are not the "artistic" type that hangs out at the Tacheles across the street. "What you see is what you get," he said. Whatever that means, what you do get here are such rarities as margaritas, daiquiris, and homemade brownies. It's open daily from noon to 3am, and a beer costs 4 DM ($2.65) for .3 liter.

Silberstein

Oranienburger Strasse 27. ☎ **28 12 095**. S-Bahn: Oranienburger Strasse, less than a 4-minute walk.

This is the trendiest, hippest, and most sophisticated bar on Oranienburger Strasse, located in the shadows of the newly renovated synagogue. It's decorated in minimalist style, with a bare floor, modern art on the walls, and high-backed chairs that are artsy but uncomfortable. If you like them, though, you can buy them: everything in the bar is for sale, including the tables and artwork. In summer, you can sit out back in the courtyard and watch the artists at work. Occasionally the bar transforms into a disco, for which there's a 5-DM ($3.35) admission price. Otherwise, a beer here costs 4 DM ($2.65) for .3 liter. It opens at 4pm Monday to Friday and at noon Saturday and Sunday—the closing hour is whenever the staff has had enough, usually the wee hours of the morn.

Tacheles

Oranienburger Strasse. S-Bahn: Oranienburger Strasse, about a 1-minute walk. U-Bahn: Oranienburger Tor, a 1-minute walk.

This place is so alternative that for several years it didn't have a telephone or a sign outside its door and didn't seem likely to make it through another year. No wonder: The building itself is a massive bombed-out department store, built in 1907–08 as a state-of-the-art store with an impressive 14 entrances and 12 elevators. Heavily damaged in World War II, it was taken over by a group of artists in 1990, who registered it as an historic landmark and turned many of its sadly neglected rooms into studios, exhibition space, and venues for performances. Still in an extraordinary state of disrepair and lacking heat and most of its window panes, it has a cafe on the ground floor, popular with the cutting edge of Berlin's avant-garde and a must for a night out on Oranienburger Strasse. Slightly tamer than it was a few years ago, it can at times still boast a fairly bizarre atmosphere, where characters from *Star Wars* would feel right at home. Its name, by the way, comes from Yiddish, meaning "straight talk." The cafe is open daily from 10am to at least 4am, and a bottle of Beck's beer costs 4 DM ($2.65).

Verkehrs-Beruhigte O(st)Zone

Auguststrasse. S-Bahn: Oranienburger Strasse, a couple minutes' walk. U-Bahn: Oranienburger Tor, a 1-minute walk.

Located on the corner of Auguststrasse and Oranienburger Strasse, this bar is a comfortable place for a drink. Its name is a play on words:

Verkehrs-Beruhigte Zone means a pedestrian-only street; Ost-zone refers to East Berlin. True to its name, a Trabant (East German car) is part of the bar's decoration, along with newspapers plastered to the ceiling and a portrait of ousted Honecker behind the bar. A .4-liter beer costs 3.50 DM ($2.35), and opening hours are from 9am daily, closing at irregular hours at night.

NEAR NOLLENDORFPLATZ

Cafe Sidney
Winterfeldstrasse 40. ☎ **216 52 53**. U-Bahn: Nollendorfplatz, a 5-minute walk.

This modern and breezy cafe/bar stands on a square called Winterfeldplatz, famous for its morning market on Wednesday and Saturday. Decorated with palm trees and featuring two pool tables and split-level seating, it opens at 8am on Wednesday and Saturday, 9am the rest of the week, and serves breakfast until 5pm. Closing hours are 2am Sunday through Thursday and 4am Friday and Saturday. A half liter of beer is 6 DM ($4). and a glass of wine is 5 DM ($3.35).

Slumberland
Winterfeldplatz. ☎ **216 53 49**. U-Bahn: Nollendorfplatz, about a 5-minute walk.

Everyone seems to drop by here after they've been to the Saturday market on Winterfeldplatz. Slumberland is at its most crowded, however, in the very late hours, when many people come here after other bars have closed down. It plays African, Caribbean, reggae, and calypso music, and even has a real sand floor, along with fake banana trees and palms, to set the mood. Beer prices start at 4.50 DM ($3) for a .4 liter, wine at 5 DM ($3.35). It's open Sunday to Friday from 8pm to 4am, and on Saturday from 11am to 6pm and 9pm to 4am.

Café Swing
Nollendorfplatz 3-4. ☎ **216 61 37**. U-Bahn: Nollendorfplatz, a 1-minute walk.

Popular with a young, student crowd, this cafe is about as informal and casual as it gets. It offers outdoor seating in summer, and every Saturday evening (and sometimes Friday as well) there's free live music starting at 1am. The paintings on the wall are bright and slightly jarring—not the kind of place in which you'd want to nurse a hangover. Beer prices start at 4.50 DM ($3) for a .4 liter. It's open daily from about 10:30am to 3am.

IN KREUZBERG

Kreuzberg used to be the insider's tip for Berlin's alternative nightlife scene. Although there's still plenty of that, parts of Kreuzberg have become fashionable and yuppified, as Berlin's professional crowds claim areas of their own. Partiers in search of the radical should head toward Wiener Strasse.

Café Fontane
Fontanepromenade 1. ☎ **691 33 45**. U-Bahn: Südstern, a 1-minute walk.

This modern and trendy bar features split-level seating, palm trees, a billiard table, a large window facade, and an outdoor terrace. It's a great place to watch the sun set over the treetops of the park across the street.

In addition to American and Mexican food, it offers Beck's on tap for 5.50 DM ($3.65) for a half liter; a cup of coffee is 2.80 DM ($1.85). It opens daily at 9am, closing at 4am weekdays and 5am Friday and Saturday nights.

Leydicke
Mansteinstrasse 4. ☎ **216 29 73**. U-Bahn: Yorckstrasse. Bus 119 from the Ku'damm to Mansteinstrasse stop.

Opened in 1877, this bar is one of the oldest drinking establishments in Berlin and features an antique bar and shelving, wainscot, and ceiling. It makes and sells its own wines and liqueurs, produced from fruit brought in from western Germany. Wine by the glass starts at 6 DM ($4). It's open Monday to Friday from 5pm to midnight, Saturday from 2pm to midnight, and Sunday from 6pm to midnight.

Madonna
Wiener Strasse 22. ☎ **611 69 43**. U-Bahn: Görlitzer Bahnhof. Bus 129.

Anyone familiar with Berlin's bar scene has either been here or heard of this place, by far the most well-known establishment on Wiener Strasse. It attracts students, the young working class, and punks, and if you want to dress like everyone else here, wear either denim or leather. Although singer Madonna may first come to mind, its namesake is the other Madonna, present in several religious and sacrilegious statues that decorate the place (including a half-naked mannequin wearing a cross), along with fake stained-glass windows. A bottle of Beck's beer, which is all everyone seems to drink, costs 3.50 DM ($2.35). The place is open daily from noon to about 3am (to 4am on weekends).

Morena
Wiener Strasse 22. ☎ **611 69 43**. U-Bahn: Görlitzer Bahnhof. Bus 129.

This is Wiener Strasse's funkiest, coolest bar, where hair styles range from dreadlocks to bleached orange, long hair to shaved heads, and where nose studs are so common they're almost passé. Crowded even during the day, especially in nice weather when you can sit outside. A bottle of Beck's beer is 4 DM ($2.65), and it's open from 9am to 3am daily.

Wienerblut
Wiener Strasse 14. ☎ **618 90 23**. U-Bahn: Görlitzer Bahnhof.

Rustic punk may be the best way to describe this typical Kreuzberg bar, popular with young people who strive for the unkempt, casual look in hairstyles and clothing. Earrings for men are an absolute must. There's nothing refined about this alternative hangout, unless you count the red lights above the bar that cast a bloodlike glow over the place (Wienerblut means Viennese blood, a play on Wiener Strasse). Diversions include a Foosball and a pinball table. Beer prices start at 3.50 DM ($2.35) for a third of a liter. It's open from 5pm to 3am on weekdays, to 5am on weekends.

Café Wunderbar
Körtestrasse 38. ☎ **692 11 20**. U-Bahn: Südstern, a 1-minute walk.

Impressions

In the Berlin cafes and restaurants the busy time is from midnight on till three. Yet most of the people who frequent them are up again at seven. Either the Berliner has solved the great problem of modern life, how to do without sleep, or, with Carlyle, he must be looking forward to eternity.
—Jerome K. Jerome, 1900

This is the most casual watering hole in the area, simple and pleasant with blue-and-white walls, a pool table, pinball and video games, and a window facade with a view of a towering church. Hearty breakfasts, including various kinds of scrambled eggs, are served until 3pm. A half-liter of beer is 5 DM ($3.35); a cup of coffee is 2.80 DM ($1.85). It's open Monday to Thursday from 11am to 3am and Friday to Sunday from 11am to 4am.

BEER GARDENS

Loretta's Garden
Lietzenburgerstrasse 89. ☎ **882 33 54**. U-Bahn: Uhlandstrasse, about a 5-minute walk.

This huge beer garden, located a few minutes' walk south of the Ku'damm in the heart of the city, seats about 6,000 people under a spread of trees. It's open from April to the end of September, daily from 10am to 1am. You fetch your own beer here, with half-liter mugs costing 6.50 DM ($4.35). Stalls sell food ranging from American spareribs and barbecued chicken to crepes.

Luise
Königin-Luise-Strasse 40. ☎ **832 84 87**. U-Bahn: Dahlem-Dorf, a 1-minute walk.

Located in Dahlem not far from the area's many museums, Luise is a popular watering hole with several hundred seats outdoors. In addition to .4-liter mugs of beer selling for 5.50 DM ($3.65), it also offers Weissbier, a wheat beer. It's open when the weather is fine, from 10am to 11pm.

GAY BARS

Andreas Kneipe
Ansbacher Strasse 29. ☎ **218 32 57**. U-Bahn: Wittenbergplatz, a couple minutes' walk.

This well-known gay bar has been here more than a quarter century. It's popular for both its location just off Wittenbergplatz and its laid-back atmosphere. Almost anyone—including women and straight couples—can feel comfortable among the mixed clientele. A beer costs 3.20 DM ($2.15) for .3 liter. It's open daily from 11am to 4am.

Tom's Bar
Corner of Motzstrasse and Eisenacher Strasse. ☎ **213 45 20**. U-Bahn: Nollendorfplatz, a 4-minute walk.

This large bar attracts men from their 20s to 40s. Pictures of men adorn the walls, a glass display case advertises a leather shop, and pornographic films are shown on a large screen in the back room. In the basement is a "contact" room. It's open daily from 10pm to 6am.

FOR WOMEN ONLY

Extra Dry
Pariser Strasse 3. ☎ **885 22 06**. U-Bahn: Spichernstrasse, a 1-minute walk.

This cafe is *for women only* and is certainly one of the best women's cafes in Berlin. Clean, modern, and nicely furnished, Extra Dry does not serve alcohol; instead, it offers milk shakes, fruit cocktails, and light snacks. This cafe is a good place for women traveling alone or tired of the usual bar scene; here you can sit and write letters if that's what you feel like doing. The service is friendly. Extra Dry is open Sunday and Tuesday through Thursday from 11am to 11pm, and Friday and Saturday from 11am to midnight.

Pour Elle
Kalckreuthstrasse 10. ☎ **218 75 33**. U-Bahn: Nollendorfplatz, about a 5-minute walk.

This establishment for women only features two bars and a dance floor. It's open Wednesday through Sunday from 9pm to 5am.

4 More Entertainment

MOVIES

You won't have any trouble finding a cinema showing the latest movies from Hollywood, dubbed, unfortunately for visitors, in German. Luckily, Berlin's main cinematic attraction lies in its "Off-Ku'damm" cinemas, those specializing in the classics of film history as well as new German and international productions of independent filmmakers. Check *tip* or *zitty* for listings of current films. (*OF*) means that the film is in the original language, and (*OmU*) means that the film has German subtitles. You can also call the following cinemas to ask what's currently being shown.

Arsenal
Welserstrasse 25. ☎ **218 68 48**. Tickets 10 DM ($6.65). U-Bahn: Wittenbergplatz. Bus 119, 219.

This is the original Off-Ku'damm cinema, and since the 1970s it has been paving the way for alternative programs. Arsenal specializes in retrospectives, film series, and experimental and avant-garde films from around the world, often in the original language.

Filmmuseum Potsdam
Marstall, Potsdam. ☎ **0331/27181-0**. Tickets 6 DM ($4) adults, 4 DM ($2.65) students and senior citizens. S-Bahn: Potsdam-Stadt, then a 5-minute walk.

Located in Potsdam's film museum, this cinema shows classics, little-known films, and more recent releases, both German and international.

Kino Zeughaus
Deutsches Historisches Museum, Unter den Linden 2. ☎ **215 02-0**. Tickets 5 DM ($3.35). Bus 100.

If you understand German, this theater in the German Historical Museum is the best place to see the German classics, retrospectives, and rarely shown films. Foreign films are also shown, usually in their original language.

Odeon

Hauptstrasse 116. ☎ **781 56 67**. Tickets 10 DM ($6.65). U-Bahn: Innsbrucker Platz.

This is the place to go if you want to see the latest Hollywood flick, since it specializes in English-language recent releases. It even sells popcorn.

CASINOS

If you wish to try your luck at the gambling tables, head toward the Europa-Center on Budapester Strasse, where you'll find the **Spielbank Berlin** (☎ **250 08 90**). Since its opening in 1975, it has witnessed an average of 1,000 guests a day, who come to play French and American roulette, blackjack, baccarat, and the one-arm bandits. Admission is 5 DM ($3.35), and a coat and tie are required for men in the winter. It's open daily from 3pm to 3am, and the nearest U-Bahn stations are Kurfürstendamm and Bahnhof Zoologischer Garten, just a couple of minutes away.

5 Late-Night Bites

If hunger strikes after midnight, there are a number of restaurants, bars, and cafes open to the early morning hours. The establishments listed in the next paragraph are described in further detail in Chapter 6, "Where to Eat." In addition, many bars listed above remain open to as late as 4am.

The following restaurants are all within walking distance of the Ku'damm: Avanti (Italian), open to 2am; Ciao Ciao (Italian), open to 2am Sunday to Thursday, and to 3am on Friday and Saturday nights; Grung Thai (Thai food), open to 3am; Orient (Middle Eastern food), open to 4am; Piccola Taormina Tavola Calda (Italian), open to 2am; Athener Grill (Greek and Italian), open to 4am during the week, and to 5am on weekends; and Jimmy's Diner (American/Mexican), open to 4am during the week, and to 6am on Friday and Saturday nights. Keep in mind, however, that these are the actual closing hours—last order is generally one hour before closing.

For dining around the clock, your best bets are these two establishments, both located near Savignyplatz within a five-minute walk of the Ku'damm.

Schwarzes Café

Kantstrasse 148. ☎ **313 80 38.** Breakfast 8–30 DM ($5.35–$20). No credit cards. Around the clock, except Tues 3am–noon. S-Bahn or U-Bahn: Savignyplatz or Uhlandstrasse, each about a 3-minute walk. BREAKFAST.

After a night of carousing this is one of the best places in town for breakfast, ranging from continental to elaborate affairs, with alcoholic coffees to boot.

Impressions

Aside from the theaters and movie houses; aside from the elegant hotels, the restaurants, cafes, and confectionary shops; aside from the countless bars, dance halls, and cabarets, which only a thick tome could list; aside from the light-flooded Friedrichstrasse, and Kurfürstendamm, and the places on Jäger and Behrensstrasse, where you find a night club in every house . . . where admission is free and a thousand shapely legs are displayed . . . aside from all this, there are two kinds of places: those one talks about and those one doesn't talk about, but frequents just the same.
—Eugen Szatmari, 1927

12. Apostol

Bleibtreustrasse 43. ☎ **312 14 33**. Courses 15–20 DM ($10–$13.35). No credit cards. Open 24 hours. S-Bahn: Savignyplatz, less than a 1-minute walk. PIZZA.

Located on a pedestrian lane that links Savignyplatz with Bleibtreustrasse, this new and trendy locale is actually tucked under the elevated S-Bahn tracks and hopes to make its mark on the Berlin scene by staying open around the clock. Food is served from 7am to 5am daily. Its walls are bathed in warm colors of sea blue and rose, accented with large murals done in the style of Rembrandt and Da Vinci—the Middle Ages meets Savigny chic. It specializes in pizzas from a stone oven but is also popular as a place to hang out with a cup of coffee or a drink. Breakfast is also available. In warm weather you can sit on the outdoor terrace.

11

Easy Excursions from Berlin

If you take only one excursion outside Berlin, it should be to Potsdam and Frederick the Great's palace of Sanssouci. In summertime, another great excursion is to the Spreewald, where you can hike or take a boat trip through a unique landscape of waterways.

1 Potsdam

15 miles SW of Berlin

Potsdam was once Germany's most important baroque town, serving both as a garrison and as a residence of Prussia's kings and royal families from the 17th to 20th centuries. The most famous of the Prussian kings was Frederick the Great, who succeeded in uniting Germany under his rule and who built himself a delightful rococo palace in Potsdam, Schloss Sanssouci. His palace still stands, surrounded by a 750-acre estate with several other magnificent structures, including the Neues Palais.

History buffs will also want to visit Cecilienhof, site of the 1945 Potsdam Conference, while fans of German film will want to see the Filmmuseum. As for Potsdam itself, although much of it was destroyed during World War II, it still has a delightful Altstadt (Old Town), including a historical Holländisches Viertel (Dutch Quarter) with houses dating from the mid-1700s. Wear your walking shoes, because this is a great town for walking. You'll want to spend the better part of a day here.

ESSENTIALS

TOURING SCHLOSS SANSSOUCI Schloss Sanssouci can be visited only by joining a guided tour, conducted only in German and often sold out by noon, especially in the summer and on weekends. Try, therefore, to schedule your trip to Potsdam on a weekday and head out early in the morning, allowing at least an hour for the trip from Berlin's center to Potsdam. If you can't get into Schloss Sanssouci, don't despair. I personally think the outside of the palace, viewed from the back below the vineyard terraces, is the most important (and most picturesque) thing to see in Potsdam. In addition, you can always visit the nearby Neues Palais. However, if you're worried about getting into the palace and wish to have a tour in English, you might consider joining an organized sightseeing tour from Berlin (see "Organized Tours" in

Chapter 7 for a list of companies offering trips to Potsdam). The disadvantage of the tours, however, is that they don't allow you to explore Potsdam, especially the Altstadt, on your own. An alternative would be to join an organized tour and then remain in Potsdam, exploring the city at your leisure and then finding your own way back to Berlin.

GETTING THERE The best way to reach Potsdam is by catching S-Bahn 3 or 7 from one of several major stations in central Berlin—including Alexanderplatz, Bahnhof Zoologischer Garten, and Charlottenburg—and riding it all the way to Potsdam-Stadt station for the price of a normal single ticket, which is 3.70 DM ($2.45).

From Potsdam-Stadt station, it's a good 40- to 50-minute walk to Schloss Sanssouci, which isn't as bad as it sounds because you'll pass through the quaint Altstadt on the way. Otherwise, an alternative is to board tram no. 91, 96, or 98 from the bridge in front of Potsdam-Stadt and take it to Luisenplatz (easily recognizable as a square with Potsdam's own Brandenburg Gate in the middle), from which the palace is a 10-minute walk. Since Potsdam is included in Greater Berlin's transportation network, regular tickets, 24-hour tickets, and weekly tickets are also valid for these tram lines and most other buses and trams throughout Potsdam.

Although not included in Berlin's transportation network, A1 is the most convenient and easiest way to reach Schloss Sanssouci. It departs every 20 minutes or so directly from in front of Potsdam-Stadt and travels to Schloss Sanssouci and then Neues Palais. The cost of this bus ticket is 3 DM ($2). Finally, the no. 695 bus, which departs from Bassinplatz in the city center and is included in Berlin's fare system, travels to both palaces.

After visiting Schloss Sanssouci and the Neues Palais, you can return to Potsdam-Stadt by boarding bus no. 695 and taking it back to Luisenplatz, transferring there to tram 91, 96, or 98; or take A1 directly back to Potsdam-Stadt. Alternatively, you can walk from Neues Palais to the Wildpark station in about eight minutes and take the local train to Potsdam-Stadt.

VISITOR INFORMATION For visitor information, contact **Potsdam-Information,** Friedrich-Ebert-Strasse 5 (☎ 0331/29 11 00 or 29 33 85), located about a five-minute walk from Potsdam-Stadt station in the heart of the city. From April to October it's open Monday to Friday from 9am to 8pm, Saturday and Sunday from 9am to 6pm; in winter it's open Monday to Friday from 10am to 6pm, Saturday and Sunday from 11am to 3pm. There's also a branch in the heart of the Altstadt at Brandenburger Strasse 18, open Monday to Friday from 10am to 6pm and Saturday from 10am to 2pm.

For information on Sanssouci, including guided-tour information and all the buildings open to the public on the massive park grounds, drop by the **Sanssouci Visitor Center**, located near Schloss Sanssouci on An der Orangerie street across from the windmill. Housed in the former royal stables built in the 19th century for Friedrich Wilhelm IV, it is open daily in March to October from 8:30am to 5pm and in winter from 9am to 4pm.

WHAT TO SEE & DO

The best way to see Potsdam is on your own two feet, starting at Bassinplatz, site of Potsdam's bus depot and the city's main market, held weekdays from 6am to 5pm and Saturdays from 6am to noon. North of Bassinplatz is one of Potsdam's oldest and most picturesque quarters, the Holländisches Viertel (Dutch Quarter), concentrated between Friedrich-Ebert-Strasse and Hebbelstrasse. Its 134 homes of gabled brick, built in the mid-1700s by and for settlers from the Low Countries, represent the largest concentration of Dutch-style homes outside Holland and are slowly being renovated. Stretching west from Bassinplatz is Brandenburger Strasse, Potsdam's most famous street. A quaint pedestrian lane lined with shops and cafes housed in beautifully restored buildings with ornate facades, it leads straight through the Altstadt, and you can walk its length in about 10 minutes. At its western end is a large stone portal, Potsdam's own Brandenburger Tor, located in the middle of a large square called Luisenplatz. From here, Allee nach Sanssouci leads to the royal estate. This is the most dramatic way to approach Schloss Sanssouci, since your first view of it includes six grassy terraces with the palace perched on top. From Schloss Sanssouci, you can reach Neues Palais by walking through the wonderful surrounding park in approximately 20 minutes.

✪ Schloss Sanssouci and Park

Zur historischen Mühle. ☎ **0331/96 94-190**. Admission 8 DM ($5.35) adults, 4 DM ($2.65) students, children, and senior citizens. Apr–Sept daily 9am–5pm (last tour); Oct, Feb, and Mar daily 9am–4pm; Nov–Jan 9am–3pm. Closed daily from 12:30–1pm; all day the first and third Mon of every month. Bus A1 or 695.

Although Potsdam was first mentioned in documents in 993 A.D. and became the second residence of the Great Elector of Brandenburg in 1660, it was under Friedrich Wilhelm I (Frederick William I) that the city blossomed into a garrison town. Credited with building the great Prussian army, Friedrich Wilhelm I was succeeded by a rather reluctant son, Friedrich II, who first tried to shirk responsibilities by fleeing to England with his friend, Lieutenant von Kette, an army officer. They were caught and tried as deserters, and Friedrich was forced to witness the beheading of his friend (some say lover) as punishment. Friedrich II thereafter conformed to his father's wishes, married, and became the third king of Prussia, to be more popularly known as Friedrich der Grosse (Frederick the Great). He doubled the size of the Prussian army and went on to make Prussia the greatest military power on the Continent.

Frederick the Great built much of Sanssouci as we know it today, created in part to satisfy his artistic and intellectual passions. Instead of being able to devote himself to the arts and the period of Enlightenment as he would have liked, Frederick the Great became involved in one war after the other, including the Silesian Wars and the Seven Years' War. He retreated to Sanssouci to meditate, pursue philosophy, and forget the worries of life. In fact, *sans souci* means "without worry."

Schloss Sanssouci (Sanssouci Palace), the summer residence of Frederick the Great, was designed by Georg von Knobelsdorff in the

1740s according to plans drawn up by the king himself. Although it looks comparatively modest and ordinary if approached from the main road and entrance, it is breathtaking if viewed from the park on the other side, for the palace sits atop six grassy terraces, cut into the side of a hill like steps in a pyramid. The terraces were once vineyards and seem to overwhelm the much smaller one-story palace. It's only after you've climbed the graceful staircases leading up through the terraces that the palace finally reveals itself, like a surprise package. Also on the top terrace is Frederick the Great's tomb.

Frederick the Great must have liked wine, because the motifs of grapes and wine are carried from the vineyards into the palace itself. Note the figures supporting the roof facing the vineyards—they look a bit tipsy and happy, as though they've just indulged in the fruits of the vine. Inside are statues of Bacchus, god of wine, as well as pictures and reliefs of grapes, vines, and people enjoying themselves. Among the guests who passed through Sanssouci was Voltaire, the great French philosopher. He stayed in Potsdam for three years, during which time he and the king spent many an evening together.

Yet Frederick the Great maintained a rather austere life, preferring to sleep in a camp bed like a soldier rather than in a royal bed. Even the Festival Hall is modestly small, noted for its inlaid marble floor in the pattern of a vineyard. The Concert Room, which contains Frederick the Great's flute, is exquisite; a stucco ceiling in the pattern of a spider web gives the illusion that the room is so light and airy that it can be held together with fragile strands. The Voltaire Room boasts hand-carved wooden reliefs painted in bright yellows, blues, reds, and other colors, as well as a chandelier with delicate porcelain flowers and brass flowers.

Schloss Sanssouci can be viewed only by joining a guided tour, which unfortunately is conducted only in German. Tours depart every 20 minutes and last 40 minutes. Remember, if you can't get into Schloss Sanssouci, head for the Neues Palais, described below.

Be sure, too, to walk through the grounds of Sanssouci Park. It's huge, with 750 acres containing a wide range of gardens, ponds, streams, and statues of Greek and mythological figures. There are, for example, the Dutch Garden, the Sicilian Garden, and the Nordic Garden, as well as the Östlicher Lustgarten (Eastern Pleasure Garden) and Westlicher Lustgarten (Western Pleasure Garden). The Orangerie, located in the Westlicher Lustgarten and reached via pathways through the Sicilian and Nordic Gardens, was built according to the style of the Italian Renaissance period to house tropical plants and later became rather elaborate accommodations for guests. Today it houses changing exhibitions and is open only from mid-May to mid-October, with an admission of 4 DM ($4). The Neue Kammern, open every day except Fridays, was built by Knobelsdorff in 1747 and also served as a guest house. My favorite room here is the fantastic Marquetry Cabinet, with walls of inlaid wood. Thirty-minute tours here, in German only, cost 5 DM ($3.35) for adults and 3 DM ($2) for students and senior citizens. The Bildergalerie (Picture Gallery), built between 1755 and 1763 to house Frederick the Great's collection, still contains

Easy Excursions

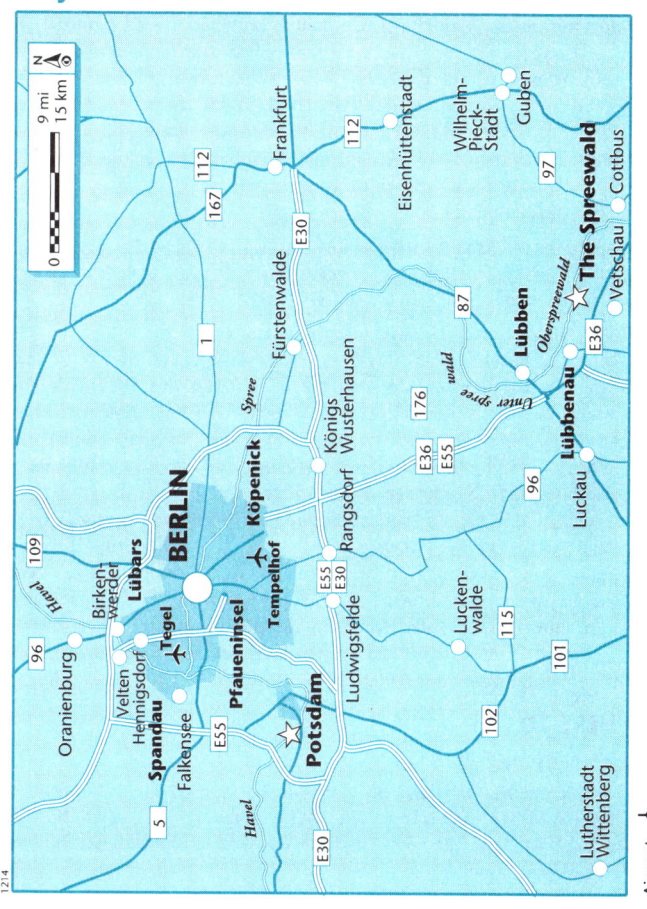

works by Italian Renaissance, Dutch, and Flemish old masters. (*Note:* It is closed until 1996 for renovation.) Finally, another interesting structure in the park is the Chinesisches Teehaus (Chinese Teahouse), built in the shape of a clover and featuring gilded statues of mandarins.

Neues Palais

Sanssouci Park. ☎ **0331/97 31 43**. Admission without guided tour, 6 DM ($4) adults, 3 DM ($2) students, children, and senior citizens; with guided tour, 8 DM ($5.35) and 4 DM ($2.65), respectively. Apr–Sept daily 9am–5pm; Oct, Feb, and Mar daily 9am–4pm; Nov–Jan 9am–3pm. Closed daily from 12:45–1:15pm; all day the second and fourth Mon of every month. Bus A1 or 695.

The largest building in Sanssouci Park, the Neues Palais was built 20 years after Schloss Sanssouci as a show of Prussian strength following the devastation of the Seven Years' War. Also serving as a summer residence for the royal Hohenzollern family, it is much more ostentatious than Schloss Sanssouci and in comparison seems grave, solemn, and humorless. Wilhelm II, Germany's last Kaiser, used it until 1918, his last year in power. When his family fled to exile in Holland, they took 60 wagons full of possessions with them from the Neues Palais.

From November through May, Neues Palais can be viewed only on guided tours, conducted in German and lasting approximately one hour. From the end of May through October, you can elect to either take a tour or walk through on your own.

Cecilienhof

Neuer Garten. ☎ **0331/96 94-224**. Admission without tour, 4 DM ($2.65) adults, 3 DM ($2) students, children, and senior citizens. May–Oct 9am–5pm; Nov–Apr 9am–4pm. Closed second and fourth Mon of every month. Bus 695.

The Neuer Garten (New Garden) was laid out at the end of the 18th century, alongside lake Heiligensee. It's the home of Cecilienhof, Potsdam's newest palace, built between 1913 and 1916 in mock-Tudor style by Kaiser Wilhelm II. It served as a royal residence of the last German crown prince and his wife, Cecilie, until the end of World War II. Its 176 rooms contain a museum, a hotel, and a restaurant. It also boasts 55 chimneys, each one different.

Cecilienhof gained everlasting fame in 1945 when it served as the headquarters of the Potsdam Conference. It was here that Truman, Stalin, and Churchill (and later Attlee of Great Britain) met to discuss the disarmament and future of a divided Germany. There's a museum here showing the conference room and the round table where the Big Three sat. Tours are offered only in German, so I recommend walking through it on your own.

WHERE TO EAT

✪ Historische Mühle

Zur Historischen Mühle. ☎ **231 10**. Soups 4–5 DM ($2.65–$3.35); main courses 10–20 DM ($6.65–$13.35). No credit cards. Apr–Oct Tues–Sun 10am–6pm; Nov–Mar Wed–Sun 10am–5pm. Directions: A 2-minute walk from Schloss Sanssouci. Bus A1 or 695. GERMAN.

Pleasantly situated in a forest of green, this German restaurant is my top choice for a meal in Potsdam and is convenient if you're visiting Schloss Sanssouci—look for it near the windmill, from which it takes its name. Start your meal with a bowl of Ukrainian Soljanka soup, followed by a main course of Schweinebraten with red cabbage and potatoes, Kasselbraten with sauerkraut and potatoes, Hungarian Gulasch, Schnitzel with mushrooms and french fries, grilled chicken, duck, Schweinshaxe, or Eisbein. If the weather is warm, you may opt instead for a beer in the restaurant's large beer garden. An alternative is the Jagdhaus, an *Imbiss* on the grounds of the restaurant selling beer and Würste, with outdoor seating. (*Note*: Closed until 1996 for renovation.)

Cafe im Drachenhaus

Maulbeerallee. ☎ **29 15 94**. Salads 13–16 DM ($8.65–$10.65); main courses 18–25 DM ($12–$16.65). No credit cards. Summer, daily 11am–7pm; winter, daily 11am–6pm. Bus A1 or 695 to Drachenhaus stop. GERMAN.

You have to be willing to climb a lot of stairs to reach this delightful place, but your efforts will be justly rewarded. After all, where else can

Potsdam

- **1** Holländisches Viertel
- **2** Potsdam Information
- **3** Ihre Frisch-Backstübe
- **4** Potsdamer Börse
- **5** Brandenburger Tor
- **6** Schloss Sanssouci
- **7** Historische Mühle
- **8** Orangerie
- **9** Neues Palais
- **10** Chinesisches Teehaus
- **11** Cecilienhof

Post Office ⊠   Church ✝   Information ⓘ

you sip a cup of coffee and eat a torte in a tiny house shaped like a Chinese pagoda? Perched atop a hill, it was built in 1770 as the living quarters of the royal vintner, but has served as a cafe since the end of the 19th century. Since it's small, you may have to wait for a table; in summer, more tables are placed outside. The food is expensive and limited—chicken breast, pork médallions, and steak are the main entrees, so come here mainly for a cup of coffee, priced at 3 DM ($2), and dessert, most costing around 4.50 DM ($3).

Ihre Frisch-Backstübe

Corner of Brandenburger Strasse and Friedrich-Ebert-Strasse. ☎ **48 21 15**. Sandwiches 3–6 DM ($2–$4). No credit cards. Mon–Fri 6:30am–6:30pm, Sat 6am–2pm, Sun 11am–5pm. Directions: A couple minutes' walk from Bassinplatz. SANDWICHES/SNACKS.

This deservedly popular bakery chain offers freshly baked breads, sandwiches, baguettes, and daily specials ranging from pizza by the slice to noodle casseroles, all on display behind the cafeteria's glass case. There are chest-high tables where you can eat your goodies, or, if you wish, order take-out and eat at one of the benches on Brandenburger Strasse.

There's a smaller branch of Ihre Frisch-Backstübe about halfway down Brandenburger Strasse, in front of Horten department store. It's an outdoor *Imbiss,* with the same open hours.

Potsdamer Börse

Brandenburger Strasse 35-36. ☎ **29 25 05**. Soups and appetizers 5–10 DM ($3.35–$6.65); main courses 10–24 DM ($6.65–$16). AE, DC, MC, V. Daily 11am–10:30pm. Directions: A 1-minute walk from the Bassinplatz bus center. GERMAN.

Just a short walk from Potsdam's main bus center in the heart of the Altstadt, this upscale restaurant served as a distillery and wine merchant's shop in the 18th century. Its menu includes soups, Sauerbraten, omelets, fish, chicken fricassee, smoked pork, roast duck, and Schnitzel. Adjoining the restaurant is the Marktklause, a German-style pub with even cheaper food and snacks, including Gulaschsuppe, Schnitzel, scrambled eggs with potatoes, and changing daily specials, with prices ranging from 2 DM ($1.35) to 12 DM ($8). It's open Monday to Saturday from 7am to midnight and Sunday from 10am to midnight.

2 The Spreewald

60 miles SE of Berlin

The Spreewald forms one of middle Europe's most unique landscapes. Here the Spree River spreads out into countless streams and canals, a labyrinth of waterways through woodlands—a bayou. Little wonder that for decades it's been a lure for city dwellers, who come here for a ride in a punt, a German version of the gondola.

Lübbenau, first settled by Slaves in the 9th or 10th century, lies in the upper Spreewald and is a convenient starting point for boat rides through the region from April to the end of October. The upper Spreewald contains about 300 miles of tree-lined canals winding through a flat countryside of meadows. Almost none of the canals is open to motorized vehicles, with the result that even barges laden with vegetables bound for market are also hand-poled.

ESSENTIALS

GETTING THERE   You can reach Lübbenau in about an hour by train from Berlin-Lichtenberg station. Trains depart every hour or so, with a round-trip ticket costing less than 30 DM ($20).

The best way to get around Lübbenau is on your own two feet; you can walk from the train station to the main boat harbor (Spreewald Hafen) in approximately 20 to 25 minutes. From the Lübbenau train station, walk straight out of the front exit of the station and continue walking straight in the same direction on Poststrasse, a tree-lined street that leads into town in about 15 minutes. It ends at the town's main square, where you'll find Lübbenau's tourist information office (look for the "I" sign). Stop at the tourist office for directions to the main harbor for boat rides. Otherwise, turn right onto Ehm-Welk-Strasse, passing the church and taking a right onto Dammstrasse, which leads to the Kahnabfahrstelle (boat departure place) and a footpath onward to Lehde. At the boat harbor, you'll find punts and boatmen to take you through the Spreewald.

VISITOR INFORMATION For information about the Spreewald and boat trips from Lübbenau, contact the Lübbenau Spreewald tourist information office at Ehm-Welk-Strasse 15 (☎ **03542/36 68**). In summer it's open daily from 9am to 6pm; winter hours are Monday to Friday from 9am to 4pm.

WHAT TO SEE & DO

BOAT TRIPS The most popular thing to do in the Spreewald is to take a boat ride through this watery wonderland. If you understand German and get a gregarious gondolier, you'll probably be regaled with tales about the Spreewald and the people who live here. Most inhabitants are Sorbs, an ethnic minority of swamp-dwelling Slavs who spoke their own language until World War II and are still proud of their traditions and culture. As you glide along the canals, you'll pass haystacks as tall as houses; poplar, ash, and weeping willow trees; and log and brick farmhouses surrounded by neat gardens. Since boats are the only means of transportation through the Spreewald, there are fireboats instead of fire trucks, and even children are ferried to school by boat.

Boat trips are offered only in good weather from April to the end of October, when boatmen gather at the landing in Lübbenau as early as 8:30am to wait for customers. If you wish to make a full day of it, try to arrive in Lübbenau by 10am. Boats can seat up to 20, but will leave for trips with as few as 8 on slow days. If there are fewer than 8, the price of the trip will be negotiated (prices are low to begin with, so the trip is still a bargain).

You can choose from several routes of varying lengths; trips range from three to eight hours. One of the most popular is the three-hour trip to **Lehde,** a Venice-style village of thatched-roof brick houses along narrow roads, with roosters crowing, canals everywhere, and family boats pulled up beside homes picturesquely situated on small islands. You can arrange for a one-hour stopover in Lehde, where you may dine or visit Lehde's **Spreewald Freiland-museum,** an open-air museum consisting of nine original farmsteads, buildings, furniture, and artifacts common to the people of the Spreewald region. The museum is open April to mid-October on Tuesday through Sunday from 9am to 5pm.

Admission is 3 DM ($2) for adults, 2 DM ($1.35) for students and senior citizens, and 1 DM (65c) for children.

The price for the three-hour boat trip to Lehde and back is 8 DM ($5.35) per adult and 4 DM ($2.65) per child. Other boat trips available include a 6$^{1}/_{2}$-hour trip to the village of Leipe, costing 14 DM ($9.35) for adults and 6 DM ($4) for children, and an 8-hour trip through the Spreewald at 16 DM ($10.65) for adults and 6 DM ($4) for children. Remember to get there early for an all-day trip; for the three-hour trip to Lehde, you should arrive at the boat harbor by 1 or 2pm at the latest.

You can also rent paddleboats if you want to strike out on your own. Two-seaters cost 6 to 8 DM ($4–$5.35) per hour or 30 DM ($20) for the whole day.

HIKES If you'd rather stick to dry land or come in the off season, you can also hike through the Spreewald. True, many paths end abruptly at one of the hundreds of canals, but that shouldn't deter you. In fact, you can even hike to Lehde on your own; it's less than 1$^{1}/_{2}$ miles from Lübbenau. You'll find the marked pathway off Dammstrasse, just past the main boat harbor, beside the Café Zum Nussbaum (look for the small green sight that says "Lehde 2,0 KM"). It's a mystical experience walking through this special bayou, as you pass small garden plots and the flora and fauna that make up the unique waterway. I especially like hiking the Spreewald in winter, when you have the place virtually to yourself.

Finally, if time permits, you might want to visit Lübbenau's **Spreewald Museum** (☎ 2472), a short walk from the boat harbor in the Schlosspark. Housed in a building dating from the mid-1700s, the museum's displays relate to the customs and traditions of the Sorbs and the history of the Spreewald, complete with various modes of transportation through the region. It's open daily from April to mid-October from 9am to 5pm. Admission is 3 DM ($2) for adults, 2 DM ($1.35) for students and senior citizens, and 1 DM (65c) for children.

IMPRESSIONS

Take, for instance, the Prussians: they are saints when compared with the French. They have every sort of excellence; they are honest, sober, hardworking, well-instructed, brave, good sons, husbands, and fathers; and yet all this is spoilt by one single fault—they are insupportable. . .
The only Prussian I ever knew who was an agreeable man was Bismarck. All others with whom I have been thrown—and I have lived for years in Germany—were proud as Scotchmen, cold as New Englanders, and touchy as only Prussians can be. I once had a friend among them. His name was Buckenbrock. Inadvertently I called him Butterbrod. We have never spoken since. —Henry Labouchère, 1871

WHERE TO EAT

The boatmen will suggest cafes and restaurants in the villages you visit. In Lehde, for example, there's the **Fröhlicher Hecht,** which first opened in 1640 as the only inn in Lehde and was owned by the same family for generations.

In Lübbenau, my favorite place for a meal is **Zum Grünen Strand der Spree,** Dammstrasse 77 (☎ 2423), located next to the boat harbor with a large outdoor terrace. Founded 100 years ago, it was the leading inn beside the boat harbor, even at the turn of the century. Its specialties are fish from the Spreewald, including carp, trout, and pike, prepared in a special Spreewald sauce. Other dishes include sausage with sauerkraut and potatoes, pork médallions with curry sauce or hollandaise, and duck with red cabbage and potatoes. Entrees range from 9 DM to 24 DM ($6–$16), and American Express, MasterCard, and Visa are accepted. It's open daily from 10am to 7pm.

Appendix

A Basic Phrases & Vocabulary

German is not a difficult language to learn, especially pronunciation. Unlike English or French, it contains no hidden surprises, and everything is pronounced exactly as it's written—according, of course, to German rules. *Ei* is always pronounced as a long *i*; thus, *nein* (which means "no") is pronounced *nine*. A *w* is pronounced *v*; a *v* is pronounced as *f*. As for those two dots over vowels, they signal a slight change in pronunciation.

English	German	Pronunciation
Hello	**Guten Tag**	goo-ten *tahk*
Goodbye	**Auf Wiedersehen**	owf *vee*-der-*zay*-en
How are you?	**Wie geht es Ihnen?**	vee *gayt* ess ee-nen
Very well	**Sehr gut**	*zayr* goot
Please	**Bitte**	*bit*-tuh
Thank you	**Danke schön**	*dahn*-keh shern
Excuse me	**Entschuldigen Sie**	en-*shool*-d-gen zee
You're welcome	**Gern geschehen**	*gehrn* geshai'en
Yes	**Ja**	yah
No	**Nein**	nine
Mr./Mrs.	**Herr/Frau**	hehr/vrow
I don't understand	**Ich verstehe nicht**	*ish* fer-*steh*-he nisht
I understand	**Ich verstehe**	*ish* fer-*steh*-he
Where is . . . ?	**Wo ist . . . ?**	voh *eest*
the station	**der Bahnhof**	deyr *bahn*-hohf
a hotel	**ein Hotel**	ain *hotel*
a restaurant	**ein Restaurant**	ain res-tow-*rahng*
the toilet	**die Toilette**	dee twah-*let*-tah
a bank	**eine Bank**	ain *bahnk*
a post office	**ein Postamt**	ain *post*-ahmt
the bus stop	**die Bus haltestelle**	dee *bus*-halte-stelle
the tourist information office	**das Fremdenverkehrsamt**	dass frem-den fer-*kerrs*-amt
To the right	**Nach rechts**	*nakh* reshts
To the left	**Nach links**	*nakh* leenks

English	German	Pronunciation
Straight ahead	**Geradeaus**	geh-rah-*deh*-ous
Ladies/Gentlemen	**Damen/Herren**	*dah*-men/ *heh*-ren
Women/Men	**Frauen/Männer**	*frow*-en/ *meh*-ner
How much does it cost?	**Wieviel kostet es?**	vee-*feel kah*-stet ess
Expensive	**Teuer**	*toy*-er
Cheap	**Billig**	*bil*-lich
The check, please	**Die Rechnung, bitte**	dee *rekh*-noong, *bit*-tuh
I would like . . .	**Ich möchte . . .**	ikh *mersh*-ta
stamps	**Briefmarken**	*breef*-mahr-ken
to eat	**essen**	*ess*-en
a room	**ein Zimmer**	ain *tzim*-mer
for one night	**für eine Nacht**	*feer* ai-neh *nakht*
Breakfast	**Frühstück**	*free*-shtick
Lunch	**Mittagessen**	*mi*-tahg-*ess*-en
Dinner	**Abendessen**	*ah*-bend-*ess*-en
Free (vacant)/ occupied	**Frei/besetzt**	*Frahy*/be-*setts*
When?	**Wann?**	vahn?
Yesterday	**Gestern**	*geh*-stern
Today	**Heute**	*hoy*-tuh
Tomorrow	**Morgen**	*more*-gen
Sunday	**Sonntag**	*zohn*-tahk
Monday	**Montag**	*mon*-tahk
Tuesday	**Dienstag**	*deens*-tahk
Wednesday	**Mittwoch**	*mitt*-voch
Thursday	**Donnerstag**	*don*-ners-tahk
Friday	**Freitag**	*frahy*-tahk
Saturday	**Samstag**	*zahmz*-tahk

Numbers

- 0 **Null** (nool)
- 1 **Eins** (aintz)
- 2 **Zwei** (tzvai)
- 3 **Drei** (dry)
- 4 **Vier** (feer)
- 5 **Fünf** (fewnf)
- 6 **Sechs** (zex)
- 7 **Sieben** (zee-ben)
- 8 **Acht** (ahkht)
- 9 **Neun** (noyn)
- 10 **Zehn** (tzayn)
- 11 **Elf** (ellf)
- 12 **Zwölf** (tzvuhlf)
- 13 **Dreizehn** (*dry*-tzayn)
- 14 **Vierzehn** (*feer*-tzayn)
- 15 **Fünfzehn** (*fewnf*-tzayn)
- 16 **Sechszehn** (*zex*-tzayn)
- 17 **Siebzehn** (*zeeb*-tzayn)
- 18 **Achtzehn** (*akh*-tzayn)
- 19 **Neunzehn** (*noyn*-tzayn)
- 20 **Zwanzig** (*tzvahn*-tzik)
- 25 **Fünfundzwanzig** (*fewnf* und *tzvahn*-tzik)
- 30 **Dreissig** (*dry*-sik)
- 40 **Vierzig** (*feer*-tzik)
- 50 **Fünfzig** (*fewnf*-tzik)
- 60 **Sechzig** (*zex*-tzik)
- 70 **Siebzig** (*zeeb*-tzik)
- 80 **Achtzig** (*akht*-tzik)
- 90 **Neunzig** (*noyn*-tzik)
- 100 **Hundert** (*hoon*-dert)
- 101 **Hunderteins** (*hoon*-dert-ahyns)
- 200 **Zweihundert** (*tzvai*-hoon-dert)
- 1,000 **Eintausend** (*ahyn*-tau-zent)

B Menu Terms

CONDIMENTS & TABLE ITEMS

Brot bread
Brötchen rolls
Butter butter
Eis ice
Pfeffer pepper
Salz salt
Senf mustard
Zucker sugar

SOUPS (SUPPE)

Erbsensuppe pea soup
Gemüsesuppe vegetable soup
Gulaschsuppe spicy Hungarian beef soup
Hühnerbrühe chicken soup
Kartoffelsuppe potato soup
Nudelsuppe noodle soup

SALADS (SALAT)

Gemischter Salat mixed salad
Gurkensalat cucumber salad
Kartoffelsalat potato salad
Kopfsalat/Grünsalat lettuce salad
Tomatensalat tomato salad

SANDWICHES (BELEGTE BROTE)

Käsebrot cheese sandwich
Schinkenbrot ham sandwich
Wurstbrot sausage sandwich

EGGS (EIER)

Bauernfrühstück "Farmer's Breakfast"—scrambled eggs with ham or sausage, onion, and potatoes
Rühreier scrambled eggs
Spiegeleier fried eggs
Verlorene Eier poached eggs

VEGETABLES (GEMUSE)

Blumenkohl cauliflower
Bohnen beans
Bratkartoffeln fried potatoes
Erbsen peas
Grüne Bohnen green beans
Gurken cucumbers
Karotten carrots
Kartoffeln potatoes

Knödel dumplings
Kohl cabbage
Reis rice
Salzkartoffeln boiled potatoes
Spargel asparagus
Spinat spinach
Tomaten tomatoes

MEATS (WURST, FLEISCH & GEFLÜGEL)
Aufschnitt cold cuts
Bockwurst Berlin sausage
Boulette meatball
Brathuhn roast chicken
Bratwurst grilled sausage
Ente duck
Kalb veal
Kaltes Geflügel cold poultry
Kassler Rippchen/Rippenspeer pork chops
Lamm lamb
Leberkäs German meatloaf
Ragout stew
Rinderbraten roast beef
Rindfleisch beef
Sauerbraten marinated beef
Schinken ham
Schweinebraten/Schweinsbraten roast pork
Tafelspitz boiled beef with vegetables
Truthahn turkey
Wiener Schnitzel veal cutlet
Wurst (plural Würste) sausage

FISH (FISCH)
Brathering grilled herring
Forelle trout
Hecht pike
Karpfen carp
Lachs salmon
Makrele mackerel
Schellfisch haddock
Seezunge sole

DESSERTS (NACHTISCH)
Blatterteiggebäck puff pastry
Bratapfel baked apple
Eis ice cream
Käse cheese
Kompott stewed fruit
Obstkuchen fruit tart

Obstsalat   fruit salad
Pfannkuchen   sugared pancakes
Pflaumenkompott   stewed plums
Rote Grütze   cooked fruits with vanilla sauce
Teegebäck   tea cakes
Torten   pastries

Fruits (Obst)

Ananas   pineapple
Apfel   apple
Apfelsinen   oranges
Bananen   bananas
Birnen   pears
Erdbeeren   strawberries
Kirschen   cherries
Pfirsiche   peaches
Weintrauben   grapes
Zitronen   lemons

Beverages

Berliner Weisse   draft wheat beer with a shot of raspberry or green woodruff syrup
Bier   beer
Bier vom Fass   draft beer
Bock Bier   dark and rich beer
Ein Dunkles   A dark beer
Ein Helles   A light beer
Pils   Light and bitter beer
Milch   Milk
Saft   juice
Sahne   cream
Schokolade   chocolate
Eine Tasse Kaffee   a cup of coffee
Eine Tasse Tee   a cup of tea
Tomatensaft   tomato juice
Wasser   water
Wein   Wine
Sekt   champagne

C Glossary of Terms

Altstadt   old town (traditional part of town or city)
Apotheke   pharmacy
Art deco   stylized art and architecture of the 1920s and 1930s
Art nouveau   highly decorative form of art, objects, and interior design with twining, flowing motifs of late 19th and early 20th centuries

Bahn   railway, train
  Bahnhof   railway station
  Hauptbahnhof   main railway station
  Stadtbahn (S-Bahn)   commuter railway
  Untergrundbahn (U-Bahn)   subway, city underground system
Baroque   ornate, decorated style of architecture in the 18th century, characterized by use of elaborate ornamentation and gilding. Also applied to art of the same period
Bauhaus   style of functional design for architecture and objects, originating in the early 20th century in Germany
Berg   mountain
Biedermeier   solid, bourgeois style of furniture design and interior decoration in the middle 19th century
Der Blaue Reiter   group of nonfigurative painters, founded in Munich in 1911 by Franz Marc and Wassily Kandinsky
Die Brücke   group of avant-garde expressionist painters originating in Dresden around 1905
Burg   fortified castle
Dom   cathedral
Drogerie   shop selling cosmetics and sundries
Expressionism   style of painting in early-20th-century Germany characterized by strong use of form and color
Gothic   medieval architectural style characterized by arches, soaring spaces, and ribbed vaulting, lasting into the 16th century; also applied to painting of the period
Jugendstil   German form of art nouveau
Kaufhaus   department store
Kirche   church
Kneipe   bar, mostly for drinking
Konditorei   cafe for coffee and pastries
Kunst   art
Oper   opera/opera house
Platz   square
Rathaus   town or city hall
Schauspielhaus   theater for plays
Schloss   palace, castle
Secession   modernist movement in German art that strongly disavowed expressionism
Stadt   town, city
Strasse   street
Tor   gateway
Turm   tower
Verkehrsamt   tourist office

D Metric Measures

Length

1 millimeter (mm)	=	0.04 inches (or less than 1/16 in.)
1 centimeter (cm)	=	0.39 inches (or under 1/2 in.)
1 meter (m)	=	1.09 yards (or about 39 inches)
1 kilometer (km)	=	0.62 miles (or about 2/3 of a mile)

To convert kilometers to miles, take the number of kilometers and multiply by .62 (for example, 25 km × .62 = 15.5 mi).

To convert miles to kilometers, take the number of miles and multiply by 1.61. (for example, 50 mi × 1.61 = 80.5km).

Capacity

| 1 liter (l) | = | 33.92 ounces or 1.06 quarts or 0.26 gallons |

To convert liters to gallons, take the number of liters and multiply by .26 (for example, 50 liters × .26 = 13 gallons).

To convert gallons to liters, take the number of gallons and multiply by 3.79 (for example, 10 gal × 3.79 = 37.9 liters).

Weight

| 1 gram (g) | = | 0.04 ounces (or about a paperclip's weight) |
| 1 kilogram (kg) | = | 2.2 pounds |

To convert kilograms to pounds, take the number of kilos and multiply by 2.2 (for example, 75kg × 2.2 = 165 pounds).

To convert pounds to kilograms, take the number of pounds and multiply by .45 (for example, 90 pounds × .45 = 40.5kg).

Temperature

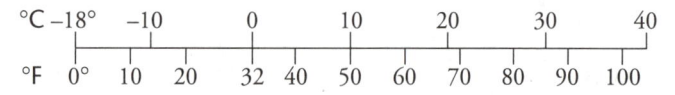

```
°C -18°   -10      0       10      20      30      40
°F   0°   10   20  32  40  50  60  70  80  90  100
```

To convert degrees C to degrees F, multiply degrees C by 9, divide by 5, then add 32 (for example, 20°C × 9/5 + 32 = 68°F).

To convert degrees F to degrees C, subtract 32 from degrees F, then multiply by 5, and divide by 9 (for example, 85°F - 32 × 5/9 = 29°C).

Index

Accommodations, 72–88
  best budget, 7–8
  camping, 3, 88
  for children, 81
  for disabled travelers, 40
  Kreuzberg, 76–77
  near the Ku'damm & Bahnhof Zoo, 73–75, 77–85, 87
  money-saving tips, 2–3
  near Rathaus Schöneberg, 76
  north of Tiergarten Park, 87–88
  near Wilmersdorfer Strasse & Bahnhof Charlottenburg, 76
  youth hostels & hotels, 3, 40, 85–88
Ägyptisches Museum (Egyptian Museum), 6, 57, 60, 116, 117, 118, 123–24, 126, 131, 132, 163
Air Travel, 2, 42–45
Alexanderplatz, 28, 29, 52, 53, 59, 119, 165
Alte Nationalgalerie (Old National Gallery), 25, 27, 117, 119, 126, 163
Altes Museum (Old Museum), 28, 126, 144, 163
Annual events, festivals and fairs, 38–39
Antikenmuseum (Museum of Antiquities), 118, 132
Architecture, 28–29, 144–45
Art museums
  Ägyptisches Museum (Egyptian Museum), 6, 57, 60, 116, 117, 118, 123–24, 126, 131, 132, 163
  Alte Nationalgalerie (Old National Gallery), 25, 27, 117, 119, 126, 163
  Altes Museum (Old Museum), 28, 126, 144, 163
  Antikenmuseum (Museum of Antiquities), 118, 132
  Bode Museum, 119, 125–26, 163
  Bröhan Museum, 57, 132–34
  Brücke-Museum, 27, 131
  East Side Gallery, 6, 138
  Filmmuseum, 145–46
  Gemäldegalerie (Picture Gallery), 58, 60, 116, 117, 118, 121–22, 129, 130, 134, 163
  Käthe-Kollwitz Museum, 25, 27, 119, 134, 154
  Kunstgewerbemuseum (Museum of Applied Arts) (Köpenick), 59, 138–39
  Kunstgewerbemuseum (Museum of Applied Arts) (Tiergarten), 57, 119, 135, 136
  Kupferstichkabinett-Sammlung de Zeichnungen und Druckgraphik (Collection of Prints and Drawings), 119, 129, 134, 137
  Museum für Indische Kunst (Museum of Indian Art), 58, 130–31

Index

Museum für Islamische Kunst (Museum of Islamic Art), 131
Museum für Ostasiatische Kunst (Museum of Far Eastern Art), 58, 131
Musikinstrumenten Museum (Museum of Musical Instruments), 57, 119, 135, 136–37
Pergamon Museum, 6, 53, 58, 116, 117, 118, 119, 120–21, 163
Skulpturengalerie (Sculpture Gallery), 58, 129–30, 134, 163

Bahnhof Charlottenburg
   accommodations, 76
   restaurants, 111–13
Bahnhof Zoologischer Garten, 47, 53, 57, 144
   accommodations, 73–75, 77–85, 88
Ballet, 186–87
Banks, 67
Bar scene, 5, 11, 193–201
Bauhaus-Archiv, 25, 29, 57, 119, 144–45
Beer gardens, 201
Berliner Dom (Berlin Cathedral), 6, 119, 126–28, 162–63, 186
Berlin International Film Festival, 28, 38, 117, 145
Berlin-Mitte (Eastern Berlin), 14, 25, 28, 29, 52, 57, 59, 116, 119, 144, 197–99
   restaurants, 100–102, 109–11, 115
   shopping, 179
   sights and attractions, 124–29
   walking tour, 156–66
Berlin Philharmonic Orchestra, 11, 26, 28, 57, 185
Berlin Wall, 6, 10, 11, 12–13, 17, 18, 21–23, 24, 29, 58, 117, 119, 128, 129, 150, 156
Bicycling, 19, 65–66
Bismarck, Otto von, 10, 15, 17, 24, 128
Boat trips, 120, 143, 147, 162, 213
Bode Museum, 119, 125–26, 163
Botanischer Garten (Botanical Garden), 141, 143
Brandenburger Tor (Brandenburg Gate), 15, 16, 17, 28, 53, 118, 119, 129, 140, 156–57
Brandt, Willy, 24
Brecht, Bertolt, 18, 24, 27, 187, 188
Bröhan Museum, 57, 132–34
Brücke-Museum, 27, 131
Bus travel
   to Berlin, 48
   within Berlin, 59, 60, 64
   for disabled travelers, 40
   organized tours, 146–47

Cabaret, 28, 188–89
Cafe scene, 11, 193–201
Cars and driving, 48–49
   to Berlin, 48
   within Berlin, 64–65
   rentals, 33, 64–65
Casinos, 203
Charlottenburg, 26, 52, 56–57, 116, 117, 131–34
Children
   accommodations for, 81
   evening entertainment, 143
   restaurants for, 97
   sights and attractions for, 142–43

travel tips for, 41
Churches and Cathedrals,
Berliner Dom (Berlin Cathedral), 6, 119, 126–28, 162–63, 186
Friedrichswerdersche Kirche, 25, 128
Kaiser-Wilhelm Gedächtniskirche (Kaiser Wilhelm Memorial Church), 6, 53, 134, 140, 150, 186
Marienkirche (Church of St. Mary), 28, 165
Climate, 37
Club scene, 188–93
Cuisine, 29–32
Currency, 34–35
Currency exchange, 5, 67
Customs, 34

Dahlem, 26, 27, 52, 57, 58, 116, 117, 118, 134
restaurants, 103
sights and attractions, 129–31
Dance clubs, 5, 67, 191–93
Disabled travelers, tips for, 39–40
Discos, 5, 191–93
Documents required for entry to Germany, 33–34

Embassies, 67–68
Emergencies, 68
Entertainment and nightlife, 4–5, 184–204
Europa-Center, 52, 53, 57, 150, 177–78
Excursions, 6, 205–15

Families, tips for, 41. *See also* Children

Fast Facts, 66–71
Fernsehturm TV Tower, 119, 139, 165
Festivals. *See* Annual events, festivals, and fairs
Film, 145–46, 202–03
Filmmuseum, 145–46
Friedrich II (Frederick the Great), 15, 16, 25, 32, 142, 161, 207–8
Friedrichswerdersche Kirche, 25, 128

Gardens. *See* Parks and Gardens
Gay Bars, 201–2
Gay travelers
information for, 51
Gedenkstätte und Museum Sachsenhausen (Memorial and Museum Sachsenhausen), 139
Gemäldegalerie (Picture Gallery), 58, 60, 116, 117, 118, 121–22, 129, 130, 134, 163
Gropius, Walter, 18, 25, 29, 58, 144

Hansaviertel (Hansa Quarter), 25, 57–58, 119, 144
Heinrich-Zille-Museum, 26, 160
Historical museums
Deutsches Historisiches Museum, 128
Gedenkstätte und Museum Sachsenhausen (Memorial and Museum Sachsenhausen), 139
Hanfmuseum (Hemp Museum), 166
Märkisches Museum, 128

Museum Berliner Arbeiterleben (Museum of Berlin Working-Class Life), 171
Museum für Vor- und Frühgeschichte (Primeval and Early History Museum), 118–19, 132, 163
Museum Haus am Checkpoint Charlie, 58, 117, 118, 124, 143
Museumsdorf Düppel, 138, 143
Topographie des Terrors, 137–38
History, 11–24
Hospitals, 68

Information sources. *See* Tourist information
Insurance, 39

KaDeWe, 6, 9, 11, 29, 119, 155, 178
Kaiser-Wilhelm Gedächtniskirche (Kaiser Wilhelm Memorial Church), 6, 53, 134, 140, 150, 186
Käthe-Kollwitz Museum, 25, 27, 119, 134, 154
Knobelsdorff, Georg Wenzeslaus von, 16, 25, 28, 161, 207
Kollwitz, Käthe, 18, 25, 27, 119, 134, 154, 161, 167, 170, 171
Köpenick, 59, 227
  sights and attractions, 138–39
Kreuzberg, 58, 116, 117, 199–201
  accommodations, 76–77
  restaurants, 104, 113–14
  sights and attractions, 137–38
Ku'damm, 5, 11, 25, 27, 53, 55–56, 57, 117, 118, 119, 140, 193–97
  accommodations, 73–75, 77–85, 88
  restaurants, 93–100, 104–109, 114–15
  walking tour, 149–56
Kunstgewerbemuseum (Museum of Applied Arts) (Köpenick), 59, 138–39
Kunstgewerbemuseum (Museum of Applied Arts) (Tiergarten), 57, 119, 134, 135, 136
Kupferstichkabinett-Sammlung de Zeichnungen und Druckgraphik (Collection of Prints and Drawings), 119, 129, 134, 137

Language, 68, 216–19
Lesbian travelers
  information for, 51
Libraries and archives, 68
Liebermann, Max, 18, 25, 26, 27
Liquor, 30, 32, 68

Mail, 69
Marienkirche (Church of St. Mary), 28, 165
Märkisches Museum, 128
Money, 34–36
Movies. *See* Film
Museum für Deutsche Völkerkunde (Museum of German Ethnology), 58, 118, 130
Museum für Indische Kunst (Museum of Indian Art), 58, 130–31

Museum für Ostasiatische Kunst (Museum of Far Eastern Art), 58, 131
Museum für Völkerkunde (Ethnological Museum), 58, 130, 143
Museum für Vor- und Frühgeschichte (Primeval and Early History Museum), 118–19, 132, 163
Museum Haus am Checkpoint Charlie, 58, 117, 118, 124, 143
Museums. *See* Art museums, historical museums, science, ethnology, and technology museums
Museumsdorf Düppel, 138, 143
Museumsinsel (Museum Island), 25, 26, 27, 28, 52, 53, 57, 58, 116, 118, 119, 144, 162
Music
  church, 6, 186
  classical, 26, 185–86
  jazz, 6, 28, 38, 117
  opera, 4, 26, 28, 57, 119, 184, 186–87
  rock 'n' roll, 28, 189–90
Music scene, 5, 6–7, 188–93
Musikinstrumenten Museum (Museum of Musical Instruments), 57, 119, 134, 135, 136–376

Neighborhoods, 56–59
Neue Nationalgalerie (New National Gallery), 25, 27, 57, 60, 117, 120, 134, 135, 136
Neues Palais (Potsdam), 205, 206, 208, 209–10
Nikolaiviertel (Nikolai Quarter), 52, 53, 57, 59, 119, 166

Parks and Gardens
  Botanischer Garten (Botanical Garden), 141, 143
  Pfaueninsel and Schloss Pfaueninsel (Peacock Island), 142
  Tiergarten park, 11, 52, 57, 119, 140–41, 143
Performance halls (listing), 185–88
Pergamon Museum, 6, 53, 58, 116, 117, 118, 119, 120–21, 163
Pfaueninsel and Schloss Pfaueninsel (Peacock Island), 142
Planning and preparing for your trip, 33–49
Police, 69
Potsdam, Germany, 25, 61, 120, 147, 205–12
  restaurants, 210–12
  sights and attractions, 205–10
Prenzlauer Berg, 59
  walking tours, 166–72
Public Transportation, 4, 59–66

Rathaus Schöneberg, 6, 17, 139–40, 146
  accommodations, 76
  restaurants, 103–4
Reichstag (Parliament), 18, 53, 57, 128–29, 157
Reinhardt, Max, 18, 24, 25, 27, 28, 187
Restaurants, 89–115
  Berlin-Mitte, 100–102, 109–11, 115
  best budget, 8–9
  for children, 97
  coffeehouses, 114–15
  by cuisine, 91–92

Dahlem, 103
late-night eating, 203–4
German/English glossary, 218–20
imbisse (food stalls), 3, 112, 118
Kreuzberg, 104, 113–14
money-saving tips, 3–4
near or on the Ku'damm, 93–100, 104–9, 114–15
Nollendorfplatz, 115
picnic fare, 11, 140
Potsdam, 210–12
near Rathaus Schöneberg, 103–104
near Schloss Charlottenburg, 113
Spreewald, 214–15
Wilmersdorfer Strasse & Bahnhof Charlottenburg, 102, 111–13
Revues, 188–89

Safety, 70
Savignyplatz, 53, 57, 151
Schinkel, Karl Friedrich, 16, 25, 28, 57, 123, 126, 127, 128, 144, 160, 162, 163, 186
Schinkel Pavilion, 25, 28, 118, 123, 144
Schlossbrücke (Palace Bridge), 25, 144, 162
Schloss Charlottenburg (Charlottenburg Palace), 6, 16, 25, 26, 28, 52, 57, 116, 117–18, 122–23, 131, 132, 144, 147
    restaurants, 113
Schloss Sanssouci and Park (Potsdam), 16, 25, 32, 120, 147, 205–6, 207–9
Schlüter, Andreas, 16, 26, 122, 128, 162, 163, 165

Science, ethnology, and technology museums
    Museum für Deutsche Völkerkunde (Museum of German Ethnology), 58, 118, 130
    Museum für Verkehr und Technic (Museum for Transport and Technology), 142
    Museum für Völkerkunde (Ethnological Museum), 58, 130, 143
Senior citizen travelers
    tips for, 4, 40–41
Shopping, 173–83
    antiques, 152, 160, 176
    art galleries, 154, 177
    best buys, 173–74
    crafts, 151, 177
    department stores and malls, 6, 152, 177–79
    fashion, 152, 179
    flea markets, 6, 11, 27, 58, 119, 120, 160, 176–77, 182
    food, 6, 9, 29, 119, 155, 179–80
    gifts/souvenirs, 180–81
    jewelry, 152
    kitchenwares, 181
    markets, 181–82
    money-saving tips, 5
    perfume, 152, 183
    porcelain, 150, 155, 183
Sights and attractions, 4–7, 116–72
    itineraries, 117–20
Single travelers, tips for, 40
Skulpturengalerie (Sculpture Gallery), 58, 129–30, 134, 163
Spreewald, Germany, 6, 53, 120, 147, 212–15

Student travelers, tips for, 3, 33, 41–42, 51
Subways, 59, 60, 61–64
    for disabled travelers, 40, 61–64
    for women travelers, 61–64
Swimming, 143, 148

Taxis, 64
    for disabled travelers, 40
Telephones, 70
Temperatures, average monthly, 37
Theater, 4, 27–28, 187–88
Tiergarten, 25, 26, 27, 53, 57, 58, 116, 119
    accommodations, 88
    sights and attractions, 134–37
Tiergarten park, 11, 52, 57, 119, 140–41, 143
Topographie des Terrors, 137–38
Tourist information, 33, 50–51
Tours, organized
    by boat, 147, 162
    by bus, 146–47
    walking, 147–48
Train travel, 46–48
    for disabled travelers, 40

Unter den Linden, 5, 11, 15, 16, 25, 26, 28, 52, 53, 57, 118, 119, 157, 160, 161

Walking tours, 147–72
Wannsee Beach, 11, 53, 61, 120, 143, 147, 148
Wilmersdorfer Strasse
    accommodations, 76
    restaurants, 102, 111–13
    shopping, 179
Women travelers, tips for, 40–41, 51–52, 61–64, 202

Zeughaus (Arsenal), 16, 26, 28, 161–62
Zille, Heinrich, 18, 26, 27, 160
Zoologischer Garten (Berlin Zoo) and Aquarium, 11, 19, 57, 60, 141, 143, 150

Welcome to Berlin, welcome to Pizza Hut!

3,– DM voucher

Use this 3,– DM voucher with your visit to one of our Berlin restaurants.

Pizza Hut

Only 1 voucher per person with any pizza or pasta meal. (Not valid with buffets and discounted menus.)

Taste it - you`ll love it!

Kurfürstendamm 146 · Kurfürstendamm 203 · Hauptstraße 139

We are Always in Season in Berlin and throughout Germany

Kemwel has the right car rentals at the right prices. Rates starting from 3 days with unlimited mileage.

Get a $10 calling card FREE with your car rental.

Kemwel
1-800-678-0-678

Name _____

Street _____

City _____ State _____

Zip _____ Tel: ( ) _____

Place Stamp Here

The Kemwel Group, Inc.
106 Calvert Street
Harrison, NY 10528-3199

DERCAR

DER TRAVEL SERVICES

A division of DER Travel Services
Serving travelers in Europe since 1917

Drive into eastern Europe with any Opel model!

DISCOUNT ON RENTALS OF ONE WEEK OR MORE

$5 Off Opel Corsa
$10 Off Opel Astra
$15 Off Opel Vectra
$20 Off Opel Vectra Stationwagon
$25 Off Long-term Rentals, any Opel model (2 weeks or more)

For reservations phone toll-free
1-800-782-2424, Press 3

Terms & Conditions

I. Minimum rental is 7 days.
2. Reservations must be made and the rental must be fully prepaid in the U.S.
3. Certificate may be used to reduce DERCar's pre-paid rental rates on any basic or inclusive rental. Certificate must be mailed to DER after reservation is made by phone.
4. Certificate is valid one time only. It cannot be exchanged for cash or negotiated and may not be combined with any other offer, discount or promotion.
5. All DER Car terms and conditions in its car rental brochure apply, including minimum rental age of 25.

Mail to: DERCar Expires 12/31/96
9501 W. Devon Avenue   DER
Rosemont, IL 60018   Booking #_____

Name _____

Address _____

City _____State_____

Zip _____Phone (   )_____

$10 Off
Your Next Affordable Europe Rental!

PC #66920
Offer expires 12/31/96

Hertz®

Book an Affordable Europe Nonprepaid rate and use this certificate to receive $10 off your rental charges. If you prefer to pay in advance, use this certificate to receive $10 off any optional services you elect. Please read the important information on the back of this certificate. For reservations contact your travel agent, or call Hertz, toll-free: 1-800-654-3001.

Terms and Conditions:
1. Offer is available at participating locations in Europe.
2. Minimum rental period is three days.
3. Reservations must be made in the U.S. prior to departure on an Affordable Europe rate plan, using **PC #66920**. Advance reservation requirement is 8 hours before departure, or 14 days prior to departure for mailed vouchers.
4. Certificate may only be used as an allowance toward rental charges, including optional service charges, such as collision damage waiver, insurance services, refueling, luggage racks, baby seats, etc. paid at time of rental. Offer cannot be applied to charges prepaid before departure.
5. Certificate must be presented and surrendered at time of rental. It is valid one time for a value up to $10. U.S. dollar amount will be calculated in local currency at the exchange rate applicable at time of rental.
6. Certificate can neither be exchanged for cash nor negotiated.
7. Certificate may not be combined with any other offer, discount or promotion. Offer is not available on rentals reserved through tour operators, or on corporate/contract rates.
8. Standard Affordable Europe, intercity rules and restrictions apply.
9. Minimum rental age is 25. All renters must present a valid driver's license held for at least one year prior to rental.

Hertz®
Hertz rents Fords and other fine cars.

SAVE 10% at

CHOICE HOTELS
INTERNATIONAL

Friendship **Econo Lodge** **Rodeway**

The next time you're traveling, make a reservation at any **Sleep, Comfort, Quality, Clarion, Friendship, Econo Lodge** or **Rodeway** Inn, Hotel or Suite and ask for **"The Travelers' Discount"** -- you'll **SAVE 10%** on your night's stay!

Over 1,400 hotels offer a free continental breakfast and children 18 and younger stay free when sharing the same room as their parents.

For reservations,
call the toll-free numbers on the back!

FOR RESERVATIONS CALL:

- Sleep — 1-800-62-SLEEP
- Comfort — 1-800-228-5150
- Quality — 1-800-228-5151
- Clarion — 1-800-CLARION
- Econo Lodge — 1-800-55-ECONO
- Friendship — 1-800-453-4511
- Rodeway — 1-800-228-2000

Advance reservations through the toll free number required.
Discounts are based on availability at participating hotels and cannot be used in conjunction with other discounts or promotions.

Valuable discount coupon
good for 15% OFF
your first order from

Magellan's
CATALOG OF TRAVEL ESSENTIALS

*If it makes travel more comfortable,
safe and rewarding, we have it!*

**Phone 1-800-962-4943
for a FREE CATALOG**

Mention this coupon when you place
your first order and receive 15% OFF.

PO Box 5485-AF, Santa Barbara, CA 93150

NOTES

NOTES

NOTES

NOTES

Now Save Money on All Your Travels by Joining

Frommer's
TRAVEL BOOK CLUB

The Advantages of Membership:
1. Your choice of any **TWO FREE BOOKS**.
2. Your own subscription to the **TRIPS & TRAVEL** quarterly newsletter, where you'll discover the best buys in travel, the hottest vacation spots, the latest travel trends, world-class events and festivals, and much more.
3. A **30% DISCOUNT** on any additional books you order through the club.
4. **DOMESTIC TRIP-ROUTING KITS** (available for a small additional fee). We'll send you a detailed map highlighting the most direct or scenic route to your destination, anywhere in North America.

Here's all you have to do to join:
Send in your annual membership fee of $25.00 ($35.00 Canada/Foreign) with your name, address, and selections on the form below. Or call 815/734-1104 to use your credit card.

Send all orders to:

FROMMER'S TRAVEL BOOK CLUB
P.O. Box 473 • Mt. Morris, IL 61054-0473 • ☎ 815/734-1104

YES! I want to take advantage of this opportunity to join Frommer's Travel Book Club.

[ ] My check for $25.00 ($35.00 for Canadian or foreign orders) is enclosed.
All orders must be prepaid in U.S. funds only. Please make checks payable to Frommer's Travel Book Club.

[ ] Please charge my credit card: [ ] Visa or [ ] Mastercard

Credit card number: _____

Expiration date: ___ / ___ / ___

Signature: _____

Or call 815/734-1104 to use your credit card by phone.

Name: _____

Address: _____

City: _____ State: _____ Zip code: _____

Phone number (in case we have a question regarding your order): _____

Please indicate your choices for TWO FREE books (*see following pages*):

Book 1 - Code: _____   Title: _____

Book 2 - Code: _____   Title: _____

For information on ordering additional titles, see your first issue of the *Trips & Travel* newsletter.

Allow 4–6 weeks for delivery for all items. Prices of books, membership fee, and publication dates are subject to change without notice. All orders are subject to acceptance and availability.

AC1

The following Frommer's guides are available from your favorite bookstore, or you can use the order form on the preceding page to request them as part of your membership in Frommer's Travel Book Club.

FROMMER'S COMPLETE TRAVEL GUIDES
(Comprehensive guides to sightseeing, dining and accommodations, with selections in all price ranges—from deluxe to budget)

Acapulco/Ixtapa/Taxco, 2nd Ed.	C157	Italy '96 (avail. 11/95)	C183
Alaska '94-'95	C131	Jamaica/Barbados, 2nd Ed.	C149
Arizona '95	C166	Japan '94-'95	C144
Australia '94-'95	C147	Maui, 1st Ed.	C153
Austria, 6th Ed.	C162	Nepal, 3rd Ed. (avail. 11/95)	C184
Bahamas '96 (avail. 8/95)	C172	New England '95	C165
Belgium/Holland/Luxembourg, 4th Ed.	C170	New Mexico, 3rd Ed.	C167
Bermuda '96 (avail. 8/95)	C174	New York State, 4th Ed.	C133
California '95	C164	Northwest, 5th Ed.	C140
Canada '94-'95	C145	Portugal '94-'95	C141
Caribbean '96 (avail. 9/95)	C173	Puerto Rico '95-'96	C151
Carolinas/Georgia, 2nd Ed.	C128	Puerto Vallarta/Manzanillo/ Guadalajara, 2nd Ed.	C135
Colorado '96 (avail. 11/95)	C179	Scandinavia, 16th Ed.	C169
Costa Rica, 1st Ed.	C161	Scotland '94-'95	C146
Cruises '95-'96	C150	South Pacific '94-'95	C138
Delaware/Maryland '94-'95	C136	Spain, 16th Ed.	C163
England '96 (avail. 10/95)	C180	Switzerland, 7th Ed. (avail. 9/95)	C177
Florida '96 (avail. 9/95)	C181	Thailand, 2nd Ed.	C154
France '96 (avail. 11/95)	C182	U.S.A., 4th Ed.	C156
Germany '96 (avail. 9/95)	C176	Virgin Islands, 3rd Ed. (avail. 8/95)	C175
Honolulu/Waikiki/Oahu, 4th Ed. (avail. 10/95)	C178	Virginia '94-'95	C142
Ireland, 1st Ed.	C168	Yucatán '95-'96	C155

FROMMER'S $-A-DAY GUIDES
(Dream Vacations at Down-to-Earth Prices)

Australia on $45 '95-'96	D122	Ireland on $45 '94-'95	D118
Berlin from $50, 3rd Ed. (avail. 10/95)	D137	Israel on $45, 15th Ed.	D130
Caribbean from $60, 1st Ed. (avail. 9/95)	D133	London from $55 '96 (avail. 11/95)	D136
Costa Rica/Guatemala/Belize on $35, 3rd Ed.	D126	Madrid on $50 '94-'95	D119
Eastern Europe on $30, 5th Ed.	D129	Mexico from $35 '96 (avail. 10/95)	D135
England from $50 '96 (avail. 11/95)	D138	New York on $70 '94-'95	D121
Europe from $50 '96 (avail. 10/95)	D139	New Zealand from $45, 6th Ed.	D132
Greece from $45, 6th Ed.	D131	Paris on $45 '94-'95	D117
Hawaii from $60 '96 (avail. 9/95)	D134	South America on $40, 16th Ed.	D123
		Washington, D.C. on $50 '94-'95	D120

FROMMER'S COMPLETE CITY GUIDES
(Comprehensive guides to sightseeing, dining, and accommodations in all price ranges)

Amsterdam, 8th Ed.	S176	Miami '95-'96	S149
Athens, 10th Ed.	S174	Minneapolis/St. Paul, 4th Ed.	S159
Atlanta & the Summer Olympic		Montréal/Québec City '95	S166
Games '96 (avail. 11/95)	S181	Nashville/Memphis, 1st Ed.	S141
Atlantic City/Cape May,		New Orleans '96 (avail. 10/95)	S182
5th Ed.	S130	New York City '96 (avail. 11/95)	S183
Bangkok, 2nd Ed.	S147	Paris '96 (avail. 9/95)	S180
Barcelona '93-'94	S115	Philadelphia, 8th Ed.	S167
Berlin, 3rd Ed.	S162	Prague, 1st Ed.	S143
Boston '95	S160	Rome, 10th Ed.	S168
Budapest, 1st Ed.	S139	St. Louis/Kansas City, 2nd Ed.	S127
Chicago '95	S169	San Antonio/Austin, 1st Ed.	S177
Denver/Boulder/		San Diego '95	S158
Colorado Springs, 3rd Ed.	S154	San Francisco '96 (avail. 10/95)	S184
Disney World/Orlando '96		Santa Fe/Taos/	
(avail. 9/95)	S178	Albuquerque '95	S172
Dublin, 2nd Ed.	S157	Seattle/Portland '94-'95	S137
Hong Kong '94-'95	S140	Sydney, 4th Ed.	S171
Las Vegas '95	S163	Tampa/St. Petersburg, 3rd Ed.	S146
London '96 (avail. 9/95)	S179	Tokyo '94-'95	S144
Los Angeles '95	S164	Toronto, 3rd Ed.	S173
Madrid/Costa del Sol, 2nd Ed.	S165	Vancouver/Victoria '94-'95	S142
Mexico City, 1st Ed.	S175	Washington, D.C. '95	S153

FROMMER'S FAMILY GUIDES
(Guides to family-friendly hotels, restaurants, activities, and attractions)

California with Kids	F105	San Francisco with Kids	F104
Los Angeles with Kids	F103	Washington, D.C. with Kids	F102
New York City with Kids	F101		

FROMMER'S WALKING TOURS
(Memorable strolls through colorful and historic neighborhoods, accompanied by detailed directions and maps)

Berlin	W100	San Francisco, 2nd Ed.	W115
Chicago	W107	Spain's Favorite Cities	
England's Favorite Cities	W108	(avail. 9/95)	W116
London, 2nd Ed.	W111	Tokyo	W109
Montréal/Québec City	W106	Venice	W110
New York, 2nd Ed.	W113	Washington, D.C., 2nd Ed.	W114
Paris, 2nd Ed.	W112		

FROMMER'S AMERICA ON WHEELS
(Guides for travelers who are exploring the U.S.A. by car, featuring a brand-new rating system for accommodations and full-color road maps)

Arizona/New Mexico	A100	Florida	A102
California/Nevada	A101	Mid-Atlantic	A103

FROMMER'S SPECIAL-INTEREST TITLES

Arthur Frommer's Branson!	P107	Frommer's Where to	
Arthur Frommer's New World		Stay U.S.A., 11th Ed.	P102
of Travel (avail. 11/95)	P112	National Park Guide, 29th Ed.	P106
Frommer's Caribbean		USA Today Golf	
Hideaways (avail. 9/95)	P110	Tournament Guide	P113
Frommer's America's 100		USA Today Minor League	
Best-Loved State Parks	P109	Baseball Book	P111

FROMMER'S BEST BEACH VACATIONS

(The top places to sun, stroll, shop, stay, play, party, and swim—with each beach rated for beauty, swimming, sand, and amenities)

California (avail. 10/95)	G100	Hawaii (avail. 10/95)	G102
Florida (avail. 10/95)	G101		

FROMMER'S BED & BREAKFAST GUIDES

(Selective guides with four-color photos and full descriptions of the best inns in each region)

California	B100	Hawaii	B105
Caribbean	B101	Pacific Northwest	B106
East Coast	B102	Rockies	B107
Eastern United States	B103	Southwest	B108
Great American Cities	B104		

FROMMER'S IRREVERENT GUIDES

(Wickedly honest guides for sophisticated travelers and those who want to be)

Chicago (avail. 11/95)	I100	New Orleans (avail. 11/95)	I103
London (avail. 11/95)	I101	San Francisco (avail. 11/95)	I104
Manhattan (avail. 11/95)	I102	Virgin Islands (avail. 11/95)	I105

FROMMER'S DRIVING TOURS

(Four-color photos and detailed maps outlining spectacular scenic driving routes)

Australia	Y100	Italy	Y108
Austria	Y101	Mexico	Y109
Britain	Y102	Scandinavia	Y110
Canada	Y103	Scotland	Y111
Florida	Y104	Spain	Y112
France	Y105	Switzerland	Y113
Germany	Y106	U.S.A.	Y114
Ireland	Y107		

FROMMER'S BORN TO SHOP

(The ultimate travel guides for discriminating shoppers—from cut-rate to couture)

Hong Kong (avail. 11/95)	Z100	London (avail. 11/95)	Z101